THE SUBJECT MATTER OF INTELLECTUAL PROPERTY

The Subject Matter of Intellectual Property

JUSTINE PILA
University of Oxford

OXFORD
UNIVERSITY PRESS

OXFORD
UNIVERSITY PRESS

Great Clarendon Street, Oxford, OX2 6DP,
United Kingdom

Oxford University Press is a department of the University of Oxford.
It furthers the University's objective of excellence in research, scholarship,
and education by publishing worldwide. Oxford is a registered trade mark of
Oxford University Press in the UK and in certain other countries

First Edition published in 2017
Impression: 1

Published in the United States of America by Oxford University Press
198 Madison Avenue, New York, NY 10016, United States of America

British Library Cataloguing in Publication Data
Data available

Library of Congress Control Number: 2017947325

ISBN 978–0–19–968861–6

Printed and bound by
CPI Group (UK) Ltd, Croydon, CR0 4YY

For Jonathan, again, and Dominique and Davita

Preface

This book reflects a longstanding interest in the subject matter that different intellectual property (IP) systems protect, and their conception by legislatures and courts. While previously that interest has led me to consider the subject matter of specific IP regimes, and in particular of the copyright and patent regimes, a central aim of the current book has been to look more broadly at the subject matter protected by all of the main species of IP. To my knowledge this has not been done previously. Indeed, beyond the confines of textbooks, it is rare to see the various IP regimes considered alongside each other and comparatively; the tendency being rather for discrete analyses undertaken within the confines of this or that IP system, and at most of the systems immediately allied to it.

Also scarce in the rich academic literature of IP are studies of its subject matter. While the particular challenges posed for law by the protection of authorial works, and of unique artistic works in particular, have long attracted the attention of IP theorists, and a series of recent appellate decisions in the United States concerning inherent patentability has drawn the attention of patent lawyers to the nature of the invention, the focus of IP scholarship has tended overwhelmingly to be elsewhere. That so little attention has been given to the subject matter of trade mark and design right protection especially is surprising, given the amount of theorizing of trade mark law in particular, and the ubiquity of trade marks and product designs in modern society.

Writing this Preface, it is difficult to not be struck by that ubiquity, and by the centrality of all types of IP subject matter to daily social and economic life. Against the background noise of an espresso machine, across the table from my younger daughter, who is reading, and while waiting to Skype with my husband in Canada, the extent of our engagement with and dependence on the subject matter to which IP rights attach could hardly be missed.

Chapters 4 and 5 of this book build on work previously published, which it has not been possible fully to reference in their body. Especially important and therefore closely reflected have been J Pila, 'An Intentional View of the Copyright Work' (2008) 71 Modern Law Review 535; J Pila, 'Copyright and its Categories of Original Works' (2010) 30 Oxford Journal of Legal Studies 299; and the chapters authored by me in J Pila and P L C Torremans, *European Intellectual Property Law* (OUP 2016). While completing the book I also wrote with Rochelle Dreyfuss the introductory chapter for R C Dreyfuss and J Pila (eds), *The Oxford Handbook of Intellectual Property Law* (OUP 2017) (entitled 'Intellectual Property Law: An Anatomical Overview'), which is no doubt apparent from sections of the latter's text.

Finally, in writing this book I have been supported and assisted by several people, some of whom I would like to acknowledge expressly. First, thanks are due to my editors at OUP for their support throughout the project. I am also grateful to Annabelle Lever for her close reading of Chapter 3, and for her helpful and generous advice and criticism. An invitation from Jonathan Herring to contribute to the BCL/MJur Medical Law and Ethics course at Oxford, and the seminar discussions about property rights in respect of body parts that followed, helped my thinking around some of the issues considered, as did discussions with Andrew Dickinson regarding the Roman Law concept of *specificatio*.

As always, my deepest thanks are due to my husband, Jonathan, whose interest in and support of my work is unfailing. I am only sorry that the difficulty of his own field of scholarship rules out any equivalent level of engagement with it by me. This book is for him, and for our daughters Dominique and Davita: each a prolific and talented author in her own right, not to mention user of IP.

Table of Contents

Table of Cases

UNITED KINGDOM

EUROPEAN UNION

European Patent Office

European Union Intellectual Property Office

General Court

Office for Harmonisation in the Internal Market

INTERNATIONAL

European Court of Human Rights

NATIONAL

Australia

Belgium

Canada

France

Germany

Netherlands

Table of Legislation

STATUTES

STATUTORY INSTRUMENTS

EUROPEAN DIRECTIVES

EUROPEAN REGULATIONS

INTERNATIONAL INSTRUMENTS

NATIONAL LEGISLATION

Australia

France

Holy See

Italy

Netherlands

New Zealand

United States

List of Abbreviations

Berne Convention	Berne Convention for the Protection of Literary and Artistic Works
CDPA	Copyright, Designs and Patents Act
CFR	Charter of Fundamental Rights of the European Union
CPC	Community Patent Convention
CPU	central processing unit
CPVO	Community Plant Variety Office
EC	European Commission
ECHR	European Convention for the Protection of Human Rights and Fundamental Freedoms
EEA Agreement	Agreement on the European Economic Area
EPC	Convention on the Grant of European Patents
EPO	European Patent Office
EU	European Union
EUIPO	European Union Intellectual Property Office
IP	intellectual property
LDMA	literary, dramatic, musical, and artistic
Lisbon Agreement	Lisbon Agreement for the Protection of Appellations of Origin and their International Registration
Madrid Agreement	Madrid Agreement for the Repression of False or Misleading Indications of Source on Goods
OHIM	Office for Harmonisation in the Internal Market (Trade Marks and Designs)
Paris Convention	Paris Convention for the Protection of Industrial Property
PDOs	protected designations of origin
PGIs	protected geographical indications
PVR	plant variety rights
Rome Convention	Rome Convention for the Protection of Performers, Producers of Phonograms and Broadcasting
TEU	Consolidated Version of the Treaty on European Union
TFEU	Treaty on the Functioning of the European Union
TRIPs Agreement	Agreement on Trade-related Aspects of Intellectual Property Rights
TSGs	traditional specialities guaranteed
UK	United Kingdom
UPC Agreement	Agreement on a Unified Patent Court
UPOV	Union for the Protection of New Varieties of Plants
WACs	works of artistic craftsmanship
WCT	WIPO Copyright Treaty

1

Definitions and Intellectual Property Subject Matter

1. Definitions and Intellectual Property Subject Matter

Despite a rich academic literature in the field of intellectual property (IP), there has been little conceptual analysis of the subject matter that IP rights protect, and in reflection of this, little attention paid to the meaning of the terms used to denote those subject matter, such as 'invention', 'authorial work', 'trade mark', and 'design'. Instead, and reflecting perhaps the widespread concern over the impact of IP rights on third parties, scholarly attention has tended overwhelmingly to focus on the doctrinal mechanisms within each regime by which the law seeks to mediate competing rights and interests in respect of those subject matter. The result has sometimes seemed to be an interest in everything *but* the subject matter that IP protects—from the secondary requirements for the subsistence or grant of IP rights, to the definition and scope of those rights and the tests for their infringement, the public policy and morality exclusions from protectability, the exceptions and limitations to IP protection, and issues surrounding the exploitation and enforcement of IP rights. In addition, to the extent that attention *has* been paid to IP subject matter, its focus has tended to be confined to one or more discrete categories of subject matter protected by a single regime, such as the artistic work within copyright, with little or no attempt to relate them *inter se*.[1] Further, such studies have largely avoided any attempt to define the terms used

[1] Most of the studies of individual categories of IP subject matter from the past two decades have focused on the subject matter of copyright and patent protection. In the field of copyright see eg Anne Barron's and David Booton's articles on different categories of copyright-protectable subject matter (eg A Barron, 'Copyright Law and the Claims of Art' (2002) 4 Intellectual Property Quarterly 369 (comparing the classification of visual arts by copyright law and certain theories of art, and arguing for greater attention within copyright to creative work rather than authorship); D Booton, 'Framing Pictures: Defining Art in UK Copyright Law' [2003] Intellectual Property Quarterly 38 (drawing on philosophical literature to study use of the 'artistic work' concept in UK copyright law, including the nature of the objects that it denotes and their difference from the objects denoted by the term 'literary work'); A Barron, 'The Legal Properties of Film' (2004) 67 Modern Law Review 177 (using a comparative and historical analysis of legal and non-legal conceptions of the film to support a Marxist conception of film copyright); A Barron, 'Copyright Law's Musical Work' (2006) 15 Social and Legal

to denote such subject matter, whether with reference to equivalent language or to the subject matter that the terms denote,[2] mirroring the practice of legislatures and courts themselves.[3]

This practice may be attributed to several factors. One is the difficulty of the terms in question; words such as 'art' and 'literature' eluding accepted definition even within the non-legal disciplines devoted to theorizing them, and sometimes being described by experts within those disciplines as indefinable.[4] Another is the past tendency of legislators to believe that the definition of such words is most appropriately left to the courts to undertake in the context of individual cases.[5] And a third is the tendency of the courts in turn to eschew the necessity and value of general definitions, whether due to a belief that the terms in question can be used and understood adequately without them, or to a belief that the pursuit of such definitions is unproductive.[6]

Another possible explanation for the eschewal by academics in particular of attempts to define the terms denoting IP subject matter might be concerns about

Studies 101 (using a study of 18th century case law to offer an account of the development of the category of 'musical works' protected by copyright and its impact on social conceptions of the musical work concept). In the field of patent law see eg the study of the historical social and economic conditions, technical developments, and doctrinal themes that helped to support the distinction between idea and embodiment on which modern patent doctrine depends by Alain Pottage and Brad Sherman (A Pottage and B Sherman, *Figures of Invention: A History of Modern Patent Law* (OUP 2010)), and the historical study of the exclusions from patentability by Sigrid Sterckx and Julian Cockbain (S Sterckx and J Cockbain, *Exclusions from Patentability–How Far Has the European Patent Office Eroded Boundaries?* (CUP 2012)). A notable recent work in the field of trade mark law is Deven Desai's and Spencer Waller's analysis of the shift in the focus of trade mark protection from marks to brands (DR Desai and S Waller, 'Brands, Competition, and the Law' [2010] Brigham Young University Law Review 1425)).

[2] The distinction between these two types of definition is referred to by Richard Robinson as the distinction between word:word and word:thing definitions: see R Robinson, *Definition* (OUP 1963).

[3] This is remarked upon in some of the works cited in n 1. See eg Barron, 'The Legal Properties of Film' (n 1) 192 ('determining what qualifies as a copyright work has been the single most troublesome task for copyright law in the UK'); Pottage and Sherman (n 1) 3 ('modern patent lawyers so rarely ask the question: *what is the invention?* [and w]hile patent doctrine assumes that there is such a thing as the invention, it avoids any precise definition of that thing'); see Desai and Waller (n 1) 1432 ('Despite the rich business literature on brands and branding, the question of what is a brand or what makes a brand has received little attention in legal literature').

[4] See eg B Bourbon, 'What Is a Poem?' (2007) 105 Modern Philology 27. Even more elusive are understandings of the essential nature of, for example, literature. See eg R Howell, 'Ontology and the Nature of the Literary Work' (2002) 60 The Journal of Aesthetics and Art Criticism 67. Robinson describes such claims as reflecting the 'emotional or volitional force' attracted by words such as 'art': see Robinson (n 2) 47.

[5] See eg H L Deb vol 495 cols 610-11 (29 March 1988) (deciding not to resolve by legislation the question of whether a reporter's verbatim transcript of another's spoken words might be an original literary work within the meaning of UK law so as 'to merit copyright', but rather to leave it to the courts to decide in any given case).

[6] Something of this latter view can be seen in the academic literature as well. For example, in their book *Figures of Invention: A History of Modern Patent Law* (n 1), Pottage and Sherman suggest that the absence of any 'conceptual' definition of 'the invention' in patent law has been productive in allowing for definition of that term 'at the level of practice' by means of an 'equivocation between different senses of "invention" [that] allows lawyers to develop a more responsive set of resources for addressing the economic and social complexities of innovation' (3).

the dangers of reifying the concepts that those terms signify, and thereby adding to the sense of their (and of intellectual property's) inevitability. Indeed, the search for definition in law in general has been described as entailing a sacrifice of life to logic, and as risking the law's enslavement to its own abstractions.[7] In the field of IP particularly, this fear of reification and its consequences connects to a wider academic sensibility to the historical contingency of IP by reason of its basis in the social, intellectual, economic, and technological contexts of particular times and places,[8] and to the complex ways in which the law and its definitions influence the interpretation of cultural forms and interact with the culture of modern societies in general.[9]

One claim of this book is that, as valid as this latter sensibility in particular is, the law and theory of IP can only benefit from attempts to define directly the terms used to denote the subject matter that IP rights protect—whether or not by such classical definitional methods as formulating a list of necessary and sufficient conditions for the terms' proper application.[10] The most obvious reason is the transparency that definitions bring and the knowledge they generate, and the value of each in a discipline such as law particularly. Indeed, where the terms to be defined denote objects of such importance to daily life as images, medicines, product designs, and commercial emblems or logotypes, and it is on the basis of the law's understanding of those objects—including its understanding of their similarities and differences—that the rules regulating their use are organized and applied, these results of the definitional exercise can only be positive. Beyond this, and depending on the nature and purpose of the definitions sought, one value of seeking them in law especially lies in their provision of a tool not just for ordering, but for clarifying and explicating legal principles in the light of their context and its requirements.[11] Add to this the arguments for intelligibility in law more generally,[12] and one has a compelling case for definitional activity of the type herein supported and undertaken.

[7] See H Cairns, 'A Note on Legal Definitions' (1936) 36 Columbia Law Review 1099, 1100 (the use of such 'precise and technical language' as one might expect to find in a definition can only result in the sacrifice of life to logic, and make lawyers 'the slaves of their own abstractions'; quoting W S Holdsworth, *A History of English Law* (3rd edn, Methuen & Co 1923) 481).

[8] See eg C Seville, 'The Emergence and Development of Intellectual Property Law in Western Europe' in R C Dreyfuss and J Pila (eds), *The Oxford Handbook of Intellectual Property Law* (OUP 2017) http://www.oxfordhandbooks.com/view/10.1093/oxfordhb/9780198758457.001.0001/oxfordhb-9780198758457 (last accessed 5 June 2017). A classic text in the field of copyright is M Rose, *Authors and Owners: The Invention of Copyright* (Harvard University Press 1993).

[9] For a discussion see J M Gaines, *Contested Culture: The Image, the Voice, and the Law* (University of North Carolina Press 1991).

[10] According to Robinson (n 2) 89, in some cases the specification of such a list would do violence to the accepted extension or common meaning by excluding from it members that properly belong in it or admitting into it things that properly belong outside of it.

[11] Cf, in relation to the exercise of defining the concept of law itself, G Lamond, 'Coercion and the Nature of Law' (2001) 7 Legal Theory 35, 38 ('A theory of law ... must lend a degree of order to this material and actively fashion it. The essential features of law are the product, then, of a theory that makes sense of our existing understanding of legal systems').

[12] See Robinson (n 2) 34 ('It is irrational for an author to refuse to try to say what he meant by a certain word in a certain place, and irrational for his interpreter to refuse to do this for him. He may properly say that he no longer knows what he meant by the word. He may also properly say that, although he believes he means something by the word, he is unable at present to find any other words

2. Specific Definitional Aims and Methods

2.1 An Indicative (Nominal Word: Thing Definitional) Exercise

It has been suggested that the ultimate purpose of defining the terms used to denote the subject matter protectable by each IP regime is to promote understanding and analysis of that regime and of intellectual property in general. This says nothing, however, about the more immediate purpose of definition, or the method by which it is appropriately undertaken. The immediate purpose of the definitional exercise undertaken in this book is to understand the ways in which the legal terms denoting the subject matter protectable by IP rights have recently been used by legal authorities in the field. To that end, the aim will be less to formulate equivalent language with which the terms might in any context be replaced, than to identify and understand the objects that those terms are understood by the authorities in question to denote.[13] Consistent with the study's jurisdictional focus, the authorities whose use of the terms will be prioritized are European and UK legal officials, including primarily European and UK legislators and judges. It is, thus, in broad terms at least, a search for definition in the second ('word:thing') of the two nominal senses distinguished by Richard Robinson[14] with which this book is concerned, and in particular, a search for words sufficient to connote or convey the abstract idea to which the terms are annexed[15] in the recent history of their use by European and UK intellectual property officials.[16]

In undertaking this search, three types of knowledge will be generated.[17] The first is knowledge of the existence of the 'rule or custom or habit' by which the relevant terms have recently been 'used as a sign of a certain thing'.[18] The second is knowledge of the existence of the terms themselves. And the third and most elusive is knowledge of the objects denoted by the terms. As stated by Robinson with respect to the last of these forms of knowledge promoted by word-thing definitional exercises in general:

> Even if we are somewhat familiar with the thing before we learn the definition, the definition may give us new knowledge of the thing in that it abstracts it and sets it off from the rest of the world in a way which we probably had not done before unless we already had some other word for that thing.[19]

to mean the same thing, that is, he is unable to think of any method of defining his word. But he may not simply declare that he is under no obligation to define the word; for that would be equivalent to saying that he has a right to publish unintelligibilities').

[13] H L A Hart, *The Concept of Law* (Clarendon Press 1961) 14. [14] See n 2.

[15] J Locke, *An Essay Concerning Human Understanding* (1689) (Hayes Barton Press 2005) 383.

[16] See Robinson (n 2) 36. ('No brief lexical definition of a word, then, is likely to embrace the multiplicity of uses the word has had at different times or even at one time').

[17] These three types of knowledge are described by Robinson as provided by nominal word-thing definitions: see Robinson (n 2) 31–33.

[18] ibid 31. [19] ibid 33.

Thus described, the definitional exercise undertaken in this book may be cast as indicative in the sense of indicating the objects denoted by the terms in practice. In the language of H L A Hart, it reflects a belief in the potential for such an exercise to supply a map, however incomplete, of the field of IP, both by making explicit the latent principles that guide official uses of each of the terms in question, and by exhibiting relationships between the phenomena in respect of which such terms are used and other phenomena.[20] Consistent with this, the pursuit of word:thing rather than word:word definitions[21] underlines that the focus of the exercise is not merely on words, but also on the realities of the objects that they are used to talk about,[22] and that its result will be definitions that are in large measure descriptive in the sense of fitting with the way in which the terms are actually used in authoritative legal (intellectual property) practice.

One consequence of defining the terms in question with reference to their recent use by IP legal officials is to heed the academic sensibility described above by underlining the nature of IP subject matter (and of IP more generally) as a 'folk concept', namely, and as defined by Brian Tamanaha in his discussion of conceptions of law in pluralistic societies, that which people within a given group have come to see and label as such.[23] The reason is its concern with what legal officials have recently seen and labelled as 'inventions', 'authorial works', 'trade marks', 'designs', and the like, which concern is fully consistent with, and indeed assumes, that those perceptions and labels will differ at different times and in different legal and social communities.

2.2 An Explicative and Reconstructive (Conceptual Definitional) Exercise

In addition to promoting understanding of how the terms to be defined have recently been used by European and UK legal authorities, the purpose of this book is, as suggested above, to use the definitional exercise as an opportunity to clarify the understanding of the terms reflected by such use having regard to and within the confines of the legal and policy contexts in which they exist and are applied.[24] This can be explained with reference to a further distinction drawn by Robinson between lexical and stipulative definitions. Clearly, authoritative legal (including legislative) definitions of 'invention', 'authorial work', 'trade mark', and 'design' are stipulative rather than lexical, in the sense of comprising commands regarding the meaning that such terms are to be understood in IP law as having. They therefore lack the truth-value of lexical definitions; it being possible to speak of a legislative definition of 'trade mark', for example, as valid or invalid, but not as true or false. However, and as Robinson explains, while stipulative definitions lack the truth-value of lexical definitions, they

[20] Hart (n 13) 14. [21] See n 2. [22] Hart (n 13) 14.

[23] B Z Tamanaha, 'Understanding Legal Pluralism: Past to Present, Local to Global' (2008) 30 Sydney Law Review 375, 396.

[24] See A Gupta, 'Definitions' in E N Zalta (ed), *The Stanford Encyclopedia of Philosophy* (Summer 2015 edn) para 1.5.

nonetheless entail a commitment to using terms in and only in the senses stipulated by their definition.[25] It is this implied commitment entailed by stipulative definition that enables criticism of the courts, for example, for using the terms that denote different IP subject matter in a manner inconsistent with IP legislation, including the nature, aims, and values of the rights and systems that such legislation creates. Hence the extension of the definitional exercise undertaken in the current study beyond descriptions of the use of the terms 'invention', 'authorial work', etc, by legal officials to explications and even reconstructions of such use having regard to and within the limits permitted by this commitment and correlative duty.

In its explicative and reconstructive aims, the method adopted in the following chapters may be said to reflect in part the conceptual definitional approach attributed to Immanuel Kant, according to which definition 'is reached partly by an analysis of usage, and partly by a decision which makes the concept more precise'.[26] Hence, and consistent with what was said above, the result sought to be achieved is a study that reflects the fact that what matters in and for law is less the meaning of words than the analysis of the concepts that they signify, and the name that properly expresses those concepts; and less the lexical task of reporting how words are standardly used than the analytic task of explicating such use in the light of its legal and policy contexts specifically. In pursuing this end the method adopted may be said to take a leaf from Ronald Dworkin's work regarding conceptions of law in general and of legal principles in particular.[27] The reason is its treatment of the definitional exercise as involving a search for understanding of current law that reflects the past decisions of courts and legislatures interpreted in their most (contextually) appropriate light, consistent with and in recognition of the duty entailed by the stipulative nature of legal definition described above. By construing it in this way, the definitional task is harnessed for the dual purposes of ordering and clarifying the principles of IP in the sense earlier outlined.

A further premise of this approach is a view of the terms 'authorial work', 'invention', 'trade mark', and 'design' as terms of historical and theoretical significance, consistent with the critical legal studies view that '[t]he mapping of a discipline is both an historical and a theoretical project'.[28] The terms are also treated as denoting analytic and organizational concepts, in recognition of their use in fact to denote those objects regarded as appropriate for a certain type of legal (intellectual property) protection, and of their deliberate construction to pursue the goals of such protection in a manner consistent with the wider context in which those goals exist.

[25] Robinson (n 2) 64–65.
[26] L W Beck, 'Kant's Theory of Definition' (1956) 65 The Philosophical Review 179, 180.
[27] See R Dworkin, *Law's Empire* (Harvard University Press 1986).
[28] P Goodrich, 'Intellection and Indiscipline' (2009) 36 Journal of Law and Society 460, 460.

2.3 An Analytic and Synthetic (Definitional) Exercise that Proceeds in Three Stages

Consistent with the definitional aims above, different methods are deployed throughout the following chapters to track the use of different terms. These include an analytic method, focusing on the shared and differentiating properties—the *genus* and *differentia*—of the objects that the terms are used to denote, and a synthetic method, focusing on the means by which those objects come to exist.[29] In all cases, however, the ultimate aim of the study is to indicate and explicate the law's understanding of the terms by considering their central uses by the relevant legal officials, having regard to the relevant legal and policy contexts of such use, and the commitment of the law to defining the terms in question in (and only in) a given (authoritative legal) sense.

To this end, the study undertaken in the following chapters proceeds in three main stages.

2.3.1 An Overview of the Nature, Aims, and Values of Intellectual Property Rights and Systems

At the first stage, undertaken in Chapter 2, the context in which the relevant terms fall to be defined is considered, with a particular focus on the nature, aims, and values of IP rights and systems in Europe and the United Kingdom. Here the original aims of the European statutory IP regimes are discussed, and shown to remain largely unchanged today. In the case of patents, copyright, and designs, these aims have historically been to promote and reward the creation and/or introduction to the public of certain intangible objects of perceived value to society, and to support industry and commerce by regulating access to those subject matter after they have entered the public realm, in addition to protecting the rights and interests of creators. In the case of trade marks, they have been to protect the public from misrepresentations regarding the origin of goods and services in trade, and in so doing to support competition and efficiency within the marketplace.

With respect to its nature specifically: IP is a type of property conferring temporary exclusionary rights in respect of the objects it exists to protect. The property status of IP is a matter of positive law, and a reflection of the exclusionary nature of the rights it confers and their presumptive transferability. In combination, it is these two features of IP rights that account for their potential economic value, and their conception as economic rights, whatever the perceived arguments and/or justification(s) for their existence.

More difficult is to understand the nature of the objects to which IP rights attach. In the language of contemporary European IP law and policy, those objects are 'intellectual creations', the protection of which is described as necessary to generate employment and wealth, promote the production and distribution of goods

[29] For a discussion of the synthetic method of definition see Robinson (n 2) 100.

and services, support innovation and competition, and facilitate creativity, innovation, development, and solutions to global (health, environmental, and other) challenges—in addition to ensuring to creators sufficient protection to enable their intellectual work to flourish, and to protect their personal rights and interests as creators, including their dignity. Consistent with the position described above in respect of the terms 'invention', 'authorial work', 'trade mark', and 'design', however, no definition of the term 'intellectual creation' in European or UK law and policy exists. Hence the question posed in Chapter 2 of how the commitment to protecting such subject matter in pursuit of the various instrumentalist and deontological objectives outlined previously translates in practice, and what *are* the subject matter to which IP rights in law are understood by legal officials to be capable of attaching.

2.3.2 A Theoretical Framework for Thinking about Intellectual Property and Related Definitional Questions

This leads to the second stage of the current enquiry, where a theoretical framework for thinking about the subject matter protectable by IP in general is proposed, and certain questions for understanding the subject matter in the context of the definitional exercise described above are derived. The framework is adapted from existing European and UK law with the assistance of certain metaphysical devices. Those devices are the category, the property, the type/token distinction, and the artifact. Considered together, they support a paradigmatic conception of each of the subject matter protectable by IP as an artifact type distinguished by its properties and arranged by legislatures and courts into categories reflecting those properties. While not without its analytic and normative difficulties, the fit between this framework and the subject matter that IP rights protect makes it a useful heuristic device. The questions proposed on its basis to guide the relevant definitional exercise are four-fold, and concern respectively: the nature of the (categories of) subject matter denoted by the terms 'invention', 'authorial work', 'trade mark', and 'design' (and thus protectable by the main IP regimes), including their essential properties; the means by which each subject matter is individuated within the relevant regime; the relationship between each subject matter and its concrete instances; and the manner in which the existence of a subject matter and its instances is known for the purposes of IP.[30]

In legal theoretical terms, the formulation of the four questions above with the assistance of current law and insights from philosophy as part of the definitional exercise earlier outlined can be said to reflect a recognition of and concern to do justice to the different (external and internal) points of view that exist with respect to both the terms to be defined and the subject matter that they denote. Specifically,

[30] The specific questions are as follows: (a) What are the (categories of) subject matter protected by the regime—ie what are the essential properties of the subject matter (as distinct, for example, from its accidental properties)? (b) How is each subject matter individuated? (c) What is the relationship between each subject matter and its tokens? (d) How is the existence of each subject matter and its tokens known?

and somewhat unusually for IP scholarship, it can be said to reflect a recognition of and concern to do justice to the points of view of two groups of people: first, those detached and uncommitted observers of IP regimes; and second, those users of IP laws and systems who are also committed to them in the sense of accepting their rules and principles as standards to be applied and maintained.[31] It also reflects the characteristic dependence of the law in general on other disciplines in the pursuit of its social policy aims.[32] Within IP law itself, that dependence can be seen from the extent of legal officials' reliance on science, aesthetics, and marketing when accessing the various domains that it regulates. This is apparent from the emphasis placed on hypothetical expert perspectives, and from the courts' reservation to themselves of a freedom more generally to take evidence from different persons within different non-legal disciplines when deciding whether a given object is an 'invention', 'design', 'authorial work', 'trade mark', or other type of artifact protectable by IP. In this regard again, the law recognizes and seeks to do justice to the external and internal perspectives on the meaning of such terms and the nature of the subject matter that they denote.

Returning to the choice of philosophical devices to emphasize: an artifact is defined within philosophy as an object the existence and character of which depends on the productive actions and intentions of one or more human beings, referred to as the authors of the object in question.[33] Thus conceived, it fits closely to the legal conception of certain IP subject matter at least, including most obviously the authorial work protected by copyright. Moreover, the idea of an intangible object owing its existence and character to the actions and intentions of one or more human beings that underlies it is helpful in focusing attention on two central features of IP subject matter. The first of these features is their intangibility, and the second is their origination in an act of human creation (requiring a certain talent or capacity[34]) in one or both of two recognized (common law) legal senses. According to the first of these senses, based on the non-IP case of *Doodeward v Spence*,[35] for property rights to exist in respect of an object derived from nature, the object must be the result of a transformative act that gives rise to something new, in the sense of something that is different from the thing acted upon. According to the second, based on the non-IP case of *Yearworth v North Bristol NHS Trust*,[36] for property rights to exist in respect of an object derived from nature, the object must be the result either of a transformative act in the *Doodeward* sense, or of an act that gives rise to something that supports a new use, in the sense of a use that is different from the use supported by the thing acted upon.

[31] See Hart (n 13) 86–88, 99–102. [32] Goodrich (n 28).

[33] See generally R Hilpinen, 'Artifact' in E N Zalta (ed), *The Stanford Encyclopedia of Philosophy* (Winter 2011 edn).

[34] See in this connection the distinction drawn by Charles Beitz in his discussion of distributive justice between property rights (in the form of possessory claims) in respect of personal capacities and talents on the one hand and other natural resources on the other: C R Beitz, 'Justice and International Relations' (1975) 4 Philosophy and Public Affairs 360.

[35] *Doodeward v Spence* [1908] HCA 45, (1908) 6 CLR 406 (*Doodeward*).

[36] *Yearworth v North Bristol NHS Trust* [2009] EWCA Civ 37, [2010] QB 1 (*Yearworth*).

It is possible to see the different views reflected in these common law personal property cases as reflecting different understandings of the requirements for acquiring ownership by specification (*specificatio*).[37] In Roman law, *specificatio* was applied to determine the ownership of the results of five industrial processes—agriculture, smithying, tailoring, carpentry, and apothecary—and interpreted to require the creation of a new species (*nova species*) from pre-existing materials.[38] In order for such a species to exist, the new object needed to reflect a sufficiently significant and irreversible change from the pre-existing materials.[39] If and only if it did would the object be recognized as capable of separate ownership, whether by reason of: its nature as a *res nullius* susceptible of exclusive occupation; the accession to it of the pre-existing materials by means of human labour and skill; or recognition of the practical difficulty of identifying the pre-existing materials in the new object.[40] Viewed in the light of these principles, which exist also in the modern law of some jurisdictions, the *Doodeward* and *Yearworth* cases can be seen to reflect a disagreement over the scope of *specificatio*, and what exactly is required for a *nova species* to be said to exist.[41]

Closely related to the concept of the artifact is the distinction drawn by some philosophers between tokens and types. While not without its difficulties, this distinction represents a useful heuristic device for IP. The reason is its assistance in elucidating further the intangible nature of the subject matter that IP rights protect, including their difference from the tangible objects protected by other forms of property, and the ways in which IP rights operate in practice. For example, as descriptive or abstract concepts in the form of types, each IP subject matter is capable of repeated instantiation or exemplification in a variety of concrete forms or instances, as tokens. Subject matter that are not so capable, such as the non-repeatable method of creating a more beautiful dove considered by the Bundesgerichtshof in 1969, will generally (for that reason) be ineligible for protection by intellectual property rights. And just as types are recognized within philosophy as capable of being instantiated perfectly and imperfectly, the law recognizes that even imperfect instantiations of a given type may be sufficient to infringe the IP rights in respect of it. For these reasons, the view of IP subject matter as types, and of their concrete instances as tokens, has analytic value for IP, whether or not it is supported fully by philosophers.

Of further use and importance for IP are the devices of categories and properties.

[37] Gaius 2.79 and Justinian 2.1.5. The discussion here relies on C van der Merwe, '*Nova Species*' (2004) 2 Roman Legal Tradition 96. I am grateful to Andrew Dickinson for alerting me to this article.

[38] C van der Merwe, '*Nova Species*' (2004) 2 Roman Legal Tradition 96, 99.

[39] ibid 98 ff. [40] ibid.

[41] The position supported in the *Yearworth* case is perhaps consistent with the position argued for but rejected in a modern Scottish case discussed by van der Merwe (n 38) 97–98, *Kinloch Damph Ltd v Nordvic Salmon Farms Ltd* (1999) Outer House Cases LEXIS (30 June 1999). That case involved a proprietary claim in respect of salmon that had been grown, with the assistance of the defenders' feeding and husbandry, from smolt (young salmon in embryonic state). According to the court, since the defenders' investment of effort and material in growing the salmon did not entail the transformation by human effort of materials to create a new substance, there was no *nova species* in respect of which they could be said to have a valid ownership claim.

The use of categories in particular is ubiquitous in IP, from the copyright distinction between literary, dramatic, musical, and artistic works, to the conception of trade marks as signs that indicate the commercial origin of certain goods or services. In many IP regimes, categories can be seen to operate in either or both of two ways: first, to denote differences between subject matter of a certain type; and second, to denote systems of subject matter by sorting every member of a certain type that exists. However they operate, the nature and extent of their use by legal officials in identifying and understanding the subject matter protectable by different species of IP supports the legal realist idea that organizing concepts into categories is a central and inevitable part of the search for legal knowledge and understanding, in addition to being an important means by which the courts and legislatures seek to ensure that the law develops in a normatively desirable way. So too by recognizing and expressing the properties that certain objects do and do not possess, the organization of subject matter according to different categorical schemes supports the analytic definitional method described above by helping to identify the shared and differentiating properties of the objects that the terms in question are used by legal officials to denote in practice. At the very least, and regardless of whether categories and properties have the centrality to legal understanding and development that some theorists claim, viewing IP through their lens is helpful in engaging with and ordering its rights and subject matter specifically.

2.3.3 Defining the Terms in Question

It remains to explain the third and final of the definitional stages to be undertaken. Here, officials' use of the legislative terms that denote the subject matter protectable by IP regimes is considered in detail, and the results of that consideration used to answer the four questions outlined previously.[42] The primary focus is on the meaning of the terms in question: 'invention', 'plant variety', 'authorial work', 'trade mark', 'goodwill', 'designation of origin', 'geographical indication', and 'design', with reference also to the terms used to denote the subject matter (such as phonograms and first fixations of films) protectable by related rights. As explained above, the aim is to define each of these terms with reference to the objects that they denote, and with a view to indicating and explicating the meaning reflected in their use by the relevant (European and UK) IP legal officials particularly. At the conclusion of each chapter, the definitions in question are presented as answers to the four questions above,[43] and thus with reference to the categories and properties of the subject matter protectable by each IP regime, the methods by which those subject matter are individuated within each regime, the relationship between each subject matter and its concrete instances or tokens, and the manner in which each subject matter and its tokens is known. In the course of answering these questions, regard is also had to the suitability of the terms deployed by the legislatures and courts to denote the subject matter, and to the rules or habits by which those terms are used

[42] See n 30. [43] ibid.

as a sign of a certain thing; albeit these ordinarily being apparent from the legislative stipulations themselves.

3. Definitions of 'Invention', 'Authorial Work', 'Trade Mark', and 'Design', etc

The conclusions reached from the third stage of the definitional exercise described above may be summarized as follows.

3.1 'Invention': An Idea for a Product or Process that Is Technical (Europe) or Technically Inventive (UK), and that May (But Need Not) be Intended for a Specific Purpose

The term that is used to denote, and that appropriately denotes, the subject matter protectable by patent right is 'invention'. In modern law, this term denotes an (a) idea of a person (b) for an individual product or process (c) that is technical (Europe) or technically inventive (UK), in the sense of being the causal, perceivable, and repeatable result of some purposive human (Europe) and inventive (UK) action on the material world to control the forces of nature. Thus defined, the essential properties of the objects denoted by the term 'invention' are their abstract nature (as ideas), and their capacity to support repeated instantiation in the real or material world as a technical (Europe) or technically inventive (UK) product or process. In addition, a 'product' in this sense is understood to be a physical or concrete object that exists independent of the method by which it is made,[44] and a 'process' is understood to be a series of steps resulting in a particular end. Either may also be limited in its identity by the particular use or end result intended for it, in which case it will be a purpose-limited product or process, as appropriate.

These (European and UK) definitions of the term 'invention' conform closely to the paradigmatic conception of IP protectable subject matter as artifact types above. The reason is their intangibility, and their dependence for existence on the productive actions and intentions of one or more human beings, denoted by the term 'inventor'. The definitions also reflect a view of the subject matter protectable by patents as human creations. In the case of the European definition, the conception of 'creation' supported reflects the less restrictive conception derived from the *Yearworth* case. This is in contrast to the position of other jurisdictions, such as the United States, which define 'invention' to denote creations in the more restrictive *Doodeward* sense of requiring (an idea for) a transformative human act, accounting for the exclusion from protection of isolated genetic sequences and a range of methods that have been treated as protectable by European legislative and judicial authorities. The position of UK law in this regard is currently unclear. On the one hand, the UK conception of the invention has long had sympathies in the direction of the US conception.

[44] *Kirin-Amgen Inc v Hoechst Marion Roussel Ltd* [2004] UKHL 46, [2005] RPC 169 [88].

On the other hand, the UK conception has been constrained by the European authorities with which it is required to conform. This is apparent not only from the European legislative provisions requiring the availability of patents for isolated products, but also from the European legislative provisions requiring the availability of patents for previously available subject matter for a specific purpose on the basis of the intention of the user with respect to it.

3.2 'Plant Variety': A Type of Invention in the European Conception

Similarly for the law's definition of the term used to denote the subject matter protectable by plant variety right: 'plant variety'. In Europe and the UK, this term is used to denote every plant group that is (a) distinguishable from other plant groups by its expression of at least one genotype characteristic (distinct), (b) largely the same in its essential properties (homogenous), and (c) stable, in the sense of retaining those properties after each propagation cycle. Thus defined, the essential properties of the plant variety are the same as those of the invention within the meaning of European patent law, namely, its abstract nature (as an idea for a technical product), and its capacity to support repeated instantiation in the material world (by derivation of the product); albeit the product in the case of a variety being plant material that expresses the characteristics defining of a (distinct, homogeneous, and stable) plant grouping specifically. As a result, a plant variety is a type of invention in the European conception outlined previously.

3.3 'Authorial Work': An Expressive Object that Has a Certain Expressive Form and History of Production (Conceived Differently by European and UK Legal Officials)

Moving to the copyright regime: the term that is used in European law to denote, and that appropriately denotes, the subject matter protectable by copyright is 'authorial work'. By contrast, in UK law the relevant terms are 'original literary work', 'original dramatic work', 'original musical work', and 'original artistic work'. 'Authorial work' denotes an original expressive production in the literary, artistic, or scientific domain, and thus covers the family of objects denoted by the terms 'original literary work', 'original dramatic work', 'original musical work', and 'original artistic work', among other original works. The essential properties of these categories of authorial works within the meaning of both European and UK law are: (a) their possession of a certain (in the UK, literary, dramatic, musical, or artistic (LDMA)) expressive form; and (b) the history of their production. With respect to (b), the relevant property may be more specifically described as the property of having derived from a process involving the exercise of free and creative choices by one or more persons to produce a bounded expressive object that reflects those persons' personality or personal touch (Europe), or the property of having been produced by the exercise of independent skill and labour and intended and/or accepted—or at least, not *not* intended and/or accepted—by society to exist as an authorial work of LDMA type (UK). Once again, this definition conforms closely to the paradigmatic conception of IP subject matter above, and further reflects a view of the subject matter protectable by copyright as a creation in the more restrictive of the two senses described previously. This is in contrast to the non-authorial subject matter protectable by related rights, which still conform to the paradigmatic idea of IP subject matter, but which reflect the less restrictive common law conception of the objects capable of attracting property rights.

3.4 'Trade Mark': An Expressive Object Intended and Suitable for Use to Distinguish Goods or Services

With respect to the trade mark regime: the term that is used to denote the subject matter protectable by registered trade mark is alternatively 'sign' or 'trade mark'. Despite recent academic suggestions to the contrary, the latter of these terms is most appropriate having regard to the nature of the objects that registered trade mark right is understood to protect.

A 'trade mark' within the conception of European and UK legal officials is an (a) expressive object (b) that is (i) intended for use and capable of being used to distinguish the goods or services of one or more commercial undertakings from those of others, and (ii) capable of being represented in a manner that is clear, precise, self-contained, easily accessible, intelligible, durable, and objective in the trade mark register. In addition, for a subject matter to be a trade mark, its essential characteristics must not consist exclusively of functional, technical, or aesthetic characteristics of goods. Thus defined, the essential properties of trade marks are: (a) their possession of certain expressive qualities; (b) the intention of their putative deviser to use them to indicate a distinguishing feature of certain goods or services; and (c) their capacity to support such intended use. To exist as such, trade marks must also be inherently unsuitable for the limited-term protections afforded by the patent, copyright, and design right regimes respectively. On this view, trade marks are purpose-limited expressive objects that combine features of the subject matter protectable as authorial works and purpose-limited inventions. They therefore conform to the paradigmatic idea of an artifact considered previously. They are also creations in the second and more expansive of the *Doodeward* and *Yearworth* senses on the basis that their production involves the making of an expressive object available as a mark of commercial origin without any necessity for a transformative human act. They are thus constituted as such both by their expressive properties (being the properties of the sign) and by the intention of the trade mark applicant or owner (to use the object manifesting those properties for a certain purpose), underlining once again their existence as a hybrid of the work and invention.

It remains to consider the specific manner in which trade marks distinguish the goods or services to which they relate. For the most part, they do so by indicating that the goods or services in question have a certain commercial origin, thereby enabling consumers of the goods or services to repeat or avoid their prior purchasing experiences. Exceptions exist, however, in the case of collective and certification marks, each of which is stipulated by UK legislation to be a type of trade mark. In the case of these subject matter, the expressive object indicates not the goods' or services' commercial origin, but rather their originator's association with a particular collective and their certification by a particular authority respectively.

3.5 'Designation of Origin' and 'Geographical Indication': A Trade Mark

Closely related to the protection conferred by registered trade mark right is that conferred by protected designations of origin (PDOs) and protected geographical indications (PGIs) respectively. In Europe and the UK, the subject matter entitled to PDO and PGI protection are denoted by the terms 'designation of origin' and 'geographical indication'. Subject to certain minor exceptions, each is defined as a type of trade mark within the conception outlined previously, and more specifically, as a purpose-limited sign (comprising a name) that is capable of distinguishing and intended for use to distinguish certain goods (currently comprising but not needing conceptually to comprise agricultural products and foodstuffs). To exist as such, PDOs and PGIs must also be inherently unsuited to the protection offered by other IP regimes (including particularly the plant variety and trade mark regimes). As with collective and certification marks, however, the manner in which PDOs and PGIs distinguish the goods to which they relate is different from the manner in which regular trade marks distinguish them: rather than distinguishing them with reference to commercial origin, PDOs and PGIs distinguish them with reference to the *terroir* properties that they express.

3.6 'Goodwill': An 'Attractive Force Which Brings in Custom'[45]

In stark contrast to the subject matter considered to this point is that understood by UK legal authorities to be denoted by the term 'goodwill'. While the protection conferred in respect of goodwill by means of the passing off action is closely related to that conferred by registered trade mark, the subject matter of that protection is very different. It is also difficult to fit within the paradigmatic idea of IP protectable subject matter considered previously, much less within either of the two common law senses of human creation. According to that conception, the term 'goodwill' denotes the attractive force or favourable regard that the public has for the provider of goods or services, as demonstrated by the trader's custom. While goodwill thus defined is instantiated in a similar range of concrete objects and events as other IP subject matter, and therefore has tokens, it is not as such a type.

[45] *Inland Revenue Commissioners v Muller & Co's Margarine Ltd* [1901] AC 217 (HL) 224 (Lord Macnaughten), cited with approval in *Reckitt & Colman Products Ltd v Borden Inc* [1990] UKHL 12, [1990] RPC 341 (Lord Jauncey).

3.7 'Design': A Type of Authorial Work that (in the Conception of Unregistered UK Design Law) Has a Different History of Production

The last of the terms considered in this book are those used to denote the subject matter protectable by registered and unregistered design rights. In the UK and Europe, this subject matter is denoted simply by the term 'design'. In legal officials' usage, this term encompasses the subject matter of registered and unregistered design right, and is perhaps better replaced with the terms 'registered design' and 'unregistered design' respectively.

In Europe, both of the terms 'registered design' and 'unregistered design' are understood to refer to an appearance of the external features of a product or product part, including those features of a part intended for assembly in a complex product that remain visible during the product's normal use, and excluding any features that are not the product of free and creative choices by the subject matter's putative designer. Thus defined, the subject matter denoted by the terms in question are original artistic works within the meaning of EU copyright, being comprised of the same formal and historical properties. While UK legal officials support the same conception of the subject matter denoted by the term 'registered design', they define the term 'unregistered design' differently. In UK legal usage, 'unregistered design' denotes an original work comprising a specific and individual appearance of the external or internal shape or configuration of a product or product part—being the appearance of a product or product part excluding any surface decoration—produced by a person exercising independent labour and skill, and excluding any aspects of appearance attributable to interoperability or interchange requirements. Thus conceived, an unregistered design within the meaning of UK law is a type of original artistic work within the meaning of traditional UK copyright authorities—albeit excluding the requirement for an authorial work's history of production. This is hardly surprising given that that requirement was formulated precisely to exclude from copyright those designs and other subject matter that possess the formal properties of original literary and artistic works but are nonetheless not appropriately conceived, for reasons related to the intention of their creator and view of society regarding their nature, as works of literary and artistic authorship.

Notwithstanding the complexity of these definitions of the terms 'registered design' and 'unregistered design', it is clear from the relevant authorities that the objects denoted by each—like those denoted by the term 'original artistic work' in UK copyright law—are expressive objects of visual significance that depend for their existence on the productive actions and intentions of one or more human beings, referred to as the 'designers' of the objects in question. As such, and as for original artistic works, they conform closely to the paradigmatic view of IP subject matter, and reflect the more restrictive of the two conceptions of a creation considered previously. While their combined expressive and functional nature makes it tempting to conceive them as purpose-limited expressive objects in the manner of trade marks, the nature of their purpose–namely, instantiation by incorporation in or application to individual products–serves paradoxically to underline their similarity to authorial works, accounting for the view of such products as merely the media through which designs are realized. The reason is that the category of objects understood to be denoted by the terms in question contains only those objects that result from a transformative act on the part of one or more natural persons giving rise to new properties of visual significance in the sense either of properties that differ from those which existed previously or—for the objects denoted by the term 'unregistered design' in UK law—of properties that can be said to have originated with the relevant persons. Nonetheless, and given the ability of applicants for registered design right at least to decide the level of generality at which their subject matter is defined (with a view to determining the precise scope of their IP protection) particularly, it is possible to conceive the objects denoted by the term 'registered design' as comprising ideas for the addition of certain properties of visual significance to a product or product part, in addition to original works within the meaning of copyright, bringing them closer conceptually to the inventions protectable by patent grant—and more specifically, to the purpose-limited expressive objects protectable by registered trade mark.

It is apparent from this overview of the definitions of the terms used to denote the subject matter protectable by IP rights that, with the exception of goodwill, each conforms closely to the paradigmatic idea of IP subject matter considered previously, and comprises a human creation in one or other of the two common law senses derived from the *Doodeward* and *Yearworth* cases. Important are the purposive actions, and in some cases the wider intentions, of certain individuals, and the existence of an object capable of attribution to them. Where they differ is in the nature of the actions and intentions required. In the case of authorial works and designs, the law requires a human act that is sufficiently transformative to produce an expressive object the formal and historical (including intentional) properties of which differentiate it from the thing or things acted upon. By contrast, in the case of inventions (as conceived by European legal officials at least), plant varieties, trade marks, and related rights subject matter, the law requires only an act sufficient to make an existing object available in a state that supports a new purpose, being a purpose that differs from that supported by the use of object in its original state. The result is an understanding of the relevant subject matter as comprising certain abstract (ideational) or expressive (formal)—in addition to certain historical, including intentional—properties.

3.8 The Method by which Each Subject Matter Is Individuated within Intellectual Property

Every subject matter to which an IP right attaches must be capable of being distinguished as an individual subject matter of relevant type. For industrial property rights such as patents, trade marks, and registered designs, this generally requires that the subject matter be capable of being distinguished *qua* invention, trade mark, and design etc from the application for protection. One explanation for this requirement is the rule of law consideration that the monopoly-like restrictions on individual freedoms that these industrial property rights impose must be defined sufficiently clearly for the public to be able to organize their lives without infringing others' rights. In addition, there is the contractual nature of industrial property rights as consideration for the disclosure of a valuable object (such as an invention or product design), or for the commitment to use a valuable object (such as a trade mark). In combination, these considerations explain the need for a person to apply formally for the grant of the rights in question, and to provide as part of their application a definition or description of the subject matter for which protection is sought that is sufficient to enable its identification as a discrete object of relevant type.

It is possible to read in the statutory provisions governing the identification of these industrial property subject matter two different notions and requirements for evidence of their existence. The first, reflected in the requirement for definition and/or description, is metaphysical individuation, according to which an object is individuated by 'whatever it is that makes it the single object that it is'.[46] The second, reflected in the requirement for a disclosure sufficient to enable the subject matter to be identified, is epistemic individuation, according to which an object is individuated by the ability of a certain intelligent individual to single it out 'as a distinct object of perception'.[47] With respect to the question 'how is each IP-protectable subject matter individuated?', the answer in the context of the registrable rights above is then: metaphysically, by asking what idea for a technical or technically inventive product or process is described in the patent document, what purpose-limited expressive object is represented in the application for registered trade mark protection, or what appearance of the external features of a product or product part is represented in the application for registered design protection; and also epistemologically, by asking what does the hypothetical persons on whom patent, trade mark, and design laws rely understand the idea, expressive object, or appearance as a distinct object of perception to be?[48]

Within these three industrial property fields, the second of these conceptions and methods of individuation can be said to have especial importance. This is apparent in those areas concerned with establishing the identity of a subject matter *qua* invention, trade mark, or registered design, including novelty and infringement (in patent law), the relative grounds of refusal of registration for trade marks that are identical or confusingly similar to an earlier trade mark and infringement (in trade mark law), and novelty and individual character (in design law). In each of these areas it is clear that the identity of an individual subject matter depends primarily on the perception of a certain hypothetical person, being the skilled technical addressee of the invention in patent law, the well-informed and reasonably observant and circumspect average consumer of the relevant goods or services in trade mark law, and the informed user of the products to which the design relates in design law. Put differently, it is clear that the ability of a certain hypothetical intelligent individual to single out each subject matter for which protection is sought as a distinct object of perception is central to its legal status as a subject matter of protectable type.

[46] E J Lowe, 'Individuation' in M L Loux and D W Zimmerman (eds), *The Oxford Handbook of Metaphysics* (OUP 2005) 75.

[47] ibid. [48] ibid.

An important distinction exists between trade marks on the one hand and PDOs and PGIs on the other in relation to the method by which subject matter are individuated within each regime. That distinction relates to the different ways in which the goods and services in respect of which each type of IP right is registered are specified. For trade marks, the goods and services must be specified clearly and precisely by the applicant in her trade mark application with reference to certain classes of goods and services. Trade marks are then individuated on the basis in part of the goods or services thus specified. However, while PDOs and PGIs are also individuated on the basis in part of the goods in respect of which they are registered, consistent with their nature as purpose-limited signs, the manner in which those goods are specified is different, in reflection of the different nature of the subject matter protectable as PDO or PGI. As seen previously, the subject matter protectable as PDOs and PGIs is a sign of use to indicate a product's embodiment of certain *terroir* properties. It follows from this that the individuation of the protected subject matter depends on the identification of both the sign (ie the product name) and the products that originate from the geographical area and embody the associated characteristics designated by it. Within Europe, both are published in a Database of Origin and Registration (DOOR). In addition to listing the name comprising the designation or indication, the DOOR lists the type of product in respect of which the name is registered, and the conditions with which individual products of that type must comply in order to be marked with the PDO or PGI. Those conditions, contained in the product specification required by legislation, then provide the basis for determining whether the PDO or PGI may be used in respect of a particular product, and the scope of protection conferred by the PDO or PGI on its beneficiaries. Thus conceived, the role of the product specification is very similar to that of the patent claims and plant variety description. As for trade marks, however, PDOs and PGIs are otherwise individuated with reference to the image that they produce in the mind of the well informed and reasonably observant and circumspect average consumer.

Slightly different is the method by which subject matter are individuated within the fields of copyright, unregistered design right, and plant variety right. Here the same reliance is not placed on the perspective of a hypothetical intelligent individual when deciding whether a subject matter is an individual object of protectable type as in the fields of industrial property rights considered previously. Nonetheless, even in these fields the method by which subject matter are individuated depends essentially on what legal officials would single out as distinct objects of perception. In addition, where a subject matter *is* directed to a specialist audience, as in the case of instructions for weaving fabric (which may be protected as a graphic work), the courts will consider how it is perceived in fact by that audience. Given this, individuation in the epistemic sense is also of central importance in these fields. Indeed, the primary difference in them might be the closer correspondence between the metaphysical and epistemic senses of individuation that exists (in comparison with the correspondence between them that exists in the patent, trade mark, and registered design right fields) owing to the absence of an equivalent 'hypothetical intelligent individual' construct through which the process of individuation is required to be filtered.

3.9 The Relationship between Each Subject Matter and Its Tokens

The precise relationship between each category of protectable subject matter and its tokens differs according to the species of IP.

Beginning with patents: each protected idea is instantiated in the individual products or processes to which it relates, and in the definition of it contained in the patent application and register. None of these tokens reproduces the invention as such, but rather represents it, or an invention that is materially the same as it. While the products by which an invention may be instantiated are physical objects, the processes are sequences of steps (ie occurrences), and the definition is a materially recorded literary work. Thus, the tokens of a single invention can differ ontologically.

Similarly in the case of plant varieties, each subject matter is instantiated in material that expresses the genotype characteristics of the variety, and in the official description of those characteristics contained in the plant variety right register. For plant varieties, such instantiations are construed to allow for a certain tolerance range, which may be greater than that allowed for the tokens of inventions. This has been rationalized with reference to varieties' existence as living objects, and the dependence of official descriptions and manifestations of their defining characteristics on a variety of environmental, technological, and legal factors (such as soil, use of fertilizers, temperature and light conditions, and plant variety examination guidelines) the changing nature of which, legal officials have recognized, will often lead a given variety to manifest (or be described as manifesting) different characteristics at different times.

As with the tokens of inventions, the tokens of plant varieties do not reproduce the subject matter protectable by plant variety right as such, but rather represent it. While the products by which a variety may be instantiated are physical objects, the official description is a materially recorded intangible expressive object in the form of a literary work, making the tokens of varieties essentially different, as for the tokens of inventions in general.

The relationship between the works protected by copyright and their individual tokens is slightly different. While tokens can instantiate the protected work by representing it, as for the tokens of an invention or plant variety, they can also instantiate the work by reproducing it. Examples of a token representing the work include a musical score and dramatic script, each of which contains instructions for realizing the musical and dramatic work respectively. Examples of a token reproducing the work include a recreation of a photograph or drawing. Even artistic works can be represented rather than reproduced, however, as in the case of a textual description of a graphic work. Since in all cases a protected work is instantiated in its tokens, the work is the object or occurrence that the tokens instantiate.

As the example of a textual description of a graphic work makes clear, the tokens of an authorial work need not have the same expressive properties by virtue of their ability to represent rather than reproduce the work. However, tokens of works all share a causal connection to the protected work due to the law's requirement that any copyright-infringing act be the result of (direct or indirect) access by the putative infringer to the protected subject matter.

Each registered trade mark, PDO, or PGI is instantiated in the manner in part of an authorial work. Thus, the tokens of a given trade mark, PDO, or PGI have in common their expressive form, consistent with their nature as expressive objects. However, merely reproducing or representing a trade mark, PDO, or PGI in recorded verbal or written form will not suffice to instantiate it as such by reason of its purpose-limited nature. Thus, a person who writes 'just do it' to her colleague will not thereby instantiate the trade mark JUST DO IT. Rather, for the slogan to be instantiated *qua* trade mark it must be represented as such and, in particular, it must be represented as a mark of commercial origin or certification etc for goods or services of the same type as those for which the slogan is registered. The same applies mutatis mutandis with respect to PDOs and PGIs.

That leaves the relationship between each registered and unregistered design and its tokens. Registered designs are realized or instantiated by application to or incorporation in an individual product or product part. As with product inventions, the design is thus instantiated in or exemplified by the products or product parts to which it relates, and in the representation of it contained in the design right application and document. The same applies for unregistered designs, with the difference that they also share a causal connection to the protected design, owing to the requirement that any infringing act involve a subject matter derived from that design, similar to the position in copyright.

3.10 Establishing the Existence of Each Subject Matter and Its Tokens

As with the relationship between each IP subject matter and its tokens, so too the method of establishing the existence of each differs according to the species of IP and the nature of the subject matter in question.

In patent law, the existence of a patented invention is known by reason of and reference to its textual definition and description in the patent application and register, while the existence of an invention in general may be known by means of any source of information sufficient to establish its essential properties. The existence of one or more of an invention's (other) properly and improperly formed tokens is known from the existence of a product or process that the hypothetical skilled addressee of the invention would understand to fall within its scope, including (if the invention is patented) within the scope of the definition of the invention contained in the patent claims, in the sense of manifesting materially the same physical properties as the product or process to which the invention relates and, for purpose-limited inventions, the same intention with respect to the purpose of its use. In plant variety right law, by contrast, the existence of a protected variety is known to the authorities by the existence of a token in the form of a sample of the variety, the deposit of which is necessary to secure plant variety right protection, and to the public by its textual description in the register, while the existence of a variety in general may be known by means of any source of information sufficient to establish its essential properties. The existence of one or more of a variety's (other) properly and improperly formed tokens is also known from the existence of a product that the relevant authorities understand to fall within the scope of the variety—including (if the variety is protected) within the scope of the official description of the variety contained in the register—tolerating such variations as appropriate having regard to the scientific, environmental, technological, and legal factors above.

Similarly in copyright, the existence of an authorial work must be established by such evidence as exists, including in the United Kingdom that provided by the material record of the work that triggered its protection (if such record has not been lost or destroyed). The existence of one or more of a work's properly and improperly formed tokens is similarly known from the existence of a thing or event, in the form of a performance or other act of communication, that the court would understand to incorporate or involve the whole or a (substantial) part of the essential properties of the protected work that it has accepted to exist and to have been derived from it.

In trade mark law, the existence of a trade mark is known by reason of and reference to its representation in the register, as for the existence of an invention in patent law. The existence of one or more of its properly or improperly formed tokens is known from the registration or use of a subject matter that the hypothetical reasonably observant and circumspect average consumer of the relevant goods or services would understand to be identical or confusingly similar to the protected trade mark in respect of identical or confusingly similar goods or services. The same applies mutatis mutandis with respect to PDOs and PGIs, except that the existence of one or more properly or improperly formed tokens of such subject matter is known from the registration or use of a subject matter that the hypothetical reasonably observant and circumspect average consumer of the relevant goods would understand to *evoke* the same type of product in respect of which the PDO or PGI is registered.

And finally, in design law, the existence of a registered design is known by reason of and reference to its representation in the design documentation, and the existence of an unregistered design must be established by evidence, as for the existence of an authorial work. More difficult is the position with respect to the properly and improperly formed tokens of each. One or more of the tokens of a registered design is known from the existence of a product that, or a part of which, produces the same overall visual impression in the mind of the informed user of the products to which the design relates as the impression produced by the design represented in the design documentation. While the tokens of an unregistered design are established in the same way for the purposes of unregistered Community design right, for the purposes of unregistered UK design right they are established from the existence of a product that incorporates the whole or a substantial part of the protected design. For both (Community and UK) titles of unregistered design right, the producer of the tokens of a design must also be shown to have derived them directly or indirectly from the design itself.

4. Conclusions

Despite the tendency to treat them as separate, the various subject matter protectable by the different species of IP have much in common. For example, the plant variety is a type of invention as conceived by European legal officials, and the design is a type of authorial work, albeit—and in the case of the unregistered design in its UK conception—with a different history of production than the history of an authorial work's production. That leaves the trade mark and other product designations such as PDOs and PGIs, which are hybrid work-inventions in the form of purpose-limited expressive objects.

Conceived in these terms, IP subject matter are all creations, and in particular intellectual creations, in one or other of the two common law senses described previously. Authorial works and designs satisfy the restrictive conception reflected in the *Doodeward* case, while trade marks, plant varieties, and inventions (as understood by European legal officials) satisfy the more expansive conception reflected in *Yearworth* instead. Whether Europe will amend its definition of the invention to reflect the more restrictive sense of creation in the manner of other common law jurisdictions recently remains to be seen. The question must be asked, however, as to the justification for offering different levels of protection by means of the patent and plant variety right regimes for the same subject matter, and whether the difference in the secondary requirements for such protection offers a sufficient explanation for this differential treatment. The same question is raised by the similarity between those subject matter that are 'inventions' grace only of European legal officials' expansive conception of creation on the one hand, and the phonograms and other subject matter protectable by related rights on the other.

Understanding legal officials' use of the terms stipulated by legislation to denote the subject matter protectable by each of the main IP regimes is essential for the reasons given at the outset of this chapter: namely, to enable the field to be ordered and clarified within the limits imposed by the stipulative nature of legal definition and by the nature, aims, and values of IP in general. A central aim of any such process is (or ought to be) to ensure that, however widely or narrowly the scope of IP protection is cast, its primary reference point remains the individual subject matter to which the property rights attach, conceived as a subject matter of relevant (protectable) type. Thus, for example, it is the conception of a trade mark as a purpose-limited expressive object inherently unsuited to protection by design, copyright, or patent protection that is the appropriate starting point for determining the nature and scope of the rights that are afforded with respect to each sign for which a registered trade mark is granted.

One issue that defining the terms denoting the subject matter protectable by each IP regime helps bring into focus is the precise relationship between the requirement for the existence of a subject matter of protectable type on the one hand, and the requirement for its fulfilment of certain secondary requirements (or its possession of certain accidental properties) on the other. This issue raises the further question of whether the scope of protection conferred in respect of a given subject matter ought, as a matter of policy, to be defined with reference to the protectable subject matter *simpliciter*, or rather with reference to that subject matter possessing some or all of the secondary properties that the law requires it to possess in order to secure protection. This relates back to the question above regarding the consistency of treating similar subject matter (such as certain inventions and plant varieties) differently, and the coherence of an IP system that fails to recognize that the subject matter protectable by a given regime are a subset of or closely analogous to the subject matter protectable by another regime. While answering these questions is not among the aims of this book, offering a map by defining the terms used to denote the subject matter that each IP regime protects with reference to conceptions of those subject matter is a first step to enabling these and related questions to be posed and addressed.

2

An Overview of Intellectual Property Rights and Systems

1. Introduction

The stipulative nature of authoritative legal definition requires that legal officials' understanding of the terms used to denote the subject matter of intellectual property (IP) be understood in the context of IP law as a whole, including the nature, aims, and values of the rights and systems that it creates.[1] Hence the focus of the current chapter on those rights and systems as they have developed and exist in the United Kingdom and Europe today. In the course of this discussion certain distinctions of importance for IP law are identified, including the distinction between industrial and authorial property, the distinction between registered and unregistered rights, the distinction between IP rights and IP legislation, and the distinction between IP rights and IP subject matter, respectively.

2. Intellectual Property Law in England and France before the 1880s

The patent system was the first statutory IP system to be created. It was established by a 1474 Venetian Act that offered protection for contrivances as such people 'who have most clever minds' might devise and invent. According to its terms:

> There are men in this city, and also there come other persons every day from different places by reason of its greatness and goodness, who have most clever minds, capable of devising and inventing all kinds of ingenious contrivances. And should it be legislated that the works and contrivances invented by them could not be copied and made by others so that they are deprived of their honour, men of such kind would exert their minds, invent and make things that would be of no small utility and benefit to our State. Therefore, the decision

[1] See ch 1 s 2.2.

has been made that, by authority of this Council, any person in this city who makes any new and ingenious contrivances not made heretofore in our Dominion, shall, as soon as it is perfected so that it can be used and exercised, give notice of the same to the office of our Provveditori di Comun, having been forbidden up to ten years to any other person in any territory and place of ours to make a contrivance in the form and resemblance of that one without the consent and license of the author. And if nevertheless someone should make it, the aforesaid author and inventor will have the liberty to cite him before any office of this city, which office will force the aforesaid infringer to pay him the sum of one hundred ducats and immediately destroy the contrivance. But our Government will be free, at its complete discretion, to take and use for its needs any of the said contrivances and instruments, with this condition, however, that no one other than the authors shall operate them.[2]

In 1623 an English counterpart to this statute permitted grants of privilege by the Crown to the 'true and first inventor and inventors' of any 'manner of new manufactures ... not contrary to the Lawe nor mischievous to the State, by raisinge prices of Commodities at home, or hurt of Trade, or generallie inconvenient'.[3] The grants were to last for fourteen years and prevent others during that period from working (using) or making the patented subject matter.[4] Striking is the law's resemblance to the Venetian Act, including in the content, scope, term, and beneficiaries of the protection it envisaged, the requirement for application to and approval by a state authority and, most importantly for present purposes, the subject matter for which it offered or approved protection. Under the Venetian Act that subject matter was the category of new and ingenious contrivances perfected for use and exercise, and under the Statute of Monopolies it was the category of manners of new manufacture not contrary to law nor mischievous to the state.

The Statute of Monopolies became the blueprint for patent laws throughout the common law world, and is still the explicit basis for the patent laws of Australia and New Zealand.[5] It and the Venetian Act by which it was influenced also served as early models for other emergent IP regimes in Europe. Two related ideas can be seen to have been central. One is the idea of rewarding and encouraging the introduction into the public sphere of creations of value through the promise of a right to prevent others from making or using those creations for a limited period. (In the case of the Statute of Monopolies, that period corresponded to two seven-year terms of an industrial apprenticeship, being an estimate of the time required to train locals in the working of the patented object.) And the second was the idea of promoting trade and commerce by regulating access to such creations following their entry to market.

The same ideas can be seen to have underpinned the emergence of the copyright regime. Postdating the Venetian Patent Act by nearly 200 years, the first copyright legislation of 1710—the English Statute of Anne[6]—recognized the right of

[2] Venetian Statute on Industrial Brevets 1474, in L Bently and M Kretschmer (eds), *Primary Sources on Copyright (1450–1900)* (Arts and Humanities Research Council 2008) www.copyrighthistory.org. For a commentary see J Kostylo, 'Commentary on the Venetian Statute on Industrial Brevets (1474)' in Bently and Kretschmer (ibid).

[3] Statute of Monopolies 1623 (Eng) (Statute of Monopolies).

[4] ibid s VI.

[5] See Patents Act 2013 (NZ) s 14(a); Patents Act 1990 (Aus) s 18(1)(a).

[6] Statute of Anne 1710 (Eng) (Statute of Anne).

authors to prevent third parties from printing, reprinting, or importing within or into Britain any book they had created for a renewable term of fourteen years from the day of first publication, subject to the book having been deposited for use by certain public libraries. Mirroring again the early patent acts' focus on the introduction to the public of creations of value, the title and preamble of the Statute of Anne described its purpose as being to encourage learning and 'Learned Men to Compose and Write useful Books' by protecting authors and their families from ruinous piracy. So too the idea of promoting trade and commerce by regulating access to books and other printed materials is clearly visible in the history of the copyright regime. For example, the Statute of Anne was introduced in England to replace the pre-copyright printers' system of the 16th and 17th centuries. By operation of that system, the English Crown had regulated the trade in printed materials by conferring monopoly rights in respect of the then recently introduced printing technology in exchange for an undertaking by their beneficiaries only to print materials approved for publication by the Crown. While the Statute of Anne replaced that system, it preserved the rights of printers acquired under it for a limited period and—in its focus on the printing, reprinting, and importing of books—reflected the same concern with regulating access to printed works and technologies.

Once accepted, these ideas of rewarding and encouraging the public dissemination of creations of value and promoting trade through the regulation of access to them spread to other areas of industry and human activity. In 18th century France, for example, monopoly rights similar to those conferred on the stationers' company and other printing guilds of Europe were conferred on the *Conseil des Prud'hommes* in respect of weaving looms to protect their silk weaving industry before being replaced by general laws recognizing designers as having property rights in respect of their creations. The first law of this type was introduced in England by the Calico Printers' Act 1787[7] for the express purpose of encouraging 'the arts of designing and printing linens, cottons, calicoes and muslins' by preventing unauthorized copies and imitations of new and original fabric patterns for a limited, two-month period.[8] According to its terms, any person who invented, designed, and printed—or caused to be invented, designed, and printed—a new and original pattern or patterns for printing linens, cottons, calicos, and muslins, acquired the right to prevent others from doing the same, or from publishing, selling, or exposing for sale any linen, cotton, calico, or muslin featuring the pattern(s).

The same transition from the grant of individual privileges to the recognition of property rights as a means of rewarding and encouraging the introduction to the public of useful intellectual objects is reflected in the history of the lesser known IP system concerning plant varieties. For example, an 1833 Papal Edict declared that:

[7] Calico Printers' Act 1787 (Eng).

[8] The full title of the Act was 'An Act for the Encouragement of the Arts of Designing and Printing Linens, Cottons, Calicos and Muslins by vesting the properties thereof in the Designers, Printers and Proprietors for a limited time'.

Deserving men who have applied their intelligence and industry to the discovery of new products and to the invention, improvement or introduction of new types of culture or technical solutions, or of new methods for their use, deserve to have the rewards of their research and their discoveries guaranteed to them to the same extent as the rewards deriving from science, letters or the fine arts. We have already provided sufficiently, in Our Edict of September 23, 1826, for means of guaranteeing the ownership of scientific and literary works, and We have now to concern ourselves with guaranteeing also the ownership of those works that relate to the progress of agriculture and its techniques by a more reliable and more expeditious method than that practiced hitherto with respect to the grant of specific exclusive privileges.[9]

According to André Heitz, under this provision any person 'who for instance discovered a natural product or found or introduced an important new type of agricultural plant in the Papal States was granted an exclusive property right,' which right lasted from five to fifteen years, and prevented others during that period from working the product or plant.[10] That right was subject to an obligation on the part of its beneficiary to work the product or plant himself within one year following the grant. It was also conditional upon the working of the product or plant not causing harm to local economic activity or public safety, health, and well-being, mirroring the position in respect of inventions under the Statute of Monopolies.[11]

That brings us to the trade mark regime, the history of which is similar to that of other IP regimes in having emerged out of a pre-property system aimed at supporting the organization of industry through the regulation of guild monopolies. For example, the governing charters of the merchant guilds of medieval Europe had routinely required the affixing of two marks on merchants' goods—one of the guild under whose monopoly the goods were produced, and one of the individual merchant within that guild responsible for producing them—as a means of tracing their origins in the event of the goods being defective or otherwise produced in breach of guild monopoly rules. (A similar practice of affixing authors' names to printed materials was later deployed under the pre-copyright stationers' system as a means of attributing responsibility for the materials' content.) In the 17th century case of *Southern v How*,[12] an English court supported this practice by declaring that traders were prohibited from affixing others' signs of origin to their own goods on the ground that doing so would deceive the public as to their goods' provenance. That principle received legislative recognition in the context of different trades in the 17th, 18th, and 19th centuries, and in the first general trade mark legislation of 1875.[13] The result was a form of protection that differed from the

[9] A Heitz, 'The History of Plant Variety Protection' in *The First Twenty-Five Years of the International Convention for the Protection of New Varieties of Plants: December 2, 1961–December 2, 1986* (UPOV 1987) 53, 60.

[10] ibid.

[11] ibid. It took nearly 100 years for another plant variety right regime to emerge, and not in Europe but rather the United States, with the Plant Patent Act of 1930. That Act introduced a *sui generis* system for the protection of plant varieties similar in its substantive terms to the system later introduced by a collection of European and other states in 1961 as the International Convention for the Protection of New Varieties of Plants (UPOV Convention).

[12] Southern v How (1618) Pop R 143, 79 ER 1243 (KB).

[13] Trade Marks Registration Act 1875 (UK).

protection conferred by copyright, patents, designs, and plant varieties in its focus on preventing the deceit of consumers rather than rewarding and encouraging the introduction to the public of valuable creations and discoveries. It also served a different commercial role: rather than establishing a market for such creations and discoveries (the intangible nature of which would otherwise have deprived them of economic value by enabling their reproduction and exploitation by third parties at marginal cost), trade mark protection sought primarily to support the function of signs in communicating information to consumers regarding the goods to which they were attached.[14] At the same time, by supporting this function trade mark law promoted trade and commerce by facilitating informed and efficient purchasing decisions and fair competition among traders within the marketplace.

In conclusion, the original IP regimes in England can be understood as having emerged in broadly similar circumstances, while having been driven by somewhat different, albeit overlapping, aims and ideas. The central aims of the earliest patent, copyright, industrial designs, and plant variety rights regimes were to reward and encourage the introduction to the public of socially valuable creations and discoveries in the form of contrivances and manners of new manufacture, books, fabric designs, and agricultural products, and thereby to promote industry and commerce by supporting the establishment and smooth functioning of markets in respect of them. The central aims of the trade mark regime, by contrast, were to protect the consuming public from misrepresentations regarding the origin of goods in trade, and in doing so to promote a competitive and well-functioning marketplace. Despite these differences, the subject matter protectable by each species of IP was similar in its intangible (informational or expressive) nature.

3. Early Deontological and Instrumentalist Arguments for Intellectual Property

Of note regarding the characterization of the aims of different IP regimes in Section 2 is its public policy and public benefit focus, consistent with the terms of each founding IP instrument. In addition, however, implicit in the idea of rewarding those who introduce new objects of value to the public is the idea of such persons as *deserving* to be rewarded. This idea of desert is also reflected in the description of the beneficiaries of early IP legislation as 'men ... who have most clever minds' (Venetian Patent Act), 'true ... inventors' (Statute of Monopolies), 'learned men' (Statute of Anne), and 'deserving men' (1833 Papal Edict), and gives the early English IP legislation a certain normative ambivalence in its focus on both individual and communitarian values and interests.

[14] M Lehmann, 'The Theory of Property Rights and the Protection of Intellectual and Industrial Property' [1985] International Review of Industrial Property and Copyright Law 525, 531–32; see also R A Posner, 'The Law and Economics of Intellectual Property' (2002) Daedalus 5, 8.

The idea of IP as promoting individual as well as communitarian values and interests references the two main theories and traditions of IP recognition and protection among European states. According to the first of these, IP rights are granted by the state to secure certain public benefits, such as creating an environment conducive to innovation, expression, and creation, and/or supporting a smooth and efficient market in intellectual creations and related goods and services. According to the second, IP rights exist for deontological rather than instrumentalist ends, in recognition of the moral or natural law rights that individuals have to exclude others from the results and benefits of their intellectual labours.

The choice between deontological and instrumentalist conceptions of IP has importance for understandings of the subject matter that IP protects. For example, if IP rights are moral or natural law rights owed to individuals by reason of their acts of intellectual creation or discovery, they will only legitimately be granted in respect of intellectual creations and discoveries properly conceived. By contrast, if IP rights are instruments of the state for securing certain public benefit ends, their grant will be justified in any situation in which it is necessary and effective to secure those ends. In the first model, it is the existence of a certain type of subject matter that serves as the primary reference point for deciding whether rights do and should exist. By contrast, in the second model it is the necessity for and efficacy of the rights in securing the relevant ends that is the primary determinant of whether a given grant is justified. The point is underlined by the terms of the earliest French and English IP statutes. The earliest French IP enactments of the 1790s followed the assertion of property protection in the 1789 Declaration of the Rights of Man as 'inviolable and sacred',[15] and conferred temporary exclusionary rights on those who had made 'any discovery or new invention, in any kind of industry',[16] and to '[a]uthors of writings of all kinds, composers of music, painters and designers who make engravings or drawings'.[17] By contrast, and as seen above, the earliest English IP enactments of the 17th and 18th centuries granted or approved the grant of rights in respect of similar types of subject matter—manners of new manufacture, books, and fabric designs—to support manufacturing and encourage the arts of writing and design. It is from this difference that the association of deontological and instrumentalist theories of IP protection with the English (common law) and French (civil law) traditions respectively derives.

[15] Déclaration des Droits de l'Homme et du Citoyen de 1789 art 17 ('Les propriétés étant un droit inviolable et sacré, nul ne peut en être privé, si ce n'est lorsque la nécessité publique, légalement constatée, l'exige évidemment, et sous la condition d'une juste et préalable indemnité').

[16] Décret relatif aux brevets d'invention 1790 art 1 ('Toute découverte ou nouvelle invention, dans tous les genres d'industrie, est la propriété de son auteur; en consequence, la loi lui en garantit la pleine et entière jouissance, suivant le mode et pour les termes qui seront ci-après déterminés').

[17] Décret relatif aux droit de propriété des auteurs d'écrits en tout genre, des compositeurs de musique, des peintres et des dessinateurs 1793 art 1 ('Les auteurs d'écrits en tout genre, les compositeurs de musique, les peintres et les dessinateurs qui feront graver des tableaux ou dessins, jouiront, durant leur vie entière, du droit exclusive de vendre, faire vendre, distribuer leurs ouvrages dans le territoire de la République, et d'en céder la propriété en tout ou en partie').

4. The Great (Paris and Berne) Conventions of the 1880s

A challenge for European countries in the 19th and early 20th centuries, and for the EU since its creation in the 1950s, has been to define rules and standards of IP protection that respect, in the sense of being consistent with, these different deontological and instrumentalist—and common and civil law—traditions. The first steps to that end were taken with the great conventions of the 1880s—the Paris Convention for the Protection of Industrial Property,[18] and the Berne Convention for the Protection of Literary and Artistic Property,[19] of 1883 and 1886 respectively—each of which created a Union of states committed to the non-discriminatory treatment of the citizens of other Union states, and to the recognition of certain minimum standards of IP protection.[20]

The focus of the Paris Convention is on the recognition and protection of industrial property. According to Article 1(3), 'industrial property' within the meaning of the Convention is to be 'understood in the broadest sense', and in particular to 'apply not only to industry and commerce proper, but likewise to agricultural and extractive industries and to all manufactured or natural products, for example, wines, grain, tobacco leaf, fruit, cattle, minerals, mineral waters, beer, flowers, and flour'. Article 1(2) defines the object of industrial property protection exhaustively as comprising 'patents, utility models, industrial designs, trade marks, service marks, trade names, and indications of source or appellations of origin, and the repression of unfair competition'. Beyond this definition, the Convention is largely silent on the subject matter to be protected by each industrial property regime, except on the question of what signs might be registered or used as trade marks. Prohibited is the registration or use without authorization of emblems (including flags) of member states, and official signs and hallmarks indicating control and warranty adopted by member states.[21] Required is the protection of service and collective marks, and of trade names.[22]

More expansive are the provisions of the Berne Convention regarding the subject matter to be protected by literary and artistic property. For example, Article 2 requires the protection by copyright of literary and artistic works, and defines that category to include 'every production in the literary, scientific and artistic domain, whatever may be the mode or form of its expression', including (by express provision) derivative works (translations, adaptations, arrangements of music, and other alterations of literary or artistic works), and collections of works or of data, and

[18] Paris Convention for the Protection of Industrial Property (adopted 20 March 1883, last revised 14 July 1967) 828 UNTS 305, as amended (Paris Convention).

[19] Berne Convention for the Protection of Literary and Artistic Works (adopted 9 September 1886, last revised 24 July 1971) 828 UNTS 221, as amended (Berne Convention).

[20] For a fuller discussion of these Conventions see S Ricketson, 'The Emergence and Development of the International Intellectual Property System' in R C Dreyfuss and J Pila (eds), *The Oxford Handbook of Intellectual Property Law* (OUP 2017) http://www.oxfordhandbooks.com/view/10.1093/oxfordhb/9780198758457.001.0001/oxfordhb-9780198758457 (last accessed 5 June 2017).

[21] Paris Convention art 6*ter*.

[22] ibid arts 6*sexies*, 7*bis*, and 8.

excluding (by further express provision) news of the day and miscellaneous facts having the character of press information. A number of additional categories of subject matter are also left for protection by literary and artistic property at the discretion of Berne Union states, including official legislative, administrative, and legal texts and their official translations, and works of applied art.

Having established a subject matter of relevance, application of the Paris and Berne Conventions generally depends on showing the individual claimant to be a national of, or resident or domiciled in, a Paris or Berne Union state, so as to be entitled under each Convention to seek protection in the territories of its other Union states.[23] The protection to which the claimant is then entitled is the same protection afforded under the domestic laws of the state in which protection is sought—including the rights specially provided for by the Paris or Berne Convention itself.[24] In the case of the Paris Convention, the most important of these for registered IP rights—patents, utility models, trade marks, and industrial designs—are the rights of priority, which give a claimant a period of time after first filing for protection in his own country in which to file for protection for the same subject matter in other Paris Union countries.[25] Beyond this, the rights specially conferred by the Paris Convention are comparatively limited. For patents they include: the right of the inventor to be identified as such in the patent document;[26] the right not to be denied a patent by reason of restrictions under local law;[27] the right not to have a patent revoked for failure to work the invention in certain circumstances;[28] the right not to be required to mark patented products as patented;[29] the right to enjoy a grace period for the payment of renewal fees and the restoration of a lapsed patent;[30] the right to use patented contrivances on ships, aircraft, and vehicles temporarily entering the territory of a Union state without infringement;[31] the right to enforce a process patent obtained in a country into which goods manufactured in accordance with the patent are imported under the local law of the country of importation;[32] and the right to temporary protection for patented inventions in respect of goods exhibited at official or officially recognized international exhibitions.[33] So too the rights specially conferred in respect of the other forms of industrial property governed by the Paris Convention are limited—barely touching on the central issues raised by the existence of each regime, such as the nature of the subject matter protected, the protection conferred in respect of that subject matter, the requirements for obtaining such protection, and the period for which the protection lasts.[34]

Considerably more detailed in this regard are the provisions of the Berne Convention. As amended, it prohibits the making of protection of foreign authors and works subject to any formality,[35] such as deposit, registration, or publication,

[23] See Ricketson (n 20). [24] Paris Convention art 2(1); Berne Convention art 5(1).
[25] Paris Convention arts 4A–4I. [26] ibid art 4*ter*. [27] ibid art *4quater*.
[28] ibid art 5A. [29] ibid art 5D. [30] ibid art 5*bis*. [31] ibid art 5*ter*.
[32] ibid art 5*quater*. [33] ibid art 11. [34] See Ricketson (n 20).
[35] Berne Convention art 5(2).

as the Statute of Anne had done. It also defines: the category of subject matter entitled to protection—'literary and artistic works'—to 'include every production in the literary, scientific and artistic domain', as seen above;[36] the exclusive rights that must be accorded to authors in respect of such subject matter to include the moral rights of paternity (authorial attribution) and integrity,[37] and the economic rights of reproduction, translation, public performance and recitation, broadcasting, adaptation, and cinematographic adaptation and performance/communication,[38] lasting (with some exceptions) for the life of the author plus 50 years; [39] and the exceptions that Union states may recognize to these rights to cover the use of an authorial work for specific purposes, including those of news reporting, education, quotation, and review,[40] and 'in certain special cases' where the use 'does not conflict with a normal exploitation of the work and does not unreasonably prejudice the legitimate interests of the author'.[41]

Since their introduction in the late 19th century, and most recent revisions in the 1960s and 1970s, the Paris and Berne Conventions have been adopted as the basis for further international instruments in the field of IP. These include the 1961 Rome Convention,[42] requiring the protection of performances, phonograms, and broadcasts by rights analogous to copyright (so-called 'neighbouring rights' or 'related rights'), and the 1996 WIPO Copyright and Performers and Phonograms Treaties,[43] extending and updating copyright and related rights for the digital environment. They also include the 1994 TRIPs Agreement.[44] In the field of copyright and related rights, this Agreement endorses the subject matter provisions of the Berne Convention,[45] and makes further provision for the protection of computer programs, whether in source or object code, as literary works, and for the protection of compilations of data or other material, whether in machine readable or other form. In the field of industrial property, the Agreement similarly affirms and extends the provisions of the Paris Convention, including by defining the categories of subject matter requiring protection by the law of trade marks, geographical indications, and patents respectively. Under Article 15(1) of the TRIPs Agreement, for example, trade marks are defined to include:

> Any sign, or any combination of signs, capable of distinguishing the goods or serves of one undertaking from those of other undertakings, shall be capable of constituting a trademark. Such signs, in particular words including personal names, letters, numerals, figurative elements and combinations of colours as well as any combination of such signs, shall be eligible for registration as trademarks. Where signs are not inherently capable of distinguishing

[36] ibid art 2(1). [37] ibid art 6*bis*. [38] ibid arts 9–14. [39] ibid art 7(1).

[40] ibid arts 10 and 10*bis*. [41] ibid art 9(2).

[42] Rome Convention for the Protection of Performers, Producers of Phonograms and Broadcasting (adopted 26 October 1961) 496 UNTS 72 (Rome Convention).

[43] WIPO Copyright Treaty (opened for signature 20 December 1996, entered into force 6 March 2002) 36 ILM 65; WIPO Performances and Phonograms Treaty (opened for signature 20 December 1996, entered into force 20 May 2002) 36 ILM 76.

[44] Agreement on Trade-related Aspects of Intellectual Property Rights (opened for signature 15 December 1993, entered into force 1 January 1995) 1869 UNTS 299 (TRIPs Agreement).

[45] ibid art 9(1).

the relevant goods or services, Members may make registrability depend on distinctiveness acquired through use. Members may require, as a condition of registration, that signs be visually perceptible.

This is followed in Article 22(1) by a definition of geographical indications as 'indications which identify a good as originating in the territory of a Member, or a region or locality in that territory, where a given quality, reputation or other characteristic of the good is essentially attributable to its geographical origin', and in Article 27 by a requirement that patents be made 'available for any inventions, whether products or processes, in all fields of technology'.

5. Intellectual Property Law in Europe and the United Kingdom Today

5.1 Constitutional Values and Intellectual Property

5.1.1 Europe

The purpose of the three primary fields of IP in the United States, formally speaking at least, can be readily ascertained from the constitutional provisions by which Congress is empowered to introduce IP legislation. For copyright and patents this is Article I, section 8, clause 8 of the Constitution, which grants Congress the power:

To promote the progress of science and useful arts, by securing for limited times to authors and inventors the exclusive right to their respective writings and discoveries.

For trade marks it is Article I, section 8, clause 3, which grants Congress the power '[t]o regulate Commerce with foreign Nations, and among the several States, and with the Indian Tribes.'[46]

In the EU, equivalent constitutional provisions governing the basis and exercise of EU legislative authority in IP may be found in the EU Treaties and Charter of Fundamental Rights.[47] Under the Treaties, the EU legislature is empowered to introduce harmonizing directives in any field if necessary to support the establishment and functioning of the internal market.[48] It may also introduce regulations establishing unitary IP rights,[49] and negotiate and enter international agreements concerning IP.[50] In exercising each of these competences, the EU is constrained by the requirements of subsidiarity and proportionality,[51] the values of 'respect for human dignity, freedom, democracy, equality, the rule of law and respect for human

[46] In the 19th century, in the *Trade-Mark Cases* 100 US 82 (1879), the Supreme Court struck down US trade mark legislation introduced in reliance on cl 8 as *ultra vires*. Since then federal trade mark legislation in the US has been based on the commerce clause (ie cl 3).

[47] Charter of Fundamental Rights of the European Union [2010] OJ C 83/389 (CFR).

[48] Consolidated Version of the Treaty on the Functioning of the European Union [2012] OJ C 326/47 (TFEU) art 114.

[49] ibid art 118. [50] ibid art 216.

[51] Consolidated Version of the Treaty on European Union [2012] OJ C 326/13 (TEU) art 5(1).

rights, including the rights of persons belonging to minorities' on which European Union is based, and the need to act in accordance with the Union's aims.[52] Those aims are set out at length in Article 3 of the TEU as follows:

1. The Union's aim is to promote peace, its values and the well-being of its peoples.
2. The Union shall offer its citizens an area of freedom, security and justice without internal frontiers, in which the free movement of persons is ensured in conjunction with appropriate measures with respect to external border controls, asylum, immigration and the prevention and combating of crime.
3. The Union shall establish an internal market. It shall work for the sustainable development of Europe based on balanced economic growth and price stability, a highly competitive social market economy, aiming at full employment and social progress, and a high level of protection and improvement of the quality of the environment. It shall promote scientific and technological advance.

   It shall combat social exclusion and discrimination, and shall promote social justice and protection, equality between women and men, solidarity between generations and protection of the rights of the child.

   It shall promote economic, social and territorial cohesion, and solidarity among Member States.

   It shall respect its rich cultural and linguistic diversity, and shall ensure that Europe's cultural heritage is safeguarded and enhanced.
4. The Union shall establish an economic and monetary union whose currency is the euro.
5. In its relations with the wider world, the Union shall uphold and promote its values and interests and contribute to the protection of its citizens. It shall contribute to peace, security, the sustainable development of the Earth, solidarity and mutual respect among peoples, free and fair trade, eradication of poverty and the protection of human rights, in particular the rights of the child, as well as to the strict observance and the development of international law, including respect for the principles of the United Nations Charter.
6. The Union shall pursue its objectives by appropriate means commensurate with the competences which are conferred upon it in the Treaties.

Also important in EU law is the CFR, which shares the status of the Treaties, and serves as a further statement of the values on which European Union is based, and expression of the general principles with which EU legal measures must comply.[53] Of especial significance for IP among its provisions are those requiring the protection of human dignity,[54] privacy,[55] and freedom of expression, including the pluralism of the media,[56] freedom of the arts and sciences,[57] education,[58] freedom to choose an occupation and conduct a business,[59] intellectual property,[60] integration of persons with disabilities,[61] and environmental and consumer protection.[62]

Already from this introduction one can see the complexity of the European constitutional landscape and the range of values that underpin the European legal order and that are required to inform its legislation, including in the field of IP. They

[52] ibid arts 1–5. [53] ibid art 6(1). [54] CFR art 1. [55] ibid art 7.
[56] ibid art 11. [57] ibid art 13. [58] ibid art 14. [59] ibid arts 15 and 16.
[60] ibid art 17(2). [61] ibid art 26. [62] ibid arts 37 and 38.

include the political values of subsidiarity,[63] the need to preserve the sovereignty of EU Member States in areas in which the EU does not enjoy competence,[64] and the need to respect European cultural and linguistic diversity, and ensure that Europe's cultural heritage is safeguarded and enhanced.[65] They also include the establishment and functioning of an internal market, including the promotion of sustainable development for Europe and of scientific and technological advance, and the recognition and protection of a wide variety of fundamental rights, freedoms, and interests.

5.1.2 The United Kingdom

In the UK, the absence of a written constitution or bill of rights makes it more difficult to identify the constitutional values underpinning and otherwise informing the UK intellectual property regime. In the field of industrial property, the first patent legislation, the Statute of Monopolies 1623—which has been described recently by a court as quasi-constitutional legislation[66]—established the power of the state to grant patents for inventions as an exception to the general legal prohibition against the grant of monopolies, justified on the instrumentalist and deontological grounds considered previously. The proviso that they not be 'contrary to the Lawe nor mischievous to the State, by raisinge prices of Commodities at home, or hurt of Trade, or generallie inconvenient' reflected clearly the concern of the state that such grants for inventions as were made not be contrary to other laws nor to the public interest. From the late 19th century this proviso was supported by an express power of the patent office to refuse to grant a patent on grounds of morality,[67] creating a potential opening for the courts to consider the limits of IP laws with reference to public interest considerations, although the power was rarely invoked. What was invoked as limiting IP laws from the late 1960s was *EU* constitutionalism, and particularly the EU Treaties' free movement and competition provisions.[68] Across all spheres of intellectual property, and in each of the EU's Member States, those provisions were applied directly in IP cases to support the exhaustion of IP rights in respect of individual products following their sale within EU territory by or with the consent of the IP rights holder.[69] The provisions also had an indirect influence on UK IP cases as a result of most EU legislation in the field of IP having been introduced under the EU's harmonization competence conferred by (what is now) Article 114 of the TFEU. Since EU legislation is interpreted purposively, having regard (among other things) to the aims as stated in the instrument's recitals,[70] and since the recitals of any instrument introduced in reliance on Article 114 must make clear its

[63] See TEU art 5(3). [64] ibid art 5(2). [65] ibid art 3(3).

[66] *Oakley Inc v Animal Ltd* [2005] EWHC 210 (Ch) [23]–[25] (Mr Prescott QC).

[67] Patents, Designs, and Trade Marks Act 1883 (UK) s 86 ('The comptroller may refuse to grant a patent for an invention ... of which the use would, in his opinion, be contrary to law or morality').

[68] Under the current Treaties see TFEU arts 34–36 and 101–102.

[69] See eg Case C–16/74 *Centrafarm v Winthrop* [1974] ECR 1183.

[70] See eg Case C–283/81 *Srl CILFIT and Lanificio di Gavardo SpA v Ministry of Health* [1982] ECR 3415.

harmonization aims in order to avoid repeal for lack of constitutionality, the EU IP laws by which the UK courts have been bound invariably emphasize the EU Treaty values of harmonization.

Two events from the 1960s tested the constitutional values of the UK's IP systems. The first, affecting the patent realm, was the invention of modern technology, which enabled scientists for the first time to isolate human genes and other human biological material, and to use them as the basis for the creation of useful therapeutic and other products. By the time of its invention, the Statute of Monopolies-based patent system had been replaced by a new system based on the European Patent Convention of 1973.[71] At a constitutional level, the effect of this replacement was to detach the system from its Statute of Monopolies roots and make European harmonization—achieved via consistency with the decision-making of the European Patent Office (EPO)—a central and explicit reference point for the development of UK patent rules and principles.[72] The question thus arose as to the constitutional values governing the EPC and EPO specifically; and the answer reflected in the Office's response to biotech patenting was that such values were limited and undeveloped. The EPC was a standalone international legal instrument that did not form part of any general legal order, and that was therefore not subject to the human rights or other public law principles and values constitutive of such orders. With limited exceptions, such principles and values as were to be taken into account when interpreting its provisions were confined to those given direct or indirect expression in the articles of the EPC, such as the Article 53(a) provision that patents not be granted for inventions (the commercial exploitation of which) was contrary to public policy or morality.[73] In the absence of any clear reference point for interpreting this provision, however, the EPO construed it narrowly, as only supporting the exclusion from protection of subject matter such as a letter bomb that would be universally regarded as outrageous.[74] That was despite its earlier indication that the provision would support the assessment of an invention from a public interest perspective, including having regard to principles of environmentalism, animal welfarism, and public health.[75]

The second disruptive technology to emerge in the 1970s was digital technology. The early suggestion of international instruments such as the WIPO's WCT and WPPT was that digital technology did not require any significant adaptation of traditional (Berne and Rome Convention) principles. In the UK, however, the conclusion of these instruments coincided with the introduction of the Human

[71] Convention on the Grant of European Patents (opened for signature 5 October 1973, entered into force 1 January 1977) 1065 UNTS 199, as amended (EPC). The new EPC-based system of UK patent law was introduced by the Patents Act 1977 (UK).

[72] ibid s 130(7) (requiring so far as practicable the substantive provisions of the Patents Act 1977 to be interpreted consistently with the interpretation of the corresponding provisions of the EPC).

[73] EPC art 53(a).

[74] *Howard Florey/Relaxin* [1995] EPOR 541 (Opp Div); see also T356/93 *PGS/Glutamine synthesase inhibitors* [1995] EPOR 357.

[75] See T19/90 *Harvard/Onco-mouse* [1990] EPOR 501.

Rights Act of 1998, implementing the European Convention of Human Rights.[76] That Act required that, '[s]o far as it possible to do so, primary legislation and subordinate legislation must be read and given effect in a way that is compatible with the Convention rights' defined in section 1(1),[77] including the rights to freedom of expression,[78] and to the peaceful enjoyment of one's possessions.[79] Soon after its passage, the Court of Appeal of England and Wales declared the Act to have increased the importance of ensuring that individual freedom of expression rights were not trampled by copyright. With this in mind it recognized a residual judicial power to allow the unauthorized reproduction (or other copyright use) of a work on freedom of expression grounds notwithstanding the absence of any express provision in the UK's Copyright, Designs and Patents Act 1988[80] to that effect.[81] Whether the decision resulted in any substantive change to the law is unclear, but that was certainly the implication of the Court's reasoning at the time.[82]

From these early nods to constitutionalism in the patent and copyright fields, the position has changed dramatically on account of EU legislation. Unlike the ECHR and Human Rights Act 1998, and the EPC morality/public interest provisions, there can be no doubt about the EU's counterpart human rights instrument having triggered a substantive change to UK IP laws and systems, albeit (and to date) indirectly only, through the EU Regulations and Directives influenced by it, and the decisions of the EU Court of Justice in the IP field in which it has been invoked as an interpretative mechanism.[83] In combination with the free movement and other provisions of the EU Treaties, this impact has effected a shift in UK IP law and its underpinning values to the point that we can now say that there is little difference between the constitutional values that inform EU and UK IP law respectively.

5.2 European Commission Policies and Intellectual Property

Within the EU legal order, the task of translating these constitutional values into IP policies and laws falls to the European Commission and Council. Starting with policy, an insight into the result can be gleaned from the Commission's description of IP as 'a key driver for growth and innovation', and a means of 'enhanc[ing]

[76] European Convention for the Protection of Human Rights and Fundamental Freedoms (opened for signature 4 November 1950, entered into force 3 September 1953) 213 UNTS 221, as amended (ECHR).

[77] Human Rights Act 1998 (UK) s 3(1).

[78] ECHR art 10.

[79] ibid First Protocol art 1.

[80] Copyright, Designs and Patents Act 1988 (UK) (CDPA).

[81] *Ashdown v Telegraph Group Ltd* [2001] EWCA Civ 1142, [2002] QB 546 [58] ('Now that the Human Rights Act is in force, there is the clearest public interest in giving effect to the right of freedom of expression in those rare cases where this right trumps the rights conferred by the Copyright Act. In such circumstances, we consider that s.171(3) of the Act permits the defence of public interest to be raised').

[82] On the ambivalent significance of *Ashdown* see J Griffiths, 'Copyright Law After Ashdown—Time to Deal Fairly with the Public' [2002] European Intellectual Property Review 240.

[83] See eg Case C–201/13 *Deckmyn v Vandersteen* ECLI:EU:C:2014:2132; Case C–34/10 *Brüstle v Greenpeace eV* [2011] ECR I–09821; and the other cases cited in J Pila and P L C Torremans, *European Intellectual Property Law* (OUP 2016) 50.

the EU's industrial competitiveness globally.'[84] Intellectual property rights, the Commission has said, 'are one of the principal means through which companies, creators, and inventors generate returns on their investment in knowledge, innovation, and creativity.'[85] Exactly *why* companies, creators, and inventors ought to be given the opportunity through the grant of property rights to generate returns on their investment in knowledge, innovation, and creativity is not made clear by the Commission. The implication of its statement, however, supported by other European Commission policy documents, and by the recitals of European IP legislation, is that the reasons lie in a mix of instrumentalist and deontological thinking. For example, the Commission Communication from which the above excerpt is taken continues as follows:

> A recent study has estimated that IPR-intensive sectors account for around 39% of EU GDP [Gross Domestic Product] (worth some EUR 4.7 trillion annually) and, taking indirect jobs into account, up to 35% of all jobs. In practical terms, through the granting of temporary exclusive rights, IP is directly linked to the production and distribution of new and authentic goods and services, from which all citizens benefit. The key to achieving these goals is an optimal and economically efficient IP 'infrastructure' which spans the legal recognition, registration, utilisation and balanced enforcement of all forms of IPRs.
>
> The EU needs innovation to stay competitive relative to countries with lower labour, energy and raw materials costs, and must create the conditions that stimulate innovation so that European businesses can help us trade our way out of the crisis. This is why knowledge-based industries play a core role in the 'Global Europe' and 'Europe 2020' strategies.
>
> Intellectual creations need protection if creativity and innovation are to flourish, and this is the role of IPRs, which also play an important function in promoting development and in addressing some of today's global challenges. For developing countries, a pragmatic and flexible approach will help them maximise the potential of their own intellectual assets and further their integration into international trade, while achieving broader societal welfare.[86]

Reflected in this statement is a view of IP rights as instruments for achieving the public benefit ends of generating jobs and wealth, promoting the production and distribution of goods and services, supporting innovation and competition with other states, and promoting creativity, innovation, development, and solutions to global (health, environmental, and other) challenges; and as means for ensuring to creators of intellectual products sufficient protection to enable their creative work 'to flourish'. This breadth of objectives for IP is consistent with and helps to explain the view of the Director of WIPO recently that changes in the context in which IP rights are exploited—including the rise of intangibles in the so-called knowledge economy, the geopolitical shift from West to East, and the empowerment of state actors via the Internet and other means—have given them a new role beyond their traditional roles of recognizing and protecting private

[84] European Commission, Communication from the Commission to the European Parliament, the Council and the European Economic and Social Committee: Trade, growth and intellectual property—Strategy for the protection and enforcement of intellectual property rights in third countries, COM(2014) 389 final 2.

[85] ibid. [86] ibid.

rights, and encouraging creation and the dissemination of its results.[87] In that role, Francis Gurry argued, IP rights regulate competition, ensure equilibrium between competing interests (including the interests of states), and operate as a financing mechanism.[88]

Also made clear in the statement of the European Commission above is its view of the nature of IP rights, including the subject matter to which those rights attach. Specifically, we are told that IP involves 'the granting of temporary exclusive rights' in respect of 'intellectual creations'. In addition, it is apparent that the temporary exclusive rights in question are understood by the European Commission to be property rights, consistent with Article 17 of the CFR (which recognizes the protection of property—including intellectual property—as a fundamental right), and with the wider acceptance by supranational and domestic European courts, including the European Court of Human Rights,[89] of the property status of IP rights as a matter of positive law, whatever the difference between IP and other species of property.

By way of conclusion, we can therefore say that the purpose of IP law in Europe is to build on the traditions of Member States by recognizing and protecting exclusive rights in respect of intellectual creations in a way that reflects and promotes EU Treaty and CFR values. Importantly, European IP law is not starting from scratch: it has centuries of domestic and international IP jurisprudence behind it that takes the recognition and protection of IP rights, defined differently having regard to a range of third party and social rights and interests, as a given. Nor does European IP law displace the laws of EU Member States or the international measures to which those States were, before 1957, already parties: rather, it builds on them to support the internal market and economy, and the recognition and protection of European fundamental rights and interests. Given this we can say that EU IP law supports a diversity of instrumentalist and deontological values and objectives in a multi-level (domestic, European, and international) system of governance.

Each of these aspects of the context of the European law of intellectual property constrains as much as motivates that law's development. For example, and as has been seen, the EU Treaties and CFR bind the legislature and courts in their law-making and decision-making in the field of IP. In addition, however, the domestic traditions of IP protection, and the international measures to which the EU and its Member States have adhered, represent further constraints on EU law-making and decision-making in IP, albeit of a secondary order to those represented by primary EU legal instruments.

[87] F Gurry, 'Re-thinking the Role of Intellectual Property', paper delivered at the University of Melbourne (August 2013) http://www.wipo.int/export/sites/www/about-wipo/en/dgo/speeches/pdf/dg_speech_melbourne_2013.pdf (last accessed 5 June 2017).

[88] ibid.

[89] See eg *Anheuser-Busch Inc v Portugal* (2007) 45 EHRR 36 (Grand Chamber).

5.3 Intellectual Property Legislation

The question arises of how the EU view of IP rights (as temporary exclusive rights in respect of intellectual creations that aim to build on the traditions of Member States by recognizing and protecting such rights in a way that reflects and promotes EU Treaty and CFR values) finds expression in European IP measures specifically. The starting point for considering this must be European IP legislation itself, an overview of which should also offer a preliminary answer to the question regarding the implications of the nature and purpose of IP rights for (EU legal) conceptions of the subject matter that they protect.

5.3.1 Copyright and Related Rights

The legislative basis of the European copyright system is a series of intersecting and overlapping directives, all of which have been introduced in reliance on the EU's internal market competence[90] for the purpose of harmonizing domestic copyright and related rights laws in support of the establishment and functioning of the internal market. The directives are a combination of vertical instruments, dealing with specific rights or subject matter, and horizontal instruments, dealing with rights and subject matter in general. They build on the 1971 Berne Convention Act, and with the EU Treaty and CFR provisions, represent a well-developed European copyright system that is also extensive in coverage. The directives in question are as follows:

- The Software Directive,[91] governing the recognition and protection by copyright of computer programs;
- The Satellite Broadcasting and Cable Retransmission Directive,[92] governing the satellite broadcasting and cable retransmission of programmes containing copyright and related rights subject matter;
- The Term Directive,[93] governing the duration of copyright and related rights, and the protection by copyright of photographs;
- The Database Directive,[94] governing the recognition and protection by copyright and related rights of databases;

[90] TFEU art 114.

[91] Council Directive 91/250/EEC of 14 May 1991 on the legal protection of computer programs [1991] OJ L 122/42, replaced by Directive 2009/24/EC of the European Parliament and of the Council of 23 April 2009 on the legal protection of computer programs [2009] OJ L 111/16.

[92] Council Directive 93/83/EEC of 27 September 1993 on the coordination of certain rules concerning copyright and rights related to copyright applicable to satellite broadcasting and cable retransmission [1993] OJ L 248/15.

[93] Council Directive 93/98/EEC of 29 October 1993 harmonising the term of protection of copyright and certain related rights [1993] OJ L 290/9, replaced by Directive 2006/116/EC of the European Parliament and of the Council of 12 December 2006 on the term of protection of copyright and certain related rights [2006] OJ L 372/12.

[94] Directive 96/9/EC of the European Parliament and of the Council of 11 March 1996 on the legal protection of databases [1996] OJ L 77/20.

- The Resale Right Directive,[95] governing the right of authors of certain artistic works to be remunerated upon the re-sale of the original realization of their works;
- The Enforcement Directive,[96] governing the enforcement of IP rights;
- The Information Society Directive,[97] governing the recognition and protection by copyright and related rights of authorial works, phonograms, first film and performance fixations, and broadcasts;
- The Orphan Works Directive,[98] governing the recognition and protection of third party rights in respect of orphan works; and
- The Collective Rights Management Directive,[99] governing the collective management and exploitation of copyright and related rights.

As directives, Member States are required to implement each of these instruments as to the result to be achieved,[100] and to interpret domestic law so far as possible to be consistent with them.[101] According to the Court of Justice, this requires domestic courts to construe domestic law falling within their scope 'in the light of the wording and the purpose of [the relevant] directive.'[102] Questions arising in domestic copyright and related rights proceedings that raise a matter of EU law that is not *acte clair* may or must (depending on the court) be referred to the Court of Justice for preliminary determination under the EU Treaties.[103] When answering those questions, the European Court will interpret the governing directive in the light of its purpose and wider context, including to ensure consistency so far as possible with international instruments.[104] Of especial importance in this regard, aside from the Berne Convention, are the 1961 Rome Convention and the 1996 WIPO Copyright Treaties, which with Berne comprise an international code of copyright that sits above the European system.

From the European system there has developed a body of substantive copyright and related rights principles—an *acquis communautaire*—the outlines of which may be summarized as follows.

[95] Directive 2001/84/EC of the European Parliament and of the Council of 27 September 2001 on the resale right for the benefit of the author of an original work of art [2001] OJ L 272/32.

[96] Directive 2004/48/EC of the European Parliament and of the Council of 29 April 2004 on the enforcement of intellectual property rights [2004] OJ L 195/16 (Enforcement Directive).

[97] Directive 2001/29/EC of the European Parliament and of the Council of 22 May 2001 on the harmonisation of certain aspects of copyright and related rights in the information society [2002] OJ L 167/10 (Information Society Directive).

[98] Directive 2012/28/EU of the European Parliament and of the Council of 25 October 2012 on certain permitted uses of orphan works [2012] OJ L 299/5.

[99] Directive 2014/26/EU of the European Parliament and of the Council of 26 February 2014 on collective management of copyright and related rights and multi-territorial licensing of rights in musical works for online use in the internal market [2014] OJ L 84/72.

[100] TFEU art 288.

[101] Case C–106/89 *Marleasing SA v La Comercial Internacional de Alimentación SA* [1990] ECR I–4135 (*Marleasing*).

[102] ibid [8]. [103] TFEU art 267.

[104] See eg Case C–306/05 *SGAE v Rafael Hoteles SA* [2006] ECR I–11519 [35].

1. Any person who authors a work is entitled to copyright—a bundle of temporary exclusive rights—in respect of the work. So too those responsible for a performance, broadcast, phonogram, a first film, performance or broadcast fixation, or a database that is the product of significant commercial investment, are entitled to a corresponding bundle of temporary exclusive rights—related rights—in respect of the relevant subject matter.
2. Copyright in an authorial work or related rights in a related rights subject matter subsists automatically upon the work's or subject matter's creation. Each species of right takes effect as an object of property that may be exploited in accordance with the domestic laws of each Member State, subject (in the manner of all objects of domestic property rights) to the free movement, competition, and other laws of the EU Treaties.
3. The bundle of exclusionary rights comprising copyright lasts for the life of the author plus seventy years, and includes the exclusive rights to reproduce the work, to communicate the work to the public, to rent and lend publicly the work, and for certain works of art, to profit from re-sales of the first realization of the work. The nature of the rights conferred by related rights are similar, although last for between twenty-five and seventy years from creation of the protected subject matter.
4. The bundle of exclusionary rights comprising copyright and related rights are subject to certain exceptions and limitations, including exceptions and limitations aimed at protecting the fundamental rights and interests of third parties and the general public, such as freedom of expression, education, and the integration of persons with disabilities.
5. Copyright and related rights are enforceable by a mix of civil and criminal law sanctions and measures, and may be the subject of compulsory licensing.

Of these general European copyright and related rights principles the first has especial relevance for present purposes. It identifies clearly the subject matter of European copyright and related rights protection as authorial works, performances, broadcasts, phonograms, first film, performance, and broadcast fixations, and databases. These are plainly not exclusively technical legal categories, in the manner of 'intellectual property' for example, and nor it seems clear were they intended by the EU legislature to be understood to be. Having said that, EU legislation does not make their relationship to non-legal, including ordinary language conceptions, of authorial works and other subject matter clear, raising the question as to the proper understanding of that relationship, and the means by which the nature and boundaries of each category of subject matter is appropriately defined. On one view, consistent with the nature and purpose of European IP law above, the categories of authorial works and related rights subject matter should contain such subject matter—including such 'intellectual creations' specifically—as domestic IP traditions, international IP instruments, and European IP law and policy suggest they should contain. On another view, which may not be inconsistent with this, and which can also be reconciled with the understanding of the nature and purpose of European IP law outlined above, the primary reference point for understanding the nature of authorial works and related rights subject matter should be contemporary, non-legal conceptions of each. According to this latter perspective, for example, the category of authorial works should be defined to include all those subject matter that are understood outside of law to be works of authorship. As a practical matter, this second view would require law-makers and decision-makers to look beyond positive law when deciding what subject matter copyright and related rights protect, and identify a particular section of society whose view on this question ought to be prioritized.

On its face, and as this overview demonstrates, EU copyright and related rights legislation is largely consistent with the EU view of IP rights above. Specifically, it supports the recognition and protection of transferable exclusionary rights for authors in respect of their works (intellectual creations), subject to the protection of competing CFR values in the exceptions and limitations to those rights particularly, and in a way that supports the traditions of EU Member States through the use of indirectly effective EU directives rather than directly effective regulations. By offering related rights protection for performances, broadcasts, and other recordings, transmissions, and presentations of expressive content, it also supports and rewards investment in the creative arts more generally. This is consistent with the emphasis placed in the recitals of the EU's Information Society Directive on: the importance of copyright and related rights to 'intellectual creation',[105] including as a means for ensuring 'the maintenance and development of creativity',[106] the financing of 'European cultural creativity',[107] and the safeguarding of 'the independence and dignity of artistic creators and performers';[108] and the importance of the harmonization of copyright and related rights to furthering the goals of the internal market and undistorted competition,[109] and ensuring 'compliance with the fundamental principles of law'.[110]

In the UK, copyright and related rights are governed by the CDPA. This Act is an amended version of the 1911 Copyright Act,[111] introduced to consolidate previous British copyright legislation and to implement Britain's obligations under the Berne Convention. Given this common heritage in Berne, it is unsurprising that the CDPA is largely consistent with EU copyright and related rights legislation, despite its core provisions predating that legislation. The main differences of current relevance lie in the CDPA's use of the term 'copyright', its description of the subject matter in which copyright subsists, and its definition of the rights conferred in respect of that subject matter. Regarding the first and second of these differences, section 1(1) of the CDPA describes copyright as 'a property right which subsists in accordance with this Part in the following descriptions of work—

(a) original literary, dramatic, musical or artistic works,

(b) sound recordings, films or broadcasts, and

(c) the typographical arrangement of published editions'.

[105] Information Society Directive recital 9. [106] ibid. [107] ibid recital 11.
[108] ibid. [109] ibid recital 1. [110] ibid recital 3.
[111] An Act to amend and consolidate the Law relating to Copyright 1911 (UK).

Thus, instead of literary and artistic property and related rights, the CDPA refers only to copyright, and instead of subsisting in authorial works as a general category, the CDPA recognizes copyright in the European sense of literary and artistic property as subsisting in (and only in) original literary, dramatic, musical, and artistic works, each of which categories is further defined in sections 3 to 4 of the CDPA. Regarding the third difference, section 2 of the CDPA, in conjunction with Chapter IV, extends and supplements the economic rights provided for by EU legislation, including by recognizing and protecting authors' non-transferable moral rights of paternity, integrity, and privacy, consistent with Article 6*bis* of the Berne Convention.[112]

Despite its historical roots in the printers' industrial rights of copy from the 16th and 17th centuries, and especially since the introduction of the EU copyright directives, the British copyright regime reflects the same general policy motivations as the EU copyright regime reflects, including, increasingly, the same concern with protecting third party fundamental rights and interests by means of exceptions and limitations to authors' rights.

5.3.2 Industrial Property Rights

The legislative basis of the European industrial property system is also rather fragmented. It includes separate instruments for a number of different species of right, including patents, trade marks, designs, trade secrets, and plant variety rights, which it is appropriate to consider separately.

5.3.2.1 Patents

The legislative basis of the European patent system is a combination of EU and non-EU instruments. The centrepiece is the EPC, which introduces a system for the grant of national patents in any number of the thirty-eight EPC Contracting States, supported by harmonized legal rules governing the requirements for a valid patent grant, and enforced by European patent offices and tribunals. This system is supplemented by the EU Biotech Directive[113] and Supplementary Protection Certificate Regulations,[114] introduced under Article 114 of the TFEU, and governing for EU Member States the grant and enforcement of patents for biotechnological subject matter and the grant of supplementary protection for certain previously patented products. Building on this EPC and EU framework is the

[112] The rights are: to be identified as author or director of the work (for certain literary, dramatic, musical, and artistic works, and films: s 77(1)); to object to the derogatory treatment of the work (for certain literary, dramatic, musical, and artistic works, and films: s 80(1)); and to protect the privacy of the work (for certain photographs and films: s 85(1)).

[113] Council Directive 98/44/EC on the legal protection of biotechnological inventions [1998] OJ L 213/13 (Biotech Directive).

[114] Regulation (EC) No 1610/96 of the European Parliament and of the Council of 23 July 1996 concerning the creation of a supplementary protection certificate for plant protection products [1996] OJ L 198/30; Regulation (EC) No 469/2009 of the European Parliament and of the Council of 6 May 2009 concerning the supplementary protection certificate for medicinal products [2009] OJ L 152/1.

unitary (EU) patent package of 2012/13, comprising two EU Regulations[115] and a non-EU Unified Patent Court Agreement.[116] When—or perhaps *if*[117]—it is implemented, the unitary patent package will enable the registration of patents granted under the EPC as unitary patents, conferring uniform and unitary protection throughout the territories of thirteen or more participating EU Member States.[118] It will also establish a European patent court having exclusive competence with respect to such patents, Supplementary Protection Certificates, and other European (EPC) patents,[119] subject to a seven-year opt-out period,[120] and be supported by European rules defining the rights conferred by a patent and the exceptions to them.[121] Those rules reproduce and extend earlier provisions of the Community Patent Convention 1975 (CPC) that was signed but never ratified by the original six and later additional EEC States,[122] and can be expected to be construed in the light of the existing interpretation of those provisions by the domestic courts of EU Member States.[123]

From this European system has developed a body of substantive patent law principles, the outlines of which may be summarized as follows.

1. Any person who devises an invention that is new, inventive, and susceptible of industrial application, and who is the first to file an application for a patent in respect of that invention supported by a description sufficient to enable it to be worked, is entitled to a patent—a bundle of temporary exclusive rights—in respect of it.
2. A patent is valid from notification of its grant and given retrospective operation from the date of filing. It takes effect as an object of property that may be exploited in accordance with the domestic laws of each Member State,

115 Regulation (EU) No 1257/2012 of the European Parliament and of the Council of 17 December 2012 implementing enhanced cooperation in the area of the creation of unitary patent protection [2012] OJ L 361/1 (UP Regulation); Council Regulation (EU) No 1260/2012 of 17 December 2012 implementing enhanced cooperation in the area of the creation of unitary patent protection with regard to the applicable translation arrangements [2012] OJ L 361/89.

116 Agreement on a Unified Patent Court [2013] OJ C 175/1 (UPC Agreement).

117 The likelihood of the unitary patent package being implemented was uncertain following the UK's decision in June 2016 to leave the European Union, though many supporters of the package remained optimistic that it would still be implemented, with some even envisaging the possibility of UK participation in the system post-Brexit (see eg W Tilmann, 'A possible way for a non-EU UK to participate in the Unitary Patent and Unified Patent Court?' *IPKat blog* (28 June 2016) http://ipkitten.blogspot.co.uk/2016/06/a-possible-way-for-non-eu-uk-to.html (last accessed 5 June 2017); A Ohly and R Streinz, 'Can the UK Stay in the UPC system after Brexit?' [2017] GRUR International 1). In November 2016, the UK government announced that it would ratify the UPC Agreement while still an EU Member State, enabling fulfilment of the requirements for the system's establishment (which include ratification by the UK). The Prime Minister's subsequent calling of a general election for June 2017 delayed the projected timeframe for this ratification, and consequently for the system's establishment, which will now not take place before 2018.

118 UP Regulation arts 3(2) and 18(2).

119 UPC Agreement art 32.

120 ibid art 83(1).

121 ibid arts 25–30.

122 Convention for the European Patent for the common market (opened for signature 15 December 1975) arts 29–32; see also 89/695/EEC: Agreement relating to Community patents [1989] OJ L 401/1 arts 25–28.

123 See UPC Agreement art 24(1)(e).

subject once again to the free movement, competition, and other laws of the EU Treaties.

3. The bundle of exclusionary rights conferred by a patent lasts for a maximum period of 20 years (from the filing date), and includes the exclusive right to prevent others (in the case of a product invention) from making, offering, putting on the market, and using the product and (in the case of a process invention) from using the process, among other things.
4. The bundle of exclusionary rights conferred by a patent are subject to certain exceptions and limitations, including exceptions and limitations aimed at preventing the patenting of subject matter the commercialization of which would be contrary to fundamental rights such as human dignity, and at enabling research and the continuation of certain prior lawful uses of the invention.
5. Patents are enforceable by a mix of civil and criminal law sanctions and measures, and may be the subject of compulsory licensing.

As this outline makes clear, in Europe the structure of patent law continues to follow closely that of copyright and related rights, more than 300 years after the Statute of Anne, and notwithstanding the difference in the nature of the: protected subject matter (inventions rather than authorial works and recordings, transmissions, and presentations of them); rights conferred (limited monopolies rather than derivation rights); and requirements for grant (disclosure, examination, and registration rather than mere creation). In relation to the EU view of IP rights and the implications of the nature and purpose of IP rights for patentable subject matter specifically, European patent legislation—explicitly in the case of the Biotech Directive and Unitary Patent Regulations—supports the conception of IP rights as subsisting in respect of intellectual creations, in the form of products and processes devised by an inventor and reflecting her 'creative efforts',[124] having regard to EU Treaty and CFR values and policies, including those relating to the promotion of the internal market (accounting for the unitary patent package),[125] scientific and technological development (accounting for the conception of inventions as relating to fields of technology, the availability of patents, and the limits on patent scope and term),[126] and the protection of human dignity (accounting for the exclusion from protection of certain subject matter, such as uses of human embryos for industrial or commercial purposes).[127] The view of patents as both reward and incentive is also further reflected in the presumptive restriction of their availability to the first of an invention's potentially many independent inventors (or their employers) to make the invention available to the public,[128] and in the right of an inventor to be identified as such in the patent document.[129]

[124] Biotech Directive recital 46.
[125] UP Regulation arts 1, 2, and 4.
[126] Biotech Directive recitals 10–12 and 20–23.
[127] ibid recitals 16 and 38, and art 6(2)(c).
[128] See EPC arts 52(1) and 54(1).
[129] ibid art 62.

A notable feature of the European patent landscape is the EPC: a non-EU but nonetheless (by virtue of its aims and membership) European instrument with extensive substantive legal coverage and its own supporting administrative and judicial (or quasi-judicial) branches. This instrument and the European patent system it creates sit alongside the EU patent system established by the Biotech Directive and Supplementary Protection Certificate Regulations, and alongside the hybrid EU/supranational system created by the UPP. The result is a degree of fragmentation and complexity that one does not see to the same extent in other areas of IP. On the other hand, since the instruments are complementary rather than competing, and are subject to a relatively clear hierarchy of legal sources and norms for EU Member States especially, few if any real conflicts of legal principle can be said to exist.

At the domestic (UK) level, the substantive provisions of the European patent regime are reflected in corresponding provisions of the Patents Act 1977. That Act was introduced for the express purpose of implementing the three main European and international patent instruments concluded during the 1970s: the EPC; the CPC; and the international Patent Cooperation Treaty of 1977.[130] Consistent with this harmonizing aim, section 130(7)—transposed from a resolution annexed to the CPC[131]—requires that its substantive law provisions be interpreted, so far as practicable, to be consistent with the interpretation of the corresponding provisions of the EPC, CPC, and PCT respectively. According to the UK courts, this has four main consequences for any tribunal interpreting a provision of domestic law for which there exists a corresponding EPC provision. The first is to make the relevant EPC provision the source of law to which the tribunal should in its judgments refer. (According to Lord Justice Jacob in *Aerotel Ltd v Telco Holdings*,[132] referring to European legislative provisions rather than to their UK counterparts promotes harmonization by making UK case law more comprehensible to the domestic courts of other European states, and thus more likely to be taken into account.[133]) The second consequence is to require that individual provisions of patent legislation be construed according to international treaty interpretive principles, as set down in the Vienna Convention on the Law of Treaties,[134] thus allowing 'more room for a teleological interpretation' than traditional British interpretive principles allow for.[135] The third is to require that relevant decisions of the Boards of the European

[130] Patent Cooperation Treaty (opened for signature 19 June 1970, entered into force 24 January 1978) 1160 UNTS 231.

[131] Resolution on the adjustment of national patent law.

[132] *Aerotel Ltd v Telco Holdings; Macrossan's Patent Application* [2006] EWCA Civ 1371, [2007] RPC 7.

[133] ibid [6].

[134] Vienna Convention on the Law of Treaties (adopted 27 January 1980) 1155 UNTS 331.

[135] *CFPH's Application* [2005] EWHC 1589 (Pat), [2006] RPC 5 [26] and [27] ('British Acts of Parliament are written by professional parliamentary draftsmen according to certain well-understood semantic conventions, in principle allowing meaning to be expressed tightly. In contrast, an international convention such as the European Patent Convention may be drafted by a committee not all of whose members speak the same mother-tongue and none of whom may be aware of, or care about, the aforesaid semantic conventions. Indeed the Convention is expressed in three languages, all equally authentic. It is therefore not surprising that the methods of interpretation to be applied to such an

Patent Office be considered and treated as having 'great persuasive authority', both as decisions of expert courts, and consistent with the aims of European legal harmonization.[136] And finally, according to the UK courts, section 130(7) requires that conflicts between European and appellate UK authority be resolved in favour of the UK authority, provided that authority gives 'tolerably clear guidance' and is not 'inconsistent with clear guidance from the Board' that is not 'wrong'.[137]

Of course, in so far as EU regulations and directives in the patent field are concerned, UK courts are required to give them direct and indirect effect respectively, and will remain so until the United Kingdom ceases to be a Member State of the EU.[138]

5.3.2.2 Trade Marks

Whereas the focus of the European copyright and related rights system is on protecting the creations of authors and others and supporting the creative industries, and the focus of the European patent system is on protecting the creations of inventors and supporting research and development in fields of technology, the focus of the European trade mark system is on protecting the marketing assets of European businesses in order to support growth and competition within the internal market particularly. This explains the early interest of trade mark law and its harmonization and unification to the EU and, in reflection of that interest, the existence since 1989 of an EU directive harmonizing the domestic trade mark laws of EU Member States,[139] and the existence since 1993 of an EU regulation establishing a unitary (EU) trade mark title and system with effect throughout their territory.[140]

international instrument are not the same. In particular, there is more room for a teleological interpretation. It may have its problems, of course—in particular, how to ascertain the *telos*, or purpose').

136 *Merrell Dow Pharmaceuticals Inc v HB Norton & Co Ltd* [1995] UKHL 14, [1996] RPC 76 [12]. Cf C Floyd, 'Novelty under the Patents Act 1977: the State of the Art after *Merrell Dow*' [1996] EIPR 480, 480 (criticising the UK courts' tendency 'to treat the decisions of the Appeal Boards of the [EPO] on matters relating to the interpretation of the EPC as if they were a supranational court like the ECJ, when in fact they are the decisions of a limb of the granting office itself').

137 *Symbian v Comptroller-General of Patents* [2008] EWCA Civ 1066, [2009] RPC 1 [36]. See also *Eli Lilly v Human Genome Sciences Inc* [2010] EWCA Civ 33, [2010] RPC 14 [40] and [41] (rejecting counsel's argument that the UK courts must follow 'standards' set for the application of 'pure principles of law' by the EPO, in addition to those principles themselves).

138 TFEU art 288; *Marleasing* (n 101). Considering the *Marleasing* obligation in the patent context, the UK courts have described it as 'a strong duty of interpretation', akin to the courts' 'duty under section 3 of the Human Rights Act 1998 to interpret domestic legislation as far as possible in a manner which is compatible with Convention rights under the European Convention on Human Rights': *SAS Institute Inc v World Programming Ltd* [2010] EWHC 1829, [2011] RPC 1 [163] (Arnold J, citing *R (IDT Card Services Ireland Ltd) v Commissioners for Her Majesty's Revenue and Customs* [2006] EWCA Civ 29, [2006] STC 1252 [73]–[92] (Arden LJ)).

139 Originally First Council Directive 89/104/EEC of 21 December 1988 to approximate the laws of the Member States relating to trade marks [1989] OJ L 40/1; now Directive (EU) 2015/2436 of the European Parliament and of the Council of 16 December 2015 to approximate the laws of the Member States relating to trade marks [2015] OJ L 336/1 (Trade Marks Directive).

140 Originally Council Regulation (EC) No 40/94 of 20 December 1993 on the Community trade mark [1994] OJ L 11/1; now Council Regulation (EC) No 207/2009 of 26 February 2009 on the Community trade mark [2009] OJ L 78/1, as amended (Trade Mark Regulation).

In combination, these instruments support the following general principles of substantive European trade mark law.

1. Any person may by application register a trade mark, namely, a sign capable of being represented, and of distinguishing the goods or services of one undertaking from those of others, in respect of one or more classes of goods and services, provided (among other things) that the sign (a) does not designate a characteristic of the relevant goods or services, (b) has not become customary in the language or trade, (c) is not a shape resulting from, necessitated by, or giving substantial value to the relevant goods, (d) is not contrary to public policy or morality, (e) would not deceive the public, and (f) does not conflict with the rights conferred by existing EU or Member State trade marks.
2. A trade mark confers protection from notice of its registration but must, for that registration to remain valid, be put to genuine use by or with the consent of the trade mark owner within EU territory less than five years after registration, and remain in use without periods of interruption lasting five or more years.
3. Registered trade marks take effect as objects of property that may be exploited in accordance with the domestic laws of the Member State in which their owner is seated, domiciled, or otherwise established.
4. The rights conferred by a registered trade mark last indefinitely, for renewable registration periods of 10 years, and include the exclusive right to prevent others in the course of trade from using any sign that is:
   - Identical to the registered mark and used in respect of identical goods or services;
   - Identical or similar to the registered mark, used in respect of similar or identical goods or services, and likely by reason of the relevant identity or similarity to cause confusion on the part of the public in the territory in which the mark is used; or
   - Identical or similar to the registered mark in situations in which the use takes unfair advantage of, or is detrimental to, the distinctive character or repute of the registered mark.
5. The rights conferred by registration of a trade mark are subject to certain limitations, including limitations aimed at ensuring the free movement of goods placed on the market by or with the consent of the trade mark owner, and limitations aimed at enabling third parties to use, in the course of trade and in accordance with honest industrial or commercial practices: their name or address; signs or indications that are not distinctive or that concern characteristics of the relevant goods or services; and registered marks in comparative advertising.
6. Trade marks are enforceable by a mix of civil and criminal law sanctions and measures, and may be the subject of licensing, but not of compulsory licensing.

At the domestic level, these principles find expression in the Trade Marks Act 1994 (UK), governing the registration and protection of national trade marks. They are also supplemented in the UK by the common law action of passing off, which potentially limits the use that can be made of another person's unregistered trade mark or other embodiment of goodwill. For such an action to succeed, a claimant must be able to show that she has goodwill in respect of the mark or object that has been harmed by the defendant's misrepresentative use of it.[141]

As seen in section 2, trade mark law is different in nature from copyright and patent law, consistent with the different nature of trade marks themselves. Absent here is a concern with rewarding and promoting creation and discovery, and present instead is a concern with protecting consumers from the harm caused by the use of signs associated with a particular trade origin in connection with goods or services having a different origin, and promoting fair and honest commercial practices. Aside from the recitals to the Trade Mark Regulation and Trade Marks Directive,[142] this can be seen from the legislation's operative provisions themselves, including: their definition of the subject matter capable of registration as a trade mark (signs capable of distinguishing the goods or services of one undertaking from those of others[143]); their rules of entitlement (any person can register a trade mark, regardless of whether she is the creator of the mark as an expressive object, and notwithstanding the inability of any trader to be regarded as the creator of the trade origin that a mark signifies[144]); their restriction of registration to trade marks in 'genuine use' as such;[145] and their restriction of the rights conferred by registration of a mark to the rights to exclude others from using the mark in a manner harmful to consumers or contrary to honest commercial practices.[146] For all of these reasons, trade marks have been described as outliers in the galaxy of IP rights: modern trade mark law being concerned not with ensuring protection to intellectual creations and discoveries, and supporting innovation and creativity, but rather with ensuring protection to traders' marketing assets, and supporting fair competition and consumer protection in the marketplace, consistent with its aims historically.[147] Nonetheless, those aims fall squarely within the general aims of the EU specified in Article 3 of the TEU, including its commitment to establishing an internal market and working for the sustainable development of Europe based (among other things) on a highly competitive social market economy, and are consistent also with the EU's commitment under Article 38 of the CFR to ensuring 'a high level of consumer protection'—and perhaps, with its recognition under Article 16 of the freedom of persons to conduct a business. More importantly for present purposes, the subject matter protectable by trade marks comprise an expressive object (in the form of a sign) of use for an informational purpose (distinguishing the goods or services of one trader from those of others), and is in this sense closely related to the authorial works and technological ideas protectable by the copyright and patent regimes respectively.

[141] *Reckitt & Colman Products Ltd v Borden Inc* [1990]UKHL 12, [1990] RPC 341.

[142] See eg Trade Marks Directive recitals 16 and 27; Trade Mark Regulation recital 8.

[143] Trade Marks Directive art 3; Trade Mark Regulation art 4.

[144] Trade Marks Directive art 28(2); Trade Mark Regulation art 5.

[145] Trade Marks Directive art 16; Trade Mark Regulation art 15.

[146] Trade Marks Directive art 10; Trade Mark Regulation art 9.

[147] See eg Posner (n 14) 8 ('A third very common form of intellectual property, trademarks, is misnamed, and I will not discuss it extensively. Trademarks are merely identifiers, designed to protect consumers from being misled regarding the origin or quality of particular products or services. There are many interesting legal and economic issues concerning trademarks, but they are not centrally issues of property').

5.3.2.3 Designs, Plant Variety Rights, and Trade Secrets

The legislative basis of the European design right system is, like that of the trade mark system, an EU regulation (creating unitary registered and unregistered EU design rights)[148] and an EU directive (harmonizing the domestic registered design right laws of all EU Member States).[149] In substance registered and unregistered EU design rights are similar to patents and copyright respectively, with the correspondence between unregistered design right and copyright being particularly strong in the UK.[150] This similarity of design right protection to that conferred by patents and copyright is notwithstanding the ability of designs to function in the market as trade marks, and subject to the important exception that unregistered EU design right does not subsist automatically in a design upon creation, as with copyright and unregistered UK design right,[151] but rather from when the design is made available to the public.[152] These points notwithstanding, registered and unregistered design rights fall squarely within the conception of IP rights above as bundles of temporary exclusive rights in respect of an intellectual creation; with the details of their specific regulation reflecting the hybrid creative-industrial nature of the subject matter they protect. Thus, under the Designs Regulation, consistent also with the substantive law provisions of the Designs Directive, any person who designs the appearance of the whole or part of a product and either (a) makes the design available to the public, or (b) applies to register the design with the appropriate authorities, is entitled to rights in respect of that appearance to the extent that it is new and has 'individual character' as against the prior art.[153] Rights derived from publication last for three years (from publication), and rights derived from registration last for up to five successive five-year periods of registration (from the filing date).[154] However so derived, design rights take effect as objects of property that may be exploited in accordance with the domestic laws of the Member State in which their owner is established.[155] The rights conferred by registered design right include the right to use the design and prevent third parties from using it without consent, including by making or otherwise dealing commercially with a product incorporating the design or to which the design has been applied.[156] By contrast, the rights conferred by unregistered design right include the right to do those acts with respect to a copy of the design only.[157] As with authors and inventors, designers have the right to be recognized as such.[158] Regardless of their source, design rights are subject to certain

[148] Council Regulation (EC) No 6/2002 of 12 December 2001 on Community designs, as amended [2006] OJ L 386/14 (Designs Regulation).

[149] Directive 98/71/EC of the European Parliament and of the Council of 13 October 1998 on the legal protection of designs [1998] OJ L 289/28 (Designs Directive).

[150] See CDPA Part III (governing unregistered UK design right).

[151] Designs Regulation art 11(1).

[152] See CDPA s 213(6) (providing for the subsistence of UK unregistered design right in designs once recorded in a design document or incorporated in/applied to an article).

[153] Designs Regulation arts 4(1) and 1(2); also Designs Directive art 3(2).

[154] Designs Regulation arts 11 and 12; also Designs Directive art 10.

[155] Designs Regulation arts 27 and 34.

[156] ibid art 19(1); also Designs Directive art 12(1).

[157] Designs Regulation art 19(2).

[158] ibid art 18.

limitations, including limitations aimed at enabling acts done privately and for non-commercial purposes, teaching, and the continuation of prior lawful uses of the protected subject matter.[159] Finally, design rights are enforceable by a mix of civil and criminal law sanctions and measures,[160] and may be the subject of licensing, but not of compulsory licensing.[161]

Also referable to the EU view of IP rights above are those conferred under the European plant variety rights (PVR) system in respect of plant varieties. Established in 1994 by a regulation,[162] the PVR system enables any person who has either bred or discovered and developed a previously non-commercialized plant variety that is distinct, uniform, and stable to obtain a Community PVR in respect of it,[163] subject to deposit of a sample, provision of an appropriate denomination for the variety, substantive examination for fulfilment of the criteria above, and registration of the right. Once granted, such a PVR enables the breeder or discoverer and developer to prevent others from a range of acts in respect of the variety and its propagating material, including producing or reproducing it, and offering it for sale or otherwise commercializing it.[164] That right lasts for twenty-five years or, for vine and tree varieties, for thirty years from the end of the calendar year in which the grant was made,[165] and is subject to certain exceptions, including an exception to enable farmers to use for propagating purposes in the field, on their own holding, the product of a harvest they have obtained by planting propagating material of certain types of protected variety.[166] In addition, however, both the PVR owner and third parties must use the denomination provided by the applicant correctly in association with the variety, even after expiration of the right.[167] As with most other IP rights, plant variety rights may be licensed, including compulsorily.[168]

As with the Papal Edit of the 19th century referred to in section 2, the modern PVR system protects discoveries as well as creations, and in this sense might be said to differ from the other IP systems considered previously. However, while plant varieties may not be creations in the sense in which authorial works and perhaps inventions are accepted to be, they will often be the product of financial and intellectual investment on the part of their breeder or discoverer, and are also of substantial value to society as a source of food for humans and agriculturally important animals. This, combined with the limited opportunities that breeders and discoverers would have in the absence of IP rights to recoup their investment (owing to the capacity of seeds to be freely propagated at zero cost), and the negative impact on farmers and other third parties that would be caused by restricting access to varieties

[159] ibid arts 20–23; also Designs Directive arts 13 and 15.

[160] Enforcement Directive.

[161] But see Registered Designs Act 1949 (UK) ss 11A and AB (authorizing the Registrar to cancel or amend terms of UK registered design right licences in the public interest).

[162] Council Regulation (EC) No 2100/94 of 27 July 1994 on Community plant variety rights [1994] OJ L 227/1 (CPVR Regulation); see also the Plant Varieties Act 1997 (UK) (governing the grant of UK plant variety rights).

[163] CPVR Regulation arts 6, 10, and 11. [164] ibid art 13. [165] ibid art 19.

[166] ibid art 14. [167] ibid art 17. [168] ibid art 29.

completely, is generally regarded as making them suitable for IP protection.[169] In this respect, plant varieties are similar to trade marks, the protection of which by IP proceeds from a similar logic. In the EU policy terms above, PVRs can also be said to promote the production and distribution of goods and services, support competition with other states, and promote innovation and solutions to global health and environmental challenges; in addition to supporting fair competition and consumer protection in the manner of trade marks through their naming rights and obligations specifically.

That leaves the European system governing the protection of confidential information, and in particular trade secrets and information of a private nature.

The protection of private information has long been recognized in the EU by means of the Article 7 CFR right to privacy. By contrast, the protection of trade secrets was only recently given a statutory footing, with the adoption in May 2016 of the Directive on the protection of undisclosed know-how and business information (trade secrets) against their unlawful acquisition, use, and disclosure.[170] Under its terms—which are expressed as being subject, among other things, to the right to freedom of expression and information under the CFR[171]—any person who is in lawful control of commercially valuable information outside the public realm can prevent the unauthorized acquisition of that information by means of dishonest commercial practices.[172]

In the UK, these and the Directive's other provisions governing enforcement of individuals' duties of confidence will supplement the common law action of breach of confidence. Under that action, third parties are prohibited from disclosing any sufficiently particular information that (a) is confidential, (b) has been communicated in circumstances importing an obligation of confidence, and (c) the disclosure of which would be to the detriment of the person communicating it.[173] In recent years this action has been extended by the House of Lords, in the light of the Article 8 ECHR and Article 7 CFR right to privacy above, to support a new tort of misuse of private information.[174] As a result, any person deemed to have a reasonable expectation of privacy in respect of information—by reason either of the information's private nature, or the impact on the person of its disclosure—will be able to protect that privacy by restraining disclosure of the information unless doing so would be disproportionate having regard to some competing right or interest. According to Lord Hoffmann in *Campbell*, recognition of the new tort represented 'a shift in the centre of gravity of the action for breach of confidence' from an action based on a duty or obligation of good faith (much like that which

[169] See Pila and Torremans (n 83) 220–21.

[170] Directive (EU) 2016/943 of the European Parliament and of the Council of 8 June 2016 on the protection of undisclosed know-how and business information (trade secrets) against their unlawful acquisition, use and disclosure [2016] OJ L 157/1 (Trade Secrets Directive).

[171] ibid recitals 19, 21, and 34, and arts 1(2) and 5.

[172] ibid arts 2–5.

[173] *Coco v AN Clark (Engineers) Ltd* [1969] RPC 41 (ChD).

[174] *Campbell v Mirror Group Newspapers Ltd* [2004] UKHL 22, [2004] 2 AC 457.

underpins the Trade Secrets Directive) to an action based on a right to the esteem and respect of other people.[175]

The precise nature of the rights and obligations created by the traditional UK breach of confidence action, including the proper place of that obligation in any discussion of intellectual property, has long been a matter of academic and juridical debate and controversy. No doubt the rights and obligations created by the Trade Secrets Directive will give rise to similar discussion and disagreement. Despite or perhaps consistent with this, the recitals of the Directive cast its aim as being to offer a complementary or alternative form of protection for 'the results of innovation' to that provided by patents, design rights, and copyright.[176] The effect, the Directive states, will be to enable 'creators and innovators to derive profit from their creation or innovation',[177] and thereby to promote innovation, creativity, economic growth, and competitiveness within EU territory.[178]

5.4 Conclusion

Supranational and domestic laws and legal systems inevitably differ in their centres of gravity: the one oriented around harmonization, and the other oriented around the protection of substantive rights and interests. Despite this, such is the nature of the EU legal order, and of EU IP laws and policies, that there now exists little difference between the values that inform the EU and UK IP regimes respectively, and the substantive provisions of EU and UK IP legislation in which those values find their most direct expression. The starting point of each is a view of IP rights as limited exclusionary rights in respect of 'intellectual creations' the definition of which reflects and promotes EU Treaty and CFR values. The difficulty concerns the nature of the intellectual creations to which IP rights attach, which include a range of expressive and other objects that, while closely related inter se, are not obviously 'intellectual creations' in the ordinary sense of that phrase.

6. Distinctions of Importance to Intellectual Property Rights[179]

6.1 The Distinction between Industrial, Authorial, and Other Species of Intellectual Property

As their full titles suggest, the Paris and Berne Conventions divide the field of IP into the two subcategories of industrial property (covering patents, designs, trade marks, and unfair competition) and literary and artistic property (covering copyright) respectively. The continued importance of the Conventions since the 19th

[175] ibid [51]; cf [85] (Lord Hope of Craighead). [176] Trade Secrets Directive recital 1.
[177] ibid recital 2. [178] ibid recitals 1–4.
[179] See further R C Dreyfuss and J Pila, 'Intellectual Property Law: An Anatomical Overview' in Dreyfuss and Pila (eds), *The Oxford Handbook of Intellectual Property Law* (n 20).

century has ensured the persistence of this distinction, formally at least. The question therefore arises of its meaning and substantive significance if any.

According to Stephen Ladas, while literary and artistic property in the sense of the Berne Convention denotes the rights of authors of all forms of literary and artistic creations, industrial property in the sense of the Paris Convention is merely a collective name for an aggregate of rights referring to the industrial or commercial activity of a person.[180] With the purpose of furthering his economic interest, Ladas wrote,

> a man invents, creates, devises or uses different things. He invents a new product or a new process of manufacture. He creates a new design or model. He adopts a distinctive mark for his goods, or uses a trade name or the name of the place where his business is established and so forth. It is to all these aspects of a man's activity that the name 'industrial property' is applied.[181]

Of course, many authorial creations will be commercialized, and many more will be made with the subjective intent of furthering their creator's economic interests. However, neither of these facts deprives a poem or other authorial work of its essentially expressive nature and, as a consequence of that nature, of its inherently subjective significance. Conversely, while many useful methods and contrivances, signs of origin, and industrial designs will be made with the subjective intent of producing something of aesthetic value, each has an essentially (inherently) industrial or commercial nature in the sense of deriving its significance, in an objective sense, from its deployment in the industrial or commercial realm. Each has in this sense a certain instrumental value or significance that authorial creations lack.

Beyond this understanding of the distinction between authorial and industrial subject matter lie many conceptual and definitional difficulties. The paradigmatic type of industrial property subject matter is the invention: an idea for an object (product or method) of practical use, such as the knife (an object for cutting) or method of distillation (steps for separating mixtures of liquids). In addition to their industrial or commercial nature, inventions differ from literary, artistic, and other expressive objects in being products of the 'anonymous collective inertial motion' that drives scientific but not artistic communities.[182] In practical terms this gives each invention an element of inevitability: if Graham Bell had not devised the telephone in 1876—an act for which he sought (and was later granted) a US patent claiming an 'apparatus for transmitting vocal or other sounds telegraphically'[183]—one of the number of other people working in the field would almost certainly have devised it soon after. By contrast are authorial expressions, the subjective and non-cumulative nature of which means that they might never have been created. Among other things, this explains the tendency to describe authorial works as *original* in

[180] S P Ladas, *Patents, Trademarks, and Related Rights: National and International Protection, Volume 1* (Harvard University Press 1975) 2.

[181] ibid.

[182] G Steiner, *Grammars of Creation: Originating in the Gifford Lectures for 1990* (Yale University Press 2001) 29.

[183] *Improvement in Telegraphy*, US Patent US174465 A (filed 14 February 1876).

the sense of being unique on the one hand, and inventions as *new* in the sense of not having previously been known and *inventive* in the sense of not having been obvious from what was known previously on the other.

It has been suggested that inventions are a paradigmatic type of industrial property subject matter. So too they and authorial works may be described as paradigmatic types of intellectual creations, and their regulation by different intellectual property regimes explained with reference to certain essential differences between them. However, and as we have seen, there are also other intellectual property regimes regulating other categories of subject matter, raising the question as to the essential nature of and differences between those categories. As outlined above, the regimes in question include: the product design right regime, protecting aspects of the appearance of manufactured products; the trade mark regime, protecting signs of commercial origin in the course of trade; the plant variety right regime, protecting previously non-commercialized varieties of plant; and the trade secret regime, protecting industrial or commercial information of confidence.

As a formal matter, three of these four additional species of IP are industrial property rights by virtue of their inclusion in the Paris Convention; albeit indirectly for trade secrets by virtue of the Convention's provisions requiring the repression of unfair competition.[184] And so too, substantively, each regime regulates a type of expressive or informational subject matter that derives its significance from its deployment in the industrial or commercial realm, and for this reason may be defined as industrial property regimes in the sense defined by Ladas. Having said that, and as has been seen, the subject matter of each is on its face rather different. For example, only inventions and designs suggest the existence of an intellectual creation. By way of contrast, and conventionally at least, trade marks are signs that have come or have the capacity to come through their use in trade to indicate the commercial origin of certain goods or services to consumers, and are hardly intellectual creations of the trader or consumers in the manner of a design or invention. Similarly for the other species of right lying outside the Paris and Berne Conventions but accepted nonetheless as forms of intellectual property, which seem to sit uncomfortably alongside copyright, patent, and design rights owing to the resistance of their subject matter to categorization as intellectual creations. For example, related rights and plant variety rights protect recordings, transmissions, and presentations of expression and previously non-commercialised varieties of plants respectively, each of which is defined in part precisely by its failure to constitute an intellectual creation, and thus by its perceived failure to merit the protection conferred on authors and inventors by the copyright and patent regimes. Understanding the significance of these characteristics and differences for the regulation and protection of each type of subject matter has been and remains a central challenge for the law and theory of intellectual property.

One thing to emerge from this discussion is the extent to which the nature of IP law, including the distinction between its different branches and species of IP,

[184] Paris Convention art 1(2).

depends on the nature of the subject matter that it protects: authorial works, in the case of copyright; inventions, in the case of patent law; plant varieties, in the case of plant variety rights; recordings, transmissions, and presentations of authorial works and other expression, in the case of related rights; and signs of commercial origin, in the case of trade marks. Perhaps the most difficult IP subject matter (and therefore IP right) from a conceptual standpoint are designs and confidential information, including trade secrets. The reason in the case of designs is their dual authorial and industrial nature: while a dress, chair, or kettle might plausibly be treated as a work of creative expression, its functional nature and industrial method of production distinguishes it from paradigmatic authorial works. It is considerations such as these that have historically led countries to deny functional items the protection of copyright, preferring instead to offer them more limited protection in the form of a *sui generis* right for their specific aspects of design.

Confidential information, including trade secrets and in some jurisdictions privacy rights, has given rise to similar conceptual challenges. Few countries regard information as capable of supporting property rights as such. However, if the information is confidential or private in nature—as for example with information relating to a person or to the client lists of a trader—its use by third parties may be restricted in order to protect its confidentiality or privacy. In such cases, it is less the information itself than its quality of confidence or privacy that is the subject of the relevant right. So too in the case of the *sui generis* data exclusivity and database rights—allied to patent and copyright law—the subject matter of the relevant IP right is not the data specifically, but rather their exclusivity and—for the database right—the arrangement by means of which a certain selection of data is presented. Thus, while the objectives of these and related forms of (trade secret and confidentiality) protection may be consistent with the IP policy and aims of the EU more generally, it is difficult to locate their subject matter within the family of subject matter protectable by other IP regimes. Indeed, the European Commission expressly denies the nature of trade secrets as a species of intellectual property for the following reason:

> The holder of a trade secret does not have an exclusive right over its creation. He cannot prevent competitors from copying and using the same solutions – reverse engineering (the process of discovering the technological principles of a device, object or system through analysis of its structure, function and operation) is entirely lawful. Trade secrets are only legally protected in instances where someone has obtained the confidential information by illegitimate means (e.g. through spying, theft or bribery).[185]

Given this, and notwithstanding their common treatment in books on intellectual property, the subject matter of trade secret and confidentiality protection will not be considered further in the current study.

[185] European Commission, 'Frequently Asked Questions: Protection against the Unlawful Acquisition of Undisclosed Know-how and Business Information (Trade Secrets)' https://ec.europa.eu/growth/industry/intellectual-property/trade-secrets/faq_en (last accessed 5 June 2017).

6.2 The Distinction between Registered and Unregistered Intellectual Property Rights

The choice between deontological and instrumentalist conceptions of IP is sometimes associated with the choice between automatically subsisting and registrable IP rights. As has been seen, the earliest IP regimes made the recognition of IP rights conditional upon their registration by the state following a successful application for their grant. This was true of the Venetian and English patent systems of the 15th and 17th centuries, and of the English industrial design right system of the 18th century. Similarly, the Statute of Anne recognized the subsistence of rights only upon the publication, and following the deposit and registration, of a book, while the early trade mark systems required the use in trade of the relevant sign of origin. Today trade marks are registrable rights, as are patents, plant variety rights, and registered design right, while copyright subsists automatically upon creation of a work, and unregistered design right subsists on creation or publication of the design. To some extent it is possible to associate this distinction with a different view of the rights themselves. For example, rights that subsist automatically, upon the creation or publication of an object, are sometimes seen as arising from nature, while rights that are granted by the state upon application and examination are sometimes seen as arising from a decision by the state that their recognition and protection will be of public benefit. However, it is clear that this distinction is imperfect. For example, even the Statute of Anne was cast in instrumentalist terms, as encouraging 'learning' and the composing of useful books. In addition, early patent acts required application and registration, but no substantive examination, suggesting that provided the applicant satisfied certain formalities the grant would be made. Further, registration systems are easily and frequently conceived as protecting creators as much as the public, since they make it easier for creators to establish their entitlement to protection and inform the public of the existence of their rights. Finally, even substantive examination of an application for IP protection can be seen as consistent with a natural law conception of that protection, since its point will always be to establish that the requirements for protection have been satisfied and thereby limit protection to those who (are perceived to) merit it on whatever (deontological or instrumentalist) grounds. At the end of the day, and as with legal systems in general, the fact that IP systems serve certain ends or values by means of registration and other requirements does not enable a conclusion that those ends or values are what justify the systems' existence.

6.3 The Distinction between Intellectual Property Rights and Legislation

It is common to use the terms 'copyright', 'patents', 'trade marks', 'design rights', and 'plant variety rights' to denote both a species of IP and the legislation in which it is defined. For example, one typically uses the term 'copyright' to denote both an author's rights and a legislative regime. However appropriate this may be, it ignores an important difference between the two that derives from the fact that, whereas copyright *qua* author's right is an entitlement of an individual based in considerations of utility and deontology, copyright *qua* legislation is the mechanism by which the state identifies and reconciles the competing rights and interests of all individuals—including authors and third parties—as well as of society in respect of authorial subject matter. As such, copyright *qua* legislation is protective of both authors' and third parties'/societal interests. That is one reason why the call by critics of digital copyright for a completely self-regulated Internet, in which access to authorial works is regulated by private ordering (contractual and technological protection) mechanisms rather than by property, has generally failed to convince: namely, since the market is incapable of ensuring access conditions that take account of the rights and interests of all parties and of society. In effect, then, the distinction between IP rights and IP legislation can be said to reflect a distinction between conceptions of IP as private right and conceptions of IP as regulatory tool respectively.[186] Alternatively, it can be said to underline that the definition of IP rights is informed as much by third party and societal rights and interests as by the rights and interests of the IP rights' presumptive beneficiaries.

6.4 The Distinction between Intellectual Property Rights and Subject Matter

A final distinction to be drawn is between IP rights and subject matter. Outside IP, in the area of real and personal property, the tangibility of the objects to which property rights attach lessens the importance of this distinction, and arguably subverts it by counting possession of the object as among the incidents of property. In IP, the intangibility of IP subject matter precludes any corresponding possessory rights or talk of 'ownership'. For these reasons, it is important to distinguish clearly between the rights that IP confers and the subject matter to which those rights relate; and to remember, for example, that while an author or trade mark owner will own IP rights in respect of her work or sign, she will not, with certain limited exceptions,[187] own the work or sign itself.

7. Conclusion

Statutory IP laws began to emerge in Europe from the 15th century as means of promoting and rewarding the introduction to the public of certain intellectual creations and discoveries of social value. Of especial interest among the early IP regimes were those introduced in France immediately following the Declaration of the Rights of Man in 1789. While reflecting the same appreciation of the social value

[186] Cf M A Lemley, 'The Regulatory Turn in IP' (2013) 36 Harvard Journal of Law & Public Policy 109; R P Merges, 'What Kind of Rights are Intellectual Property Rights?' in Dreyfuss and Pila (eds), *Handbook of Intellectual Property Law* (n 20) (rejecting the view of IP as a regulatory tool).

[187] One such exception is the ownership rights created in respect of employee-devised inventions as between employer and employee by the Patents Act 1977 (UK) s 39.

of intellectual creations and the consequential desirability of encouraging them, the French laws additionally underlined the rights of the individuals who created them, supporting the development of a tradition of IP focused more squarely on deontological than instrumentalist values and considerations. Nonetheless, those traditions were sufficiently compatible to enable their supporting states to agree to harmonize their laws in accordance with the Paris and Berne Conventions in the 19th century, which Conventions remain foundational to the international and European IP systems of today.

Historically in Europe, IP rights were exclusive rights granted in respect of specific types of expressive and informational subject matter: contrivances and manners of new manufacture, books, patterns for printing linens, cottons, calicos, and muslins, agricultural products, and signs of commercial origin. For most of these subject matter, such rights were a means of rewarding and encouraging the introduction of valuable creations and discoveries to the public realm and promoting industry and commerce by regulating access to objects the intangible nature of which would have otherwise made it difficult to establish and maintain a market in respect of them. For signs of commercial origin, by contrast, they protected the public from misrepresentations regarding the origin of goods in trade, and in doing so promoted competition and efficiency in the marketplace. To these ends the earliest European and English IP regimes conferred on the inventors or importers of contrivances and manners of new manufactures, the authors of books, the designers of new fabric designs, the discovers of new agricultural products, and the traders who affixed signs to their goods to indicate the goods' commercial origin, exclusive rights for a limited period to prevent third parties from reproducing, importing, publishing, and/or using the protected subject matter within local territory without the permission of the recognized beneficiary.

Today, intellectual property laws cover a wider spectrum of subject matter, reach more deeply into the lives of citizens, and are vastly more complex than they were in their earliest days. Nonetheless, the essential nature and purpose of IP rights remain largely unchanged. At the European level, IP rights are conceived as temporary exclusive rights in respect of different categories of 'intellectual creation', broadly defined to include discoveries and other informational products of innovation and creativity, much as they were defined historically. Reflecting its supranational nature and the global environment in which it operates, the EU seeks through the regulation of IP rights to build on the traditions of its Member States in a manner that is consistent with both its international commitments and its particular economic and social values and aims. The result of this particular objective may be described as two-fold. The first is a view of IP rights as instruments for achieving certain public benefit ends, including generating jobs and wealth, promoting the production and distribution of goods and services, supporting innovation and competition with other states, and promoting creativity, innovation, development, and solutions to global (health, environmental, and other) challenges. And the second is a belief in the value of IP rights as means for ensuring to creators and innovators of intellectual (informational and expressive) products sufficient protection for the benefits of their creative and innovative labours to enable their work to flourish.

That leaves the nature of IP rights themselves. As the term 'intellectual property' suggests, IP rights are property rights in respect of discrete intellectual objects. Their property status is widely recognized as a matter of positive law, consistent with their exclusionary nature and (with exceptions) their transferability, and has been affirmed by the European Court of Human Rights and the EU legislature through the recognition of IP in the property clause of the CFR. So too the concern of IP rights with 'intellectual creations' is widely recognized. According to the European Commission in the communication from July 2014 excerpted above, for example:[188]

> Intellectual creations need protection if creativity and innovation are to flourish, and this is the role of IPRs, which also play an important function in promoting development and in addressing some of today's global challenges.

The question that remains is how this commitment to protecting intellectual creations, supporting creativity and innovation, promoting development, and addressing today's global challenges, is reflected in the range of subject matter to which IP rights attach, which is the question addressed in the following chapters.

[188] See text accompanying n 86.

3

A Framework for Thinking about Intellectual Property Subject Matter

1. Introduction

A central question for all intellectual property (IP) regimes is what subject matter to protect and, having answered that question, how to determine whether a given subject matter is of a type identified as eligible for protection. When considering the law's response to these questions, certain devices of philosophy offer analytic assistance. These devices are categories, properties, types/tokens, and artifacts. When taken together they suggest a framework for thinking about the subject matter protectable by IP regimes. Specifically, they support a paradigmatic or focal conception of IP subject matter as artifact types distinguished by their properties and arranged by the legislature and courts into categories reflecting those properties. In the current chapter this conception and its analytic value for the UK and European laws of IP are considered. In the course of doing so certain distinctions of importance for IP subject matter specifically are highlighted, complementing the distinctions of importance for IP rights discussed in Chapter 2. These include: the distinction between the essential and (salient but) accidental properties of IP subject matter; the distinction between IP subject matter and their concrete instances; the distinction between transformative and non-transformative intellectual creations as protectable IP subject matter; and the distinction between metaphysical and epistemic understandings of the individuation of IP subject matter.

My aim in this chapter is considerably more modest than formulating a theory of the subject matter protectable by IP rights currently. Nonetheless, and as with such a theory, for a framework of the type herein proposed to be of value it must reflect, in general terms at least, the reality of the subject matter that the main IP regimes protect. It might be objected that any framework devised in this way will support certain views and values of the current intellectual property system that ought not to be supported. These might include the view of IP law in general as something that is natural or inevitable, and inherently good for individuals and societies in the myriad ways it claims to be. They might also include the reification of individualistic conceptions of human creation, and the tendency that modern IP regimes have towards increased proprietization of the expressive and scientific domains.[1] Suffice it to say that my aim is not to support these views or values. As stated previously, it is clear that the law and subject matter of intellectual property, like the law in general and its conception of the diverse other objects that it regulates, represent only what we currently perceive and label them to be.[2] However, there is no inconsistency between recognizing this and trying to understand better the law that exists by means of such theoretical devices as one has to hand.

A related objection that might be made is that importing analytic categories into law from philosophy and using those categories as lenses through which to view and order different IP regimes will distract attention from the aims and values of IP, and from (what ought to be) the concern of law-makers to define and conceive the subject matter that IP rights protect with a view to pursuing and protecting those aims and values specifically. The suggestion here is that this ought not to be the case. As seen in Chapter 2, modern IP systems pursue a range of economic and social objectives, from promoting efficient and competitive markets to enabling creators' intellectual work to flourish and protecting their personal rights and interests. Central to its pursuit of these objectives today, as historically, is a conception of the nature of IP rights as limited rights of property that subsist in or are made available by the state in respect of certain expressive and informational subject matter of perceived value to society, referred to by EU law-makers as 'intellectual creations'. This conception of IP rights, and of the subject matter to which they appropriately attach, informs and constrains understandings of the aims and values of IP systems as much as those aims and values inform and constrain conceptions of IP subject matter themselves. So, while it is clearly the case that IP subject matter ought to be understood in the context of IP systems as a whole, this does not preclude the use of other disciplines to elucidate their nature, including their nature as objects of property rights in the form (paradigmatically at least) of intellectual creations specifically. Indeed, the fact that authorial works, inventions, designs, and trade marks etc are not exclusively legal constructs (in the manner of property), but rather objects that exist outside of law as an aspect of the social and economic life of all modern communities, makes it inevitable and desirable that IP law] draw on other disciplines in understanding them.

[1] For a discussion see P Drahos, *A Philosophy of Intellectual Property* (Dartmouth 1996) esp 201–202.

[2] In relation to the law in general see B Z Tamanaha, 'Understanding Legal Pluralism: Past to Present, Local to Global' (2008) 30 Sydney Law Review 375, 396 (describing law as a 'folk concept' in the sense of being 'what people within social groups have come to see and label as "law"', and thus not appropriately studied as a scientific category).

2. Intellectual Property Subject Matter as Artifacts

According to Article 27(2) of the Universal Declaration of Human Rights,[3] '[e]veryone has the right to the protection of the moral and material interests resulting from any scientific, literary or artistic production of which he is the author'. As a basis for the recognition of intellectual property rights, this article supports a conception of IP subject matter as artifacts, namely, and as defined by philosophers, objects the existence and character of which depend on the productive actions and intentions of one or more human beings, being the authors of the object in question.[4] This definition brings to mind the conception of IP subject matter supported by the European legal definition of copyright works, according to which copyright subsists in any work that expresses the intellectual creation of an author in the sense of resulting from her exercise of formative freedom in the production of a bounded expressive object that bears her personal mark.[5] While not all IP subject matter will represent as close a fit to the philosophical conception of artifacts above as authorial works, that conception is nonetheless helpful in offering an analytic frame of reference when thinking about legal conceptions of IP subject matter more generally. At its heart is the idea of an intangible object that owes its existence and character to the actions and intentions of one or more human beings.

2.1 Intellectual Property Subject Matter as Intangible Objects

Broadly speaking, and consistent with the language of property theory, an intangible object is an object that lacks an essential concrete or material form. An example may be offered from the 19th century case of *Walter v Lane*.[6] That case involved two objects, each of which was potentially capable of supporting property rights. The first was a tangible object, in the form of a written record of a speech composed and delivered by Lord Rosebery to a public audience, and comprising a collection of words printed on paper in shorthand notation by a reporter. And the second was an intangible object, in the form of the speech of Lord Rosebery that the written record contained. There was no question in *Walter v Lane* that the reporter owned the written record of the speech. What was in question, however, was whether he had property rights in respect of the literary record produced by his shorthand. If and only if he did have such rights could he succeed in his claim against the defendant in the case for having infringed his literary copyright by reproducing his report of Lord Rosebery's speech. According to a majority of the House of Lords,

[3] Universal Declaration of Human Rights, UN Doc A/810 (10 December 1948).

[4] See generally R Hilpinen, 'Artifact' in E N Zalta (ed), *The Stanford Encyclopedia of Philosophy* (Winter 2011 edn).

[5] See Case C–145/10 *Painer v Standard Verlags GmbH* [2011] ECR I–12533 (*Painer*) and the other cases discussed in ch 5.

[6] *Walter v Lane* [1900] AC 539 (HL) (*Walter v Lane*).

the reporter did have the rights he claimed, namely, copyright in his record as an intangible work of authorship. Only Lord Robertson disagreed, deciding that the only intangible work of authorship was the speech of Lord Rosebery itself, of which Lord Rosebery was the sole creator.[7]

It is the intangible nature of authorial works and other IP subject matter that makes IP rights so conceptually difficult, and their protection by property rights so controversial. In the case of tangible objects, property rights are recognized in consequence of the objects' capacity to support exclusive possession or occupation: the possession or occupation of a tangible object founding a prima facie claim to ownership. To justify this from a social policy perspective, we might note that such properties make the objects rivalrous and exhaustible—only a limited number of people can use them at any particular time (making them rivalrous), and each person's use of them depletes their availability for use by others (making them exhaustible)—which in turn make the recognition of property rights in respect of them desirable as a means of preventing the social conflict, inefficiencies, and waste that would otherwise be caused by people fighting over them and using them simultaneously. By recognizing and enforcing rights of exclusion in respect of them, it might be said, the state limits this conflict and encourages people to direct their investment to other resources in respect of which they have the exclusive rights of exploitation conferred by property. Conversely, if IP subject matter is neither rivalrous nor exhaustible, the same risks of social conflict and overexploitation ought not to exist by recognizing the freedom of all persons to access them, thereby rendering the traditional justifications for recognizing and enforcing property rights inapplicable. In addition, where the objects in question are intangible in nature, as for ideas, facts, turns of phrase, and chemical formulae, restricting this freedom can have the effect of fencing off parts of the public realm from authorized use, and thereby preventing people from using basic elements of humanistic and scientific expression, and from accessing such 'public goods'[8] as medicines and news items. This impact of the exclusionary rights of IP underlines the importance of ensuring that their recognition and enforcement by the state are clearly justified on deontological, instrumental, or other grounds and, even if they are found to be so justified, of carefully defining the subject matter to which they attach.

2.2 Intellectual Property Subject Matter as Intellectual Creations

In a recent discussion of the Berne and Paris Conventions,[9] Sam Ricketson remarked upon their difference in focus. While the Berne Convention focuses on securing

[7] For a detailed discussion of the case see J Pila, 'An Intentional View of the Copyright Work' (2008) 71 Modern Law Review 535.

[8] On the nature of public goods see J Rawls, *A Theory of Justice* (Harvard University Press 1971).

[9] S Ricketson, 'The Emergence and Development of the International Intellectual Property System' in R C Dreyfuss and J Pila (eds), *The Oxford Handbook of Intellectual Property Law* (OUP 2017) http://www.oxfordhandbooks.com/view/10.1093/oxfordhb/9780198758457.001.0001/oxfordhb-9780198758457 (last accessed 5 June 2017).

rights for a certain class of people—authors—the Paris Convention focuses on securing protection for a certain class of object—industrial property—where by 'industrial property' is meant subject matter related

[n]ot only to industry and commerce proper, but likewise to agricultural and extractive industries and to all manufactured or natural products, for example, wines, grain, tobacco leaf, fruit, cattle, minerals, mineral waters, beer, flowers, and flour.[10]

The distinction between securing rights for a category of people and securing protection for a category of objects might be viewed as pointing to two different types of property law reasoning. According to the second, which is more prevalent in the field of personal property, one starts from the existence of a thing, such as a bicycle or a chair, and reasons to its ownership by the person in possession of it. According to the first, which is more prevalent in the field of intellectual property, and which underpins the view of IP subject matter as artifacts considered in section 2.1, one starts from a person and reasons to exclusionary rights in respect of the objects created by her, such as a poem, medicine, suit design, or variety of plant. By requiring an act of intellectual creation to justify IP rights, the law underlines an important restriction on the scope of IP, in modern times at least, which is its inability to protect any form of subject matter the existence of which cannot be attributed to one or more natural persons.

That intellectual property denotes property rights in respect of intellectual creations might be regarded as implicit in the phrase 'intellectual property', and as in any case consistent with the central arguments for its recognition and protection. For example, when the members of the King's Bench in *Millar v Taylor*[11] were asked to decide whether common law property attached to works of literary authorship, they reasoned from the general principles governing the subsistence of rights of property. To that end they considered three alternative criteria for the recognition of property rights. According to the first, property rights attach to objects of value. According to the second, property rights attach to objects capable of exclusive occupation. And according to the third, property rights attach to products of human labour. A majority of the court supported the third of these criteria, reasoning in the result that since literary works are products of literary labour, they are protected by property rights vesting in their creators at common law, independent of their value and notwithstanding their absence of any essential concrete or material form.[12]

[10] Paris Convention for the Protection of Industrial Property (adopted 20 March 1883, last revised 14 July 1967) 828 UNTS 305, as amended (Paris Convention) art 1(3).

[11] *Millar v Taylor* (1769) 4 Burr 2303 (KB).

[12] See eg ibid 2398 (reporting the statement by Lord Mansfield that the basis for literary property in published and unpublished works at common law was the argument that: 'it is just, that an author should reap the pecuniary profits of his own ingenuity and labour[;] that another should not use his name, without his consent[;] that he should judge when to publish, or whether he ever will publish[; that] he should not only choose the time, but the manner of publication; how many; what volume; what print[; that] he should choose to whose care he will trust the accuracy and correctness of the impression; in whose honesty he will confide, not to foist in additions: with other reasons of the same effect'); *contra* 2362–2363 (Yates J in dissent, supporting a view of property as existing in respect of objects capable of exclusive occupation only).

The argument from Locke, accepted by a majority of the judges in *Millar v Taylor*, that a person who labours to create an object has property rights in respect of the object by virtue of her ownership of her body, and therefore of her labour, underpins the nature of IP subject matter as artifacts. Given this, its prevalence in UK and European copyright jurisprudence in particular is not surprising. However, so too other theories of IP proceed from a view of IP rights as triggered by a human act resulting in an object of protectable type. An example is the theory of utility, according to which IP rights are instruments of the state granted to encourage the creation and dissemination of objects of value for society. Another is the theory of desert, according to which IP rights reward those who labour to create objects in recognition of the value of their labour and/or of the resulting objects. And a further one is the theory of autonomy, according to which IP rights recognize and protect the emotional and/or financial needs of those who labour to create intellectual products.[13] Crucial for each of these theories is the idea of a human act triggering a claim to IP protection in respect of a resulting object, which object is the artifact to which the IP rights attach.

Conceiving intellectual property reasoning as proceeding from a human act to exclusionary rights in respect of a resulting object draws attention to the two perennial questions for IP law and policy. The first is what types of act justify exclusionary rights and, closely related to this, to what and for whose benefit do those rights attach. And the second is how the rights conferred ought to be conceived, defined, and capable of exploitation; and, closely related to this, which institutions ought to be entrusted with their administration and enforcement.

In relation to the first of these questions, two perspectives may be offered from the common law jurisprudence regarding personal property rights in respect of human body parts.[14] The first derives from the early 20th century case of *Doodeward v Spence*,[15] which involved a claim to the ownership of a stillborn two-headed foetus that had been preserved by the claimant in spirits. According to Griffith CJ in the High Court of Australia, since the claimant had exercised work or skill to transform the (lawfully obtained) stillborn into something different from the foetus, he owned the resulting object.[16] Implicit in the chief justice's reasoning is that a transformative act of human labour or skill that gives rise to something new, in the sense of something that is materially and irreversibly changed from the thing acted upon, will justify property rights in respect of the new object

[13] For a detailed discussion see J Pila and P L C Torremans, *European Intellectual Property Law* (OUP 2016) ch 3.

[14] I am grateful to Jonathan Herring and Imogen Goold for drawing my attention to these cases.

[15] *Doodeward v Spence* [1908] HCA 45, (1908) 6 CLR 406 (*Doodeward*).

[16] ibid 414 (Griffith CJ, finding: 'I entertain no doubt that, when a person has by the lawful exercise of work or skill so dealt with a human body or part of a human body in his lawful possession that it has acquired some attributes differentiating it from a mere corpse awaiting burial, he acquires a right to retain possession of it, at least as against any person not entitled to have it delivered to him for the purpose of burial, but subject, of course, to any positive law which forbids its retention under the particular circumstances').

as a creation of the claimant.[17] Different was the view supported by the Court of Appeal for England and Wales in the 2009 case of *Yearworth v North Bristol NHS Trust*.[18] According to the Court of Appeal in that case, restricting ownership to human body parts transformed by work or skill in accordance with the *Doodeward* principle would not have been 'entirely logical'.[19] Hence its decision in *Yearworth* that the use of one's body to generate and ejaculate sperm was sufficient to confer ownership rights in respect of the sperm thus generated and ejaculated. Implicit in this reasoning is that making a material object (such as sperm) available in a state that supports a new use, in the sense of a use that is different from the use supported by the object in its previous state, is sufficient to justify the conferral of rights in respect of the object in that state.

The disagreement expressed in these common law property cases can be viewed in different ways. On one reading, it concerns the question of what exactly an act of human creation entails: only the transformation of a pre-existing object into something that is materially different in its essential properties, or also the making of a pre-existing object available in a state in which it supports a different use or purpose? On another reading, the disagreement concerns the more general question of what *types* of human act trigger the existence of property: only acts of human creation, or also acts that, while involving no creation, nonetheless enable something to be done with an object that could not be done with it previously? This can be understood in Aristotelian terms with reference to the different causes of or explanations for the objects in respect of which property rights are claimed to exist. For example, an object transformed from a pre-existing object will have a different formal cause from that of the object transformed: different things will make each object what it is. By contrast, an object made available in a state in which it supports a new or improved use may have the same formal cause as the object in its original state, but will have a different efficient and final cause from that object: each will be due to a different cause (ie have a different origin), and each will be for (ie in pursuit of) a different end.

The same disagreements can be seen to exist in IP; albeit the objects protected by IP having an exemplary rather than a formal cause in the Aristotelian sense by reason of their intangibility, and thus being the objects that they are by reason of the idea or plan that they represent, rather than by reason of their formal properties. Under European patent law, for example, any person who acts upon the world by controlling the forces of nature to produce a causal, perceivable, and repeatable result is potentially entitled to a patent, whether for the method of acting upon the world or the result produced by implementing it.[20] That principle explains the availability of patents for a product that a person has isolated from its natural environment on the basis that the act of isolation represents a human intervention in the world justifying the recognition of intellectual property rights in respect of the product by reason, in part at least, of the new purpose that the product in its

[17] This reasoning reflects the requirements for the existence of a *nova species* according to the Roman Law principle of *specificatio*: see ch 1, text associated with n 39.

[18] *Yearworth v North Bristol NHS Trust* [2009] EWCA Civ 37, [2010] QB 1 (*Yearworth*).

[19] ibid [45].

[20] G2/07 and G1/08 *Essentially Biological Processes* [2011] EPOR 27.

isolated form supports. European patent tribunals have long recognized this,[21] as more recently has the EU legislature. By provision of Article 5(2) of the Biotech Directive,[22] for example, an element isolated from the human body, including a gene or partial sequence of a gene, is an invention for which a patent may be granted, subject to the disclosure of a function that the isolated element supports.[23] The resulting position and the reasoning underlying it are consistent with the logic of the *Yearworth* case. They do not, however, enjoy universal support. For example, according to the superior courts of the United States and Australia, the mere act of isolating a product from its natural environment is not sufficient to support a patent, since such act does not involve the creation of anything new, ie and as the courts in question understood the concept of 'newness' in the relevant cases, anything materially different from that which had existed previously.[24] This position and the reasoning supporting it are consistent with the logic of the *Doodeward* case, and imply a requirement for an act of human transformation beyond the mere making available of an object in a new or different state. The result is divergent views in different jurisdictions regarding the acts that justify patent grants. So too in copyright: according to the well-established position of the UK courts, for a person to be an author who benefits from copyright, she must have exercised skill and labour in the creation of an authorial (literary, dramatic, musical, or artistic) work.[25] Similarly under European law, and as previously seen, only a person who exercises free and creative choices in the creation of a work that bears her personal mark is perceived to merit the title author and the resulting protections of copyright.[26] Implicit in both UK and European principles is the *Doodeward* idea that to be entitled to copyright a person must transform an existing object to create something new, in the sense of something materially different from the object transformed. Once again, this position may be contrasted with the position previously supported by courts in other jurisdictions, that exercising labour to make existing information available to the public in a new and useful state—as occurs, for example, in the production of an exhaustive, alphabetically arranged telephone directory for a particular geographical area—is enough to trigger copyright in respect of the information in that state.[27]

Even if the recognition and protection of IP rights are confined in certain regimes and jurisdictions to subject matter the existence of which can be attributed to an act of intellectual creation in the *Doodeward* sense, and/or such subject matter is treated as paradigmatic of the subject matter protectable by IP

[21] See eg *Howard Florey/Relaxin* [1995] EPOR 541 (Opp Div).

[22] Directive 98/44/EC of the European Parliament and of the Council of 6 July 1998 on the legal protection of biotechnological inventions [1998] OJ L 213/13 (Biotech Directive).

[23] ibid art 3(2).

[24] See *Association for Molecular Pathology v Myriad Genetics, Inc* 133 S Ct 2107 (2013); *D'Arcy v Myriad Genetics, Inc* [2015] HCA 35, (2015) 89 ALJR 924.

[25] *Walter v Lane* (n 6); *Sawkins v Hyperion Records* [2005] EWCA Civ 565, [2005] RPC 32 (*Sawkins*). While the courts are clear on the need for skill *and* labour, this can be reconciled with the *Doodeward* reference to skill *or* labour by an understanding of the labour required for the relevant transformative act.

[26] See eg *Painer* (n 5) [94].

[27] See eg *Desktop Marketing Systems Pty Ltd v Telstra Corp Ltd* [2002] FCAFC 112.

(by reason for example of its fit with the concept of an artifact), there remains the question of whether other subject matter not originating in such an act might nonetheless be eligible for protection by (certain types of) intellectual property. This question has been universally answered in the affirmative. This is apparent inter alia from: the protection by related ('neighbouring') rights of recordings and transmissions—in the form of films, phonograms, broadcasts, and performances—of authorial works and other expressive content; the protection by plant variety rights of newly commercialized varieties of plant; and the protection by registered trade mark of expressive objects suitable and intended for use in trade to indicate the commercial origin of certain goods or services.[28] Since each of the human acts triggering the IP rights in question—recording or transmitting expressive content, breeding or discovering the existence of a variety of plant, and associating an expressive object with the goods or services of a certain origin—involves making a pre-existing object available in a state that supports a new use, namely, preservation and distribution of the expression, commercialization and distribution of the plant variety, and designation of the commercial origin of goods and services, each can be regarded as a human act of intellectual creation in and only in the *Yearworth* sense. Whether an object not owing its existence to an act of intellectual creation in this or the *Doodeward* sense might (or ought) nonetheless (to) be protected by intellectual property, however, must be doubted.

It is possible to attribute some of the greatest errors in IP decision-making to a failure by the courts to be clear on what types of human act are required for a species of IP to exist, and to insist on the occurrence of such an act before supporting such existence. An example is the House of Lords decision in *Walter v Lane*, discussed above, which was affirmed as the leading authority on the copyright subsistence requirement of originality in 2009 by the Court of Appeal of England and Wales in *Sawkins v Hyperion Records*.[29] According to the court in *Walter v Lane*, since the verbatim record of Lord Roseberry's spoken words created by the reporter was a book within the meaning of 19th century UK copyright legislation, it was protected by literary copyright. In addition, since it was assumed that every book must have an author, and that every copyright must have an owner, the House of Lords had little option but to decide that the reporter responsible for bringing the book into existence by recording on paper the words that Lord Rosebery had spoken was an author entitled to copyright. Only Lord Robertson in dissent rejected this conclusion by reasoning that began not with the existence of a book entitled to copyright, but rather with the non-existence of any human act of intellectual creation beyond that undertaken by Lord Rosebery in conceiving his speech. The result was a finding by Lord Robertson that the act of the reporter himself—which involved the exercise of skill and labour in the creation of a verbatim record of Lord Rosebery's speech—was not an act of authorial creation as could justify the recognition for

[28] See ch 2. [29] See *Sawkins* (n 25) [33] (Mummery LJ).

his benefit of literary copyright; and consequently, that the verbatim record of another's speech was not an artifact as might be capable of supporting rights of intellectual property.

3. Intellectual Property Subject Matter as Types

As has been seen, IP subject matter can be conceived as intangible objects resulting from human acts of (intellectual) creation more or less widely defined. When considering further the nature of these artifacts, another metaphysical device that may usefully be invoked, and that can be seen to underpin law-making and decision-making in IP, is the distinction between a type and its tokens or particulars. This distinction is helpful in elucidating more fully the intangible nature of IP subject matter, including their difference from the tangible objects protected by the law of personal property, and the way in which IP rights operate.

At its simplest, a type is a descriptive concept, whereas a token is a concrete instance or object instantiating that concept. As with properties (such as white) and relations (such as sister), types are generally regarded as universals, namely, qualities or characteristics that can be repeatedly and simultaneously exemplified by many distinct and concrete things. As universals, however, types are much more intimately connected with their tokens than properties or relations are connected with their particulars. As remarked by Richard Wollheim in 1968, this is reflected in our tendency to 'think and talk of the type as though it were itself a kind of token, though a peculiarly important or pre-eminent one'.[30]

Authorial works are often used to explain the type/token distinction. An example given by Linda Wetzel in her essay on the distinction[31] is the sentence 'Rose is a rose is a rose is a rose' from the poem *Sacred Emily* by Gertrude Stein, which contains three word types ('rose', 'is', and 'a'), four tokens of the word type 'rose', and three tokens of each of the word types 'is' and 'a'. As this example suggests, types are abstract and unique, whereas tokens are concrete objects comprised, for example, of ink on paper.[32] Hence the importance of the type/token distinction for intellectual property, as a more nuanced version of the intangible/tangible object distinction discussed above. For example, authorial works such as Erik Satie's*Gymnopédie No1* and inventions such as the Onco-mouse[33] are each protectable by IP rights as abstract concepts or descriptions that exist separate from their performances (for *Gymnopédie No1*) and the individual mice having their properties (for the Onco-mouse). Seeing such subject matter as types offers

[30] L Wetzel, 'Types and Tokens' in E N Zalta (ed), *The Stanford Encyclopedia of Philosophy* (Spring 2014 edn) para 3, quoting from R Wollheim, *Art and Its Objects* (Harper and Row 1968) 76.

[31] See Wetzel (n 30) para 1.1. For a more detailed account of the type/token distinction by Wetzel see L Wetzel, *Types and Tokens: On Abstract Objects* (The MIT Press 2009).

[32] See Wetzel (n 30) para 1.1.

[33] The Onco-mouse is the transgenic non-human eukaryotic animal into whose germ and somatic cells an activated oncogene sequence has been inserted.

an explanation for the German Federal Court of Justice's (Bundesgerichtshof's) decision in the 1969 *Red Dove* case[34] that the act of creating a more beautiful dove by a combination of selection and breeding techniques could not support a patent because of its non-repeatability. Explaining the decision in terms of the type/token distinction, we would note that the non-repeatability of the act deprived both it and the dove of the qualities of a type, by preventing it from being instantiated repeatedly. As the German court said, to grant a patent for such a subject matter would be to confer a kind of monopoly unknown to patent law, namely, one that excluded others from use of a token, in the form of the dove that the applicants succeeded on one occasion by following certain steps to create, for which there existed no type. In 2005 the Court of Appeal of England and Wales similarly supported a view of the authorial works protected by copyright as types. That occurred in *Sawkins v Hyperion Records*, where Lord Justice Mummery emphasized the distinction that exists in law between a musical work and the written score on which it is or may be recorded. Bringing to mind the definition of artifact discussed above, Lord Justice Mummery defined a musical work as a combination of sounds intended for realization in performance, and musical copyright as subsisting in works thus defined, independent of any material recording or other fixation of them. In his judgment:

> Music must be distinguished from the fact and form of its fixation as a record of a musical composition. The score is the traditional and convenient form of fixation of the music and conforms to the requirement that a copyright work must be recorded in some material form. But the fixation in the written score or on a record is not in itself the music in which copyright subsists. There is no reason why, for example, a recording of a person's spontaneous singing, whistling or humming or improvisations of sounds by a group of people with or without musical instruments should not be 'music' for copyright purposes.[35]

On the view expressed in *Sawkins*, musical works (and by implication other intellectual creations) are universals in the Platonic (realist) sense specifically, namely, abstract objects that are capable of repeated exemplification by concrete particulars, but that exist separate from and independent of those particulars.[36] This view of IP subject matter is consistent also with the decision in *Red Dove* that the non-repeatability of the method of producing the dove deprived it of the qualities of an invention protectable by IP rights; and with the court's further emphasis in that case on the absence of any need for the method *qua* invention to have been applied to produce a dove in order to be recognized and protected as such. However, and as philosophers have pointed out in respect of works of art, the view of intellectual creations as abstract and predicable of things sits uncomfortably with our intuitive tendency, referred to already, of regarding them as existing *in* their individual instances.[37] Taking that tendency seriously might lead us to the Aristotelian view

[34] Case X ZB 15/67 *Red Dove* [1969] GRUR 672, [1970] 1 International Review of Industrial Property and Copyright Law 136 (Bundesgerichtshof) (*Red Dove*).

[35] See *Sawkins* (n 25) [53].

[36] This definition reflects the view of universals supported by Platonic realists. For a general discussion of it and other views of universals see D M Armstrong, *Universals: An Opinionated Introduction* (Westview Press 1989).

[37] See Wetzel (n 30) para 3.

that, rather than being abstract, universals (and therefore IP subject matter) exist in and only in time and space, meaning for authorial works that they exist in and only in all of the specific occasions of their performance and reproduction. On this view, for example, *Gymnopédie No 1* would exist in and only in the written scores representing it, the sound recordings of its various performances, and the occasions of those performances (and of the performances of its sound recordings) respectively. If all of the written scores and sound recordings of the work in the world were destroyed, the piece would not exist, except on the occurrence and for the duration of any performance of it.

So too the signs protected by trade marks—be they words such as 'Nike', slogans such as 'Just do it' or images such as the Nike swoosh—are types (or legisigns) that, according to Charles Sanders Peirce who coined the type/token distinction, do not themselves exist but rather determine things that do exist in the form of tokens (or sinsigns).[38] Indeed, this Peircean distinction between legisigns and sinsigns forms the basis of the semiotic theories and concepts that have been widely deployed by IP scholars to explain the aims and functions of trade marks.[39] Central among the concepts is that of the sign itself: the words, images, and other objects that may be registered as trade marks. As linguists have emphasized, the meanings of signs do not inhere within the objects themselves, but rather are invested in those objects by those who engage with and interpret them. Also central among the concepts deployed to explain trade marks are the signifier and signified. The signifier is the literal, visual, or other form that a particular sign takes, and the signified is the meaning that it (the sign) signifies. The relevance of these concepts for trade marks will be obvious when one considers their nature and how they operate. As described earlier, trade marks are signs used in trade to denote the commercial origin of goods and services. They also operate as reputational externalities for the trader of the goods or services with which they are associated, and as objects to which certain meanings associated with those goods or services (and the trader responsible for them) attach. Trade marks are thus readily conceivable as signs in the preceding semiotic sense of deriving their value from that which they signify in the mind of those members of the public who engage with and thereby interpret them.

Another aspect of IP law that may be clarified by conceiving IP subject matter as types is the nature of IP rights themselves, and how they function. For example, by viewing IP subject matter as types we can see that when IP law restricts the unauthorized reproduction of an authorial work or product design, or the making of an invention, it is in substance restricting the unauthorized production of tokens of the protected subject matter *qua* type. So too in the case of trade marks: when the law restricts the unauthorized use of a mark in the course of trade, it is in substance restricting the unauthorized use of the mark *qua* sign, ie as a signifier of a particular

[38] See ibid para 4.1.3.

[39] See eg B Beebe, 'The Semiotic Analysis of Trademark Law' (2004) 51 UCLA Law Review 621; M Pulos, 'A Semiotic Solution to the Propertization Problem of Trademark' (2006) 53 UCLA Law Review 850; A Lang, 'A Case for Applying the Theoretical Semiotics in the Practice of Trade Mark Law' (2008) 21 International Journal for the Semiotics of Law 6.

meaning, be it the origin of the relevant goods or services to which it is affixed or something else.

In sum, characterizing IP subject matter as types and IP rights as aimed at excluding third parties from the unauthorized use of their tokens is helpful, both in facilitating understanding of the subject matter that IP law protects, and in supporting critical evaluation of that protection. It also enables us to draw on the extensive philosophical work that has been done regarding the nature and identity conditions of types and tokens in considering the subject matter that are and ought to be protected by IP having regard to the rights that such protection confers on their individual beneficiaries.

When discussing IP subject matter as types it is appropriate to note the uncertainty among philosophers as to whether every such subject matter is a type properly conceived. For example, according to Wetzel, an oil painting such as the *Mona Lisa* is not a type for which there can exist many tokens.[40] Rather, there is and perhaps can only be one token of such a painting.[41] So too, according to Nicholas Wolterstorff, works such as paintings and sculptures are not types—in his phenomenology, performance works (of which there can be a performance) or object works (of which there can be an impression, casting, or example)—but rather physical objects.[42] However, even if we accept this to be correct, it does not render the type/token distinction inapplicable or unhelpful for IP. The important question is not whether every IP subject matter is recognized by philosophers to be a type properly conceived. Rather, what matters is whether the subject matter protected by IP rights on the one hand, and the copies of those subject matter from which third parties are excluded by IP rights on the other, fit the type/token distinction sufficiently to make that distinction a useful heuristic device. Also important in this context is the concept of 'normative characterisation', discussed below.[43] Drawing on this concept, one might describe the act of categorizing an object as a type in IP as a means of supporting the law's development in a normatively desirable way. For example, and consistent with EU jurisprudence particularly, since copyright is an author's right, we might believe it to be unfair and otherwise undesirable to treat authors differently according to the nature of the authorial works that they create. So the Court of Justice suggested in *Painer*, when it decided that the realism of photographic portraits does not require or permit that they be given less extensive protection than other works of authorship.[44] Similarly in *Copydan Båndkopi v Nokia Danmark A/S*,[45] the Court of Justice held that the fundamental right of equality before the law[46] requires that the EU private copying exception to copyright be interpreted to ensure equal treatment of different media and technologies, so as to prohibit national compensation rules that discriminate, without any justification, between

[40] See Wetzel (n 30) para 2.2. [41] ibid.

[42] See N Wolterstorff, 'Toward an Ontology of Art Works' (1975) 9 Noüs 115.

[43] See n 100 and associated text. [44] See *Painer* (n 5) [95]–[98].

[45] Case C–463/12 *Copydan Båndkopi v Nokia Danmark A/S* ECLI:EU:C:2015:144 (*Copydan*).

[46] Charter of Fundamental Rights of the European Union [2010] OJ C 83/389 art 20.

different categories of economic operators or users of protected subject matter.[47] This commitment to equal (non-discriminatory) treatment of authors and other prospective IP beneficiaries (including the users of IP subject matter) dates to the 19th century, and may be one reason for the law's concern to treat unique works of visual art, such as oil paintings, as types, in the same way as other works of artistic, literary, musical, and dramatic authorship for most copyright purposes, while also subjecting them to special treatment in recognition of their differences (consistent with the legal requirement of equality). Thus, IP law protects and conceives a painting as a work of authorship of which there can be any number of copies in the form, for example, of a recreation or photograph of the painting. However, it also recognizes the authors of certain unique works of art, including paintings, as having a resale right or *droit de suite* in recognition that copies of such works have a less proximate relationship to the originals than for copies and originals of other authorial works,[48] and that the IP rights in respect of these unique works of art will therefore be of considerably less commercial value than the personal property rights in respect of their first material embodiment, which rights will often be held by someone other than the works' creator.

The example of performances raises another issue regarding tokens that any attempt to order or theorize the subject matter protected by IP must address. That issue is whether, instead of exemplifying or instantiating types, tokens are more accurately conceived as representing them as abstract particulars, in the way that a map of a country represents rather than reproduces the country.[49] While this may be difficult to accept for the tokens of object works—ie and in Wolterstorff's conception above, works of which there can be an impression, casting, or example—it makes sense for written fixations of performance works, such as musical scores and dramatic scripts, which contain instructions for the realization of the musical or dramatic work that is their type, and which are thus more accurately conceived as representations of that type than as reproductions of it.[50] So too for the written fixations of other subject matter protected by IP, such as inventions, which similarly comprise instructions for the realization of a product or process, and are similarly best conceived as representations of the relevant type rather than reproductions of it. In the field of copyright, the UK courts can be seen to have recognized this in their acceptance that a musical score, as a token of a musical work,

[47] See *Copydan* (n 45) [30]–[33].

[48] Directive 2001/84/EC of the European Parliament and of the Council of 27 September 2001 on the resale right for the benefit of the author of an original work of art [2001] OJ L 272/32.

[49] See Wetzel (n 30) para 5.

[50] Cf Wolterstorff (n 42), who sees dramatic works as performance works only, on the basis that the script provides instructions for performing the play and is therefore not a copy of the work, but who suggests that musical works might be both performance *and* object works; the latter if the score is regarded as being to a musical work what a copy of a literary work is to a literary work. Wolterstorff further categorizes phonograms as objects of object works (akin to impressions of a print) of which there can be copies, and films as both performance works *and* object works, except that each performance involves (a showing of) a copy, in contrast to other performance works (which can be performed from memory).

includes not only the printed notes on the score, but all other markings aimed at facilitating those notes' realization in performance.[51] So too the UK and European legislatures, which accept the possibility of a token being different in form from other tokens of the same type by, for example, treating different language versions of a literary work as tokens of the translated work (in addition to being types in their own right).[52] Also, in the field of unregistered UK design right, the tokens of product configurations have been held to include the schematic depictions of the nature and arrangement of the components of a product in whole or part,[53] which depictions perform precisely the function of a map of a country.[54] Given this, the law can be said to have committed to a theory of tokens as representations rather than exemplifications in the case of certain subject matter.

Other aspects of the philosophical work concerning the type/token distinction that have potential importance for IP include the view of philosophers such as Wolterstorff that a type in the philosophical sense above might also be a kind, ie a thing of which there are examples, and even a norm kind, ie a kind for which it is possible to have properly and improperly formed examples.[55] For example, 'A rose is a rose is a rose is a rose' is an improperly formed example of the line from the poem by Stein referred to previously. From a legal perspective, characterizing IP subject matter as norm kinds is desirable, since extending any rights of Stein in respect of *Sacred Emily* to imperfect examples of her poem prevents third parties from avoiding liability for infringing any rights that she has in respect of that poem by changing a single word, as in the example given. For this reason, there are compelling policy arguments for committing to a view of authorial works, inventions, signs, designs, and other IP subject matter as norm kinds in this sense, regardless of our position when standing in the discipline of philosophy, to prevent the law from applying arbitrarily. In the UK and Europe, that commitment can be seen in the definition of intellectual property rights and infringement. For example, under sections 16(3) and 226(2) of the CDPA, the copyright subsisting in a work and the unregistered design right subsisting in a design are infringed by reproducing the whole or a substantial part of the work and design, just as under the Patents Act 1977 (UK) and registered design right legislation, a patent for a product and registered design right for the appearance of a product shape is generally infringed by making a product that embodies the same inventive concept as the product (for the patent) and that produces the same

[51] See *Sawkins* (n 25) [55] and [56] (Mummery LJ).

[52] The same applies for other adaptations of a work; adaptation being among the rights reserved exclusively to the owner of a copyright work under the domestic laws of all European states, consistent with art 8 of the Berne Convention for the Protection of Literary and Artistic Works (adopted 9 September 1886, last revised 24 July 1971) 828 UNTS 221, as amended (requiring Berne Union states to recognize authors of literary and artistic works as enjoying 'the exclusive right of making and of authorizing the translation of their works throughout the term of protection of their rights in the original works'). See eg Copyright, Designs and Patents Act 1988 (UK) (CDPA) s 16.

[53] *Mackie Designs Inc v Behringer Specialised Studio Equipment (UK) Ltd* [1999] RPC 717 (Ch).

[54] H Laddie and others, *The Modern Law of Copyright and Designs* (3rd edn, Butterworths 2000) paras 53.6–10.

[55] See Wetzel (n 30) para 4.1.2. For a more detailed discussion of Wolterstorff's argument see Wolterstorff (n 42).

overall visual impression as the appearance (for the design right).[56] Similarly under the Trade Marks Act 1994 (UK), the rights conferred by a registered trade mark are infringed by use of a mark that is identical or similar to the mark registered. The point underlines again the importance of viewing legal characterization as a partly normative process, and of undertaking that process with its normative consequences in mind. On the question of who decides what is and is not an example of a given subject matter: while one might expect it to be the subject matter's creator, as the person having primary responsibility and authority with respect to it,[57] any reliance on her judgement would need to be mediated to ensure fair and objective decision-making. And so it is that the law approximates or objectifies the creator's perspective by adopting an internal point of view with respect to each subject matter that prioritizes the normative conventions applicable with respect to objects of its type. The significance of and necessity for doing so is well illustrated by Neil MacCormick's discussion of the Lilliputians' discovery and description of Gulliver's 'wonderful kind of engine' in Jonathan Swift's *Gulliver's Travels*.[58] Knowing only what they can observe from its form and behaviour, the Lilliputians do not know that the engine is a watch, although they manage to describe it sufficiently to convey to readers familiar with watches that it is one. As MacCormick remarks, invoking a distinction of H L A Hart:[59]

> We look upon these wonderful engines 'from the internal point of view', from the point of view of those who understand and work with that complex set of normative conventions in terms of which we can use these artefacts to measure the passage of time and thus to synchronize and co-ordinate activities with each other to a remarkably high degree of accuracy. By contrast, the Lilliputians are outsiders. They are unaware of those conventional norms which for us make sense of our use of watches. Accordingly they can (for the moment at any rate) only appreciate Gulliver's watch and his use of it at the level of observable, or, rather, sensible phenomena ... Theirs is, by contrast with ours, an 'external point of view'. It is 'external' in respect of the set of conventional norms in question.[60]

That the law adopts the 'internal point of view' with respect to IP subject matter, including when deciding what are and are not correctly or incorrectly formed examples of them, can be seen from its reliance on the construct of a hypothetical

[56] See *Schütz (UK) Ltd v Werit UK Ltd* [2013] UKSC 16, [2013] RPC 6 (in relation to patents); Council Regulation (EC) No 6/2002 of 12 December 2001 on Community designs [2002] OJ L 3/1 (Designs Regulation) art 10, and Directive 98/71/EC of the European Parliament of the Council of 13 October 1998 on the legal protection of designs [1998] OJ L 289/28 (Designs Directive) art 9 (in relation to design right).

[57] On the idea of authorship entailing (moral) responsibility in general see R Nozick, 'Coercion' in M Morgenbesser, P Suppes, and M T White (eds), *Philosophy, Science, and Method: Essays in Honor of Ernest Nagel* (St Martin's Press 1969) 440. As seen in ch 2 s 2, in the pre-modern printing and trademark systems of England and Europe, authorial designation and the affixing of guild and merchant marks was required as a means of denoting responsibility for the contents of printed works and the quality of traded goods.

[58] N MacCormick, *Legal Reasoning and Legal Theory* (OUP 1994).

[59] See H L A Hart, *The Concept of Law* (Clarendon Press 1961) 86 ff.

[60] See MacCormick (n 58) 276.

person for whom the subject matter is presumed to have been intended when deciding issues of infringement. In patent law that person is referred to as the 'skilled addressee', and represents the community of people skilled in the art of technology to which the invention relates. In trade mark law she is referred to as the 'average consumer', and represents the community of people involved in making purchasing decisions about goods or services of the type for which the trade mark is registered. And in European design law she is referred to as the 'informed user' of the product(s) in or to which the design is intended to be incorporated or applied. Different is the approach adopted in copyright and unregistered UK design right, where what determines whether a subject matter is or is not a properly or improperly formed example of an authorial work or design is not the view of the art-regarding or design-regarding community for which the work or design was intended, but rather the extent to which the subject matter reflects the expressive properties that make the work or design the subject matter that it is. Despite these differences, in all cases the focus can be said to be on the final cause of the protected subject matter in the Aristotelian sense referred to previously, namely, the end in pursuit of which the act of creation was done, and from which society is perceived to benefit. In the case of authorial works and designs as conceived by unregistered UK design right law, the final cause will be the production of the specific work or design as an expressive object. In the case of (other) industrial property subject matter, by contrast, the final cause will be the production of an object supporting a certain use in the commercial or industrial realm.[61] The result might be said to be the law's prioritizing of different notions and requirements for evidence of a subject matter's existence and principles for its individuation. For authorial works and UK unregistered design right subject matter, the concept of metaphysical individuation can be seen to be prioritized, according to which an object is individuated by 'whatever it is that makes it the single object that it is',[62] reflecting the close conformity of such works' final with their formal causes.[63] By contrast, for the subject matter protected by industrial property, the concept of epistemic individuation can be seen to be prioritized, according to which an object is individuated by the ability of a certain intelligent individual to single it out 'as a distinct object of perception'.[64] In all cases an internal point of view is adopted with respect to the relevant subject matter, being the point of view of 'those who understand and work with that complex set of normative conventions'[65] in terms of which subject matter of the relevant type are used and experienced in society.

Another view of types of potential relevance for IP subject matter casts them as theoretical objects having the sole or primary function of unifying all of the tokens of a given description.[66] In law, as noted above, we would describe those tokens as

[61] This is consistent with the industrial nature of each, on which see ch 2 s 6.1.

[62] See E J Lowe, 'Individuation' in M L Loux and D W Zimmerman (eds), *The Oxford Handbook of Metaphysics* (OUP 2005) 75.

[63] For example, the final cause of an expressive work such as a poem will be production of the poem, while its formal cause will be the arrangement of the words of which the poem is comprised.

[64] Lowe (n 62) 75. [65] See n 60. [66] See Wetzel (n 30) para 5.

representing the concrete objects from which third parties are excluded by IP rights existing in respect of the relevant subject matter. For example, identifying Stein's *Sacred Emily* as a type could be said in law to unify all of the written copies, performances, and other concrete instances of it that third parties must not, by reason of the copyright subsisting in it, produce or exploit. This view could support a conception of types as universals in the Aristotelian (non-Platonic) sense above as existing in their concrete instances, and also has the benefit of avoiding the epistemological problem created by seeing types as abstract objects not located anywhere in space or time.[67] Having said that, it is difficult to accept from a legal perspective, since it implies that IP rights exist in respect of things that do not per se exist.

A proximate view to that of types as existing in and for the purpose of unifying the tokens of a given type that the law might be said more readily to support is the conceptualist one that IP subject matter do not exist as general *things*, such as an invention or sign, but only as general *ideas*, which ideas can then be applied to more than one thing (token or particular).[68] Applied to words, Wetzel explains, 'the thesis would be that words are not abstract objects "out there", but objects in the mind', whose existence is then contingent on having been thought of.[69] This thesis fits well with the law's view of patentable subject matter (inventions) as ideas for achieving a practical end that, to be protected, must be represented by a description in writing but not instantiated or exemplified in any concrete form. By defining the infringement of the resulting IP rights in terms that require the unauthorized use of a token or particular of the invention, the law in effect acknowledges that, while inventions are ideas existing in the mind, none of the IP rights existing in respect of them can be infringed by the mere act of thinking.[70]

In sum, and notwithstanding certain philosophical caveats, IP subject matter and their material instances can be conceived as types and tokens respectively. Put differently, there can be seen to exist a strong general fit between the type/token distinction and the subject matter protected by—and the rights conferred in respect of those subject matter on the owners of—intellectual property. Given this, we can posit a legal commitment to a view of IP subject matter as types, regardless of whether they are accepted by philosophers to be, and in this conception as norm kinds, namely, objects of which there are properly and improperly formed examples. Further, we can point to the law's acceptance of IP subject matter as existing independent of their concrete instances, either as Platonic entities or as ideas, and to its protection of them as such, even as it makes clear their close relationship to those instances. And finally, we can cast our expectations regarding any account of IP subject matter in the terms suggested for theories of types and tokens respectively, and accordingly expect from such an account an understanding of what each

[67] ibid. [68] See ibid para 7.1. [69] ibid.

[70] See eg L Hoffmann, 'Software Patents', paper delivered at the 23rd Annual IPSANZ Conference (11 September 2009) (on file with author) [10] ('All patents are based on ideas, ideas about how to do things. You can have a monopoly of the product or process which embodies your idea. You obviously cannot have a monopoly of the idea itself because that would mean that to enforce your patent you would have to be able to stop other people from thinking').

IP type and its individual tokens are, including their relationship, and by what methods we can know about and individuate them.[71] In this way the distinction between types and tokens can be used to help make sense of legal conceptions of the subject matter currently protected by IP and to facilitate critical engagement with them.

4. Categories of Intellectual Property Subject Matter

Conceiving IP subject matter as different artifact types draws attention to the role of categories as a further metaphysical device of importance within the field of intellectual property. For example, identifying subject matter suitable for protection by copyright requires that a distinction be drawn between authorial and non-authorial subject matter. Similarly, the type/token distinction discussed in section 3 is at base a mechanism for sorting different objects into different categories.

Categories are and have always been ubiquitous in IP. For example, the 1908 (Berlin Act) version of the Berne Convention 1886 required the recognition of copyright subsistence in the two categories of literary and artistic works as original or authorial works. According to Article 2 of the Convention, included within the categories of literary and artistic works were several specific types or sub-categories of works, namely:

> Writings; dramatic or dramatico-musical works, choreographic works and entertainments in dumb show . . .; musical compositions with or without words; works of drawing, painting, architecture, sculpture, engraving and lithography; illustrations, geographical charts; plans, sketches, and plastic works relative to geography, topography, architecture or science[; and] [t]ranslations, adaptations, arrangements of music and other reproductions in an altered form of literary or artistic work as well as collections of different works.

Added to these were works of art applied to industrial purposes, in so far as the domestic legislation of each country allowed for their protection, and photographic works and works produced by a process analogous to photography. It is on the further revised version of this international definition of copyright subject matter that the current EU law of copyright and related rights builds and depends. For example, under the early EU copyright directives, Member States were required to recognize copyright as subsisting in a number of categories of subject matter, such as original databases, computer programs, and photographs, as literary and artistic works within the meaning of the Berne Convention,[72] and

[71] Wetzel (n 30) para 4.2.

[72] See Directive 96/9/EC of the European Parliament and of the Council of 11 March 1996 on the legal protection of databases [1996] OJ L 77/20 art 3 (implementing Berne Convention art 2(5)); Directive 2009/24/EC of the European Parliament and of the Council of 23 April 2009 on the legal protection of computer programs [2009] OJ L 111/16 art 1(1); Directive 2006/116/EC of the European Parliament and of the Council of 12 December 2006 on the term of protection of copyright and certain related rights [2006] OJ L 372/12 (Term Directive) art 6(1) (implementing Berne Convention art 2(1)).

to protect the rights of authors of all such literary and artistic works for the life of the author plus seventy years.[73] While the requirement imposed by the later Information Society Directive on Member States to recognize authors as having certain rights in respect of their works has been interpreted as supporting a general EU legal principle of copyright subsistence in respect of the general category of authorial works,[74] the starting point for interpretation and application of that category is the same categories of subject matter recognized in Article 2 of the Berne Convention. In addition, the test formulated by the Court of Justice for determining whether a given subject matter is an authorial work within the meaning of the Directive depends on the preliminary categorization of the subject matter as a work of a certain type. According to its test, for a subject matter to be an authorial work the subject matter must: (a) be a type of subject matter that leaves scope for the exercise of formative freedom in its production; and (b) be the product of a person's exercise of that formative freedom that bears her personal mark.[75] In order to satisfy the first of these requirements, the subject matter at issue must be categorized according to type, which categorization then informs the courts' determination of the second requirement. The result is a conception of authorial works that is sensitive to the differences between different categories of subject matter. For example, and as the Court of Justice has held, the claim that a particular photograph is an authorial work must be assessed in the light of the scope for formative freedom that photography in general affords,[76] just as the claim that a particular arrangement of words is an authorial work must be assessed in the light of the nature of literary authorship.[77] A similar approach to deciding the inherent protectability of a given subject matter is taken in the field of registered and unregistered design right. Under EU legal principles, for example, a subject matter will only be a design protectable by either title of (registered or unregistered) Community design right if it is a type of subject matter that leaves scope for formative freedom in its creation, which scope has been exploited by the putative designer in the particular case—not to produce a work that bears

[73] Term Directive art 1(1).

[74] This follows the decision of the Court of Justice in Case C-5/08 *Infopaq International A/S v Danske Dagblades Forening* [2009] ECR I–06569 (*Infopaq*) [37] that 'copyright within the meaning of article 2(a) of Directive 2001/29 is liable to apply only in relating to a subject-matter which is original in the sense that it is its author's own intellectual creation'. While this statement does not support the subsistence of copyright in *any* subject matter that is original in the sense specified, the Court of Justice has subsequently built on it to support such subsistence. See eg Joined Cases C–403/08 and C–429/08 *Football Association Premier League Ltd v GC Leisure* and *Murphy v Media Protection Services Ltd* [2011] ECR I–09083 [98] and [99] (deciding that sporting events 'cannot be regarded as intellectual creations classifiable as works within the meaning of the Copyright Directive' and '[a]ccordingly ... cannot be protected under copyright').

[75] See *Painer* (n 5) [85]–[94]. [76] ibid.

[77] See eg *Infopaq* (n 74) [44] and [45] (describing the nature of a newspaper article as an author's own intellectual creation as evidenced by 'the form, the manner in which the subject is presented and the linguistic expression'; and rejecting the capacity of individual words to support (literary) copyright on the basis that '[i]t is only through the choice, sequence and combination of those words that the author may express his creativity in an original manner and achieve a result which is an intellectual creation').

her personal mark (as in copyright), but rather to produce an appearance of the whole or part of a product that creates an overall visual impression in the mind of the notional informed user of the product that differs from that created in her mind by previously available designs.[78]

Categories also play an explicit role in the UK law of copyright. The reason is section 1(1) of the CDPA, the original 1911 version of which was introduced to consolidate the then existing UK law of copyright in accordance with the requirements of the Berne Convention. In its current form, section 1(1) declares copyright in the UK to subsist in eight categories of subject matter: original literary, dramatic, musical, and artistic works; sound recordings, films, and broadcasts; and typographical arrangements of published editions. In section 4(1), the category of (original) artistic works is further defined to mean graphic works, photographs, sculptures, collages, works of architecture, and works of artistic craftsmanship.

Despite their similar provenance, the categories of UK copyright law might be said to operate in a different way than the way in which the categories of EU copyright law operate. Specifically, it might be said that, while the categories of UK law denote *differences between* subject matter, the categories of EU and international law denote *systems of* subject matter. Starting from this position, we would cast the premise of EU and international law to be the Aristotelian idea that every existing object in the world can be categorized, and treat Article 2 of the Berne Convention as the result of its drafters' attempt to identify all of the authorial works that exist by creating an inventory of such works as objects. By contrast, treating the CDPA as based on an understanding of category differences would involve reading section 1 of the CDPA (and the associated jurisprudence of the UK courts) not as an inventory of authorial works as such, but rather as an acknowledgement by the legislature that there exist certain types of authorial works—namely, literary, dramatic, musical, and artistic works—that are substantively, ontologically, different, and that must therefore be distinguished.[79]

So too, beyond copyright and related rights in other fields of IP, one can observe the ubiquity of categories and their performance of either or both of these differentiating and systematizing roles. For example, under Article 52 of the European Patent Convention,[80] consistent with the EU Biotech Directive, and reproduced in section 1(1) of the Patents Act 1977, protectable subject matter is denoted by the general category of inventions, corresponding to the EU copyright category of authorial works. Under the same legislation, that category is defined negatively,

[78] See ch 7 s 2.3.

[79] This view of section 1 of the CDPA as denoting differences between rather than systems of subject matter can be supported by the fact that, while confining authors' rights to works of literary, dramatic, musical, or artistic type, UK law recognizes the existence of other types of authorial works, which are consequently ineligible for protection by copyright. See eg *Creation Records v News Group Newspapers Ltd* [1997] EMLR 444 (Ch) (denying copyright to an original work of authorship in the form of a photographic scene on the basis of its failure to be a literary, dramatic, musical, or artistic work within the meaning of the CDPA).

[80] Convention on the Grant of European Patents (opened for signature 5 October 1973, entered into force 1 January 1977) 1065 UNTS 199, as amended (EPC).

with reference to a list of further subject matter that are not 'as such' inventions, namely: '(a) discoveries, scientific theories and mathematical methods; (b) aesthetic creations; (c) schemes, rules and methods for performing mental acts, playing games or doing business, and programs for computers; [and] (d) presentations of information'.[81] In addition, and focusing on the subject matter that *are* inventions, section 60 of the Patents Act 1977 organizes the general class of subject matter for which a patent may be granted into the two sub-categories of products and processes. By defining patent rights differently with respect to each, the legislation supports the view of these categories as denoting fundamentally different objects. Within each sub-category of product and process lie further sub-categories recognized by the courts, such as uses and purpose-limited processes (processes for a specific purpose) within the category of processes. And finally, patent jurisprudence requires that each invention for which a patent is sought and granted be organized and perceived with reference to the mechanical, chemical, or other field of technology to which it relates.[82]

Considering the nature of category differences, some philosophers, such as Michael Dummett, have argued that categorical concepts are not merely capable of being distinguished, but must (for cognitive reasons) be distinguished, since they are necessary for us even to identify 'things', and therefore cannot be derived from considering things pre-identified without regard to categories.[83] We cannot refer to, discover, or single out objects at all, Dummett has claimed, except by way of distinguishing the identity conditions criterially associated with the proper use of different sortal terms and names such as, in the case we are considering, 'literary', 'dramatic', 'artistic', and 'musical'.[84]

The view of philosophers that categorization is inherent in the process of discovery is shared by many legal theorists, including especially supporters of legal taxonomy. According to Peter Birks, for example, the organization of concepts into categories is the inevitable result of the search for legal understanding or knowledge.[85] To reason, he argues, is to order and classify. Whether or not one accepts this and Dummett's claim that categories are essential to thinking, it is important in suggesting as a benefit of categories for IP the deeper understanding of its subject matter that they facilitate. That benefit can readily be perceived by reflecting on the way in which works of literature, art, drama, and music are differentiated in human and social experience, both by reason of their different aspects of form and the different means by and context in which we engage with them. For example, and of relevance to the field of copyright, art theorists have

[81] Patents Act 1977 (UK) (Patents Act) s 1(2).

[82] This is ensured, inter alia, by the mechanism of the notional addressee skilled in the art to which a claimed invention relates that is used to assess the invention's patentability, discussed below.

[83] A Thomasson, 'Categories' in E N Zalta (ed), *The Stanford Encyclopedia of Philosophy* (Fall 2013 edn) para 2.3.

[84] ibid.

[85] See P Birks, 'Introduction' in P Birks (ed), *English Private Law, Volume 1* (OUP 2000) xxxi–xxxxii.

considered the psychology of art appreciation, and convincingly argued that the perception of an authorial work *qua* work requires that it be perceived in relation to a category.[86] The premise of this view, as I have elsewhere discussed, is that formalist conceptions of art— 'the seemingly common-sense notion that aesthetic judgements about works of art are to be based solely on what can be perceived in them, how they look or sound'—are 'seriously misleading';[87] that while works *are* to be judged solely with reference to their form, it is first necessary that they be perceived correctly.[88] The reason is the dependence of our aesthetic judgements about individual works on the categories with reference to which the works are perceived, and the variability of their properties relative to those categories. Hence the two issues of importance for art theory, which are also the issues that occupy the courts in copyright: how correctly to identify the category of a work, and how to perceive the work relative to that category.[89] Further, and as seen previously, the categories in question are not merely 'local' categories such as expressionist and surrealist, but also broader categories of art, music, drama, and literature.

A similar analysis can be offered for the subject matter protectable by industrial property rights, supporting a similar claim for the appropriateness of dividing industrial property subject matter such as inventions and trade marks into categories. What matters in the patent field is less psychology than science, and the cumulative nature of invention. As we saw in Chapter 2, a distinguishing feature of scientific and technological work is the way in which it builds on existing states of knowledge in a particular scientific or technological field, and the consequential need for such work and its results to be perceived relative to the existing knowledge of the field to which it relates. In patent law, the background knowledge of relevance is referred to as the 'state of the art' or 'prior art' of the relevant invention,[90] and the need for inventions to be perceived relative to it is ensured, among other things, by the legal requirement that they be individuated epistemically and, in particular, that they be perceived adopting the mantle of the notional skilled addressee: the person skilled in the art to which they relate.[91] Hence the two issues of importance for scientific theory, which are also the issues that occupy the courts in patent law: how correctly to identify the field or art of an invention, and how to perceive the invention relative to that field.

[86] See K Walton, 'Categories of Art' (1970) 79 Philosophical Review 344. On the value of this theory for copyright see J Pila, 'Copyright and Its Categories of Original Works' (2010) 30 Oxford Journal of Legal Studies 229.

[87] See Walton (n 86) 367.

[88] ibid. Walton adds that 'examining a work with the senses can by itself reveal neither how it is correct to perceive it, nor how to perceive it that way'.

[89] See Pila (n 86) 244.

[90] See eg EPC art 54(2) (defining the 'state of the art' for a particular invention 'to comprise everything made available to the public' before the date on which a European patent for the invention was sought).

[91] See eg EPC art 56 (defining an inventive invention as one that 'having regard to the state of the art . . . is not obvious to a person skilled in the art'). On the role and identity of the skilled addressee see Pila and Torremans (n 13) 138.

In the trade mark realm, by contrast, psychology is important, along with trade practices and the requirements of the trade mark register. For example, trade marks can only be registered in respect of one or more (clearly and precisely identified[92]) categories of goods and services, which categories must be designated in the trade mark application[93] and conform to the international taxonomic system referred to as the Nice Classification.[94] This requirement for the registration of signs in respect of specified categories of goods and services reflects the nature of the trade mark itself, as a sign intended and suitable for use to signify the commercial origin of the trade mark owner's goods or services in trade, and the function of the trade mark register to enable third parties to identify each subject matter registered as a trade mark and the scope of the protection that its registration confers. The international nature of the Nice Classification also reduces the legal uncertainty and inefficiencies that would result from permitting individual applicants and/or states to devise their own system of categories.

Categories inform the conception and assessment for protection of individual trade marks in another way too. When deciding whether a given subject matter is a trade mark, decision-makers begin by deciding whether or not the subject matter is a sign, and if it is, which of a number of judicially formulated categories of sign it falls within. This process of sorting subject matter *qua* signs into different categories according to their different expressive forms and properties directly informs the further assessment of their protectability, including specifically of their distinctive character. Principles of category neutrality and equal treatment of signs notwithstanding, different types of signs such as colours, tastes, shapes, smells, figures, sounds, words, and slogans have been recognized by the courts to be more or less capable of distinguishing the origin of goods or services in trade, and more or less appropriate for monopolization from a policy perspective. As in the copyright and design right fields, the result is an approach to identifying protectable subject matter that relies substantially on categories, and that is sensitive to the need to engage with subject matter differently according to their essential and differentiating properties.

That this should be the case is hardly surprising. Specifically, if one accepts the thesis that authorial works, inventions, trade marks, and other IP subject matter are differentiated in human and social experience, one is likely to accept that any law aimed at recognizing and protecting individual rights in respect of them will

[92] Case C–307/10 *Chartered Institute of Patent Attorneys v Registrar of Trade Marks* ECLI:EU:C:2012:361 [43] and [59].

[93] See eg Council Regulation (EC) No 207/2009 of 26 February 2009 on the Community trade mark [2009] OJ L 78/1, as amended (Trade Mark Regulation) art 26(1)(c); Commission Regulation (EC) No 2868/95 of 13 December 1995 implementing Council Regulation (EC) No 40/94 on the Community trade mark [1995] OJ L 303/1, as amended (EUTM Implementing Regulations) art 1, rule 1(c).

[94] See eg EUTM Implementing Regulations art 1, rule 12(d). The Nice Classification consists of the 45 classes of goods and services contained in the Nice Agreement Concerning the International Classification of Goods and Services for the Purposes of the Registration of Marks (current edition 11–2017).

seek to express and reflect these differences. This is consistent with the idea above of assessing IP subject matter from the internal point of view, and is true, as suggested previously, regardless of whether one is prepared to commit to the thesis that there exists a unique, true, and complete system of categories for the subject matter protected by each IP regime: all that is required is a belief that categorization can be helpful in IP by providing 'a framework within which existence questions can be answered in a systematic and wholesale way'.[95]

A closely related benefit of categories emphasized by legal realists particularly derives from their role beyond the reflection of legal knowledge in its construction.[96] By understanding this role, realists argue, legal categorization can help to ensure that the law develops in a normatively desirable way.[97] In addition, by identifying the human values that underlie particular legal categories, and rethinking the legal rules that best promote those values, legal categories can be explained and developed in a way that accentuates their normative desirability while remaining attuned to their particular social context.[98] And finally, by keeping legal categories sufficiently narrow to ensure their reflection of human experience and situation in human contexts, they can be appropriately tailored to and focused on serving human needs.[99]

Once again, the role of categories in supporting the development of the law in a normatively desirable way—well captured by the concept of 'normative characterisation' that is used by Mark Freedland and Nicola Kountouris in their employment law scholarship to express the idea of the essential and integral link that exists between the legal classification of personal work relations and its consequences[100]—can be readily related and explained with reference to IP. For example, legal conceptions of IP subject matter offer obvious mechanisms for ensuring that the scope of IP protection is defined in a manner that reflects particular policy considerations. Thus, in copyright and design law, one way of restricting protection to forms of expression rather than to ideas would be to define the subject matter that copyright and design right protect in a formalistic way with a view to ensuring that non-literal copying is incapable of infringing copyright,[101] and that only shapes (rather than

[95] Thomasson (n 83) para 1.5.

[96] H Dagan, 'Legal Realism and the Taxonomy of Private Law' in C E F Rickett and R Grantham (eds), *Structure and Justification in Private Law: Essays for Peter Birks* (Hart Publishing 2008) 147.

[97] ibid 156. [98] ibid 161–162. [99] ibid 162–163.

[100] M R Freedland and N Kountouris, *The Legal Construction of Personal Work Relations* (OUP 2011) 6 ('We suggest the terminology of "normative characterization" to ... capture the essential connectedness between identifying the legal character of a given personal work relation and making normative propositions about that relation').

[101] Traces of such formalism can be seen in both EU and UK copyright jurisprudence. In relation to EU jurisprudence see eg *Infopaq* (n 74) [45] (supporting a conception of literary works as selections and arrangements of words). In relation to UK jurisprudence see the discussion in Pila (n 86). Academics concerned to limit the scope of copyright protection to a right of literal copying have also done so by less direct analytical routes. See eg R Tushnet, 'Worth a Thousand Words: The Images of Copyright Law' (2012) 125 Harvard Law Review 683 (arguing that the nature of images in particular requires '[g]reater epistemic humility' on the part of IP law, which in turn supports limiting artistic copyright in respect of them to a right of literal or near-literal reproduction).

shapes and configurations) of products can be protected by design right.[102] So too in patent law, one way of restricting protection to subject matter that advances technology would be to define the subject matter capable of supporting a patent as subject matter that represents a technological advance, in the sense of a technological contribution to the prior art.[103] And finally, in trade mark law, one way of restricting protection to signs of use in trade to indicate the commercial origin of goods and services would be to define the subject matter capable of supporting registration as a mark to those capable of distinguishing goods and services in trade and/or in genuine use to that end.[104]

In conclusion, categories are an important aspect of all IP regimes. Consistent with our discussion in Chapter 2, we might also describe them as a desirable aspect for at least two related reasons. One is the substantive, ontological differences that exist between the subject matter protected by and within different IP regimes, and the need for categories of IP rights (such as patents and copyright) and subject matter (such as inventions and authorial works) to express and reflect these differences in a way that satisfies basic rule of law requirements, such as clarity. The other is the need for categories to answer the question of what exists, and more specific to IP, the question of what products of human (intellectual) creation the law ought to protect and not protect. A central issue for the courts and legislatures then becomes how to draw and conceive the resulting legal categories of IP rights and subject matter, and what if any weight to give when drawing them to normative considerations of IP and wider social and legal policy.

5. Properties of Intellectual Property Subject Matter

The discussion above, including the reference to the identity conditions associated with the use of different sortal terms and names, underlines a further point regarding the UK and European legal categories of IP subject matter, namely, that the objects denoted by those categories can be understood with reference to the properties that characterize and differentiate them inter se. Put differently, categories can be compared to properties: the members of a category corresponding to the

[102] Such formalism exists in EU design right jurisprudence, but not in the jurisprudence of unregistered UK design right, which recognizes the subsistence of design right in the 'configuration' of articles as well as in their shape, where by 'configuration' is meant the nature and arrangement of an article's components rather than its physical geometry: CDPA s 213(2); *Mackie Designs Inc v Behringer Specialised Studio Equipment (UK) Ltd* [1999] RPC 717 (Ch).

[103] As it is defined under UK law. See eg *Symbian v Comptroller-General of Patents* [2008] EWCA Civ 1066, [2009] RPC 1 [11] (*Symbian*). While European law accepts as inherently patentable any subject matter that is technical in nature, regardless of the contribution it makes, it also limits patentability to subject matter that are inventive by reason of their technical aspects specifically: see eg T154/04 (*Estimating Sales Activity/DUNS LICENSING ASSOCIATES*) [2007] EPOR 38 (*Duns Licensing*); G3/08 (*Programs for Computers*) [2010] EPOR 36 (*Programs for Computers*).

[104] As is in law done: see eg Trade Mark Regulation arts 4 and 15; Directive (EU) 2015/2436 of the European Parliament and of the Council of 16 December 2015 to approximate the laws of the Member States relating to trade marks [2015] OJ L 336/1 (Trade Marks Directive) arts 3 and 16.

instances of one or more properties such that the category is an extension of the same.[105] Thus, we might say that each of the members of (or subject matter falling within) a specific category exemplify certain essential properties that differ from those exemplified by the members of (or subject matter falling within) another category, and that the point of the categories is to recognize and express these differences[106] and, in doing so, to stipulate certain definitions of the subject matter to which IP rights attach. In this sense, discussion of properties helps to explain and account for the existence of categories of subject matter and of the subject matter contained within them. In so doing it also supports the formulation of definitions of different types of IP subject matter. Even if such definitions need to be 'open' in order to be able to adapt to reflect changing social contexts and experiences, including by accommodating borderline cases, they are nonetheless important in enabling different types of IP subject matter to be located within a family of objects,[107] and in supporting the principled development of the various IP regimes with a view, among other things, to limiting the scope for their conferral of overlapping protection.

This can again be illustrated with reference to the subject matter protected by the main IP regimes. For example, and consistent with the discussion above, we might identify the intellectual creation as the *genus* of subject matter protectable by IP, and the property of being the appearance of the whole or part of a product as that which differentiates the subject matter protectable by registered design right from the subject matter protectable by other IP regimes. That property should then inform the principles by which subject matter are individuated as designs, such that any disagreement over the questions 'is x a design?' or 'what makes it true that x is a design?' will be determined with reference to it.[108] As the *differentia* of subject matter protectable by registered design right, however, no object exemplifying this property should be eligible for overlapping protection by a different species of IP. This creates an immediate issue for the law of artistic copyright due to its conception of artistic works as objects of visual significance.[109] If visual significance were the only differentiating property of the artistic work, and the appearance of the whole or part of a product were the only differentiating property of the design, there would be a problem by reason of the overlap thereby produced between the categories of copyright and design right subject matter, which overlap would, in

[105] F Orilia and C Swoyer, 'Properties' in E N Zalta (ed), *The Stanford Encyclopedia of Philosophy* (Spring 2016 edn) para 1.1.4 .

[106] ibid.

[107] See Hart (n 59) 14–15 (discussing the use of simple forms of definition in law, including 'open' definitions).

[108] See M Murphy, 'Defect and Deviance in Natural Law Jurisprudence' in M Klatt (ed), *Institutionalized Reason* (OUP 2012) 45, 59 (discussing the non-defectiveness conditions of artifactual kinds such as a paper clip as the means by which disputes over the question 'what makes it true that x is a paper clip?' are resolved).

[109] See eg *Interlego AG v Tyco Industries Inc* [1989] AC 217 (Privy Council) 258 ('What is important about a drawing is what is visually significant and the re-drawing of an existing drawing with a few minimal visual alterations does not make it an original *artistic* work' (emphasis in original)).

the absence of legal correction, create an entitlement to simultaneous protection of the same properties of a single subject matter by different species of property.

Moving from the question of which if any properties differentiate the subject matter of different IP regimes to focus instead on what differentiates the subject matter within each regime: UK copyright law offers the clearest demonstration of the law's reliance on the differentiating properties of subject matter due to its statutory distinction between the four categories of protectable work above, and the definition of each type of work as having certain formal (expressive) characteristics. For example, literary works are defined as having the property of being 'written, spoken or sung',[110] dramatic works are defined as having the property of being works of action capable of performance before an audience,[111] musical works are defined as having the property of combining sounds for listening to,[112] and artistic works, as just seen, are defined as having the property of being visually significant.[113] To the extent that the properties of literary works overlap with those of musical and dramatic works, so as to enable a subject matter to be protected by both literary and musical or dramatic copyright, the legislation removes the overlap by providing for the work's protection by musical or dramatic copyright only, thus preserving the mutual exclusivity of the categories. The need for a fuller understanding of LDMA works than these statutory definitions provide is suggested immediately by the reality of the subject matter that exist. These include subject matter that possess the expressive properties of LDMA works specified by the legislation but are difficult to accept as authorial works (such as a painted house or fence), and subject matter that fail to possess the specified properties of a given statutory category of work but are nonetheless accepted (by art-regarding society at least) as works of the relevant type (such as John Cage's *4'33"*[114]). Nonetheless, the statutory definitions of original LDMA works above demonstrate the prominent reliance on properties to differentiate the four categories of authorial works protectable by UK copyright.

While most prominent in copyright, categories and therefore properties also play a central role within each of the other IP regimes, consistent with the legal taxonomic thesis described previously. For example, UK and European patent law define protectable subject matter as those objects falling within the general category of inventions,[115] and further distinguish between those inventions having the property of being a product and those inventions having the property of being a process,[116] defining the rights conferred with respect to each differently.[117] In so doing they highlight two further categories of foundational importance for patent systems, as well as the role of properties in legislative conceptions of patentable subject matter. That role is also apparent in the courts' discussion of the general category of

[110] CDPA s 3(1). [111] *Norowzian v Arks Ltd (No 2)* [2000] FSR 363 (CA) 367.

[112] See *Sawkins* (n 25) [53] ('as indicated in the dictionaries, the essence of music is combining sounds for listening to').

[113] See n 109.

[114] This is Cage's famous 'silent piece' or 'silent prayer' for piano, in which no sounds are intentionally made by the pianist for the duration of the composition's three movements.

[115] EPC art 52(1)–(3); Patents Act s 1(1) and (2). [116] Patents Act s 60. [117] ibid.

inventions, which has been defined in the UK and Europe as including any subject matter having the property of being technical and any subject matter having the property of making a technical contribution to the prior art respectively.[118]

Focusing on the properties of the objects falling within different categories of IP subject matter raises a host of further difficulties, some of which have been considered already in the discussion of categories, such as the nature of properties, whether the properties of objects denoted by different categories are universals or rather particulars,[119] and the implications of the answers for IP subject matter and the objects by which they are exemplified. A further important distinction is between the primary and secondary properties of an object. Primary properties are those objective features of the object that are also fundamental to its existence in the sense of explaining why the object has the other properties that it has.[120] This distinction can be seen to be important in patent law, where product inventions are generally defined with reference to their physical properties, which we might consequently regard as their primary and fundamental properties, among other reasons since they determine the object's function, consistent with the discussion of formal and final causes previously. Another distinction of importance for conceptions of the subject matter protectable by IP is the distinction between purely qualitative and not purely qualitative properties.[121] For example, the property of being original in the sense of European and UK copyright law involves the person alleged to be the author of the work and is therefore contingent on the existence of that person, enabling it to be described as a property that is not purely qualitative.[122] So too the property of having individual character in the sense defined by European design law is not purely qualitative, since it depends on the production of an overall impression in the mind of a notional informed user that differs from the impression produced on that person by previously accessible subject matter.[123]

Another way of expressing the distinction between purely qualitative and not purely qualitative properties might be by distinguishing between intrinsic and external (or relational) properties. For example, the property of being inventive is an external property, since it depends on the relation of the inventive object to other objects: being inventive is instantiated by an invention because of its distance from (and thus its relation to) other inventions. Even the property of being technical instantiated by an invention might be said to depend on the invention's relation to other things, being the material world from which it was derived by human action. Indeed, the conception of IP subject matter as intellectual creations in either of the two senses above[124] suggests that every such subject matter will be constituted in part at least by the history of its individual production, and thus by

[118] See n 103. [119] On this distinction see Orilia and Swoyer (n 105) para 1.1.
[120] ibid para 7.15. [121] ibid para 7.12.
[122] See *University of London Press v University Tutorial Press* [1916] 2 Ch 601 (ChD) 608–609 ('the Act does not require that the expression must be in an original or novel form, but that the work must not be copied from another work—that it should originate from the author').
[123] Designs Regulation art 6; Designs Directive art 5. [124] See s 2.2.

certain external properties, regardless of the reliance placed on their internal (eg formal) properties when deciding certain issues such as infringement.[125] In addition, and consistent with what was said earlier about perceiving IP subject matter with reference to their final causes in the Aristotelian sense, the constitutive properties of industrial property subject matter particularly might be said to include the commercial or industrial use for which they are intended, be it the manufacture of a product or commercial application of a process, the indication of the commercial origin of goods or services, or the production of goods having a certain shape and appearance.

An important further distinction drawn by philosophers is that between sortal and non-sortal properties.[126] Sortal properties have been defined as properties of a type that enable us to count objects, such as the property of being a literary work. By contrast are non-sortal or characterizing properties, such as published, which does not divide the world into a definite number of objects, but rather enables us only to divide the world into published and unpublished things.[127] Closely related to this is the distinction between the constitutive and non-constitutive properties of an object: those properties that an object must possess in order to exist as an object of relevant type, such as literary form for a literary work, and those properties that, however salient to the object from a legal perspective at least, do not determine its existence, such as the property (for a literary work) of having been materially fixed. The difficulty of drawing this distinction between constitutive and non-constitutive but salient properties—treated here as corresponding, albeit imperfectly,[128] to the distinction between essential and accidental properties—can be considered further with reference to historical conceptions of IP subject matter. For example, and as seen in Chapter 2, under the Venetian Patent Act protection was offered to 'any person in this city who makes any new and ingenious contrivances not made heretofore in our Dominion' and 'perfected so that it can be used and exercised'.[129] Contrivances are clearly specified as the subject matter of patent protection, and so the essential properties of the protected subject matter must include those physical or formal properties constituting it as a contrivance. In addition, and given the reason for our enquiry into the existence of a contrivance (to determine which persons ought and ought not to receive the protections of a limited-term monopoly in respect of it), and the ordinary language understanding of contrivances as artifacts, consistent also with the nature of IP subject matter as intellectual creations, it would be important to treat as a further essential property of the contrivance its having been created by *a* person—even if not *the* person claiming the monopoly

[125] *Contra Kirin-Amgen Inc v Hoechst Marion Roussel Ltd* [2004] UKHL 46, [2005] RPC 169 [88] ('the history of how a product was made is not an attribute which it carries around').

[126] On this distinction see Orilia and Swoyer (n 105) para 7.8. [127] ibid.

[128] But see D Miller, 'Constitutive Rules and Essential Rules' (1981) 39 Philosophical Studies: An International Journal for Philosophy in the Analytic Tradition 183 (discussing the differences between constitutive and essential rules).

[129] Venetian Statute on Industrial Brevets 1474 in L Bently and M Kretschmer (eds), *Primary Sources on Copyright (1450–1900)* (Arts and Humanities Research Council 2008) www.copyrighthistory.org (last accessed 5 June 2017). For the Statute in its entirety see ch 2, text accompanying n 1.

in respect of it—and thereby to exclude natural objects from the category of protectable subject matter. That leaves the requirements that the contrivance be 'new and ingenious', 'not made heretofore in our Dominion', and 'perfected so that it can be used and exercised'. One can clearly imagine a contrivance that is not new or ingenious, or that had previously been made within the Venetian Commonwealth. Given this, we might treat the properties of being new and ingenious, and not previously made within Venice, as salient but non-essential properties of the category of contrivances protectable by patent grant: while objects will need to possess these properties to qualify for protection, they will not need to possess them to be said to exist. Alternatively, since our enquiry is not merely into the existence of a contrivance, but rather the existence of a contrivance *qua* invention, and inventions are individuated (including by being distinguished from other inventions) with reference precisely to their novelty and ingeniousness, it would also be natural to treat these two characteristics as among their constitutive properties. That leaves the requirement that a contrivance have been perfected so as to be capable of use and exercise. Could a contrivance within the meaning of the Venetian patent laws that was not capable of use and exercise exist, or would such an object not have been a 'contrivance' properly conceived? Once again, this might depend on the principles of individuation that we adopt when deciding whether a given subject matter is a properly or improperly formed example of it. If those principles reference the contrivance's formal causes or explanations, then a subject matter incapable of realizing the end for which it was created might for that reason be said to be a defective contrivance at least, by reason of its failure to live up to a standard (effectiveness to achieve the end for which it was created) internal to all objects that fit the description 'invention'.[130]

Returning to contemporary patent law, it is the UK and European courts' disagreement regarding the distinction between an invention's essential and accidental properties that is the basis for their disagreement regarding the requirements for an invention's existence. According to the UK courts, as noted previously, an invention is any subject matter that makes a technical contribution.[131] The European Patent Office rejects this, however, on the basis that to require as an essential property of an invention that it contribute to a prior art of technology is to confuse the requirement for the existence of an invention with the secondary patentability requirements for novelty and inventive step, both of which (it maintains) denote accidental rather than essential properties of inventions properly conceived.[132] In the result, the European courts define an invention to be any subject matter that

130 This definition of non-defectiveness conditions is from Murphy (n 108) 57.

131 See n 103.

132 See eg *Duns Licensing* (n 103) [5] ('The four requirements—invention, novelty, inventive step, and susceptibility of industrial application—are essentially separate and independent criteria of patentability, which may give rise to concurrent objections. Novelty, in particular, is not a requisite of an invention within the meaning of article 52(1) EPC, but a separate requirement of patentability'); *Programs for Computers* (n 103) [10.5] (quoting from a decision of the Technical Board of Appeal explaining that the UK-endorsed 'contribution approach' raised prior art issues more appropriately considered in the context of novelty and inventive step).

has a technical character, and leave consideration of the technical contribution it makes for a later stage of the patentability enquiry, when assessing the invention's novelty and inventiveness.[133]

A similar distinction between the essential and accidental properties of an object can be drawn with respect to the subject matter protected by copyright. As seen in Chapter 2, under the first copyright legislation, the Statute of Anne, copyright was available for any book composed by an author from the date of first publication.[134] From this it might be said to follow that the essential properties of the subject matter protectable by copyright included those constituting the subject matter as the composition of an author capable of being reduced to print, and hence satisfying the description of a 'book'. Neither a printable object produced by someone other than an author, nor an authorial work incapable of being reduced to print, would satisfy this definition, with the result that both types of object would lack the essential properties of a copyright protectable subject matter. By contrast, actual reduction to print might be regarded as having been a salient but non-essential property of a book, such that any literary composition of an author not so reduced would have been regarded as a book, but a defective one not entitled to copyright protection.

As this discussion suggests, the distinction between what has been termed the essential and accidental properties of IP subject matter is not always easy to draw. The same can be seen from the requirements for copyright subsistence under current law. For example, the Berne Convention limits copyright to authorial, in the sense of original, works. In the United Kingdom, the requirement for originality is expressed as separate from the requirement for the existence of a literary, dramatic, or other protectable type of work, suggesting it to be an accidental rather than an essential property of copyright subject matter. On the other hand, if originality really *is* a synonym for authorship, as the decision in *University of London Press v University Tutorial Press*[135] suggests, it would seem to be an essential property of the copyright work, since any literary, dramatic, or other work of protectable type will by definition be a work of authorship.

It might reasonably be asked how important, if at all, the distinction between the essential and accidental properties of a subject matter really is. If the grant or subsistence of IP rights requires the presence of both, what is to be gained in practice from distinguishing them? The answer will depend in part on the object of IP protection with reference to which the rights of the IP owner are defined, and whether it is the protectable subject matter itself or the subject matter possessing also the required accidental properties. It will also depend on the ability of protectable subject matter to support rights or duties beyond those conferred by the laws of intellectual property. That they are so able is suggested by the widespread practice of regulating the use of authorial works, inventions, and other IP subject matter by private ordering (contractual) mechanisms without reference to and independent of their protection (or protectability) by IP rights. Further, and as noted already,

[133] See n 103.
[134] Statute of Anne 1710 (Eng). See ch 2, text accompanying n 3.
[135] N 122.

legal understandings of the essential properties of each type of IP subject matter can be expected to influence (and be influenced by) the method deployed at law to individuate them as such, which method is central to the determination of issues of IP ownership, scope, and infringement. And finally, given the aim of intellectual property regimes to protect and regulate access to authorial works, inventions, and other real-world objects of use and value to society, it is important to know how the law conceives those objects, among other things to be able to assess the fit between the objects being protected and regulated and the real-world objects in question.

In sum, thinking about the nature of properties can facilitate our understanding of IP subject matter in two main and closely related ways. The first is by elucidating the distinctions drawn by law-makers and decision-makers between different categories of subject matter within and across IP regimes. And the second is by elucidating the nature of the legal requirements for the existence of different IP rights, including the distinction between the requirement for the existence of a particular subject matter and the requirement that a subject matter, once found to exist, possess certain additional characteristics or qualities.

6. Conclusion

The suggestion of this chapter has been that, paradigmatically or focally at least, IP subject matter are types of artifacts having certain properties and arranged in categories that express and reflect those properties. Conceiving IP subject matter in this way is helpful in understanding and ordering the UK and EU law that exists in the context of the nature, aims, and values of IP rights and systems. It also suggests certain questions on which to focus a study of the subject matter protectable by IP. Those questions include, for each IP regime: (a) what are the (categories of) subject matter protected by the regime—ie what are the essential properties of the subject matter (as distinct, for example, from its accidental properties)? (b) how is each subject matter individuated? (c) what is the relationship between each subject matter and its tokens? And (d) how is the existence of each subject matter and its tokens known?[136] In the following chapters the subject matter protected by contemporary European and UK IP systems will be studied in the light of the analytic framework above and with a view to answering each of these four questions that that framework suggests.

[136] These are adapted from the eight questions identified by Wetzel: see Wetzel (n 30) para 4.2.2 (discussing what a theory of words and their tokens would ideally tell us).

4

The Invention and Plant Variety

1. Patents for Inventions, and Plant Variety Rights for Plant Varieties

Under UK and European legislation today, the category of patentable subject matter is denoted by the term 'invention', as it has been in English legislation since the early 19th century[1] and in case law since before the Statute of Monopolies of 1623.[2] Throughout history, English and later British law has conceived the patentable invention as an idea for a method or product that advances a particular industrial art. Variously described as a method or product of use to the public, an 'idea' or 'principle' turned to account, and a manner of manufacture, the main difficulty that has faced the courts in relation to inventions specifically has been to define their essential properties, and explain the relationship of those properties to such other properties that inventions must possess in order to be patentable. The original legislative description of inventions as manners of new manufacture implied that all inventions were methods of industrial production, ie methods of making industrially a certain product. Provided the method was sufficiently different from those that had existed previously, and that it might be of some use to society—including by not being generally inconvenient to employment or trade—it was capable of supporting a patent. Whether these properties of difference and use or utility were part of what made a subject matter an invention, however, was always unclear.

[1] See eg Letters Patent for Inventions Act 1835 (UK).

[2] Statute of Monopolies 1623 (Eng) (Statute of Monopolies). See eg *The Clothworkers of Ipswich Case* Goldbolt 252, 78 ER 147 (QB 1615) ('But if a man hath brought in a new invention and a new trade within the kingdom, in peril of his life, and consumption of his estate or stock, &c or if a man hath mad a discovery of any thing, in such cases the King of his grace and favour, in recompence of his costs and travail, may grant by charter unto him, that he only shall use such a trade or trafique for a certain time, because at first the people of the kingdom are ignorant, and have not the knowledge or skill to use it, but when that patent is expired, the King cannot make a new grant thereof, for when the trade is become common, and others have been bound apprentices in the same trade, there is no reason that such should be forbidden to use it').

The starting point for considering the invention under European and UK law today is Article 52(1) of the European Patent Convention,[3] which defines the subject matter for which European patents may be granted as 'inventions, in all fields of technology, provided that they are new, involve an inventive step and are susceptible of industrial application'. 'Inventions' within the meaning of this provision are then defined in Article 52(2) and (3) with reference to the following list of subject matter 'not [to] be regarded as inventions ... as such':

(a) discoveries, scientific theories, and mathematical methods;
(b) aesthetic creations;
(c) schemes, rules and methods for performing mental acts, playing games or doing business, and programs for computers;
(d) presentations of information.

Article 52 is the foundation of substantive European patent law, and as such is supported and supplemented by the other provisions of the EPC. It is also the starting point for the EU Biotech Directive,[4] governing the patenting of biotechnological inventions and incorporated into the EPC,[5] and for the UPC Agreement 2013,[6] supplementing the EPC with provisions governing patent rights and infringement for unitary (EU) patents specifically. Of most direct relevance to the requirement for an invention are Articles 3 and 5 of the Biotech Directive. Article 3(1) confirms the patentability of inventions (that are new, inventive, and susceptible of industrial application) 'even if' they involve biological material or processes, and Article 3(2) asserts the inherent patentability of 'biological material which is isolated from its natural environment or produced by means of a technical process ... even if it previously occurred in nature'. Consistent with this, Article 5 of the Directive distinguishes between the human body and 'the simple discovery of one of its elements, including the sequence or partial sequence of a gene', which it declares to be outside the scope of patentability, and 'an element isolated from the human body or otherwise produced by means of a technical process, including the sequence or partial sequence of a gene', which it declares to be capable of supporting a patent, 'even if the structure of that element is identical to that of a natural element'. In combination, these provisions support the Article 52(1) requirements of patentability, while also clarifying the Article 52(2) and (3) distinction between non-patentable 'discoveries ... as such' and patentable inventions in the biotechnological sphere.

[3] Convention on the Grant of European Patents (opened for signature 5 October 1973, entered into force 1 January 1977) 1065 UNTS 199, as amended (EPC).

[4] Council Directive 98/44/EC on the legal protection of biotechnological inventions [1998] OJ L 213/13 (Biotech Directive).

[5] EPC Implementing Regulations ch V.

[6] Agreement on a Unified Patent Court [2013] OJ C 175/1 (UPC Agreement).

Of especial importance among the other provisions of the EPC and UPC Agreement are the following, each of which contributes directly or indirectly to legal conceptions of the invention required by Article 52(1):

- Article 60 (corresponding to section 7 of the Patents Act), restricting the availability of patents for inventions to inventors, with an exception for inventions devised in the course of employment;
- Article 53 EPC (corresponding to sections 1(3) and 4A, and Schedule A2 section 3, of the Patents Act), excluding 'inventions the commercial exploitation of which would be contrary to "ordre public" or morality', 'plant or animal varieties or essentially biological processes for the production of plants or animals', and therapeutic, surgical and diagnostic 'methods for treatment of the human or animal body', from patent protection;
- Article 84 EPC (corresponding to section 14(5)(c) of the Patents Act), requiring that the definition of an invention in the patent claims be sufficiently supported by its description in the specification;
- Article 69 EPC (corresponding to section 125 of the Patents Act), defining the scope of the monopoly conferred by a patent as determined by the claims read in the light of the specification; and
- Article 25 UPC Agreement (corresponding to section 60 of the Patents Act), defining the rights conferred by a patent differently for product and process inventions.

In the discussion below each of these provisions is drawn upon in considering the nature of the subject matter falling within the category of inventions that Article 52 creates.

Also considered in the current chapter is the nature of the subject matter protectable by a species of IP closely related to patents. That subject matter is the plant variety, expressly excluded from patentability but nonetheless protectable by a *sui generis* legal regime similar to that created by the 1833 Papal Edit considered in Chapter 2.

2. Inventions in Europe: Subject Matter that Solves a Technical Problem Using Particular Technical Means

Two things are of immediate note about Article 52(1) of the EPC. The first is the distinction it draws between those properties that make a subject matter an invention on the one hand, being its essential properties, and those properties that make a subject matter new, inventive, and industrially applicable on the other, being its non-essential or accidental properties. And the second is its requirement that protection be granted for inventions 'in all fields of technology'. This requirement was inserted into the EPC in 2000, and implies as an essential property of inventions a certain technical character. Indeed, it was precisely to emphasize the technical nature of inventions that the phrase was inserted. This was made clear by the Administrative Council in its explanation of the insertion in 2000. According to that explanation, the phrase 'all fields of technology' would ensure consistency between Article 52(1) of the EPC and Article 27(1) of the TRIPs Agreement,[7] in particular by enshrining 'technology' 'in the basic provision of substantive European patent law, clearly defining the scope of the EPC, and making it plain that patent protection is available to *technical* inventions of all kinds'.[8] In the same explanatory remarks, the Administrative Council expressed its understanding of 'technical inventions' as 'creations in the technical field'. Inventions, it further stated, are subject matter that 'have a "technical character" or to be more precise—involve a "technical teaching", ie an instruction addressed to a skilled person as to how to solve a particular technical problem using particular technical means'.[9] It is moreover 'this understanding of the term "invention"', the Council wrote, upon which 'the patent granting practice of the [European Patent Office (EPO)] and the jurisprudence of the Boards of Appeal are based', and in the light of which the definition of 'invention' in Article 52(2) and (3) of the EPC must be read.[10] The second part of this statement is especially important in underlining the relationship between the conception of inventions as technical subject matter and the basic statutory definition of 'invention' in Article 52(2) and (3). When reading that definition, the Administrative Council made clear, one must start from the conception of 'invention' outlined above, and from the principle 'that patent protection is reserved for creations in the technical field'.[11]

The Administrative Council's understanding of the invention as a technical teaching or subject matter—supported by Articles 3 and 5 of the Biotech Directive—is consistent with and developed further in more recent EPO authorities. Of principal importance among these authorities are the decisions of the Enlarged Board of Appeal in *Programs for Computers/President's Reference*[12] and *Tomatoes/State of Israel*.[13] The focus of the first of these decisions was on the circumstances in which a computer-related subject matter will be an invention within the meaning of patent law. The answer, the Enlarged Board made clear, is when the subject matter is technical—raising the question of when exactly that will be. While the Board declined to define the term 'technical' in *Programs for Computers*, it confirmed that any subject matter involving a computer or computer-readable data storage medium (such as a CD-ROM) will have technical character, in the same way as any subject matter involving a cup, bicycle, or other man-made object will have.[14] In so doing it explicitly rejected[15] the approach taken by other Boards in past decisions of identifying the 'essence of the invention' and deciding whether that essence is technical, underlining instead the need to focus on the subject matter defined in the claims as a whole. The Board also emphasized[16] that, while computer programs and commonplace objects may be inventions on the basis of their technical character where

[7] Agreement on Trade-related Aspects of Intellectual Property Rights (opened for signature 15 December 1993, entered into force 1 January 1995) 1869 UNTS 299 (TRIPs Agreement).

[8] Administrative Council, EP Organisation Doc MR/2/00 (13 October 2000) 43 (emphasis added).

[9] ibid. [10] ibid. [11] ibid.

[12] G3/08 *Programs for Computers/President's Reference* [2010] EPOR 36 (*Programs for Computers*).

[13] Joined Cases G2/07 *Broccoli/State of Israel* and G1/08 *Tomatoes/State of Israel* [2011] EPOR 27 (*Tomatoes*).

[14] See *Programs for Computers* (n 12) [9.2]. [15] ibid [10.8.8]. [16] ibid [10.7.1].

their contribution to the art lies entirely in their non-technical features, they will lack novelty and inventive step: only those features that contribute to the technical character of an invention being taken into account when assessing its satisfaction of the other patentability requirements. Hence the Board's position that a cup decorated with a certain picture will be an invention, but lacking in technical novelty and inventiveness, and not patentable for that reason.[17] This is consistent with the principles summarized by the Technical Board in *Estimating Sales Activity/Duns Licensing Associates*,[18] as follows.

(A) Article 52(1) EPC sets out four requirements to be fulfilled by a patentable invention: there must be an invention....
(B) Having technical character is an implicit requisite of an 'invention' ... (requirement of 'technicality').
(C) Article 52(2) EPC does not exclude from patentability any subject matter or activity having technical character, even if it is related to the items listed in this provision since these items are only excluded 'as such' (Article 52(3) EPC).
(D) The four requirements—invention, novelty, inventive step, and susceptibility of industrial application—are essentially separate and independent criteria of patentability, which may give rise to concurrent objections. Novelty, in particular, is not a requisite of an invention within the meaning of Article 52(1) EPC, but a separate requirement of patentability.
(E) For examining patentability of an invention in respect of a claim, the claim must be construed to determine the technical features of the invention, ie the features which contribute to the technical character of the invention.
(F) It is legitimate to have a mix of technical and 'non-technical' features appearing in a claim, in which the non-technical features may even form a dominating part of the claimed subject matter. Novelty and inventive step, however, can be based only on technical features, which thus have to be clearly defined in the claim. Non-technical features, to the extent that they do not interact with the technical subject matter of the claim for solving a technical problem, ie non-technical features 'as such', do not provide a technical contribution to the prior art and are thus ignored in assessing novelty and inventive step ...

In *Tomatoes*, the Board considered the nature of inventions with reference to a rather different subject matter in the form of tomato plants, and the circumstances in which they and other biological material might be inventions within the meaning of the EPC. In its decision, '[h]uman intervention, to bring about a result by utilising the forces of nature, pertains to the core of what an invention is understood to be'.[19] The Board attributed this definition to the *Red Dove* decision of the German Bundesgerichtshof (Federal Court of Justice) of 1969[20] discussed in Chapter 3.[21] In that case, decided before the EPC was introduced, the Bundesgerichtshof had defined the term 'invention' as requiring a technical

[17] ibid [10.8.6].
[18] T154/04 *Estimating Sales Activity/Duns Licensing Associates* [2007] EPOR 38 (*Duns Licensing*) [5].
[19] See *Tomatoes* (n 13) [6.4.2.1].
[20] Case X ZB 15/67 *Red Dove* [1969] GRUR 672, [1970] 1 International Review of Industrial Property and Copyright Law 136 (BGH).
[21] See *Tomatoes* (n 13) [6.4.2.1].

teaching, which it characterized as 'a teaching to methodically utilize controllable natural forces to achieve a causal, perceivable result'.[22] This definition led it to confirm the availability of patents in the biological field on the same principles as in other fields, but to deny a patent for the method of making a more beautiful dove before it on the ground that the method was not repeatable. In that context, the Bundesgerichtshof held, the only subject matter for which a patent might be granted was the one-time act that had resulted in production of the dove, and the protection of that subject matter would create a type of monopoly different from that which the patent system exists to create.[23]

In conclusion, and as a result of the EBA's decisions in *Programs for Computers* and *Tomatoes*—and consistent also with the statement of the Administrative Council regarding the EPC 2000 amendment to Article 52(1) above—it can be said that in European patent law today, patentable subject matter includes all and only 'inventions' in the form of technical teachings, namely, instructions methodically to utilize controllable natural forces to achieve a causal, perceivable, repeatable result. According to the Board's jurisprudence, not only has this conception of inventions been derived from Article 52 of the EPC, it informs the interpretation of that provision, including the examples of non-inventions given in Article 52(2) and (3). Importantly, this renders the definitional value of Article 52(2) and (3) all but nugatory, since its interpretation is constrained by a prior conception of what an 'invention' is.

The circularity of the EPO's (and Administrative Council's) insistence that the Article 52(2) and (3) definition of 'invention' be read in the light of EPO jurisprudence regarding the nature of inventions as technical subject matter has led to its rejection by the UK courts, which have refused to accept that jurisprudence. Opposition to the EPO approach was expressed most strongly by Lord Justice Jacob in the 2005 decision of *Aerotel Ltd v Telco Holdings Ltd*,[24] where his Lordship described it as 'not intellectually honest' by reason of the results it supports.[25] Those results—outlined clearly in *Programs for Computers*—include the acceptance as inventions of such long-available and commonplace objects as cups and pens, as well as a range of other subject matter, such as automated (computer) systems in the field of business, that could be said on their face to fall within one or more of the list of non-inventions in Article 52(2)(c) and (3). With respect to automated business systems specifically, the Technical Board explained this position in *Controlling Pension Benefits System/PBS Partnership*[26] with reference to the character of a computer system as 'a concrete apparatus in the sense of a physical entity, man-made for

[22] *Red Dove* (n 20) [1970] 1 International Review of Industrial Property and Copyright Law 136, 138.

[23] ibid 141.

[24] *Aerotel Ltd v Telco Holdings Ltd; Macrossan's Patent Application* [2006] EWCA Civ 1371, [2007] RPC 7 (*Aerotel*).

[25] ibid [27].

[26] Case T931/95 *Controlling Pension Benefits System/PBS Partnership* [2002] EPOR 52 (*PBS Partnership*).

a utilitarian purpose', which it held to be sufficient to make it 'an invention within the meaning of Article 52(1) EPC'.[27]

2.1 Patents for Products

To describe inventions as technical teachings or instructions for solving a particular problem, as the Administrative Council has done, implies that all inventions are methods. As the EPC, Biotech Directive, and UPC Agreement make clear, however, this is not the case. The EPC makes this clear by envisaging the patenting of subject matter other than processes.[28] So too Article 25 of the UPC Agreement, mirroring section 60 of the Patents Act, defines the rights conferred by a patent differently for product and process inventions. According to Article 25(a), where the invention is a product, the patentee has the exclusive rights to prevent its owner from 'making, offering, placing on the market or using [the product], or importing or storing the product for those purposes'. By comparison, where the invention is a process, the patentee has the exclusive rights under Article 25(b) to prevent its owner from 'using [the] process ... or, where the third party knows, or should have known, that the use of the process is prohibited without the consent of the patent proprietor, offering the process for use within the territory of the Contracting Member States in which that patent has effect', and under Article 25(c) from 'offering, placing on the market, using, or importing or storing for those purposes a product obtained directly by [the] process'. Thus, European legislation makes it clear that each invention within the meaning of patent law, in addition to being a technical teaching, may be classified as either a product (that can be made and used etc), or a process (that can be used or offered for use, including for some processes to make a product).

The Biotech Directive is similarly underpinned by a distinction between product and process inventions. Aside from its explicit references to each, it suggests as the reason for the patentability of products specifically the fact of their production by technical means. Thus, and as seen already, Articles 3 and 5 assert that human genes and other biological material that are 'isolated from [their] natural environment or *otherwise* [Article 5] produced by means of a technical process' (emphasis added) are *for this reason* suitable for patent protection. The fact that they previously occurred in nature, or are identical in structure to a natural element, is expressed to be irrelevant.

Two points of importance can be taken from this. The first is that a product resulting from a technical process is for that reason technical itself, in contrast to a product resulting from a non-technical process, which is not technical. And the second is that a subject matter can be technical and identical in structure to a natural object. This explains why the US Supreme Court's decision in *Association for Molecular Pathology v Myriad Genetics Inc*[29] could not be followed by any EU

[27] ibid [5].
[28] See eg EPC art 64 (defining the protection conferred by a patent for a process specifically).
[29] *Association for Molecular Pathology v Myriad Genetics, Inc* 133 S Ct 2107 (2013) (*Myriad*).

Member State without breaching its obligations under the Biotech Directive. According to the Court in *Myriad*, an isolated DNA sequence is too similar to its natural counterpart to be regarded as a human creation, and is thus not an invention ('new ... composition of matter') within the meaning of US patent law. The basis for this decision was the Supreme Court's conception of inventions in *Diamond v Chakrabarty*[30] and—albeit this case not having been cited in *Myriad*—*Bilski v Kappos*.[31] According to the Court in *Chakrabarty*, a bacterium modified by adding four plasmids that enabled it to break down various components of crude oil was an invention on the ground that it had 'markedly different characteristics from any found in nature'.[32] In the language of US patent law, it was a 'new ... composition of matter' created by the scientists who had added the plasmids. According to the Court in *Bilski*, consistent with the reasoning governing product inventions in *Chakrabarty*, a process will be an invention if it is tied to a machine or transforms an article into a different state or thing.[33] Two readings of the significance of these cases for European law seem possible. The first is that under European law, unlike under US law, an invention need not be a human creation, but rather need only have a technical character. And the second is that under European law, unlike under US law, a subject matter will be regarded as a human creation—and thus as an invention—if it is technical, and notwithstanding its structural identity to a product of nature.

Of these two readings, the second is consistent with the statement by the Administrative Council in 2000 that 'patent protection is reserved for creations in the technical field',[34] and with the paradigmatic conception of IP subject matter as artifacts considered in Chapter 3. However, there is no clear support in EPO case law for the conception of inventions as human creations specifically.[35] In addition, the reasoning offered by the appellate courts in *Myriad* for their conflicting decisions supports very clearly a distinction between two types of human action—one reductive and the other creative—and a disagreement over the sufficiency of the former to support a patent grant. Hence the Federal Circuit's description of the act of isolating a gene in *Myriad* as involving the reduction of 'a portion of nature to concrete form'[36] and as meriting a patent on that basis, and the Supreme Court's suggestion in response that whether or not a person who first isolates a gene merits legal protection, he is not entitled to the monopoly rights of an inventor conferred by patent grant. As will be seen in Chapter 5,[37] this is essentially the view taken in copyright, where sound recordings and other fixations or 'reductions' of authorial works are recognized as worthy of legal protection by reason of their value to

30 *Diamond v Chakrabarty* 447 US 303 (1980) (*Chakrabarty*).

31 *Bilski v Kappos* 561 US 593 (2010) (*Bilski*).

32 See *Chakrabarty* (n 30) 310.

33 The Court also emphasized that, while this 'machine-or-transformation test is reliable in most cases, it is not the exclusive test': 561 US 593 (2010) 593.

34 See n 11.

35 Cf n 27 and accompanying text.

36 *Association for Molecular Pathology v Myriad Genetics, Inc* 689 F3d 1303 (Fed Cir 2012) 1331.

37 See also J Pila, 'Isolated Human Genes: The Patent Equivalent of a Non-copyrightable Sound Recording' (2014) 130 Law Quarterly Review 180.

society, but not as human creations earning the protection of authors' rights.[38] Viewing the European legal position in the light of this analysis, it might be more correctly described as being that isolated natural products are technical, and therefore inventions, even if not human creations specifically. That certainly is the view of the European legal position taken by the Supreme Court of the United States. It also reflects the Roman Law doctrine of *specificatio*, which, for obvious reasons, has especial explanatory value for this area of intellectual property.

2.2 The Statutory Categories of Non-inventions

As has been seen, the EPO begins with a conception of inventions as technical subject matter and reads the definition of 'invention' in Article 52(2) and (3) of the EPC in the light of that conception. The question that then arises is what this means for that definition specifically, and in particular, what the categories of non-inventions contained in Article 52(2) and (3) are regarded by the EPO to contain. A useful starting point for considering this is the decision of the Technical Board in *Hitachi/Auction Method*[39] that the EPO's conception of inventions as technical subject matter is sufficiently broad that the only 'activities falling within the notion of a non-invention "as such" would typically represent purely abstract concepts devoid of any technical implications'.[40]

2.2.1 Discoveries, Scientific Theories and Mathematical Methods, Schemes, Rules and Methods for Performing Mental Acts, and Presentations of Information as Such

The first example of such a 'purely abstract concept' is the discovery or realization that something exists, such as a plant bearing exotic fruit. To discover in this sense requires nothing beyond the use of one's five basic senses—sight, hearing, taste, smell, and touch—including no new idea or concept for utilizing the forces of nature to produce a causal, perceivable, and repeatable result. It accordingly lacks the technical character required for an invention under the EPC, and is rather a 'discovery as such' (and non-invention) within the meaning of Article 52(2)(a) and (3). The same reasoning explains why scientific theories and mathematical methods (statements about the natural world and how it works), other presentations of information, and schemes, rules and methods for performing mental acts, are similarly unpatentable, namely, since none involves any new idea for harnessing the forces of nature by acting upon the material world to produce a causal, perceivable,

[38] See eg Copyright, Designs and Patents Act 1988 (UK) (CDPA) s 1(1), distinguishing between original literary, dramatic, musical, and artistic works (protected against mechanical and non-mechanical copying for the life of the author plus 70 years as authorial works) and sound recordings, films, broadcasts, and typographical arrangements of published editions (protected against mechanical copying only for a lesser term as non-authorial expressive works).

[39] Case T258/03 *Hitachi/Auction Method* [2004] OJ EPO 12/575 (*Hitachi*).

[40] ibid [4.5].

and repeatable result. Given this, each fails to satisfy the European definition of the term 'invention' above. So it was that in *Zagyansky*,[41] the Technical Board found a magnetic force and theory regarding relativity and its consequences to lack the technical character required of an invention under the EPC.

Different from each of these subject matter is the discovery that an existing product—including a product of nature—has a certain useful property, or that an existing process has a certain useful effect. Such a discovery may well involve an idea for utilizing the forces of nature to produce a causal, perceivable, and repeatable result, and thus be an invention within the meaning of European law. Examples include: the discovery that aspirin contains a property of use in reducing blood pressure, which will entitle the discoverer to a patent for the product aspirin for use in treating blood pressure; and the discovery that the addition of a product to car engines to treat rust also has the effect of inhibiting friction, which will entitle the discoverer to a patent for the process of adding the product to engines to inhibit friction.[42] In the first case the invention is the old product (aspirin) for the new purpose (reducing blood pressure), and in the second case it is the old process (adding a known product to engines) for the new purpose (reducing friction). Within patent law these are understood as purpose-limited subject matter, and have special interest on account of the inclusion among their constitutive properties of their deviser's intention or purpose with respect to the object (product or process) in question.

With one exception, purpose-limited products are available only in the medical sphere, where the purpose of the product is a therapeutic, surgical, or diagnostic one.[43] The original reason for allowing patents for such 'second medical indications', as they are known, was the Article 53(c) exclusion from patentability of methods of therapy, diagnosis, and surgery, which precludes the patenting of the discovery of a new method of *using* a known product, such as a method of using aspirin for the purpose above. Since purpose-limited product patents provide similar protection without infringing this exclusion, they began to be granted in order to promote the discovery of new therapeutic uses of existing products.

The exception to the restriction of purpose-limited product claims to the medical sphere arises under recital 23 and Articles 5(3) and 9 of the Biotech Directive. Recital 23 links the requirement for an invention with the requirement for susceptibility of industrial application in the case of DNA sequences by providing that 'a mere DNA sequence without indication of a function does not contain any technical information and is therefore not a patentable invention'. The implication is that in the case of an isolated gene, the disclosure of a use—usually associated

[41] T1538/05 *Zagyansky* ECLI:EP:BA:2006:T153805.20060828.

[42] The subject matter at issue in G2/88 *Mobil/Friction Reducing Additive* [1990] EPOR 73 (*Mobil*).

[43] Purpose-limited products in the medical sphere were originally conceived as purpose-limited *processes* expressed as the use of a compound A to manufacture medicament B for the purpose of treating disease C: see G5/83 *Eisai/Second Medical Indication* [1979–85] EPOR B241. Since the insertion of art 54(4) and (5) of the EPC in 2000, however, this type of purpose-limited process is no longer recognized in the medical sphere, having been replaced with the concept of the purpose-limited product above: see G2/08 *Dosage regime/Abbott Respiratory* [2010] EPOR 26. Purpose-limited processes may still be patented, but only outside the sphere of medicine; see *Mobil* (n 42).

with the requirement for susceptibility of industrial application—is an aspect of the requirement for an invention; an implication supported by Article 9 of the Directive, which limits the protection conferred by a patent for a genetic product 'to all material, save as provided in Article 5(1), in which the product is incorporated and in which the genetic information is contained and performs its function'. As confirmed by the Court of Justice in *Monsanto Technology LLC v Cefetra BV*,[44] this prevents Member States from according genetic products the extensive protection accorded to other products, by limiting the protection that they receive from a patent to the product when performing the function that recital 23 (and Article 5(3)) requires the patentee to disclose. The result is that instead of being protected as products as such, isolated genes and other products 'containing or consisting of genetic information' are protected as purpose-limited products, namely, products of (and intended for) use for a specified purpose only.

The question arises as to the consequence of this for conception of the invention itself. Two views are plausible. The first is that the invention remains the product, but the protection it is given is limited. And the second is that the invention is the product *for the purpose*, which is then given the full protection of other types of inventions. The former might be said to raise difficulties with the TRIPs Agreement, on account of its prohibition against discrimination against inventions on the basis of their field of technology.[45] If the invention itself is the purpose-limited product, by contrast, there can be no question of discrimination since the invention is given full protection. However, the latter raises legal difficulties due to its treatment of the intention or purpose of the inventor as an essential property of the invention that must be reproduced by any user of the invention to infringe the inventor's patent rights, which conflicts with the strict liability of direct infringement of a patent under UK and other European states' domestic laws.[46]

Between perceiving the existence of a product or process (an act of discovery not invention), and perceiving that a product or process has a certain useful technical property or effect (an act of discovery *and* invention), lies a third type of discovery that might be regarded as satisfying European conceptions of the invention, notwithstanding Article 52(2)(a) and (3). This type of discovery involves perceiving that an existing product or process of nature can be made available for repeated human use, including by isolating a product (such as a human gene or an enantiomer) from its natural environment. In Europe, as noted already, isolated natural material is expressly recognized in the Biotech Directive as capable of supporting a patent on the basis of the technical process that its production (ie the material's isolation) involves, and notwithstanding the prior occurrence of the material in nature or the identity of its structure to the structure of a product of nature.

[44] Case C–428/08 *Monsanto Technology LLC v Cefetra BV* [2010] ECR I–06765.

[45] TRIPs Agreement art 27.1 ('patents shall be available and patent rights enjoyable without discrimination as to ... the field of technology').

[46] Patents Act s 60; see further *Merrell Dow Pharmaceuticals Inc v HB Norton & Co Ltd* [1995] UKHL 14, [1996] RPC 76 (*Merrell Dow*) [52].

2.2.2 Aesthetic Creations as Such

An aesthetic creation may be defined as a bounded expressive object, such as a poem or a painting, which exists (in the sense of having been intended to exist and treated by society as existing) for aesthetic enjoyment.[47] In the case of intangible works with no necessary physical form—such as a poem or a musical tune—one can readily explain such works' exclusion from patentability with reference to the definition of technical character above: they are not the product of any purposive human action on the material world utilizing natural forces to produce a causal, perceivable, and repeatable result. By contrast, works with a physical form, such as a painting or sculpture, would seem to be technical according to this definition, raising the prospect of them being inventions under European law. This is consistent with the decision of the Enlarged Board in *Programs for Computers*, referred to above, that a cup with a picture on it will possess the technical character required of an invention. However, and as also noted, the Board emphasized in that case that such a subject matter will lack the technical inventive step required to make it inventive. By parity of reasoning it seems clear that, while a sculpture, painting, or other artistic work will possess the technical character of an invention within the meaning of the EPC, since any inventive step it involves will almost certainly reside exclusively in its expressive (non-technical) features, it will also be obvious in a technical sense and therefore excluded from patentability. This is consistent with the Board's decision in *Lichtdurchlässiges Bauelement/Hettling-Denker*[48] that a work of art in the style of stained glass was not a non-invention within the meaning of Article 52(2)(b) and (3), and with the recognized patentability of such things as book-binding, paint brushes, and other means of creating aesthetic objects.[49]

2.2.3 Schemes, Rules, and Methods for Playing Games and Doing Business, and Programs for Computers as Such

Schemes, and rules and methods for playing games and doing business, are similar to discoveries and aesthetic creations in being potentially technical within the meaning of European law. For example, a method of purchasing goods over the Internet will require the use of a computer for its implementation, and will for this reason alone be regarded as an invention, as confirmed in *PBS Partnership*. However, as long as its contribution to knowledge lies in the field of purchasing (ie business), it will also be regarded by the EPO as obvious on the ground above, namely, that the art of doing business is not a *technical* art.

The examples of aesthetic creations and automated business methods further underline why programs for computers support the same analysis, namely, because

[47] Thus defined, the category of aesthetic creations includes many but not all of the authorial works protectable by copyright, the latter of which include also many creations of a non-aesthetic nature, such as databases and computer programs.

[48] T686/90 *Lichtdurchlässiges Bauelement/Hettling-Denker* ECLI:EP:BA:1993:T068690.19930621.

[49] Cf n 27 and accompanying text.

as methods for causing a device to operate, they satisfy the *Tomatoes* definition of technical. It is only when programs are alternatively conceived as intangible works of expression comprising zeros and ones that this analysis changes, supporting their exclusion from patentability on the same grounds as aesthetic creations.

2.3 Public Policy Exclusions from Patentability

2.3.1 Plant and Animal Varieties, and Essentially Biological Processes for the Production of Plants and Animals

As has been seen, Articles 3 and 5 of the Biotech Directive explain the distinction between inventions and products of nature with reference to the formers' technical character. Following a similar principle, Article 4 of the Biotech Directive excludes plant and animal varieties, and essentially biological processes for the production of plants or animals, from patentability, while also stating explicitly that 'inventions' concerning plants or animals 'shall be patentable if [their] technical feasibility … is not confined to a particular plant or animal variety',[50] as shall 'inventions which concern a microbiological or other technical process or a product obtained by means of such a process'.[51] Once again, these provisions suggest as the basis for the distinction between inventions and non-inventions the formers' technical character, and as the test of technical character (for methods) their utilization of natural forces to produce a causal, perceivable, and repeatable result, and (for products) their production by means of such a method.

As with the Biotech Directive, the EPC also excludes from patentability plant and animal varieties, and essentially biological processes for the production of plants and animals. In the EPC, however, these exclusions are located outside the general patentability provision of Article 52, in Article 53(b). There they sit alongside two further subject matter exclusions covering, respectively, inventions the commercial exploitation of which would be contrary to *ordre public* or morality, and methods of surgical, therapeutic, and diagnostic treatment practiced on the human or animal body. Despite this, and consistent with the more expansive terms of Article 4(2) and (3) of the Biotech Directive, the exclusions have been interpreted by the EPO as an expression of the distinction between (patentable) inventions and (unpatentable) discoveries, and thus as a consequence of the Article 52(1) requirement for an invention rather than any separate considerations of public policy. So it was that in *Transgenic Plant/Novartis II*,[52] the Enlarged Board of Appeal defined the category of plant varieties excluded from protection under Article 53(b) as confined to specific varieties for which *sui generis* plant breeders' rights are available, namely, 'concrete' objects or 'specific products' in the form of a particular variety resulting from biological developments and not involving any generally applicable technical

[50] Biotech Directive art 4(2).
[51] ibid art 4(3). For a definition of 'microbiological process' see ibid art 2(1)(b).
[52] G1/98 *Transgenic Plant/Novartis II* [2000] EPOR 30 (*Novartis II*).

teaching.[53] Hence the effect of Article 4(2) of the Biotech Directive, which is to confirm and entrench statutorily the EPO's reading of the EPC varieties exclusion in *Novartis II*. One result of this reading (and of the EU statutory provisions based on it) is to take genetically modified plants and animals outside the exclusion by reason of the capacity of their technical teaching to be 'implemented in an indefinite number of plant varieties'.[54]

As seen above, lack of technical character is also suggested by the terms of Article 4(3) of the Biotech Directive to be the basis for the exclusion from patentability of 'essentially biological processes for the production of plants and animals'. Under the EPC, however, that view has recently been rejected. According to the Enlarged Board in *Tomatoes*, since biological processes involve human intervention in the material world to bring about a desired result, they have technical character. Further, and contrary to the logic of *Novartis II*, the Board in *Tomatoes* held that it is precisely this reason—ie the technical character of the essentially biological processes excluded from protection by Article 53(b)—that explains the need for that exclusion. The only situation in which a technical method for producing plants or animals *will* be patentable, the Board held, is where the specific technical step 'introduces a trait into the genome or modifies a trait in the genome of the plant [or animal] produced' such that 'the process leaves the realm of the plant [or animal] breeding, which the legislator wanted to exclude from patentability'.[55] On this basis, a method of growing a plant involving a watering system or the use of a hothouse will not involve sufficient human intervention to make the method a non-biological one. The only protection available to a person who devises such a method will therefore be for the watering system or hothouse itself. While the Enlarged Board in *Tomatoes II/State of Israel* also held the plant grown by means of the method to fall outside the essentially biological process exclusion by reason of its nature as a product rather than a process, this has recently been overruled by the EP Organisation's Administration Council following intervention by the European Commission and in the interests of a 'harmonised European patent law' and 'clarity and legal certainty for users of the European patent system'.[56] In reaching its decision regarding material produced by means of an essentially biological process, the Enlarged Board in *Tomatoes II* was clearly influenced by the drafting

[53] ibid [3.1] (describing a plant variety as 'a concrete' object akin to a nail, screw or bolt, in contrast to 'an invention of general applicability' comprising 'an abstract and open definition embracing an indefinite number of individual entities' such as 'fastening means characterized in that they consist of a specific material' and 'transgenic plants … defined by certain characteristics allowing the plants to inhibit the growth of plant pathogens') [3.7] (interpreting the plant varieties exclusion as having been intended to reserve for protection by the plant variety right system 'biological developments for which the patent system was less suited … and to keep technical inventions related to plants within the patent system') and [3.10] (describing the purpose of the plant variety right system as being 'to protect specific products which are used in farming and gardening' in contrast to 'technical teachings which can be implemented in an indefinite number of plant varieties').

[54] ibid [3.10].

[55] See *Tomatoes* (n 13) 69. In G2/12 *Tomatoes II/ State of Israel* ECLI:EP:BA:2015:G000212.20150325 (*Tomatoes II*), the Enlarged Board rejected a request to 'rectify' its decision in Tomatoes while emphasising the restriction of that decision to the application EPC art 53(b) in respect of plant and animal varieties.

[56] EPO press release, 'EPO clarifies practice in the area of plant and animal patents' (29 June 2017) <https://www.epo.org/news-issues/news/2017/20170629.html> (last accessed 26 July 2017), referring

history of Article 2(b) of the Strasbourg Patent Convention, with which Article 53(b) was introduced to comply. According to the *travaux préparatoires* governing Article 2(b), the reason for excluding 'essentially' biological processes rather than only 'purely' biological processes, as had originally been proposed, was to ensure that patents would not be available for

> processes which were fundamentally of this type even if, as a *secondary* feature, 'technical' devices are involved (use of a particular type of instrument in a grafting process, or of a special greenhouse in growing a plant), it being understood that such technical devices may perfectly well be patented themselves, but not the biological process in which they are used.[57]

What the Board failed to explain in *Tomatoes II* was how its decision in that case sits with its earlier interpretation of the varieties exclusion in *Novartis II* as serving merely to reinforce the Article 52(1) requirement for an invention, and *why* technical processes for the production of plants and animals should be excluded from patentability by virtue of being 'essentially biological processes', notwithstanding their technicality.[58] Having said that, also unclear from the jurisprudence in this area, including the decision in *Novartis II* itself, is why individual plant varieties are mere concrete objects rather than embodiments of a technical teaching; and more specifically, how the apparent view of plant varieties in *Novartis II* as lacking the technical character required of inherent patentability sits with the definition of technical character in *Tomatoes*.

In fact, it seems possible that the provision governing essentially biological processes in the Strasbourg Patent Convention—which provision had the effect of excluding such processes from the harmonizing scope of the Convention rather than from patentability itself[59]—was introduced in recognition of the then view among European states that, regardless of their technical character, they were not 'inventions' properly conceived. That would explain the view of the Strasbourg drafters—repeated by the Enlarged Board in *Tomatoes II*—that merely involving a technical step does not alter the 'essentially biological' nature of a process. The implication of this reasoning is that a subject matter cannot be both a biological process and an invention, and that having some aspect of technical character is not enough to transform a subject matter from the former to the latter. As for what else might be required: again, the finding by the Board in *Tomatoes II* that a change in the genetic identity of a plant or animal attributable to the technical step is needed might suggest the requirement for a transformative human step sufficient to give rise to something that can properly be described as a human creation. In effect, this is the reasoning that the US Supreme Court deployed in *Myriad* and *Mayo Collaborative Services v Prometheus Laboratories Inc*[60] when finding that isolated

to Commission Notice on certain articles of Directive 98/44/EC of the European Parliament and of the Council on the legal protection of biotechnological inventions [2016] OJ C 411/3.

57 Committee of Experts, Memorandum by the Secretariat on the meeting held at Strasbourg from 7 to 10 November 1961, EXP/Brev (61) 8 (13 December 1961) Appendix I [6] (emphasis in original). See also Committee of Ministers, Report of the Committee of Experts to the Committee of Ministers on the meeting held at Strasbourg from 10 to 13 July 1962, CM (62) 16 (8 August 1962) [7].

58 The *travaux préparatoires* give no insight into this.

59 See J Pila, 'A Challenge to the *Novartis* Theory of European Patent History' (2009) 72 Modern Law Review 436.

60 *Mayo Collaborative Services v Prometheus Laboratories Inc* 132 S Ct 1289 (2012) (*Mayo*).

DNA sequences and methods of diagnosis, while products of human action, lack the transformative nature of human creations specifically.

In conclusion, the EPO's interpretation of Article 53(b) can be explained with reference to the requirement for an invention, albeit differently interpreted for varieties and essentially biological processes respectively. Varieties, it might be said, are excluded from patentability under Article 53(b) by reason of their failure to possess the technical character required of inventions under the EPC. By comparison, essentially biological processes would seem to be excluded from patentability under Article 53(b) notwithstanding their technical character, and by reason instead of their failure to involve a sufficiently transformative human act to make them the (intellectual) creation of their putative inventor.

2.3.2 *Inventions the Commercial Exploitation of which Would be Contrary to* Ordre Public *or Morality, and Medical and Veterinarian Methods*

The relationship between the Article 53 exclusions and the requirement for a subject matter having technical character arises also in the context of Article 53(a) and 53(c), excluding from patentability 'inventions the commercial exploitation of which would be contrary to "ordre public" or morality' and medical and veterinarian methods respectively. Notwithstanding its interpretation of the varieties exclusion, but consistent with its interpretation of the essentially biological process exclusion, the EPO has treated the first of these exclusions as applying without prejudice to the technical character of the relevant subject matter, and as thus capable of covering inventions within the meaning of Article 52(1). This is apparent from its failure to refer to the technical (or non-technical) nature of a subject matter when considering whether its commercialization would be contrary to *ordre public* or morality, and is consistent also with the use of the term 'inventions' to describe the subject matter excluded from patentability by Article 53(a). Given this, it seems safe to conclude that the historical view of inherent patentability as having a moral and public policy aspect—such that generally inconvenient subject matter were not regarded as inventions—is no longer valid.

Less clear is the position regarding medical and veterinarian methods under Article 53(c). In early drafts of the EPC, these subject matter (referred to as 'methods of therapy, including diagnostic methods') were included among the list of non-inventions contained in what is now Article 52(2) and (3). Immediately before the signing of the EPC in 1973, however, Germany proposed that they be removed from that list and excluded from patentability on the different ground of insusceptibility of industrial application. That proposal was accepted and Article 52(4) of the EPC enacted, as follows:

> Methods for treatment of the human or animal body by surgery or therapy and diagnostic methods practised on the human or animal body shall not be regarded as *inventions which are susceptible of industrial application within the meaning of paragraph 1.* This provision shall not apply to products, in particular substances or compositions, for use in any of these methods (emphasis added).

As has elsewhere been shown, the EPC drafters' uncertainty regarding the proper location of the medical and veterinarian methods exclusion reflected a wider uncertainty regarding the relationship between the requirements for an invention and susceptibility of industrial application respectively.[61] By the time the EPC was signed they seem to have settled on a view of the requirements as separate, consistent with the EPO's understanding today. However, and as seen in the discussion of purpose-limited products above, the Biotech Directive connects the two requirements by treating genetic products as purpose-limited products, and the industrial application that a patentee must disclose for any genetic product under Article 5(3) as an essential property of the product *qua* invention (ie technical subject matter) specifically. This is also consistent with current understandings of the requirement for susceptibility of industrial application itself. According to the EPO, for example, in order for that requirement to be satisfied, a patent applicant must establish that the technical basis of the subject matter is sufficiently 'sound and concrete' to enable the skilled addressee to 'recognize that its contribution to the art could lead to practical exploitation in industry'.[62]

Returning to the exclusion from patentability of medical and veterinarian methods specifically: when the EPC was amended in 2000, this exclusion was moved for a second time from Article 52(4) to its current location in Article 53(c). According to the explanatory remarks offered by the Administrative Council for that move, the reason was again to reflect the exclusion's proper legal basis, which was thought now to be public health rather than industrial applicability.[63] In the Council's statement, medical and veterinarian methods are inventions previously excluded 'by the fiction of their lack of industrial applicability', which fiction it was 'undesirable to uphold'.[64] Citing also the wording of Article 27(3)(a) of the TRIPs Agreement, the Council supported the exclusion's relocation to Article 53(c) as bringing greater coherence to the EPC without effecting any change in legal practice.[65]

The view of medical and veterinarian methods as excluded on grounds of public health is unpersuasive for several reasons. The first is that the concept of public health usually refers to human health only, and not to animal health, and yet Article 53(c) excludes veterinarian as well as medical methods.[66] In addition, if promoting public health requires the exclusion of medical methods at least, it is difficult to see why it does not also require the exclusion of medicines. And finally, the rationale of 'public health' does not sit comfortably with the EPO's interpretation of the Article 53(c) exclusions themselves. For example, in *Cygnus/Diagnostic Methods*,[67] the Enlarged Board defined the methods of diagnosis excluded from patentability by Article 53(c) as confined to methods that include each of four non-technical steps performed directly on the human or animal body—examination;

[61] J Pila, *The Requirement for an Invention* (OUP 2009) 152–53, 162.

[62] T898/05 *Hematopoietic receptor/Zymogenetics* ECLI:EP:BA:2006:T089805.20060707; also *Human Genome Sciences Inc v Eli Lilly* [2011] UKSC 51, [2012] RPC 6.

[63] Doc CA/100/00, 41. [64] ibid. [65] ibid.

[66] See eg Charter of Fundamental Rights of the European Union [2010] OJ C 83/389 art 35 ('Everyone has the right of access to preventive health care and the right to benefit from medical treatment under the conditions established by national laws and practices. A high level of human health protection shall be ensured in the definition and implementation of all the Union's policies and activities.')

[67] G1/04 *Cygnus/Diagnostic Methods* [2006] OJ EPO 334.

data gathering; comparison; and deduction—and as excluding any method that involves technical steps carried out by a device. That definition, which seems aimed at limiting the exclusion to non-technical subject matter, was supported by the Board with reference to the limited purpose of Article 53(c) to ensure the freedom of '[m]edical and veterinary practitioners ... to take the actions they consider suited to diagnose illnesses by means of investigative methods'.[68] The same policy rationale—'to free from restraint non-commercial and non-industrial medical and veterinary activities'—was relied on in *Treatment by Surgery/Medi-Physics*[69] to explain the Board's definition of the methods of surgery excluded by Article 53(c) as methods involving a substantial physical intervention on the human or animal body for which the medical profession is specifically trained and assumes responsibility,[70] and again in *Thompson/Cornea*[71] to explain the Board's definition of the methods of therapy excluded by Article 53(c) (then Article 52(4)) as methods of preventing or curing a disease or malfunction of the human or animal body, or any of the symptoms thereof.[72]

It is submitted that, having regard to these definitions, a more convincing explanation for the medical/veterinarian methods exclusion than public benefit may be a view of each of the methods in question as not being inventions after all. This explanation is clearly consistent with the EPO's definition of methods of diagnosis as comprised exclusively of non-technical steps. However, it may also be consistent with the EPO's definition of surgical and therapeutic methods as dependent for their implementation on the expertise of the medical or veterinarian profession. Consider in this regard the decision of the EPO in *Pitney Bowes/A System for Processing Mail*.[73] That case involved a method of shipping mail that involved a series of steps including the sorting of mail by a van driver by means of a predetermined system. According to the Technical Board, the method was an invention on the ground that it did not depend on 'the driver exercising a judgement of the kind usually involved in doing business'.[74] This reasoning recalls the refusal of patents by Anglo-Australian courts in the early 20th century for methods of burning timber and extinguishing fires, the steps of which would seem similarly incapable of being sufficiently predetermined as not to depend heavily on the skill and discretion of the person implementing them and located *outside* the fields of industry and technology.[75] The result can perhaps be rationalized with reference to the *Tomatoes* test

[68] ibid [4].

[69] G1/07 *Treatment by Surgery/Medi-Physics* ECLI:EP:BA:2010:G000107.20100215 [4.1].

[70] By way of contrast, it described methods of tattooing, piercing, and hair removal as not excluded by reason of their nature as uncritical methods involving a minor intervention and no substantial health risks when carried out with the required care and skill: see ibid [3.4.2.2].

[71] T24/91 *Thompson/Cornea* [1996] EPOR 19.

[72] ibid [2.4] ('It is generally accepted that the exclusions from patentability under Article 52(4) EPC are based on social-ethical and public health considerations. The intention underlying this Article is to ensure that nobody who wants to use the methods specified in this Article as part of the medical treatment of humans or animals should be prevented from this by patents.')

[73] T388/04 *Pitney Bowes/A System for Processing Mail* [2007] OJ EPO 1/16.

[74] ibid [2.3].

[75] See J Pila, 'On the European Requirement for an Invention' [2010] International Review of Intellectual Property and Competition Law 906.

of technical character itself: the need for some human action on the world utilizing the forces of nature to produce a causal, perceivable, and repeatable result suggesting the need for sufficient stability and pre-determinability to make the relevant subject matter capable of being performed by a skilled *technical* addressee.

In conclusion, the EPO currently treats the surgical and therapeutic methods excluded by Article 53(c) at least as unrelated to the requirement for an invention, and as thus not contributing anything to an understanding of that requirement or of the nature of inventions themselves. That treatment is consistent with the statement by the Administrative Council that (all) medical and veterinarian methods are inventions excluded from protection on grounds of public health. However, it is arguable that the real basis for Article 53(c)—as with the varieties exclusion of Article 53(b)—is the presumptive inability of the methods it covers to be inventions, properly conceived. That inability might be attributed to the methods' failure to satisfy the *Tomatoes* test of technicality, by reason of their exclusively non-technical steps, or their dependence on the professional (non-technical) discretion and skill of the doctors implementing them. Alternatively, and recalling the discussion of the essentially biological processes exclusion of Article 53(b), and the equivocation over the proper legal basis of the medical and veterinarian methods exclusion historically, the inability of the methods to be inventions might be attributed to the US conception of inventions—applied to a diagnostic method in *Mayo*—as requiring a sufficiently transformative act to make them human creations rather than merely an instruction for human action in a field of technology.

2.4 Conclusion

In conclusion, the inventions for which a patent may validly be granted are defined under European law as technical teachings, namely, subject matter involving technical character, in the sense of depending for their existence on some human intervention in the material world utilizing the forces of nature to produce a causal, perceivable, and repeatable result. In the jurisprudence of the EPO, this definition is both supported by the EPC and the starting point for reading its provisions on inherent patentability, including its definition of 'invention' (via a list of non-inventions) in Article 52(2) and (3). Its premise is a view of the requirement for an invention as legally and analytically separate from the further patentability requirements of novelty, inventive step, and susceptibility of industrial application respectively, such that a subject matter need not be new, inventive, or industrially applicable to be an invention within the meaning of European law.

In principle, the only exceptions to the ability of technical subject matter to support a patent are those for which express provision is made in Article 53 of the EPC. Under that Article, patents may not be granted for any subject matter—whether or not it has technical character—(a) the commercial exploitation of which would be contrary to *ordre public* or morality, (b) that is a plant or animal variety, or an essentially biological process for the production of plants or animals, or (c) that is a medical or veterinarian (diagnostic, therapeutic, or surgical) method. In the jurisprudence of the EPO, each of these exclusions—except those covering varieties and diagnostic methods, which have been related to the requirement for technical character—has been presented as having its basis in public policy. In practice, however, and with the exception of the *public ordre*/morality exclusion of Article 53(a), each may be more coherently explained with reference to the requirement for an invention after all—whether as defined in the European *Tomatoes* case, or as defined by the US Supreme Court in the line of cases including *Bilski, Myriad*, and *Mayo*.

Under European law, inventions can be products or processes, and will in either case be defined with reference to their technical properties. In some cases, they can also be purpose-limited products or processes, in which case the purpose or intention of the inventor will be a constitutive feature of the product or process *qua* invention. As the Biotech Directive in particular underlines, the recognition of purpose-limited subject matter as inventions undermines the EPO's view of the requirement for an invention as separate from the secondary patentability requirements, by treating the function or industrial application of a subject matter—its final cause in the Aristotelian sense considered in Chapter 3—as among its essential properties.

3. Inventions in the United Kingdom: Subject Matter that Make a Technical Contribution to the Art

As a starting point, it may be noted that there are two differences between the wording of section 1 and Article 52 of relevance to legal officials' definition of the term 'invention'. The first is the absence in section 1(1)—corresponding to Article 52(1) of the EPC—of the EPC 2000 reference to inventions 'in all fields of technology', presumably on the basis that the insertion of that phrase did not involve any substantive change to Article 52(1). The second is the phrase 'among other things' at the start of section 1(2)—corresponding to Article 52(2) and (3) of the EPC—which makes it clear that the list of non-inventions contained in that provision is inclusive.

However, the real difference between UK and European law in this area derives not from the wording of the legislation, but from the interpretation of that wording by the relevant judicial authorities. To date the UK courts have refused to accept the EPO's understanding of 'inventions' as technical subject matter on the basis of its stated inconsistency with Article 52(2) and (3) and established UK precedent. This is despite their obligation under section 130(7) of the Patents Act to interpret section 1 and other key Patents Act provisions—namely, sections 2 to 6, 14(3), (5) and (6), 37(5), 54, 60, 69, 72(1) and (2), 74(4), 82, 83, 100, and 125—so far as practicable to be consistent with the interpretation of the corresponding European provisions, and despite the alternative conception supported by UK precedent having itself been derived from the EPO's 1985 Guidelines for Examiners.[76] According

[76] [1985] EPO OJ 173, 117–79. See generally Pila, *The Requirement for an Invention* (n 61) 254–55.

to that alternative conception, first articulated by the Principal Examiner of the UK Patent Office in *Merrill Lynch Inc's Application*,[77] an invention within the meaning of section 1(2) of the Patents Act is any subject matter that contributes something technical to what had been known previously. Being technical is therefore not a sufficient—although almost certainly still a necessary—property of an invention in UK law. Strictly speaking, however, the courts do not ask of a subject matter 'is it technical?', but rather, 'does it make a contribution to the art that is technical?'.

In deciding whether a subject matter satisfies this test, the UK courts have adopted slightly different approaches. In *Aerotel* Lord Justice Jacob supported the following four-step test: (a) construe the claim; (b) identify the actual contribution that it (ie the claim) makes; (c) determine whether the contribution falls exclusively within the excluded subject matter of section 1(2)/Article 52(2) and (3); and (d) check that the contribution is actually technical.[78] In *Symbian v Comptroller-General of Patents*,[79] Lord Neuberger supported conflating steps (c) and (d) in the interests of moving this test closer to that of the EPO Boards by proposing that the courts ask instead: 'is the contribution technical?'—and then, when answering this question, treat Article 52(2) and (3) as a statement of what types of contribution are not technical.[80] Since *Symbian*, the courts have applied both (*Aerotel* and *Symbian*) tests, as well as variants of them. For example, in *HTC Europe Co Ltd v Apple Inc*[81] Lord Justice Floyd regarded himself as bound to 'consider whether the invention made a technical contribution to the known art, *with the rider that novel or inventive purely excluded subject matter does not count as a technical contribution*', whether or not by means of the four stage test of *Aerotel*.[82] He then identified a number of points of relevance when deciding this for computer-related subject matter specifically. They included asking 'whether the invention may be regarded as solving a problem which is essentially technical', be it a problem inside the computer (that 'will make the computer, as a computer, an improved device, for example by increasing its speed') or outside the computer (that 'will also have a relevant technical effect, for example by controlling an improved technical process').[83] In the more recent *Lantana Ltd v The Comptroller General of Patents, Design and Trade Marks*,[84] Lady Justice Arden focused on the *HTC* 'rider' by describing the requirement for an invention as a

[77] *Merrill Lynch Inc's Application* [1988] RPC 1 (Patent Office).

[78] See *Aerotel* (n 24)[40].

[79] *Symbian v Comptroller-General of Patents* [2008] EWCA Civ 1066, [2009] RPC 1 (*Symbian*).

[80] ibid [11] ('The third stage mandated in *Aerotel*, which we would have thought normally raises the crucial issue, is whether the alleged contribution is excluded by art 52(2), as limited by art 52(3). So far as we can see, there is no reason, at least in principle, why that test should not amount to the same as that identified in Duns, namely whether the contribution cannot be characterised as "technical". In effect, this can be said to involve conflating the third and fourth stages in *Aerotel*, a conflation which is easy to accept bearing in mind that it was said in *Aerotel* that the fourth stage, while required by *Merrill Lynch*, was unlikely to add anything to the third stage (a view supported by Kitchin J in *Astron Clinica Ltd v Comptroller-General* [2008] RPC 14, 49 and by Patten J in this case at 44)').

[81] *HTC Europe Co Ltd v Apple Inc* [2013] EWCA Civ 451, [2013] RPC 30 (*HTC*) .

[82] ibid [44] (emphasis added).

[83] ibid [49]; see also *AT&T Knowledge Ventures LP's Patent Application* [2009] EWHC 343 (Pat), [2009] FSR 19 (*AT&T*) [40].

[84] *Lantana Ltd v The Comptroller General of Patents, Design and Trade Marks* [2014] EWCA Civ 1463, [2015] RPC 16 (*Lantana*).

requirement for 'some identifiable inventive step' outside an Article 52(2) subject matter.[85]

While each of these approaches by the Court of Appeal in recent years is different, all support a conception of the invention as novel and/or inventive in its technical aspects. Lady Justice Arden's approach does this most directly, by requiring technical inventiveness. According to the EPO, and as seen in Chapter 3, it is the conflation of the requirement for an invention with the secondary requirements for novelty and inventiveness that makes the UK approach inappropriate.[86] However, both it and the UK courts have sought to downplay the difference between their respective positions by pointing out that the effect of both is to restrict the availability of patents to technically inventive subject matter—albeit in the UK by means of a requirement for a technically inventive subject matter, and in the EPO by means of a requirement for an inventive step in a technical field.[87]

The premise of the UK cases in this area is that a subject matter's contribution to the art is the same as its inventive step. This, however, sits uncomfortably with other UK authorities, especially those relating to the requirement for sufficient description under section 14(5)(c). According to that section, corresponding to Article 84 of the EPC, the claims of a patent in which the alleged invention is defined must 'be supported by the description' contained in the patent document. In *Fuel Oils/Exxon*,[88] the EPO interpreted this provision as expressing the general principle that 'the extent of the patent monopoly, as defined by the claims [under Article 69 of the EPC and section 125 of the Patents Act], should correspond to the technical contribution to the art in order for it to be supported or justified'.[89] Implicit is a view of the patent *description* as defining or representing the technical contribution to the art that a patent makes. Hence the need for that description to 'support' the definition of the invention contained in the claims in order for the scope of protection conferred by the patent for that invention (defined by the claims) to *correspond* to that contribution. The need for such correspondence itself derives from the contractual nature of patents, according to which the grant of a patent serves as consideration for the disclosure to the public of an invention that has been examined and found to represent some contribution to the prior art. If and only if the invention with reference to which the patent rights are defined fully captures that contribution will the consideration obtained by the patentee 'be supported or justified'.

[85] ibid [19].

[86] See eg *Duns Licensing* (n 18) [5] ('The four requirements—invention, novelty, inventive step, and susceptibility of industrial application—are essentially separate and independent criteria of patentability, which may give rise to concurrent objections. Novelty, in particular, is not a requisite of an invention within the meaning of Article 52(1) of the EPC, but a separate requirement of patentability'); *Programs for Computers* (n 12) [10.5] (quoting from a decision of the Technical Board of Appeal explaining that the UK-endorsed 'contribution approach' raised prior art issues more appropriately considered in the context of novelty and inventive step).

[87] See *Programs for Computers* (n 12) [10.7.1]; *Symbian* (n 79) [9]–[12]; *AT&T* (n 83) [35]–[38]; *HTC* (n 81) [41], [44].

[88] T409/91 *Fuel Oils/Exxon* [1994] EPOR 149 (*Exxon*).

[89] ibid [3.3].

The *Exxon* statement and legislative provision to which it relates have caused difficulty for the UK courts. In *Biogen Inc v Medeva plc*[90] the House of Lords was asked to decide whether a claim to a recombinant DNA molecule encoding for the hepatitis B (HBV) virus satisfied section 14(5)(c), and held that it did not. In Lord Hoffmann's analysis, the technical contribution to the art that the patentee had made—which his Lordship described as showing that known recombinant techniques could be used to make the HBV antigens in a prokaryotic host cell—represented 'a brilliant Napoleonic victory in cutting through the uncertainties that existed in his day to achieve the desired result', but did not 'establish any new principle that his successors had to follow if they were to achieve the same results' of making HBV antigens.[91] In that context, he held, the patentee's contribution to the art did not justify a monopoly covering all recombinant methods of making the antigens, which is what he would have received had the patent for the recombinant DNA molecule been upheld. Instead, Lord Hoffmann said, the contribution justified only a monopoly covering the particular method that the inventor had adopted and disclosed to produce the antigens. It followed in his judgment that the patent was insufficient under section 14(5)(c): while its description covered the full breadth of the claim in the sense of telling the hypothetical skilled addressee all that he needed to know to make the antigens, it was possible to envisage other means of producing the antigens that were not disclosed in the patent. In that context, Lord Hoffmann held, a monopoly granted on the basis of and defined with reference to the claim would exceed the contribution that the patentee had, through his patent description, made.[92]

Central to the logic of *Biogen* was Lord Hoffmann's connection of the contribution to the art that the patentee had made with his inventive step.[93] That connection was reinforced in Lord Hoffmann's decision by his criticism of the Court of Appeal in the proceedings below for having confused the inventive concept, 'relevant only to inventive step under section 1(1)(b)', with the 'actual subject matter of the invention (the content and scope of the claims)'.[94] According to Lord Hoffmann, the inventive concept of the *Biogen* claim was trying to express

[90] *Biogen Inc v Medeva plc* [1997] RPC 1 (HL) (*Biogen*).

[91] ibid 52.

[92] ibid especially 51–52.

[93] See also his decision in *Kirin-Amgen Inc v Hoechst Marion Roussel Ltd* [2004] UKHL 46, [2005] RPC 169 (*Kirin-Amgen*) [22] involving claims to: a recombinant DNA sequence for use in securing the expression of EPO (claim 1); EPO produced by the expression of an exogenous DNA sequence (claim 19); and EPO produced by the expression in a host cell of a DNA sequence according to claim 1 (claim 26). According to his Lordship, the invention thus claimed was only the method of making EPO by expression of an exogenous DNA sequence, and not the product EPO itself, notwithstanding the focus of claims 19 and 26. Since this corresponded to the technical contribution revealed in the patent description, no issue of insufficiency arose, underlining (Lord Hoffmann said) the sensitivity of that issue 'to the nature of the invention' claimed ([103]). The reason given by Lord Hoffmann for his narrow conception of the Amgen invention was that it represented what the skilled addressee reading each claim in its proper context—including 'on the assumption that its purpose is both to describe and demarcate an invention–a practical idea which the patentee has had for a new product or process' ([33])—would understand the patentee to have intended by his use of language to claim. While the *Kirin-Amgen* approach to identifying a claimed invention survives the Supreme Court's decision in *Actavis UK Ltd v Eli Lilly and Co* [2017] UKSC 48 (*Actavis v Eli Lilly*), the invention thus identified is no longer treated as synonymous with the scope of the patent monopoly and thus determinative of issues of patent infringement (cf *Kirin-Amgen* [70]). See further s 6.2.

[94] See *Biogen* (n 90) 10.

un-sequenced eukaryotic DNA in a prokaryotic host, and the inventive step was having and effecting this idea. That led to his Lordship's conception of the patentee's contribution to the art as showing that the HBV antigens could be made in a prokaryotic host specifically.[95]

The difficulties with this decision were exposed more than ten years later in *Generics (UK) Ltd v H Lundbeck A/S*.[96] That case involved a claim to an isolated enantiomer, and the questions of whether it was inventive and supported under section 14(5)(c). At first instance[97] Kitchin J followed the *Biogen* approach by conceiving the invention's inventive step as lying in the particular method adopted and described by the patentee for isolating the enantiomer, and its contribution to the art as showing that the enantiomer could be isolated by that method. The result was a finding that the patent was insufficient on the *Biogen* ground that its description did not cover every way of isolating the enantiomer, and would thus support a monopoly in excess of the patentee's contribution to the art.

In the Court of Appeal, however, Lord Hoffmann rejected this approach as incorrect. In his analysis, where the invention defined in the patent claims is a single product, as in *Lundbeck*, 'the technical contribution to the art is the *product* and not the process by which it was made, even if that process was the only inventive step'.[98] The result was to confirm, in the context of product patents at least, that the contribution an invention makes is not necessarily the same as its inventive step. The House of Lords in *Lundbeck* supported this on appeal, with Lord Walker explaining the difference between the inventive concept and the contribution to the art as follows:

> The expressions ['inventive concept' and 'technical contribution to the art'] are certainly connected, but I do not think it is helpful (either in considering Lord Hoffmann's opinion, or generally) to treat them as having precisely the same meaning. 'Inventive concept' is concerned with the *identification* of the core (or kernel, or essence) of the invention—the idea or principle, of more or less general application (see *Kirin-Amgen* [2005] RPC 169 paras 112–113) which entitles the inventor's achievement to be called inventive. The invention's technical contribution to the art is concerned with the *evaluation* of its inventive concept–how far forward has it carried the state of the art? The inventive concept and the technical contribution may command equal respect but that will not always be the case.[99]

It follows from this discussion that the nature of the contribution to the art that a subject matter makes and that must be technical for the subject matter to be an invention is unclear. The cases on the requirement for an invention discussed in section 1 treat it as equivalent to an invention's inventive step, making an invention any subject matter that is technically inventive, as stated in the *Lantana* case. However, this sits uncomfortably with the view of the courts in other areas. In addition, while Lord Walker in *Lundbeck* cast the difference as one of evaluation—the contribution a subject matter makes representing the *evaluation* of the inventive

[95] ibid 51.

[96] *Generics (UK) Ltd v H Lundbeck A/S* [2009] UKHL 12, [2009] RPC 13 (*Lundbeck* HL); also [2008] EWCA Civ 311, [2008] RPC 19 (*Lundbeck* CA).

[97] *Generics (UK) Ltd v H Lundbeck A/S* [2007] EWHC 1040 (Pat), [2007] RPC 32.

[98] See *Lundbeck* CA (n 96) [36].

[99] See *Lundbeck* HL (n 96) [30] (Lord Walker of Gestingthorpe).

concept that enables the invention to be called inventive[100]—the courts in that case also treated it more simply as the subject matter claimed by the patentee.

One context in which this difference might be thought to be significant is when deciding whether to disaggregate the features of a claim to identify a subject matter's contribution.[101] If the contribution to the art is the subject matter claimed, it might be said that there should be no such disaggregation. Consider for example a system for detecting fatigue in drivers:[102] that comprises (1) a camera, (2) a device transmitting data relating to fatigue indicators (eye movements and reaction speed) from the camera, and the steering wheel and brakes of a car, to a central processing unit (CPU), (3) an appropriately programmed CPU, and (4) a sound device; that depends on an algorithm that precisely encapsulates a causal link between the fatigue indicators and driver fatigue; and that enables the CPU to be programmed so that a warning sound is triggered by the device when extreme fatigue is indicated. Focusing on the subject matter as a whole, one might identify the contribution that the subject matter makes as a hardware system for generating data regarding driver fatigue and deploying that data to trigger automatically a warning sound. Thus described, its contribution would seem to be technical: it consists in the idea of automatically generating and transmitting data regarding drivers' eye movements and reaction speed, assessing the significance of the data for driver fatigue, and when a certain significance is indicated, triggering a warning sound for drivers to hear. The art thereby advanced might be described as the art of systems engineering or car manufacture. However, if the contribution were identified not from the subject matter as a whole, but rather from its inventive step, the analysis might be different. For example, in that case one might conceive the inventive step as lying in the discovery of the causal link between the relevant indictors and fatigue, and its expression by means of an algorithm.[103] If that is also the contribution, however, it is less likely to be regarded as technical, consistent with the description of mathematical methods as non-inventions in section 1(2) of the Patents Act.

This difference in approach was an issue in the *Lantana* case. There the hearing officer and trial judge focused on the features of the claimed subject matter and considered whether any single feature involved an inventive step outside the realm of section 1(2). On appeal counsel objected to that approach, saying that the contribution should have been identified from the claimed subject matter as a whole rather than from its constituent parts.[104] Adopting this approach, counsel said, the contribution would have been appropriately conceived as the provision of a better way of retrieving a document from a remote computer to a local computer.[105]

100 ibid.

101 However, in other areas of patent law, such as inventive step, the courts have treated the instruction to 'identify the inventive concept' as equivalent to the instruction to 'construe the claim' (see eg the *Windsurfing/Pozzoli* test of inventive step, discussed in s 5.1).

102 This example is taken from the Trinity Term 2011 BCL/MJur examination paper in the subject International Intellectual Property Rights.

103 This is consistent with Lord Hoffmann's remarks about the proper approach to identifying the inventive step of a subject matter in *Biogen* (n 90).

104 See *Lantana* (n 84) [30].

105 ibid.

This followed the view of past courts that 'the first task of the court' when deciding whether a subject matter is an invention 'is to construe the claim, as that is where the [alleged] invention is defined',[106] and undermined the finding of the hearing officer and trial judge that none of the features of the claim involved any inventive step.[107] The Court of Appeal rejected it, however.

Given the above, it can be said that the question of when if ever to disaggregate the claims in order to identify a subject matter's contribution to the art is a further issue of current uncertainty in UK law. In addition, even once the contribution has been identified, it remains necessary to decide its technicality. In so doing the UK courts have treated the categories of non-inventions contained in Article 52(2) and (3) as a representative sample of different 'non-technical' fields, and asked whether the contribution that a claimed subject matter makes lies in a different (non-excluded) field. In practice this has led to the refusal of protection for any subject matter that can itself be said to fall within one of the Article 52(2) and (3) categories, or to make no advance to knowledge in an art *not* represented by those categories. Examples of such subject matter have been held to include: a computer system for analyzing buy and sell securities options, held by the Court of Appeal in *Merrill Lynch Inc's Application*[108] to produce as its end result a method of doing business; a ROM device containing a program for calculating the square root of numbers, held by the Court of Appeal in *Gale's Application*[109] to be in essence a set of abstract instructions (in the form of a computer program) equivalent to a musical work; a computer system for providing and storing expert knowledge, held by the Patents Court in *Wang Laboratories Inc's Application*[110] not to make any advance beyond the mental method it performed; a computer system for identifying ships by a process of image comparison, held by the Patents Court in *Raytheon Co's Application*[111] to have as its end result a mental method; a computer system for processing digital images of crystals, held by the Court of Appeal in *Fujitsu Ltd's Application*[112] to be a mental method and thus not related to the technical arts; a networked interactive wagering system alleged (among other things) to reduce vibration, held by the Patents Court in *CFPH's Application*[113] to claim no advance beyond the art of business; an automated Internet-based lottery game, held by the Patents Court in *Shopalotto.com Ltd's Application*[114] to make no technical contribution to the art; and an automated method of acquiring documents, held by the Court of Appeal in *Aerotel* to make no contribution beyond the automation of an existing business method, which was not technical.

[106] *Gale's Application* [1991] RPC 305, 311 (Pat).

[107] The reason was that both the transmission of data across the Internet, and the remote and automatic selection of a file specified in an email and generation of an email to transmit a copy of the file back to the local computer, were part of the prior art.

[108] *Merrill Lynch Inc's Application* [1989] RPC 561 (CA).

[109] *Gale's Application* [1991] RPC 317 (CA) (*Gale's Application*).

[110] *Wang Laboratories Inc's Application* [1991] RPC 463 (Pat).

[111] *Raytheon Co's Application* [1993] RPC 427 (Pat).

[112] *Fujitsu Ltd's Application* [1997] RPC 608 (CA).

[113] *CFPH's Application* [2005] EWHC 1589 (Pat).

[114] *Shopalotto.com Ltd's Application* [2005] EWHC 2416 (Pat), [2006] RPC 7.

In *Gale's Application*, Nicholls LJ for the Court of Appeal described the effect of section 1(2) as being to confirm the pre-EPC axiom of UK patent law that patents may not be granted for ideas and discoveries, being rather confined to the industrially applicable products and processes that they support.[115] This is consistent with the *Hitachi* understanding of the Article 52(2) and (3) categories as limited to 'activities [that] typically represent purely abstract concepts devoid of any technical implications'.[116] As this suggests, no difference between the UK and EPO understandings of the categories themselves or of the meaning of 'technical' can be discerned from the cases. While the UK courts have not to date cited the definition of 'technical' supported by the Enlarged Board of Appeal in *Tomatoes*, their jurisprudence can be regarded as consistent with it.

4. Plant Varieties in Europe (Including the United Kingdom)

4.1 Introduction

As has been seen, European and UK patent legislation expressly excludes plant and animal varieties, and essentially biological processes for the production of plants or animals, from protectability by patent grant. According to the EPO, the reason for the exclusion of plant varieties specifically is the availability of alternative *sui generis* protection for such subject matter, in the form of plant variety rights (PVRs). Such protection, required internationally from the early 1960s by the UPOV Convention,[117] offered an alternative form of IP protection for plant breeders, with signatories to the Convention prohibited from awarding both patents and *sui generis* rights in respect of plant varieties.[118] So it is that European tribunals have come to interpret the plant varieties exclusion from patent protection as excluding all but only such subject matter as are eligible for protection by PVR,[119] and that patent law has become the main site for discussion of the nature of the subject matter protectable by the plant variety right regime. The effect in practice is a two-tier system of IP protection, similar to that created for expressive productions by copyright and related rights in its distinction between two types of subject matter that, while closely related in their properties, are the result of different types of human action, and thereby perceived to merit different types and levels of IP protection.[120]

Since the 1960s, the UPOV Convention has been amended, and its provisions reproduced in a European (EU) instrument. That instrument is the Community PVR Regulation,[121] which creates a system of unitary (EU) plant variety rights

[115] *Gale's Application* (n 109) 324. [116] See *Hitachi* (n 39) [4.5].

[117] International Convention for the Protection of New Varieties of Plants of 2 December 1961 (UPOV Convention).

[118] ibid art 2(1).

[119] See eg *Novartis II* (n 52) [3.6]–[3.7].

[120] See s 5.3.2.3.

[121] Council Regulation (EC) No 2100/94 of 27 July 1994 on Community plant variety rights [1994] OJ L 227/1 (CPVR Regulation).

'as the sole and exclusive form of Community industrial property rights for plant varieties'.[122] As with the unitary (EU) patent system, the EU plant variety system is without prejudice to the right of Member States to grant national property rights for plant varieties,[123] which the UK has done,[124] subject to a prohibition on the granting of a national PVR or patent for any variety in respect of which a Community PVR has been granted.[125]

4.2 The Nature of the Plant Variety

The category of subject matter for which a Community PVR may be granted is denoted by the term 'plant variety'. Under Article 5 of the CPVR Regulation, consistent with section 1 of the PV Act, 'plant variety' is defined to mean '[v]arieties of all botanical genera and species, including, inter alia, hybrids between genera or species',[126] where a 'variety' is

> a plant grouping within a single botanical taxon of the lowest known rank, which grouping, irrespective of whether the conditions for the grant of a plant variety right are fully met, can be:
>
> - defined by the expression of the characteristics that results from a given genotype or combination of genotypes,
> - distinguished from any other plant grouping by the expression of at least one of the said characteristics, and
> - considered as a unit with regard to its suitability for being propagated unchanged.[127]

This definition is an expanded version of the definition originally contained in the UPOV Convention, which defined the term 'variety' as applying to 'any cultivar, clone, line, stock or hybrid' that was 'capable of cultivation [and] sufficiently homogeneous, having regard to the particular features of its sexual reproduction or vegetative propagation', in addition to being 'stable in its essential characteristics', in the sense of remaining 'true to its description after repeated reproduction or propagation or, where the breeder has defined a particular cycle of reproduction or multiplication, at the end of each cycle'.[128] Central to this and the current European and UK definition above are the need for a multiplicity or grouping of plants that are: distinguishable from other groupings of plants by their expression of at least one genotype characteristic (distinct); largely the same in their essential properties (homogenous); and stable, in the sense of retaining those properties after

122 ibid art 1. 123 ibid art 3. 124 See Plant Varieties Act 1997 (UK) (PV Act).
125 CPVR Regulation art 92(1). 126 ibid art 5(1).
127 ibid art 5(2). See also art 5(3) and (4) (defining a plant grouping to consist 'of entire plants or parts of plants as far as such parts are capable of producing entire plants, both referred to hereinafter as "variety constituents" ', and clarifying that the expression of the characteristics referred to in art 5(2) first indent 'may be either invariable or variable between variety constituents of the same kind provided that also the level of variation results from the genotype or combination of genotypes').
128 UPOV Convention 1961 arts 2(2) and 6(1)(c) and (d).

each propagation cycle.[129] Applying this definition, the EPO has held that any subject matter comprising plants and plant propagating materials (such as seeds) that are not defined and distinguishable as a variety, as distinct for example from a species or individual form of plant, or that are defined with reference to their production or treatment by means of a process that can be applied to different varieties of plant, are not themselves plant varieties.[130] More recently, this reasoning has been reflected in the express provision of the Biotech Directive that any subject matter the technical feasibility of which 'is not confined to a particular plant or animal variety' is eligible for protection by patent grant,[131] being outside the category of subject matter eligible for protection as a plant or animal variety.

In sum, a plant variety within the meaning of European and UK law is any grouping of plants that are distinct, uniform, and stable in each of the senses above. In order to be protected by plant variety rights, they must also satisfy the separate statutory criteria of *clear* distinguishability within the meaning of Article 7 of the CPVR Regulation and section 4(2)(a) of the PV Act, *sufficient* uniformity within the meaning of Article 8 of the Regulation and section 4(2)(b) of the Act, and *sufficient* stability within the meaning of Article 9 of the Regulation and section 4(2)(c) of the Act, in addition to being novel within the meaning of Article 10 and section 4(2)(d).[132] In this sense, the plant variety properties of distinctness, uniformity, and stability are analogous to the property of inventiveness in UK patent law: in addition to needing to possess each property in order to be recognized as a variety and invention respectively, varieties and inventions must possess each property to a certain extent, in addition to satisfying other criteria, in order to be regarded as meriting the particular forms of protection conferred by the plant variety and patent regimes.[133]

5. Entitlement

5.1 Patents are for Inventors

Since inventions are ideas, they necessarily owe their existence to one or more natural persons, being the persons recognized at law to be presumptively entitled to the IP rights granted in respect of them. This is made clear in Article 60(1) of the EPC and section 7(1) of the Patents Act, which provide that only an inventor (or his successor in title) may be granted a patent, unless the invention was devised in the course of his employment. This provision is supplemented in UK law by section 7(3) of the Patents Act, which defines the inventor as 'the actual deviser of the invention'. Since only a natural person can 'actually devise' something, section

129 See T49/83 *Propagating Material/Ciba Geigy* [1984] OJ EPO 112 (*Ciba Geigy*); T320/87 *Lubrizol/Hybrid Plants* [1990] OJ EPO 71.

130 See *Ciba Geigy* (n 129) [4].

131 Biotech Directive art 4(2).

132 A1/2002–A3/2002 *Pieters Joseph en Luc BVBA v Community Plant Variety Office* (CPVO Board of Appeal, 1 April 2003).

133 ibid; see also ch 4.

7(3) makes it clear that an inventor is a natural person. This explains also Article 81 of the EPC, following Article 4*ter* of the Paris Convention,[134] which recognizes an attribution or paternity right for inventors by requiring that the inventor of an invention for which a European patent is claimed be designated in the European patent application as such.

To devise an invention in the form of 'a practical idea which the patentee has had for a new product or process'[135] is to conceive it, in the sense of having the idea, regardless of whether it is ever realized by creating the relevant product or implementing the relevant process. This is made clear in Article 69(1) of the EPC, which defines the scope of the patent monopoly conferred by a European patent as 'determined by the claims', interpreted in the light of the description and drawings. The claims, as can be seen additionally from Article 84 and section 14, 'define the matter for which protection is sought' and granted. This confirms the implication of Article 69 and section 125, that in patent law inventions are identified from a textual definition of a certain subject matter, which definition is in turn the reference point for defining the monopoly granted by the state in consideration for the disclosure of the invention by the patentee.

Therefore, only a person who independently thinks of an invention, as distinct from working or introducing an invention to the public, will be entitled to a patent for it. As seen in Chapter 2, this is contrary to the position in England before and after the Statute of Monopolies, when being the first to introduce an invention locally, by whatever means, was the act rewarded by a patent monopoly. In addition, Article 60(2) of the EPC further admits the theoretical possibility of two people independently devising the same invention and therefore being entitled to a patent for it by establishing the 'first to file' principle. According to that provision:

> If two or more persons have made an invention independently of each other, the right to a European patent therefor shall belong to the person whose European patent application has the earliest date of filing, provided that this first application has been published.

Since the jurisdiction to decide issues of entitlement under the EPC rests exclusively with the domestic courts of Contracting States (rather than with the EPO itself[136]), a fuller understanding of the concept of inventor-ship and its implications for conceptions of the invention must be sought from domestic judicial authorities. In the UK, the key authority remains the House of Lords decision in *Yeda Research and Development Co Ltd v Rhone-Poulenc Rorer International Holdings Inc.*[137] According to Lord Hoffmann in that case, the meaning of the first to file principle is not that only one of the two or more persons who independently devise an invention is properly regarded as its inventor and entitled to a patent for it. Rather, he said,

[134] Paris Convention for the Protection of Industrial Property (adopted 20 March 1883, last revised 14 July 1967) 828 UNTS 305, as amended.

[135] See *Kirin-Amgen* (n 93) [33].

[136] See the EPC's Protocol on Jurisdiction and the Recognition of Decisions in respect of the Right to the grant of a European patent, made an integral part of the EPC by art 164(1).

[137] *Yeda Research and Development Co Ltd v Rhone-Poulenc Rorer International Holdings Inc* [2007] UKHL 43, [2008] RPC 1 (*Yeda Research*).

the provision clarifies the legal position that devising an invention is not the only criterion for obtaining a patent: a person must also file an application with the relevant patent office, including a definition of the invention for which protection is sought that is clear and concise, and a description of that invention sufficient to enable the skilled addressee to work it,[138] and demonstrate that the invention she has devised satisfies the patentability requirements of novelty, inventive step, and susceptibility of industrial application. Further, while the fact of an invention having been independently devised by two or more people will ordinarily have no bearing on its industrial applicability,[139] it may affect the invention's novelty and inventive step where one of the inventors has made the invention available to the public previously, or taken the first step to doing so by filing an application for a patent for it in the UK.[140] In that case, the invention as devised by all later inventors will lack the novelty required for patentability, depriving its inventors of the right to a patent. According to Lord Hoffmann,[141] however, this does not mean that those inventors are not entitled to a patent, only that their patent will be invalid for lack of novelty. Hence his characterization of the first to file principle as one of validity rather than of entitlement.

As is clear from the earlier discussion, this understanding of Lord Hoffmann creates immediate difficulties for the UK conception of the invention as technically inventive. The reason is its premise that a person who contributes to the inventive concept of an invention will by reason of that contribution be an inventor. However, the premise of the UK conception of the invention is that not all subject matter with an inventive concept are inventions: the concept must be such as to distinguish the subject matter from the prior art so that the subject matter can be said to contribute to that art. Given the impossibility of having an inventor without an invention, this is analytically problematic.

In *Yeda Research*, the House of Lords also clarified the identity of 'the actual deviser of the invention' within the meaning of section 7(3) as being 'the natural person who "came up with the inventive concept" ' of the invention, rather than merely contributing to the claimed invention (ie the subject matter defined in the claims).[142] Since an invention cannot exist without an inventor, it follows from this statement that an invention cannot exist without an inventive concept, raising the question of what *is* an inventive concept, and how does the need for one inform legal conceptions of the invention itself?

The inventive concept—already considered in section 3—is among the most important but elusive concepts of UK patent law,[143] and arises in at least five

[138] EPC arts 83 and 84.

[139] Cf purpose-limited subject matter.

[140] See Patents Act s 2(3).

[141] See *Yeda Research* (n 137) [28].

[142] Such subject matter 'may include non-patentable integers derived from prior art': ibid [20].

[143] In *Schütz (UK) Ltd v Werit UK Ltd* [2013] UKSC 16 (*Schütz*) [69], counsel argued unsuccessfully before the Supreme Court that the inventive concept of a patent is often a controversial issue, and that there could therefore be problems if it was treated as relevant in determining whether an alleged infringer 'makes' the patented article. Lord Neuberger expressed himself to be 'unconvinced by that contention. In almost all patents, the claimed inventive concept is clearly identified or identifiable from the patent, and, if it is unclear or disputed, it will often be an issue in the proceedings anyway.'

contexts. The first is entitlement itself. The second is the requirement of section 14(5)(d) that the claim or claims of a patent 'relate to one invention or to a group of inventions that are so linked as to form a single inventive concept' (following Article 82 of the EPC). The third is the so-called *Windsurfing/Pozzoli* test[144] for assessing inventive step under section 3, which requires that one: (a) identify the 'inventive concept' of the invention—or, if there is disagreement over what it is, construe the claim in which the invention is defined; (b) identify differences between the prior art and the inventive concept (or claim); and (c) decide whether, without knowledge of the invention devised, the differences thus identified constitute steps that would have been obvious to the notional skilled addressee. The fourth is the test for deciding whether new matter has been added to patent claims by amendment in contravention of section 76 (following Article 123 of the EPC), which depends on whether the added matter discloses an inventive concept not disclosed in the claims previously.[145] Finally, the fifth is the test for 'making' a product under section 60(1)(a) of the Patents Act, which depends in part on the degree if any to which the product manufactured reflects the invention's inventive concept.[146]

According to the jurisprudence regarding these rules and requirements, and consistent also with the statement of Lord Walker from *Lundbeck* above, the inventive concept is the 'core (or kernel, or essence) of an invention—the idea or principle, of more or less general application (see *Kirin-Amgen* ...) that entitles the inventor's achievement to be called inventive', and is the basis for assessing 'how far forward' the invention has carried the prior art.[147]

An invention must have at least one inventive concept, and may have more than one. In the other direction, and as recognized explicitly by the UK courts, including by the House of Lords in *Biogen*, a single inventive concept may be shared by two or more inventions. This is apparent from Article 82 of the EPC, following rule 13.1 of the PCT Regulations, which requires that each application for a patent be confined 'to one invention only or to a group of inventions so linked as to form a single general concept'. Under section 14(5)(d) of the Patents Act, the same provision is made, with the word 'general' replaced by 'inventive'. It is this rule that permits the grant of a patent for independently claimed inventions that share an inventive concept, such as a product, a process adapted for the manufacture of that product, and a use of the product. The result is again to confirm that, while an invention must contain an inventive concept, it is not coextensive with that concept.

In conclusion, the UK law governing entitlement to a patent makes it clear that inventions are devised by natural persons coming up with an inventive concept in the sense of a practical idea, of more or less general application, for the production of a new product or implementation of a new process by purposive action on the material world. This is consistent with the EPC view of inventions as 'technical teachings' and with the *Tomatoes* definition of 'technical'. The difference is that in

[144] From *Windsurfing International Inc v Tabur Marine (Great Britain) Ltd* [1985] RPC 59 (CA) and *Pozzoli v BDMO* [2007] EWCA Civ 588, [2007] FSR 37.

[145] *Southco Inc v Dzus Fastener Europe Ltd* [1992] RPC 299 (CA).

[146] See *Schütz* (n 143) [67].

[147] See *Lundbeck* HL (n 96) [30] (citing *Kirin-Amgen* (n 93) [33]).

the view of the EPO, and as stated previously, a subject matter may be an invention without being new or inventive: novelty and non-obviousness therefore not being among the invention's essential properties. This is consistent with the view of Lord Hoffmann in *Yeda Research* that a person who independently devises an invention previously available to the public will still be an inventor under patent law, but inconsistent with the conception of inventions supported by the Court of Appeal as technically inventive subject matter.

5.2 Plant Variety Rights are also for Inventors (Referred to as 'Breeders')

Once again, the nature of the subject matter protectable by PVR accounts for the persons presumptively entitled to PVR protection. They are the one or more persons who bred or discovered and developed the variety for which protection is sought, referred to collectively as the 'breeders' of the variety, or their successors in title.[148] The only exception to this is where the variety was bred or discovered and developed in the course of employment, in which case the person entitled to UK PVR protection will be the breeders' employer, subject to contract,[149] and the person entitled to Community PVR protection will be those designated as such by the national law applicable to the employment relationship in the context of which the variety was bred or discovered and developed.[150]

Unlike the inventors of an invention, the breeders of a plant variety have no right to be recognized as such,[151] and need not be natural persons: in EU and UK law, legal persons are also accepted to be capable of breeding, or discovering and developing, a plant variety, and entitled to PVR protection on that basis. While the concept of corporate breeding or discovery and development is of course a fiction, its selective deployment in IP can be seen as an indication of different levels of personal investment in and responsibility for the existence of different IP subject matter, in the law's view at least, particularly when viewed alongside the withholding of the rights of attribution conferred on inventors and other creators by IP law. Once again then, the question arises as to what exactly is involved in breeding or discovering and developing a plant variety, and how it differs from the act of invention as conceived in patent law.

One view to emerge clearly from the treatment of plant and animal varieties in patent law is that the act of breeding or discovering and developing a plant variety does not require an act of invention as defined previously, whether in the stricter senses of US or UK law, or the more relaxed sense of European law. This was confirmed by the Board of Appeal of the Community Plant Variety Office in *Sakata Seed Co v SVS Holland BV*,[152] which described the concept of breeding as

[148] CPVR Regulation art 11(1) and (2); PV Act s 4(3). [149] PV Act s 4(4).

[150] CPVR Regulation art 11(4).

[151] While the identity of the breeder must be disclosed in the application for Community or UK PVR protection, this is an evidentiary rather than a substantive requirement aimed at helping the relevant authority to establish entitlement to the plant variety right protection.

[152] A17/2002 *Sakata Seed Co v SVS Holland BV* (CPVO Board of Appeal, 3 April 2003) (*Sakata*).

'not necessarily imply[ing] inventing something totally new'.[153] In the Community Plant Variety Office's decision, any person who comes into the lawful possession of seed samples, and then uses those samples to plant, select, and grow plants will be a 'breeder' of any variety that results, and thus entitled to Community PVR protection in respect of it.[154] In the Office's subsequent decision in *Keith E Kirsten (Pty) Ltd v Community Plant Variety Office*,[155] supported by the Board of Appeal on appeal,[156] the Office further considered the notion of 'discovery' within the meaning of EU plant variety law, and decided that it must include 'at least a minimum of activity of the person claiming to be the discoverer', with the result that a person who is merely shown a variety by another, is not properly regarded as having 'discovered' that variety so as to be potentially entitled to PVR protection for it.[157] In the Board of Appeal's decision,

> 'discover' means that somebody comes across a variety either by search or by chance, being conscious of the fact that it is a new variety, which was unknown to him before and which in his opinion is unknown to other persons as well. In this context, the additional notion that the new variety may have commercial potential is not relevant. Thus, it is possible that one and the same variety is discovered by two or more persons independently, on different moments on the same spot, or on different spots.[158]

In reaching its decision, the Board of Appeal in *Keith E Kirsten* referred to a position paper adopted by the Council of the International Union for the Protection of new Varieties of Plants (UPOV) in 2002 regarding the concept of the 'breeder' under the UPOV Convention.[159] That paper recounted the history of the entitlement provisions of the UPOV Convention, noting the preference for a broad interpretation of the concept of 'breeding' (which it treated as better denoted by the term 'improving'[160]) plant varieties, and the rejection of proposals to require 'creative selection work', or even 'effective work', as a precondition of PVR protection.[161] It also quoted approvingly from an *aide-mémoire* that had been attached to the original version of the UPOV Convention in 1961 in which all but one of certain 'classic principles of plant breeding'[162] had been accepted as breeding methodologies sufficient to support a claim to plant variety right, namely,

> (a) bulk or pedigree selection within an existing population; (b) the discovery of a natural mutation; (c) the inducing of an artificial mutation using a specific method; (d) chance cross-pollination; (e) deliberate cross-pollination; (f) any combination of the above methods.[163]

The only classic principle not included among the methods recognized by the drafters of the UPOV Convention as capable of earning PVR protection was the

[153] ibid 9. [154] ibid.

[155] A4/2003 *Re Keith E Kirsten (Pty) Ltd* (CPVO, 6 November 2003) (*Keith E Kirsten* CPVO).

[156] A1/2004 *Keith E Kirsten (Pty) Ltd v Community Plant Variety Office* (CPVO Board of Appeal, 16 December 2004) (*Keith E Kirsten* BA).

[157] See *Keith E Kirsten* CPVO (n 155) [64]. [158] See *Keith E Kirsten* BA (n 156) 6.

[159] UPOV Council (Nineteenth Extraordinary Session, Geneva, April 19, 2002), *The Notion of Breeder and Common Knowledge* Doc C(extr)/19/2 Rev (9 August 2002).

[160] ibid para 8. [161] ibid paras 9 and 11. [162] ibid para 9. [163] ibid para 5.

'introduction' of a plant, involving 'the simple multiplication and testing of an existing variety in a different environment',[164] on the basis that the material introduced by such a method would 'not be distinct from the existing known variety'.[165] The position reached in the paper was that the aim of the UPOV Convention remained as it had been previously, namely,

> to open up the system of protection to all varieties, whatever their method of breeding (thereby including the varieties that are 'discoveries'), and whatever the effort expended by the breeder to create the variety.[166]

In conclusion, a breeder within the meaning of PVR law is a person who either (a) works consciously on plant material to derive a variety, and who succeeds in that regard, or (b) 'comes across a variety either by search or by chance, being conscious of the fact that it is a new variety, which was unknown to him before and which in his opinion is unknown to other persons as well', and then plants, selects, and grows on the variety that he has come across so as to be said to have developed (as well as discovered) it.[167] Central to each method is the conception by a person of an idea for acting upon the world to produce a subject matter that satisfies the definition of 'variety' above,[168] namely, a multiplicity of grouping of plants that are distinct, homogeneous, and stable. The result is a conception of the breeder (and plant variety) that is substantially indistinct from the conception of the inventor (and invention) seen to have been supported by European law in sections 2 and 5.1 above, namely, a person who harnesses the forces of nature by acting upon the material world to produce a causal, perceivable, and repeatable result. Indeed, there is little difference between the act of discovering and developing a plant variety and the act of isolating a human gene or other product from its natural environment, confirming that a breeder and plant variety within the meaning of European PVR jurisprudence is, despite the suggestion of European patent and PVR authorities to the contrary,[169] an inventor and invention within the meaning of European patent law. The result can be seen to represent a further challenge to the European interpretation of the varieties exclusion from patentability and conception of the invention.

6. Conclusions

6.1 Introduction

The suggestion in Chapter 3 was that IP subject matter can be conceived as types of artifacts having certain properties and arranged in categories that express and reflect those properties. Conceiving IP subject matter in this way, it was said, is of analytic use in understanding the UK and European law that exists, in addition to

164 ibid para 9. 165 ibid. 166 ibid para 13.
167 See *Keith E Kirsten* BA (n 156) 9. 168 See s 4.2.
169 See eg *Novartis II* (ns 53 and 54); *Sakata* (n 152) 9.

suggesting certain questions on which to focus any study of the subject matter protectable by each IP regime. Those questions can be formulated as follows:

(a) What are the categories of subject matter protected by the regime, and what are those subject matters' essential properties?
(b) How is each subject matter individuated within the regime?
(c) What is the relationship between each subject matter and its tokens?
(d) How is the existence of each subject matter and its tokens known?

It remains to answer these questions for the patent and PVR regimes.

6.2 Inventions as Artifact Types Having Certain Properties and Arranged in Categories that Express and Reflect those Properties

(a) What are the categories of subject matter protected by the regime, and what are those subject matters' essential properties?

The main category of patentable subject matter is the category of inventions. In Europe and the UK, this category is understood to contain every (a) idea of a person (b) for an individual product or process (c) that is technical (Europe) or technically inventive (UK), in the sense of being the causal, perceivable, and repeatable result of some purposive human (Europe) and inventive (UK) action on the material world to harness the forces of nature. Thus defined, the essential properties of inventions are their abstract nature (as ideas), and their capacity to support repeated instantiation in the real or material world as a technical (Europe) or technically inventive (UK) product or process. In addition, a 'product' is understood to be a physical or concrete object that exists independent of the method by which it is made,[170] and a 'process' is understood to be a series of steps resulting in a particular end. Either can also be limited in its identity by the particular use or end result intended for it, in which case it will be a purpose-limited product or process, as appropriate.

On the basis of this understanding, the patentable invention can be said to conform closely to the paradigmatic conception of IP subject matter as an artifact considered in Chapter 3. The reason is its nature as the idea for a technical object the existence of which depends on the productive actions and intentions of one or more human beings, being the inventors of the object in question. In addition to being intangible in nature, inventions may also be described as intellectual creations in at least one of the two senses considered in Chapter 3. As conceived under European law—namely, as instructions methodically to utilize controllable natural forces to achieve a causal, perceivable, and repeatable result—inventions may be said to satisfy the more expansive view of the human acts justifying the recognition of property rights supported by the UK Court of Appeal in *Yearworth v North Bristol NHS Trust*.[171] Less clear is the position regarding inventions as conceived under UK law.

[170] See *Kirin-Amgen* (n 93) [88].
[171] *Yearworth v North Bristol NHS Trust* [2009] EWCA Civ 37, [2010] QB 1 (*Yearworth*).

By focusing on the technical nature of a subject matter's contribution to the art specifically, and treating that contribution, in cases not involving single products at least, as a subject matter's inventive concept or step, the UK courts could be said to adopt an approach that resembles more closely the approach adopted by courts in the United States than that adopted by the EPO. According to the US approach, for a subject matter to be an invention it must involve more than making a pre-existing object available in a new and useful form, or presenting previously available information or some abstract idea with the instruction to 'apply it'.[172] Specifically, it must involve an inventive concept that is sufficiently transformative to be regarded as contributing something new and different from the pre-existing object, information, or idea. Only then will it be regarded as a patent eligible composition of matter or method within the meaning of US law. As above, this is similar to the requirement of the UK courts that a subject matter involve an inventive step or concept that is technical in the European sense of not being abstract and of involving a purposive human action on the material world to produce a causal, perceivable, and repeatable result. On this basis, the UK approach might be said to align more closely to the *Doodeward v Spence*[173] view of what an act of human creation entails or of what types of human acts trigger property than to the *Yearworth* view, subject to the express legislative provisions declaring human genes and other products isolated from their natural environment to be inherently patentable.

Finally, and as seen in Chapter 3, legal conceptions of the invention as ideas that must be described to be protected, and the IP rights in which are infringed by doing any of a number of acts in relation to an individual product or process exemplifying them, reflect their view as universals in the conceptualist philosophical sense, namely, ideas that can be repeatedly applied to or expressed by means of concrete particulars. By referring to inventions as products and processes rather than as ideas, the law underlines the truth of Richard Wollheim's remark, seen in Chapter 3, that 'for much of the time we think and talk of the type as though it were itself a kind of token'.[174]

(b) How is each subject matter individuated within the regime?

Every subject matter for which a patent is sought and granted must be capable of being distinguished *qua* invention from the patent document. One explanation for this requirement is the rule of law consideration that restrictions on individual freedoms such as those that patents impose must be defined sufficiently clearly for the public to be able to organize their lives without infringing others' rights. In addition, and more specific to patent law, there is the contractual nature of patent grants, considered in Chapter 2, as consideration for the disclosure of a new and otherwise meritorious invention. In combination, these considerations explain the need for an inventor to apply for a patent and provide as part of the application a clear and concise textual definition and description of the subject matter for which

[172] *Ariosa Diagnostics, Inc v Sequenom, Inc* 788 F3d 1371 (Fed Cir 2015) 1377 (citing *Mayo* (n 60) 1294).

[173] *Doodeward v Spence* [1908] HCA 45, (1908) 6 CLR 406.

[174] R Wollheim, *Art and Its Objects* (Harper and Row 1968) 76.

protection is sought[175] sufficient to enable the invention 'to be performed by a person skilled in the art'.[176]

It is possible to read in these statutory provisions two different notions and requirements for evidence of an invention's existence. The first—reflected in the requirement for its clear and concise definition—is metaphysical individuation, according to which an object is individuated by 'whatever it is that makes it the single object that it is'.[177] The second—reflected in the requirement for a disclosure sufficient to enable a person skilled in the art to perform it—is epistemic individuation, according to which an object is individuated by the ability of a certain intelligent individual to single it out 'as a distinct object of perception'.[178]

Returning then to the question 'how is each subject matter individuated?', the answer is metaphysically—by asking what idea for a technical or technically inventive product or process is described in the patent document; and epistemologically—by asking what does the skilled addressee understand the idea thus described as a distinct object of perception to be?[179] Within patent law, the second of these conceptions and methods of individuation can be said to have especial importance. This is apparent in those areas concerned with establishing the identity of a subject matter *qua* invention—novelty and infringement—which make it clear that such identity depends on the perception of the skilled addressee.

Under European and UK law, an invention is 'new' if and only if it has not previously been made available to the public.[180] The fact that it existed previously in the public realm—inherently, by virtue of its prior existence—does not as such destroy its novelty. What matters is whether there previously existed a single source of information sufficient to enable the idea to be performed, in the sense of enabling instantiation of the product or process to which it relates by a hypothetical skilled addressee armed with common general knowledge and some capacity for experimentation but no inventiveness.[181] That also is the test for whether two patent applications are for the 'same' invention under the law of priority: namely, whether the hypothetical skilled addressee, starting with the description of the idea in the earlier patent, would be able to perform the invention defined in the claims of the later patent. The implication—made explicit by Lord Hoffmann in *Merrell Dow*—is that for an invention to lack novelty within the meaning of patent law, the public must previously have had knowledge of the invention under a description sufficient to work it.[182] This is why the prior availability to the public of a product, for example, will not be regarded as having made the product available so as to deprive it of novelty unless the information conveyed by its existence was sufficient to enable the product to be made (instantiated).[183]

[175] EPC art 84; Patents Act 1977 s 14(5)(a) to (c); cf Biotech Directive art 13.

[176] EPC art 83; Patents Act 1977 s 14(3).

[177] E J Lowe, 'Individuation' in ML Loux and DW Zimmerman (eds), *The Oxford Handbook of Metaphysics* (OUP 2005) 75.

[178] ibid. [179] ibid. [180] EPC art 54(1); Patents Act 1977 s 2(1).

[181] *Synthon v SmithKline Beecham* [2005] UKHL 59, [2006] RPC 10.

[182] See *Merrell Dow* (n 46) [41].

[183] See G1/92 *Availability to the Public* [1993] EPOR 241.

A further test of the law's understanding of how inventions are identified arises from the area of patent infringement. For a patent to be infringed, a third party must, without the permission of the patentee, do one of the acts reserved to the patentee with respect to the patented invention.[184] In practice, determining this involves two questions. The first is whether the subject matter to which the allegedly infringing act relates is the same as the patented invention, thus bringing it within the scope of the patent monopoly. And the second is whether, if it is, the allegedly infringing act is among the acts reserved exclusively to the patentee. From this it is possible to formulate an identity criterion for individual inventions that enables the determination of whether a certain subject matter X is the same as another subject matter Y such that making or using Y will infringe the patent for X. When deciding the first of these questions, courts necessarily begin with the textual definition of X in the patent claims, and proceed to interpret it with a view to deciding two things: first, the subject matter that it defines; and second, whether Y is the same. To this end, the claims must be interpreted having regard to the description and any drawings of the invention in the patent document, and with a view to balancing the interests of third parties and the patentee.[185] In the UK, the courts' approach since *Kirin-Amgen* has been to interpret the claims purposively, and in particular to ask what the hypothetical skilled addressee—reading the claims in their context, including as a demarcation of a patented invention and thus patent monopoly—would understand the claimant to have intended by his or her choice of language to mean. In *Actavis v Eli Lilly*, the Supreme Court overruled this approach by requiring that the previously single issue of material identity, adopted also in design law (as seen in Chapter 7), be treated as two separate issues of strict identity (determined by purposive construction of the claims) and equivalence (determined by analysis of the facts and expert evidence). As a result, claim construction is no longer determinative of patent scope and (thus) patent infringement, as it was under *Kirin-Amgen*. Nonetheless, since the Supreme Court in *Actavis v Eli Lilly* held that equivalence must also be assessed through the eyes of the skilled addressee, the result remains a method of answering the identity question 'is the third party's subject matter materially the same as [ie identical and equivalent to] the patented invention?' in a way that reflects the earlier understanding of what individuates a subject matter *qua* invention epistemologically.

(c) What is the relationship between each subject matter and its tokens?

Each patented idea or invention is instantiated in the individual products or processes to which it relates, and in the definition of it contained in the patent claims. Clearly, none of these tokens reproduce the invention as such, but rather represent it. While the products by which an invention may be instantiated are physical objects, the processes are occurrences, and the definition is a materially recorded literary work. Thus, even the tokens of a single invention can be essentially, ontologically, different.

184 See UPC Agreement arts 25 and 26; Patents Act s 60.
185 EPC art 69(1); Protocol on the Interpretation of Article 69 EPC art 1.

(d) How is the existence of each subject matter and of its tokens known?

In patent law, the existence of a patented invention is known by reason of and reference to its textual definition and description in the patent document itself, in accordance with and fulfilment of Articles 83 and 84 of the EPC and section 14 of the Patents Act,[186] while the existence of an invention in general may be known by means of any source of information sufficient to establish it. The existence of one or more of an invention's (other) tokens is also known in the manner above, namely, from the existence of a product or process that the skilled addressee would understand to fall within the scope of the invention—including (if the invention is patented), within the scope of the definition of the invention contained in the patent claims.

6.3 Plant Varieties as Artifact Types Having Certain Properties and Arranged in Categories that Express and Reflect those Properties

(a) What are the categories of subject matter protected by the regime, and what are those subject matters' essential properties?

The category of subject matter protectable by plant variety right is that containing plant varieties. In Europe and the UK, this category is understood to contain every plant group that is (a) distinguishable from other plant groups by its expression of at least one genotype characteristic (distinct), (b) largely the same in its essential properties (homogenous), and (c) stable, in the sense of retaining those properties after each propagation cycle. Thus defined, the essential properties of the plant variety are the same as those of the invention within the meaning of European patent law, namely, its abstract nature (as an idea for a technical product), and its capacity to support repeated instantiation in the material world (by derivation of the product); albeit the product in the case of a variety being plant material that expresses the characteristics defining of a (distinct, homogeneous, and stable) plant grouping specifically. On the basis of this understanding, the protectable plant variety conforms closely to the paradigmatic conception of IP subject matter as an artifact considered in Chapter 3, and also satisfies the *Yearworth* view of the human acts triggering the recognition of property rights, consistent with its nature as an invention within the meaning of European patent law. As ideas that must be both described[187] and instantiated[188] to be protected, and the IP rights in which are

[186] An exception exists for inventions involving the use of or concerning 'biological material which is not available to the public and which cannot be described in a patent application in such a manner as to enable the invention to be reproduced by a person skilled in the art', which material must instead be deposited in accordance with Biotech Directive art 13.

[187] CPVR Regulation art 50(1)(f) (requiring the inclusion of 'a technical description of the variety' in applications for plant variety rights).

[188] CPVR Regulation art 55(4) (requiring the provision of material expressing the characteristics of the variety for 'technical examination' for compliance with the secondary criteria of distinctiveness, uniformity, and sufficiency by the relevant PVR-granting authorities).

infringed by the unauthorized production, use, or offering of material instantiating them, plant varieties are also readily conceived as universals in the conceptualist philosophical sense, consistent once again with their nature as inventions.

(b) How is each subject matter individuated within the regime?

Every subject matter for which a PVR is sought and granted must be capable of being distinguished, on the basis of at least one of the genotype characteristics that it is described in the PVR application or register to express, from the varieties commonly known to exist on the date of application for protection. As in patent law, describing the characteristics of the variety is the initial responsibility of the applicant, who must include in her request for PVR protection: (a) the Latin and common names of the genus, species, or sub-species to which the variety belongs; (b) the characteristics of the variety that, in the applicant's opinion, differentiate it from other varieties, with a list of such other varieties if appropriate; (c) the details of any material that must be used repeatedly to produce the variety, and of any characteristics of the variety that have been genetically modified; and (d) the region and country in which the variety was bred or discovered and developed.[189] In PVR law, however, it is the examining authorities themselves who are ultimately responsible for drafting the official description of a protected variety, and who retain thereafter discretion to adapt that description (after consulting the rights holder) as required to render it 'comparable with the descriptions of other varieties of the taxon concerned'.[190] Thus, the information initially provided by the applicant serves only to inform the authorities' examination of her application, including whether it discloses a subject matter protectable by PVR, and if it does, whether that subject matter fulfils the secondary DUS (distinctness, uniformity, and stability) criteria.[191]

When a PVR is granted, the official description of the variety is entered into a public register,[192] where it performs a similar public notice and definitional role to that performed by the published definition of the patented invention in patent law. Indeed, the Bundesgerichtshof has held that the official description of a plant variety is equivalent to the definition of an invention contained in the patent claims, and supported an approach to infringement similar to that described for patents above.[193] One possible difference is that in the context of plant varieties, the scope of the monopoly conferred by the PVR extends not only to subject matter that is materially the same as the protected variety—including (by express statutory

[189] Commission Regulation (EC) No 1239/95 of 31 May 1995 establishing implementing rules for the application of Council Regulation (EC) No 2100/94 as regards proceedings before the Community Plant Variety Office art 19(2).

[190] PVR Regulation art 87(2)(b) and (4). On the scope of the Community Plant Variety Office's discretion under art 87(4) see eg A7/2007-RENV *Schrader v Community Plant Variety Office* (CPVO Board of Appeal, 2 September 2016) (*Schrader*).

[191] For an example of a case in which it was held that a subject matter had not been sufficiently substantiated as a variety see A6/2014 *The Regents of the University of California (UCR) v Community Plant Variety Office* (CPVO Board of Appeal, 29 April 2016).

[192] PVR Regulation art 87(2)(b).

[193] Case X ZR 14/07 *Lemon Symphony* (23 April 2009) (Bundesgerichtshof).

provision) constituents of the protected variety, material harvested from the protected variety, and varieties that are essentially derived from the protected variety or indistinct from it, or the production of which requires the repeated use of it[194]–but also to any subject matter that falls within the variety's 'tolerance range'. This adjustment to the scope of protection conferred by the PVR is in reflection of the living nature of varieties, and the dependence of official descriptions of their defining characteristics on a range of environmental, technological, and legal factors (such as soil, use of fertilizers, temperature and light conditions, and plant variety examination guidelines) the changing nature of which will often lead a given variety to manifest or be described as manifesting different characteristics at different times. It is in recognition of this that the Community Plant Variety Office has decided that 'every description of a variety has a tolerance range which must be taken into account when assessing [the variety's] stability';[195] and so too, the Bundesgerichtshof has held, the same 'tolerance range' must be factored in to judicial assessments of whether a certain subject matter falls within the scope of the PVR owner's monopoly.

From this discussion the following observations can be made regarding the manner in which plant varieties are individuated with the plant variety right regime. The first is that the same reliance is not placed on the perspective of experts when deciding whether a given subject matter is an individual variety as when deciding whether a subject matter is an individual invention in the patent field. As with inventions, the individuation of plant varieties is the initial responsibility of the specialist (technical) office charged with assessing the application for PVR protection, and thereafter the responsibility of a (specialist or generalist) tribunal acting with the assistance of expert evidence as required. Unlike in patent law, however, there is no requirement that the official description of a protected variety be interpreted from (and filtered through) the perspective of a notional skilled addressee, notwithstanding the subject matter's complexity, and the specialized nature of the audience to whom varieties in general are directed. The result may be a prioritizing of the view of plant varieties as needing to be capable of individuation in the metaphysical sense of being whatever it is that makes them the single varieties that they are over the view of them as needing to be capable of being singled out *qua* variety as distinct objects of perception by a certain intelligent individual. Having said that, since an essential feature of legal systems is their claim to authority, and the process of individuating the subject matter protectable by PVR falls to the 'intelligent individuals' who represent those systems, individuation in the epistemic sense is also clearly of central importance in this area. Indeed, the main difference between the methods deployed in the plant variety and patent systems may simply be the closer correspondence between the metaphysical and epistemic senses of individuation that the former supports by reason of the absence of any 'hypothetical intelligent person' construct by means of which normative considerations can be brought to

194 PVR Regulation art 13.

195 *Schrader* (n 190) [58].

bear on the questions of whether a subject matter is a single variety and if it is, what makes it the single variety that it is.

(c) What is the relationship between each subject matter and its tokens?

Each plant variety is instantiated in material that expresses the genotype characteristics of the variety, and in the official description of those characteristics contained in the PVR register, allowing for a certain tolerance range. As with the tokens of inventions, the tokens of plant varieties do not reproduce the subject matter protected by PVR as such, but rather represent it. While the products by which a variety may be instantiated are physical objects, the official description is a materially recorded expressive object in the form of a literary work, making the tokens of varieties essentially different as for the tokens of inventions above.

(d) How is the existence of each subject matter and its tokens known?

In the plant variety right regime, the existence of a protected variety is known to the authorities by the existence of a token in the form of a sample of the variety, and to the public by its textual description in the register, while the existence of a variety in general may be known by means of any source of information sufficient to establish it. The existence of one or more of a variety's (other) tokens is also known in the manner above, namely, from the existence of a product that the relevant authorities understand to fall within the scope of the variety—including (if the variety is protected), within the scope of the official description of the variety contained in the register.

5

The Authorial Work

1. Copyright Protects Authorial Works and Related Rights Protect Other Expressive Productions

1.1 Copyright Protects Authorial Works

When considering the subject matter protected by copyright under European and UK law today, it is appropriate to begin at the international level, with Article 1 of the Berne Convention on the Protection of Literary and Artistic Property.[1] That Article declares the 183 countries to which the Berne Convention applies,[2] including all EU Member States, to 'constitute a Union for the protection of the rights of authors in their literary and artistic works'. The expression 'literary and artistic works' is then defined expansively in Article 2(1) of the Convention to include '[e]very production in the literary, science and artistic domain, whatever may be the mode or form of its expression',

> such as books, pamphlets and other writings; lectures, addresses, sermons and other works of the same nature; dramatic or dramatico-musical works; choreographic works and entertainments in dumb show; musical compositions with or without words; cinematographic works to which are assimilated works expressed by a process analogous to cinematography; works of drawing, painting, architecture, sculpture, engraving and lithography; photographic works to which are assimilated works expressed by a process analogous to photography; works of applied art; illustrations, maps, plans, sketches and three-dimensional works relative to geography, topography, architecture or science.

From these two provisions emerges the principle that underpins the copyright systems of different regions and countries throughout the world, including the systems of Europe and the United Kingdom. According to that principle, copyright is a right enjoyed by authors in respect of their works.[3]

[1] Berne Convention for the Protection of Literary and Artistic Works (adopted 9 September 1886, last revised 24 July 1971) 828 UNTS 221, as amended (Berne Convention).

[2] http://www.wipo.int/treaties/en/ShowResults.jsp?treaty_id=15 (last accessed 5 June 2017).

[3] Berne Convention art 2(6) ('The works mentioned in this Article shall enjoy protection in all countries of the Union. This protection shall operate for the benefit of the author and his successors in title').

Further, and as the Berne Convention makes clear, an authorial work for copyright purposes is an expressive production of any mode or form that is original, in the sense of constituting an author's own intellectual creation. Hence the terms of Article 2(1) above, the reference throughout the Convention to authors' copyright works as their 'original works',[4] and the Convention's provision in Article 2(5) that: '[c]ollections of literary or artistic works ... which, by reason of the selection and arrangement of their contents, *constitute intellectual creations* shall be *protected as such*, without prejudice to the copyright in each of the works forming part of such collections' (emphasis added).

As noted, all twenty-eight EU Member States are members of the Union established by Article 1 of the Berne Convention. Further, the EEA Agreement[5] expressly requires EU and other EAA Member States to ratify the Berne Convention[6] by means of a provision that has been enforced in the case of EU Member States by the Court of Justice.[7] And finally, as a party to the WIPO Copyright Treaty,[8] the EU is itself required to comply with the substantive provisions of the Berne Convention.[9] For these reasons, and as the UK courts and Court of Justice have each confirmed, it is in the light of the Berne conception of copyright that UK and European copyright legislation must be read.[10]

1.2 Related Rights Protect Other Expressive Productions

Closely related to the authorial works protected by copyright are the subject matter protected by related rights. As seen in Chapter 2, these also are governed by international law, including particularly the Rome Convention,[11] which has the same effect in EU and UK law as the Berne Convention, and which requires the protection of performances of literary and artistic works,[12] recordings of sounds

[4] ibid arts 2(3), 8, 11(2), 11*ter*(2), 14(2), 14*bis*(1), and 14*ter*(1).

[5] Agreement on the European Economic Area (signed 2 May 1993, entered into force 1 January 1994) 1801 UNTS 3 (EEA Agreement).

[6] ibid Protocol 28.

[7] See Case C–13/00 *Commission v Ireland* [2002] ECR I–2943 (granting a request by the Commission for a declaration that, by failing to adhere to the Berne Convention by 1 January 1995, Ireland had breached its obligation to implement EEA Agreement Protocol 28 art 5).

[8] WIPO Copyright Treaty (opened for signature 20 December 1996, entered into force 6 March 2002) 36 ILM 65 (WCT).

[9] See ibid art 1(4) ('Contracting Parties shall comply with Articles 1 to 21 and the Appendix of the Berne Convention'); Case C–510/10 *DR, TV2 Danmark A/S v NCB–Nordisk Copyright Bureau* ECLI:EU:C:2012:244 (*DR, TV2 Danmark*).

[10] See eg *DR, TV2 Danmark* (n 9); *SAS Institute Inc v World Programming Limited* [2010] EWHC 1829 (Ch), [2011] RPC 1 (*SAS Institute* Ch) (applying the principle of consistent interpretation with relevant international agreements expounded by Lord Diplock in *The Jade* [1976] 1 All ER 920 (HL) 924).

[11] Rome Convention for the Protection of Performers, Producers of Phonograms and Broadcasting (concluded 26 October 1961) 496 UNTS 72 (Rome Convention).

[12] ibid art 3(a).

(phonograms),[13] and wireless transmissions for public reception of sounds and/or images (broadcasts),[14] by rights analogous to copyright. In addition to these Rome Convention categories are the further related rights subject matter of first fixations of cinematographic works (films) and typographical arrangements of published editions, the former of which are protected by EU and UK law and the latter of which are, for the moment at least,[15] protected by UK law only.[16]

As with authorial works, related rights subject matter are expressive objects. Unlike authorial works, however, they are not works as such, but rather occurrences (in the case of performances and broadcast transmissions), recordings of sounds or action (in the case of phonograms and films), and appearances of printed matter (in the case of typographical arrangements of published editions). In addition to being protected as expressive objects in their own right, all are capable of infringing copyright in the works performed, broadcast, recorded, or printed.

2. Authorial Works in Europe: Works that Express an Author's Own (Literary or Artistic) Intellectual Creation

2.1 Introduction

At the European level, the starting point for considering the subject matter protected by copyright is Articles 2 to 4 of the Information Society Directive. Those Articles require EU Member States to provide for certain exclusive rights (of reproduction, communication and making available to the public, and distribution) for 'authors' in respect of 'their works'.[17] This requirement follows and builds on the earlier provisions of the Term,[18] Software,[19] and Database[20] Directives requiring the protection of photographs, computer programs, and databases—if and only if they are original—as 'literary and artistic works' within the meaning of the Berne Convention.[21] For them to be 'original', the same EU legislation requires that they

[13] ibid art 3(b). [14] ibid art 3(f).

[15] But see Proposal for a Directive of the European Parliament and of the Council on Copyright in the Digital Single Market, COM(2016) 593 final art 11 (proposing related rights protection for publishers of press publications in digital use).

[16] See eg Directive 2001/29/EC of the European Parliament and of the Council of 22 May 2001 on the harmonisation of certain aspects of copyright and related rights in the information society [2002] OJ L 167/10 (Information Society Directive) art 2(d) (regarding related rights in first fixations of films); Copyright, Designs and Patents Act 1988 (UK) (CDPA) s 1(1)(b) and (c) (regarding related rights in films and typographical arrangements of published editions).

[17] Information Society Directive arts 2(a), 3(1), and 4(1).

[18] Directive 2006/116/EC of the European Parliament and of the Council of 12 December 2006 on the term of protection of copyright and certain related rights [2006] OJ L 372/12 (Term Directive).

[19] Directive 2009/24/EC of the European Parliament and of the Council of 23 April 2009 on the legal protection of computer programs [2009] OJ L 111/16 (Software Directive).

[20] Directive 96/9/EC of the European Parliament and of the Council of 11 March 1996 on the legal protection of databases [1996] OJ L 77/20 (Database Directive).

[21] See Software Directive art 1(1); Term Directive recitals 13 and 16, and art 6; Database Directive recital 28 and art 3(1).

express the intellectual creation of an author, consistent with Article 2(5) of the Berne Convention above. According to Article 6 of the Term Directive, for example:

> Photographs which are original in the sense that they are the author's own intellectual creation shall be protected in accordance with Article 1 [as a literary or artistic work within the meaning of Article 2 of the Berne Convention]. No other criteria shall be applied to determine their eligibility for protection. Member States may provide for the protection of other photographs.

Recital 16 repeats this provision, with the additional remark that a photographic work will be original if and only if 'it is the author's own intellectual creation reflecting his personality', and without regard to any other criteria 'such as merit or purpose'. The same definition of original is reflected in the Software and Database Directives. Thus, Article 3(1) of the Database Directive provides for the protection by copyright of databases that, 'by reason of the selection or arrangement of their contents, constitute the author's own intellectual creation', with no other criteria to be applied; and Article 1(3) of the Software Directive requires the protection of any computer program that 'is original in the sense that it is the author's own intellectual creation', also with no other criteria to be applied. From these three provisions it can be concluded that, as a matter of EU statutory law, the categories of subject matter protected by copyright are all original literary and artistic works within the meaning of the Berne Convention, by which is meant 'authorial works', in the sense of intellectual creations of an author reflecting her personality.

A question that arises from the EU legislation in this area is whether the subject matter protected by copyright is the work, the original work, the literary or artistic work, or the original literary or artistic work. Put differently, the question might be asked whether it is possible to have a work that is not original and/or literary or artistic in nature. The implication of the Term, Software, and Database Directives is that it is possible at least to distinguish a work from its originality. Hence the reference in the Term Directive to original and non-original photographic works, and the requirement that they be original in order to be protected by copyright. It would seem to follow from this that the copyright equivalent of the invention in patent law is the work, or the literary or artistic work, and not the original (literary or artistic) work. If this is correct, originality and authorial-ness will be accidental rather than essential properties of the subject matter protected by copyright, akin perhaps to novelty and inventive step in patent law. On the other hand, the counter-intuitiveness of a non-authorial literary or artistic work merits further consideration of this issue.

2.2 Authorial Works Have a Certain Expressive Form

European copyright law contains no definition of the term 'literary or artistic work' or 'work' as general categories of subject matter. The closest thing that EU legislation offers in this regard is a definition of databases and computer programs in the Database and Software Directives respectively, and the assimilation of each, and of photographs, with the category of literary and artistic works protected under the Berne Convention. For example, Article 1 of the Software Directive defines computer programs inclusively to 'include their preparatory design material', and requires that Member States protect them 'by copyright, as literary works within the meaning of the Berne Convention',[22] with such protection to 'apply to the expression in any form of a computer program' to the exclusion of its ideas and underlying principles.[23] Looking back to the Berne Convention itself, Article 2(1) defines '[t]he expression "literary and artistic works"' in the manner above, and as thus including 'every production in the literary, scientific and artistic domain, whatever may be the mode or form of its expression'. Read in the light of the examples of literary and artistic works offered immediately after it, this definition supports an understanding of literary works specifically as objects of literary including notational expression in whatever written, spoken, or other form they may be presented, consistent with the reference in the Software Directive to '*the expression in any form* of a computer program'.[24] This conception of the literary work protected by international and EU copyright law explains the decision of the Court of Justice in *Bezpečnostní softwarová asociace—Svaz softwarové ochrany v Ministerstvo kultury*[25] that graphic user interfaces, which by definition are objects of graphic rather than literary or notational expression, are not 'computer programs' within the meaning of European copyright law. If they are to be protected by copyright, the Court of Justice confirmed, it must therefore be as an artistic rather than as a literary work within the meaning of the Berne Convention.[26]

EU legislation also defines the database, in Article 1(2) of the Database Directive, as 'a collection of independent works, data or other materials arranged in a systematic or methodical way and individually accessible by electronic or other means', and requires the protection by copyright of any databases thus defined 'which, by reason of the selection or arrangement of their contents, constitute the author's own intellectual creation',[27] consistent with the express requirements of the Berne Convention.[28] Once again, what emerges is a conception of the database *qua* authorial work as an object of literary or artistic expression, however presented.

Finally, the Term Directive provides for the protection of photographs 'which are original in the sense that they are the author's own intellectual creation', to the exclusion of other criteria,[29] as 'literary or artistic' works within the meaning of the Berne Convention.[30] While the Directive itself offers no definition of a photograph, the Berne Convention refers in Article 2(1) above to 'photographic works to which are assimilated works expressed by a process analogous to photography', confirming the ordinary language meaning of photographs under international copyright principles as expressive objects of visual perception produced by means

[22] Software Directive art 1(1). [23] ibid art 1(2). [24] ibid (emphasis added).

[25] Case C–393/09 *Bezpečnostní softwarová asociace—Svaz softwarové ochrany v Ministerstvo kultury* [2010] ECR I–13971.

[26] ibid [46]. [27] Database Directive art 3(1).

[28] See Berne Convention art 2(5) ('collections of literary or artistic works . . . which, by reason of the selection and arrangement of their contents, constitute intellectual creations shall be protected as such, without prejudice to the copyright in each of the works forming part of such collections').

[29] Term Directive art 6. [30] ibid art 1(1).

of photographic technology. Once again, this is consistent with the Convention's definition of literary and artistic works as expressive productions of any form in the literary, scientific, or artistic domain.

In sum, for the purpose of European copyright law, authorial works are forms or modes of expression—and in particular, bounded expressive objects—in the literary, artistic, or scientific domain. This enables the immediate exclusion from protection by copyright of inventions and (other) ideas that exist solely in the mind of their creator on the ground that, even if in the literary, artistic, or scientific domain, they lack the expressive properties of a copyright work. However, while this exclusion explains the truism that copyright does not subsist in ideas, it says nothing about the analytically separate question of whether copyright protects the literary, scientific, or artistic ideas expressed in a work by preventing their unauthorized reproduction as part of the work protected by copyright. As seen above, the Software Directive expressly excludes such protection in the case of computer programs, although without prejudice to the position regarding the ideas of other types of work.

Other subject matter that might be said to lack the expressive properties of a work as defined above include perfumes and (other) objects the expressive instability or complexity of which makes them difficult objectively to identify.[31] With respect to olfactory subject matter: in some domestic European jurisdictions,[32] perfumes have been held to be ineligible for protection by copyright on the basis of their technical (rather than expressive) character. This is difficult to accept however, since even if they lack the mode or form of the subject matter listed in Article 2(1) of the Berne Convention, perfumes are plainly expressive productions in the literary, artistic, or scientific domain, and therefore fall within the scope of Article 2(1). With respect to (other) expressively unstable or complex subject matter: the exclusion of these from European copyright protection is perhaps consistent with the exclusion from legal conceptions of the invention *qua* technical teaching of subject matter that cannot be repeated in the sense of being recreated by following the steps described by the inventor, discussed in Chapter 4, and with the exclusion from legal conceptions of the trade mark *qua* sign of origin of subject matter the meaning of which cannot be repeatedly perceived and recalled, discussed in Chapter 6. Deploying similar reasoning, one might say that an expressive subject matter that is incapable of objective identification will lack the certainty of form required of a work of authorship. However, this ignores the

[31] On the protection of olfactory subject matter by copyright see further J Pila and P L C Torremans, *European Intellectual Property Law* (OUP 2016) 276–77. The subsistence of copyright in such subject matter has recently been referred to the Court of Justice for determination: see *Levola Hengelo BV v Smilde Foods BV* (Gerechtshof Arnhem-Leeuwarden 23 May 2017).

[32] See eg *Bsiri-Barbir v Haarmann & Reimer* [2006] ECDR 28 (French Cour de Cassation) (deciding that perfumes are not works of the mind but rather mere products of know-how that are accordingly ineligible for protection under French Copyright Code art L111-1); cf *Kecofa v Lâncome* [2006] ECDR 26 (Hoge Raad) (deciding that perfumes are original creations that reflect the personality of their creator and can be perceived by others that are accordingly protected by copyright under the Dutch Copyright Act 1912 art 10); *L'Oréal SA v Bellure* [2006] ECDR 16 (Cour d'appel de Paris) (supporting the subsistence of copyright in perfumes under French law on terms similar to those supported in *Kecofa*).

different nature of authorial and industrial subject matter considered in Chapter 2, and the general acceptance of an authorial work's material fixation as sufficient to establish its expressive boundaries for the purpose of copyright at least. In addition, and thinking again of olfactory subject matter, the fact that many people will lack sufficient sensory perception to be able to identify a given work may raise public policy issues regarding its suitability for protection by copyright, but ought not to affect its nature as an authorial work within the meaning of European law as such.

The definition of literary and artistic works as bounded expressive objects in the literary, artistic, or scientific domain leaves the question of whether every object having a certain expressive form, whether or not the literary or artistic (including musical or dramatic) expressive form of one of the subject matter listed in Article 2(1) of the Berne Convention, is for that reason an authorial work within the meaning of EU law. While relatively limited, the jurisprudence of the Court of Justice to date provides support for this view. The reason is its formalistic conception of copyright subject matter as selections and arrangements of words, pixels, and other expressive elements.[33] For some this might explain the prospect, noted above, of copyright subsistence in olfactory subject matter. Having said that, it is clear that merely possessing a certain expressive form is not enough to make a work an *original* literary or artistic work specifically, and thus not enough to make it an authorial work eligible for protection by copyright as a matter of EU law.

2.3 Authorial Works Have a Certain History of Production

As European legislation and the Berne Convention make clear, not all expressive productions in the literary, artistic, or scientific domain will be original, in the sense of representing the intellectual creation of a person. Thus, not all works as defined above will be the product of an act of origination or authorship. This may be why the UK legislature, in 1956, defined as works protected by copyright original literary, dramatic, musical, and artistic (LDMA) works, in addition to sound recordings, films, broadcasts, and typographical arrangements,[34] namely, since each of these subject matter is an expressive production in the literary, artistic, or scientific domain, even if they are not all capable of being works of authorship.

In contrast to UK law, however, European law neither recognizes nor permits copyright to subsist in works that are not original or authorial in nature. While non-original works may be protected, they may only be protected by rights related

[33] See eg Case C–5/08 *Infopaq International A/S v Danske Dagblades Forening* [2009] ECR I-06569 (*Infopaq*) [45]; Joined Cases C–403/08 and C–429/08 *Football Association Premier League Ltd v QC Leisure and Karen Murphy v MPS Ltd* ECLI:EU:C:2011:43 (AG) [80] (describing 'the isolated items of colour data for individual pixels' as 'comparable to individual words', in the sense that '[b]ringing those data together forms the individual frames which represent the author's own intellectual creation' in the case of a film).

[34] See Copyright Act 1956 (UK) ss 2, 3, and 12–15.

to copyright, and not by copyright itself.[35] Thus, copyright in the European sense is an author's right exclusively, supplemented by related rights in non-authorial works. This explains the tendency of scholars to treat originality as an essential (rather than an accidental) property of the work, and to define the work for European copyright purposes as a work of authorship, and in particular, and following the EU statutory and Berne Convention definitions of originality, as an 'author's own intellectual creation'.[36] Since under EU law copyright is an author's right, and the term 'work' is used to denote those subject matter that are inherently suited to protection by copyright, this view of the work for copyright purposes as a work of authorship makes conceptual sense. It also supports a conception of the authorial work in Europe as having a certain history of production.

In conclusion, and for the reasons above, the subject matter protected by European copyright law is most appropriately conceived as the authorial work in the sense of a production in the literary, scientific, or artistic domain that has a certain expressive form and that expresses the intellectual creation of an author—or, and amounting to the same thing—as an expressive production of an author. All such subject matter, but only such subject matter, are suitable for protection by copyright in its Berne conception as an author's right. The question that then remains is what does and does not fall within this category, and how are those subject matter that fall within it most appropriately conceived.

2.3.1 Authorial Works are of a Type that Leaves Scope for Creative Freedom in their Production

One type of subject matter that is not an original/authorial work within the meaning of EU law is the type that leaves no room for creative freedom in its production. According to the Court of Justice in *FAPL*,[37] for example, sporting events such as football matches 'cannot be regarded as intellectual creations classifiable as works within the meaning of the Copyright [Information Society] Directive'[38] on the ground that—in the case of football matches at least—they 'are subject to rules of the game, leaving no room for creative freedom'.[39] Central is the principle that

[35] See eg Database Directive art 7 (creating a *sui generis* database right not conditional upon originality); Term Directive art 6 (requiring the protection by copyright of original photographs, and permitting Member States to provide for the protection of 'other photographs').

[36] C Handig, 'The Copyright Term "Work:" European Harmonisation at an Unknown Level' (2009) 40 International Review of Intellectual Property and Competition Law 665. See also *Infopaq* (n 33) [33]–[34], [36] ('[The Information Society Directive] provides that authors have the exclusive right to authorize or prohibit reproduction, in whole or in part, of their works. It follows that protection of the author's right to authorize or prohibit reproduction is intended to cover "work". It is, moreover, apparent from the general scheme of the Berne Convention ... that the protection of certain subject-matters as artistic or literary works presupposes that they are intellectual creations.... In establishing a harmonized legal framework for copyright, [the Information Society Directive] is based on the same principle').

[37] Joined Cases C–403/08 and C–429/08 *Football Association Premier League Ltd v QC Leisure and Karen Murphy v MPS Ltd* [2011] ECR I–09083 (*FAPL*).

[38] ibid [98]. [39] ibid.

for a subject matter of any form to be an original work within the meaning of EU legislation, it must be of a type that leaves scope for creative freedom in its production. Where the form of a subject matter is dictated largely or exclusively by external considerations, it will fail this test, and thus be ineligible for protection. Whether a football game or other sporting event *is* thus dictated may be doubted; however, the principle remains that if it were so, it would be unsuited to protection on that basis.

The same principle was relied on by the Court in the *Painer* case[40] to explain why copyright *can* subsist in photographic portraits as works, despite the realism and simplicity of their subject matter. The reason given was that the creator of such a portrait will still need to make several creative choices during its production—including by: choosing the background, the photographic subject's position, and the lighting; deciding on the framing, the angle of view, and the atmosphere created; and choosing from a variety of developing techniques or computer software—each of which will affect the expressive form of the resulting image and thereby enable the author of that image to 'stamp the work created with his "personal touch"'.[41] Given this, the Court held, a photographic portrait is a type of work that is capable of being original, in the sense of expressing the intellectual creation of an author, and thus a type of work that is capable of being protected by copyright.[42] Once again, the decision supports the view that any type of subject matter that does not leave scope for free and creative choices in its production is not an authorial work and thus not appropriate for protection by copyright.

To date, this is the only basis on which the Court of Justice has been willing to refuse copyright protection to a given class of subject matter. For example, it was also invoked by the Court in the *Football Dataco* case[43] as the reason that not all databases are protected by copyright. In the Court's decision, where the creation of a database 'is dictated by technical considerations, rules or constraints which leave no room for creative freedom', the database will not be original, and will thus not be entitled to copyright protection.[44] While no examples of such databases were offered by the Court, they likely include local area telephone directories and football fixture lists, the expressive forms of which will invariably be dictated by such technical considerations as the need for their coverage to be exhaustive and presented alphabetically or chronologically or in some other easily accessible way, depriving their producer of the opportunity for 'creative freedom' when compiling them. And so too, in the Court's analysis in *Infopaq*, words 'considered in isolation, are not as such an intellectual creation of the author who employs them', since it is 'only through the choice, sequence and combination of those words that the author may express his creativity in an original manner and achieve a result which is an intellectual creation';[45] a decision reaffirming the centrality of the notion of expressive form and freedom to European conceptions of the copyright work.

40 Case C–145/10 *Painer v Standard Verlags GmbH* [2011] ECR I–12533 (*Painer*).

41 ibid [90]–[92]. 42 ibid [99].

43 Case C–604/10 *Football Dataco Ltd v Yahoo! UK Ltd* ECLI:EU:C:2012:115 (*Football Dataco*).

44 ibid [39]. 45 ibid [45].

In sum, while copyright under European law subsists in any expressive production of an author, whether a subject matter *is* such a production depends on more than its possession of a certain expressive form. In particular, for a subject matter to be an authorial work within the meaning of European copyright law, it must express the intellectual creation of an author, and to that end be a type of subject matter that leaves room for the exercise of free and creative choices in its production.

2.3.2 Authorial Works Reflect their Creators' Exploitation of the Scope they Leave for Creative Freedom in their Production

It is of course not sufficient for copyright protection that a work be of a type that leaves scope for the exercise of creative freedom in its production. Also required is that that scope have been exploited by the putative author to produce a work that reflects her personality or personal touch. If (and only if) it has been so exploited, the resulting work will be an authorial work entitled to the same copyright protection as other authorial works, regardless of how extensive (or otherwise) the scope for creative freedom that it afforded was. The Court of Justice has made this clear in a series of cases, including *Painer*.

The *Painer* case involved a series of photographs of Natascha Kampusch that had been taken by Eva-Maria Painer before Ms Kampusch's abduction and published without Ms Painer's permission following Ms Kampusch's escape. Also published was a photo-fit of Ms Kampusch that had been created by computer from Ms Painer's original photographs to show how Ms Kampusch might look at an older age. Among the questions referred to the CJEU in the case was whether the realism of photographic portraits means that they receive comparatively 'weaker' copyright protection, or no copyright protection at all, having regard in particular to the fundamental rights status of IP protection under European law. The Court answered this question negatively on the basis of the need to interpret authors' rights under the Information Society Directive broadly, and the absence of any indication in EU law that the extent of copyright protection 'should depend on possible differences in the degree of creative freedom in the production of various categories of works'.[46] In the Court's conclusion, provided a photographic portrait satisfies the EU test of originality, in the sense of reflecting an author's exercise of creative freedom to produce a work that bears her personal touch, it will receive the same copyright protection as other original (authorial) works.[47]

In sum, the originality of a work within the meaning of European copyright law depends on whether its subject matter leaves scope for 'sufficient formative freedom' that its creator has exploited to produce a work that bears 'his "personal touch"'.[48] The result is a two-step test of copyright subsistence that begins by considering the scope of formative freedom that the relevant type of subject matter permits, and proceeds to ask whether that scope has been exploited by the creator in the particular case to produce a work that reflects her personal touch. This is a nuanced test

[46] See *Painer* (n 40) [97]. [47] ibid [99]. [48] ibid [92].

that requires different kinds of works to be taken on their own terms for copyright subsistence purposes, while guaranteeing the same scope of protection to any work found to satisfy it. In this way it supports an expansive conception of the subject matter suitable for protection by copyright that potentially includes any bounded expressive object capable of direct perception by one or more of the five traditional human senses of sight, hearing, taste, smell, and touch, as an original expressive production in the literary, artistic, or scientific domain.

2.4 Conclusion

An authorial work within the meaning of European copyright law is any original expressive production in the literary, artistic, or scientific domain. For a subject matter to satisfy this definition it must have a certain expressive form capable of direct and objective sensory perception, and manifest the personality or 'personal touch' of the person who, by exercise of free and creative choices, created it.

3. Authorial Works in the United Kingdom: Works Created by the Exercise of Independent (Literary, Dramatic, Musical, or Artistic) Skill and Labour

3.1 Introduction

Under UK legislation today, the subject matter in which copyright subsists is defined exhaustively as original LDMA works, sound recordings, films, broadcasts, and typographical arrangements of published editions.[49] The local origins of this definition lie in the Copyright Act 1911 (UK), which was introduced to consolidate the complex array of statutory and common law rights that had emerged since the English Statute of Anne of 1710[50] to secure protection for the creators and performers of different types of LDMA subject matter, and to implement the Berne Convention.[51] Among the many changes introduced by the Act were the vesting of LDMA copyright from the point of a work's creation, rather than exclusively from its publication,[52] and the abrogation of common law rights in respect of unpublished works.[53] Another important and related change was the re-conception of the core subject matter protected by copyright to reflect the Berne Convention's requirement that Berne Union states recognize and protect by copyright 'literary and artistic works', defined (as above) to include dramatic and musical works also.[54] Thus, instead of books, including musical and dramatic compositions, engravings, drawings, and the like, copyright under the 1911 Act was declared to subsist in original LDMA works.[55] Also included within the scope of copyright subject matter

[49] CDPA s 1(1). [50] Statute of Anne 1710 (Eng), discussed in ch 2 s 2.

[51] See Law of Copyright Committee. Report of the Committee on the Law of Copyright 1910 (Cd 4976) (Gorrell Report) 2.

[52] Copyright Act 1911 (Imp) s 1(1)(b). [53] ibid s 31.

[54] Berne Convention art 2(1). [55] Copyright Act 1911 s 1(1).

under the 1911 Act was 'records, perforated rolls, and other contrivances by means of which sounds may be mechanically reproduced',[56] following the provision in Article 13 of the revised Berne Convention for the protection of recordings of musical works made before the right of musical authors to authorize such recordings was recognized.

In 1956 these statutory categories of copyright subject matter were extended to include films, broadcasts, and typographical arrangements of published editions.[57] This followed the recommendations of the Gregory Committee in 1951 that protecting films was required by the 1948 Brussels Act of the Berne Convention, regardless of their originality,[58] and that if sound recordings and films were to be protected, so too as 'a matter of natural justice' ought broadcasts and typographical arrangements to be protected, given that they also require 'considerable cost and skill' to produce.[59] The result was a distinction between the works of an 'originator' on the one hand, and the subject matter of those who exercised an originator's 'fundamental rights' to reproduce in material form or otherwise apply her works on the other.[60] According to the Committee, the rights subsisting in the latter were 'subsidiary' to the primary rights of a composer or author, and might therefore have been better referred to by a name other than 'copyright'.[61] In the resulting legislation, however, this recommendation was not adopted, with copyright instead recognized as subsisting in all eight categories of 'originator' and non-'originator' subject matter.[62] In this respect, the terminology of UK law departs from that of European law, which distinguishes between copyright for authors' works and related rights for related subject matter.[63]

The starting point for considering the subject matter protected by copyright as an author's right in the UK is section 1(1)(a) of the Copyright, Designs and Patents Act 1988. According to that provision, copyright is a property right that subsists automatically—ie without any need for registration or application—in original LDMA works. In order for copyright to subsist in a work, the work must also satisfy the relevant connecting or territorial factors under Chapter IX[64] and, for original LDM works, have been 'recorded, in writing or otherwise'.[65] It follows that in determining whether copyright subsists, one needs to ask whether there is an original LDMA work; if the work is an LDM work, whether it has been recorded; and for all works, whether it satisfies the relevant connecting or territorial factors of Chapter IX.

[56] ibid s 19. [57] Copyright Act 1956 (UK) ss 12–15.

[58] See Report of the Copyright Committee 1951 (Cmd 8662) paras 100–101.

[59] ibid paras 117 (broadcasts) and 307 (typographical arrangements).

[60] ibid paras 76–77. The Committee also underlined the trade-related aspects of intellectual property. See ibid para 3 ('There are, of course, trade interests. Indeed, the output of the United Kingdom publishing trade in 1951 has been estimated as being in the neighbourhood of £40 million, of which probably slightly more than £12 million represents exports. We believe that this trade, based on the interchange of ideas between countries, is one which is important entirely beyond its value in terms of money').

[61] ibid para 181. [62] Copyright Act 1956 (UK) ss 2, 3, and 12–15.

[63] See eg Information Society Directive arts 2–4. [64] CDPA s 1(3).

[65] ibid s 3(2).

According to UK case law, it is important to begin all copyright analyses by identifying clearly the work in which copyright is alleged to subsist. If a subject matter cannot be brought squarely within one of the section 1(1)(a) categories, it will not attract copyright protection. This was made clear in *Creation Records Ltd v News Group Newspapers Ltd*,[66] where Lloyd J rejected a claim to copyright in a photographic scene on the ground that, while the result of artistic creativity and originality, the scene could not be fitted into any of the CDPA statutory categories of work. To similar effect was the discussion in *IPC Media Ltd v Highbury-Pleasure Publishing No 2*[67] of situations involving the reproduction of features shared by a range of works—in that case, the design elements of different magazine covers and articles—and the Court's emphasis on the importance of identifying clearly a single work the copyright in which might be said to have been infringed.[68]

Also underlined by the UK cases is the importance of correctly conceiving a work once identified, and of being clear what the work does and does not comprise. For example, if a work for copyright purposes is merely a form of expression and does not include the ideas or information expressed, then the intellectual investment in conceiving ideas and deriving information for expression will not count in determining the work's entitlement to protection, nor support a claim of joint authorship in respect of it; and reproducing the ideas and information expressed in a work will not infringe its copyright. Examples of restrictively conceived works are databases and computer programs, which, for UK (as for European) copyright purposes, do not include their data (for databases) or underlying ideas, principles, functionality, programming language, or data file format (for computer programs), with the result that such elements must be excluded from copyright subsistence and infringement analyses involving these types of works.[69]

3.2 Authorial Works Have a Certain Expressive Form

The CDPA contains definitions of each of the four main categories of authorial (LDMA) works. Those definitions assume the existence of a work and set conditions for its categorization as literary, dramatic, music, or artistic. The definitions are formalistic, in that the conditions emphasize aspects of the work's form. For example, a 'literary work' is a work that 'is written, spoken or sung',[70] where 'writing' is defined to 'include[] non-literal forms of notation and code'.[71] 'Accordingly', the Act says, literary works 'include (a) a table or compilation other than a database, (b) a computer program, (c) preparatory design material for a computer program,

[66] *Creation Records Ltd v News Group Newspapers Ltd* [1997] EMLR 444 (Ch) (*Creation Records*).

[67] *IPC Media Ltd v Highbury-Pleasure Publishing No 2* [2004] EWHC 317 (Ch), [2005] FSR 20 (*IPC Media*).

[68] See also *Coffey v Warner/Chappell* [2006] EWHC 449 (Ch) (*Coffey*), where Blackburne J approved Laddie J's comments in *IPC Media* (ibid) in the context of musical works, and relied on the same to reject an allegation of copyright infringement involving the reproduction of a combination of so-called performative features—voice expression, pitch contour, and syncopation of or around a lyrical phrase.

[69] See *Football Dataco* (n 43) [46] (for databases); Software Directive art 1(2) and Case C–406/10 *SAS Institute Inc v World Programming Ltd* ECLI:EU:C:2012:259 [46] (for software).

[70] CDPA s 3(1). [71] ibid s 178.

and (d) a database'.[72] This is consistent also with section 3A(1) of the CDPA, which defines a 'database' to include collections of non-literary subject matter, following Article 1 and recital 17 of the Database Directive, and with a series of UK cases emphasizing the formal properties of literary works.[73]

'Artistic work' is also defined in the CDPA, to mean

> (a) a graphic work, photograph, sculpture or collage, irrespective of artistic quality, (b) a work of architecture, being a building or model for a building, or (c) a work of artistic craftsmanship.[74]

Similarly cast are the definitions in section 4(2) of 'building' (to include 'any fixed structure, and a part of a building or fixed structure'), 'graphic work' (to include '(a) any painting, drawing, diagram, map, chart or plan, and (b) any engraving, etching, lithograph, woodcut or similar work'), 'photograph' (to mean 'a recording of light or other radiation on any medium on which an image is produced or from which an image may by any means be produced, and which is not part of a film'), and 'sculpture' (to include 'a cast or model made for purposes of sculpture').

Interpreting this definition of 'artistic work', the courts have required a material object manifesting properties of visual significance. The requirement that the properties be visually significant comes from *Interlego v Tyco Industries*,[75] where the Privy Council described artistic copyright as 'concerned with visual image',[76] and denied it to re-drawings on the basis of their failure to manifest new properties of 'visual significance'.[77] It contrasts with the view taken in the corresponding Australian case of *Interlego AG v Croner Trading Pty Ltd*[78] that the properties of an artistic work must be visually distinctive only; the Full Federal Court in that case having criticized the UK approach as importing a requirement of novelty into the law of copyright.[79]

Consistent with the statutory definitions of individual categories of artistic work above have been the courts' understanding of those categories, including their conception of 'paintings' as images fixed in paint on a surface,[80] 'sculptures' as three-dimensional objects carved or shaped by hand,[81] 'collage' as two or more things stuck together with adhesive,[82] 'engravings' as plates the surface of which have been

[72] ibid s 3(1).

[73] See eg *The Newspaper Licensing Agency Ltd v Meltwater Holding BV* [2011] EWCA Civ 890, [2012] RPC 1 (*Meltwater*) [19] (describing a headline as 'plainly' a literary work as 'it consists of words'); *Donoghue v Allied Newspapers Ltd* [1938] 1 Ch 106 (*Donoghue*) 110 (defining a literary work as the 'form of language by which information or ideas are conveyed to an audience'); *University of London Press v University Tutorial Press* [1916] 2 Ch 601 (*ULP*) 608 (defining a literary work to mean 'work expressed in print or writing irrespective of the question of whether the quality or style is high', and as thus including mathematics papers); *Walter v Lane* [1900] AC 539 (HL) (*Walter v Lane*), affirmed in *Sawkins v Hyperion Records* [2005] EWCA Civ 565, [2005] RPC 32 (*Sawkins*) (deciding that a person who first fixes the literary work of another through the exercise of independent skill and labour is the author of that fixation and consequently entitled to literary copyright in it).

[74] CDPA s 4(1). [75] *Interlego AG v Tyco Industries Inc* [1989] AC 217 (PC) (*Interlego*).

[76] ibid 263. [77] ibid 266.

[78] *Interlego AG v Croner Trading Pty Ltd* (1992) 39 FCR 348.

[79] ibid [106]–[109]. [80] *Harpbond v Merchandising Corp* [1983] FSR 32 (CA) 46.

[81] See *Creation Records* (n 66) 449. [82] ibid 450.

cut (and the images produced from them),[83] and 'works of artistic craftsmanship' as durable, useful, handmade objects.[84] On the basis of these definitions, we might say, an artistic work is a hand-made three-dimensional object; or, more precisely, a raw material (such as paper, wood, stone etc) supporting new (created) properties of visual significance. This conception of the artistic work brings to mind the Roman Law principle of *accessio*, and the treatment of property in media as acceding to the author of any pictures on them.

In contrast to literary and artistic works, the statutory definition of 'dramatic work' is inclusive. Thus, a dramatic work includes any 'work of dance or mime'.[85] A musical work by contrast is any 'work consisting of music, exclusive of any words or action intended to be sung, spoken or performed with the music'.[86] When extrapolating from these provisions, the courts have emphasized the performative nature of musical and dramatic works without treating either as performance itself. Specifically, musical works have been defined as combinations of sounds for listening to,[87] and dramatic works as 'work[s] of action, with or without words or music, which [are] capable of being performed before an audience'.[88] Conceived in these terms, we might describe musical and dramatic works as arrangements of acoustic or behavioural elements that are stable (ie that endure) when presented in performance.[89] Hence the description of musical works in *Sawkins* as analogous to dramatic works, and as thus including all those 'elements that make some contribution to the sound of the music when performed, such as performing indications, tempo and performance practice indicators'.[90] In Lord Justice Mummery's decision, '[i]n the absence of a special statutory definition of music, ordinary usage assists: as indicated in the dictionaries, the essence of music is combining sounds for listening to'.[91] With respect to dramatic works, reference might also be made to *Norowzian*, where the Court found that dramatic copyright did not subsist in a combination of movements owing to their inability to be performed,[92] and to *Creation Records*, where the Court found that dramatic

[83] *Hi-Tech Autoparts Ltd v Towergate Two Ltd (No 2)* [2002] FSR 270 (Ch) 274–75 (applying the definition approved in *Wham-O Manufacturing Co v Lincoln Industries Ltd* [1985] RPC 127 (New Zealand Court of Appeal) (*Wham-O*) to find that artistic copyright subsisted in rubber floor mats for cars).

[84] *George Hensher Ltd v Restawile Upholstery (Lancs) Ltd* [1976] AC 64 (HL) (*Hensher v Restawile*) 77 (Lord Reid).

[85] CDPA s 3(1). [86] ibid. [87] See *Sawkins* (n 73) [53].

[88] *Norowzian v Arks Ltd (No 2)* [2000] FSR 363 (CA) 367 (*Norowzian*).

[89] Compare the anomalous decision of *Norowzian* (ibid), in which it was held that certain films—as works of action capable of performance—are also dramatic works, and hence entitled to the deeper protection of dramatic copyright in addition to film copyright.

[90] See *Sawkins* (n 73) [56].

[91] ibid [53]. See also *Beckingham v Hodgens* [2003] FSR 238 (Ch) 248 (describing 'the final musical expression' of the musical work as 'what the audience will hear'); *Stuart v Barrett* [1994] EMLR 448 (Ch) 460 (describing the musical work as a whole composition with shape and drive provided by its constituent aural elements); *Schott Musik International GmbH & Co v Colossal Records of Australia Pty Ltd* [1997] FCA 531 (defining musical works as consisting 'of a combination of sounds and noises organized in different ways as to such elements as pitch, volume, quality, duration and rhythm', quoting Sam Ricketson's *The Law of Intellectual Property* (Law Book Company 1984) [5.71]).

[92] Albeit the court in *Norowzian* (n 88), having wrongly denied the existence of a dramatic work on the ground that the work, as depicted in the material recording of it, was incapable of performance.

copyright did not subsist in a scene on the ground that it was 'inherently static' and included 'no movement, story or action'.[93] It follows from these definitions that if a work such as John Cage's *4'33"* is to be protected by UK copyright,[94] it will be protected as a dramatic work only, on the ground that it includes movements that are stable in the sense of repeating or enduring in performance, but no combination of sounds possessing the same stability.

In summary, the statutory definitions of LDMA works require that a subject matter, to be an LDMA work, possess certain aspects of LDMA form: in the case of literary works, a literary mode of presentation (writing or notation); in the case of artistic works, an artistic mode of creation (the addition of new properties of visual significance to some raw material); and in the case of musical/dramatic works, a stability of musical/dramatic composition (sounds/movements that repeat or endure in performance). Once again, however, the question arises of whether this is all that is required. If it were, copyright would be capable of subsisting in any collection of letters (as a literary work); any scribble on paper (as a drawing); any painted surface (as a painting); any hand-made three-dimensional object (as a sculpture); and any noise (as a musical work). That it is not so capable of subsisting seems clear from the cases. The question is why not, and what in addition to a particular (LDMA) form is required for the existence of an LDMA work. The difficulty of this question accounts for much of the litigation in this area of copyright law.

3.2.1 LDMA Works and Ideas—The Idea/Expression Distinction

In discussing LDMA works, a distinction is often drawn by the courts between the ideas of a work and their expression. This distinction is not statutorily entrenched in the UK, as it is in the United States, where §102(b) of the 1976 Copyright Act (17 USC) provides as follows:

> In no case does copyright protection for an original work of authorship extend to any idea, procedure, process, system, method of operation, concept, principle, or discovery, regardless of the form in which it is described, explained, illustrated, or embodied in such work.

Nonetheless, the idea/expression distinction is recognized in Article 9(2) of the TRIPs Agreement[95] and Article 2 of the WIPO Copyright Treaty—the latter of which provides that '[c]opyright protection extends to expressions and not to ideas, procedures, methods of operation or mathematical concepts as such'—and is regarded by the courts as a central tenet of UK copyright, in the context of computer programs at least.[96]

[93] See *Creation Records* (n 66) 448.

[94] See ch 3 s 5. Cage's work comprises instructions for the performance of certain actions by a person, the point of which is precisely that the person performing the actions should refrain from making any sounds.

[95] Agreement on Trade-related Aspects of Intellectual Property Rights (opened for signature 15 December 1993, entered into force 1 January 1995) 1869 UNTS 299 (TRIPs Agreement).

[96] See eg *Nova Productions Limited v Mazooma Games* [2007] EWCA Civ 219; *SAS Institute* Ch (n 10); cf *Designers Guild Ltd v Russell Williams (Textiles) Ltd* [2000] 1 WLR 2416 (HL) 2422 (*Designers Guild*).

With respect to copyright subsistence, it is well established that 'copyright does not subsist in ideas'.[97] The reason is clear, as noted in section 2: under section 1(1) of the CDPA, as under the Information Society Directive, copyright subsists only in works, and ideas are not works. Hence the statement by Lord Hoffmann in *Designers Guild* that: 'there can be no copyright in an idea which is merely in the head, which has not been expressed in copyrightable form, as in a literary, dramatic, musical or artistic work'.[98] Similarly with respect to copyright in information: copyright subsists in works, which data and other information are not, as Floyd J confirmed in *Football Dataco*.

As again noted in the discussion of EU law in section 2, it does not follow from the fact that ideas and information are not works that works are exclusively forms of expression, and do not include the ideas and information expressed. Indeed, and with the important exceptions of databases and computer programs mentioned previously, the suggestion that ideas and information are not part of an LDMA work for copyright purposes is inconsistent with the traditional UK approach to authorship and infringement, albeit not without judicial support.[99]

3.2.2 LDM Works and their Material Fixations

3.2.2.1 LDM Works Must Be Recorded to Be Protected by Copyright

By section 3(2) of the CDPA, 'copyright does not subsist in a literary, dramatic or musical work unless and until it is recorded, in writing or otherwise, and references in this Part to the time at which such a work is made are to the time at which it is so recorded'. By section 3(3):

> It is immaterial for the purposes of subsection (2) whether the work is recorded by or with the permission of the author; and where it is not recorded by the author, nothing in that subsection affects the question whether copyright subsists in the record as distinct from the work recorded.

It is clear from these provisions that the requirement for fixation of a work is an evidentiary requirement that affects neither the existence of the work nor the identity

[97] *Baigent v The Random House Group* [2007] EWCA Civ 24, [2007] FSR 24 (*Baigent*) [5].

[98] See *Designers Guild* (n 96) 2422. See also *Donoghue* (n 73) 109 ('there is no copyright in an idea, or in ideas. A person may have a brilliant idea for a story, or for a picture, or for a play, and one which appears to him to be original; but if he communicates that idea to an author or an artist or a playwright, the production which is the result of the communication of the idea to the author or the artist or the playwright is the copyright of the person who has clothed the idea in form, whether by means of a picture, a play, or a book, and the owner of the idea has no rights in that product'); *Green v Broadcasting Corporation of New Zealand* [1989] 2 All ER 1056 (PC) (deciding that a collection of dramatic features for a TV series lacked the certainty and unity of a dramatic work); *IPC Media* (n 67) (deciding that a collection of design elements from different magazine articles and covers was not an artistic work); *Baigent* (n 97) (deciding that the so-called Central Theme of the plaintiff's book was not a literary work in and of itself); and *Coffey* (n 68) (rejecting a claim of copyright infringement based on a conception of the musical work as a combination of voice expression, pitch contour and syncopation of or around a lyrical phrase).

[99] See eg *Baigent* (n 97) [7] (describing the copying of a work's ideas as unable to support a finding of infringement of its copyright).

of its author. The same has been affirmed in the cases, where a distinction has been drawn for copyright purposes between works and their material fixations, in the context at least of LDM works, reflecting their exclusively intangible nature. An example is *Sawkins*, where performance editions of 17th century musical compositions were held to be musical works distinguished from their material fixation. In the words of Lord Justice Mummery in that case:

> Music must be distinguished from the fact and form of its fixation as a record of a musical composition. The score is the traditional and convenient form of fixation of the music and conforms to the requirement that a copyright work must be recorded in some material form. But the fixation in the written score or on a record is not in itself the music in which copyright subsists. There is no reason why, for example, a recording of a person's spontaneous singing, whistling or humming or improvisations of sounds by a group of people with or without musical instruments should not be 'music' for copyright purposes.[100]

Even in *Norowzian*, where a film was held to be a dramatic work, the Court of Appeal distinguished clearly between the film and the cinematographic content (cinematographic work) that it recorded, thus maintaining the distinction between LDM works and their material fixations.

As seen in Chapters 2 and 3, it is the intangibility of copyright works that accounts for their non-rivalrous and non-depletable nature. Thus, unlike tangible objects (such as a bicycle), a novel, or other work can be used by an infinite number of people at the same time, none of whose use of the work will deplete it for future use by others. This distinction is consistent with the terms of section 3(3) of the CDPA above, and ensures (or ought to ensure[101]) that copyright in an LDM work is unaffected by the destruction of the record of the work, in addition to suggesting that where the work as created differs from the work as recorded—as in the case, for example, of a prematurely ended or otherwise imperfect recording of a speech—it is the former and not the latter that is the protected subject matter.

3.2.3 Artistic Works and their Material Fixations

While LDM works are distinguished from the fact and form of their material fixation, the same is not true, or not obviously true, for artistic works, which have a materiality (paint, paper, bricks etc) that LDM works lack, accounting for their exclusion from the fixation requirement of section 3(2).[102] This seems intuitively right—it is difficult to think of a painting without paint, a building without walls, or a collage without glue etc—but what is the result? If artistic works do not exist independent of their material fixations, does it follow that copyright in a painting extinguishes on destruction of the painted canvas? The answer would seem to be no, by reason of section 153(3) of the CDPA. According to that provision:

100 See *Sawkins* (n 73) [53]. 101 See n 92.
102 See *Abraham Moon & Sons Ltd v Thornber* [2012] EWPCC 36 [104] (*Abraham Moon*).

If the qualification requirements of this Chapter, or section 163, 165 or 168, are once satisfied in respect of a work, copyright does not cease to subsist by reason of any subsequent event.

However, to say that artistic works do not exist separate from their material fixation in the way that LDM works do is not to say that artistic works are exclusively material. In the case of a photograph, for example, the artistic work is both the paper on which the expression is recorded and the expression itself, with the result that reproducing a scene depicted in a photograph will infringe copyright in the photograph, even without mechanical copying of the photographic still.[103] This may be contrasted with the situation regarding films; a contrast that underlines the inconsistency of awarding the deep protection of copyright to photographs while awarding the shallower protection of related rights to films. Further, that the CDPA does not protect the expressive content of films (as cinematographic works) puts it in breach of the Berne Convention, and was a reason given by the Court of Appeal in *Norowzian* for its decision to treat the film in that case as a dramatic work protected by dramatic copyright, in addition to being a film protected by related rights.

3.2.4 Records of LDMA Works

Section 3(3) of the CDPA also leaves open the possibility of separate protection for records of an LDMA work. The most obvious examples of such records are sound recordings and films, both of which are protected by related rights independent of any copyright in the subject matter they record.[104] More difficult is whether LDMA copyright can subsist in a record of an LDMA work. This was the issue in *Walter v Lane*, introduced in Chapter 3.

3.2.4.1 *Walter v Lane* and the Question of Literary Copyright in Literary Transcripts

As seen in Chapter 3, the dispute in *Walter v Lane* concerned verbatim shorthand transcripts of a series of speeches that were delivered by Lord Rosebery to a small public audience in the 1890s without notes and produced by reporters in the audience for publication in *The Times* newspaper. When the defendant reproduced the published transcripts in an anthology of Lord Rosebery's speeches, he was sued for infringement of copyright subsisting in the published transcripts. Hence the question for the courts of whether the transcripts were protected by copyright.

In considering that question the House of Lords assumed from the outset that there could be no copyright in Lord Rosebery's speeches on the ground that Lord Rosebery had not recorded them. This did not mean that Lord Rosebery was not an author, but that the speeches he had authored lacked material form and were therefore not eligible for protection as 'books' within the meaning of 19th century copyright legislation. However, while Lord Rosebery's speeches may not have been books, the reporters' transcripts were assumed to be, raising the question of who

[103] See *Temple Island Collections Ltd v New English Teas* [2012] EWPCC 1 (*Temple Island*).
[104] CDPA s 1(1)(b).

their authors were. According to the House of Lords, the transcripts' authors were the reporters, for it was the reporters who had, by the exercise of independent skill and labour, produced them. This exercise of independent skill and labour was central, for it was that which made them authors rather than scribes in the sense either of having copied an existing work, or of having written the words down mechanically as they were spoken. So too the conception of the works as transcripts of the speeches rather than as the speeches themselves, for it was that which ensured that each reporter's property would be limited, and would not obstruct the freedom of other members of Lord Rosebery's audience to create their own transcripts by exercise of their own skill and labour so as to earn their own copyright.

As argued elsewhere, this reasoning is difficult to accept.[105] For a start, the emphasis on the freedom of the audience is confusing, for it is self-evident that copyright in a book will only prevent copying of the book itself. In addition, the focus on whether the reporters produced the books by skill and labour allowed their Lordships to ignore the point of that question, which was to decide whether the reporters were authors entitled to literary copyright.

Of the judges in *Walter v Lane*, only Lord Rosebery insisted on the primacy of this question. In his dissenting view, in transcribing Lord Rosebery's words each of the reporters was acting not as an author—a person who 'thinks the thoughts and chooses the words and the arrangement of them'—but as the human approximation of a phonographic instrument—'the echo, the mocking bird, the slave of the speaker'. Thus, however great their art of transcription, it was not appropriately rewarded by literary copyright.[106]

On the remaining question of whether a literary transcript is a literary work: as noted previously, the possibility is allowed by section 3(3) of the CDPA. And yet the courts' acceptance that LDM works exist independent of the fact and form of their fixation suggests that literary transcripts are merely fixations of existing literary works, and not literary works in their own right. Paradoxically, however, a key authority in support of this distinction between a work and its material fixations is *Sawkins*, where the Court of Appeal expressly affirmed *Walter v Lane* as good authority for the principle of LDMA copyright in non-servile copies of others' LDMA works.[107]

3.2.4.2 *Walter v Lane* Today

According to the Court of Appeal in *Sawkins, Walter v Lane* remains good law, notwithstanding that it was decided more than 100 years ago under very different legislation.[108] The implication is that LDMA copyright can subsist in an LDMA record of an LDMA work; a principle supported by Lord Justice Jacob in *Sawkins* for recreations of artistic works such as paintings, which he described as consistent with the public policy aims of copyright in promoting access to works.[109] However,

[105] See J Pila, 'An Intentional View of the Copyright Work' (2008) 71 Modern Law Review 535.
[106] See *Walter v Lane* (n 73) 543.
[107] See *Sawkins* (n 73) [33].
[108] ibid.
[109] ibid [83] and [87].

this is difficult to reconcile with the intangible nature of works, also emphasized in *Sawkins*.

In considering how *Walter v Lane* ought to be decided today, the starting point must be section 3(2) of the CDPA, according to which a reporter's transcripts of another's speech would trigger the vesting of copyright in the speech itself as an original literary work, which copyright would be owned by the speaker as its author. Having produced his transcript, the reporter would be free to publish it for the journalistic purpose for which it was made in reliance on section 58 of the CDPA, provided the speaker had not objected and the conditions of subsection 58(2) had otherwise been satisfied. For the reporter to have his own copyright in the transcript he would need additionally to show that it was a type of work in which copyright subsists, ie that a verbatim transcript of a speech is itself an original LDMA work within the meaning of section 1(1)(a). Given the distinction on which the CDPA is based between authorial works (entitled to copyright) and material fixations of them (entitled to related rights), however, it is difficult to see how he might do this. That difficulty is compounded by the UK courts' refusal to grant LDMA copyright solely on the basis of a subject matter's properties of LDMA form in other contexts.

3.3 Authorial Works Have a Certain History of Production

3.3.1 Authorial Works are Intended by their Creator and/or Regarded by Society to Exist as Such

The question of what, in addition to certain properties of LDMA form, is required for an LDMA work was considered forty years ago for works of artistic craftsmanship (WACs) in *Hensher v Restawile.*[110] According to the House of Lords in that case,[111] a work of artistic craftsmanship is a work of an artist-craftsman, which is not a work produced by someone who is both a craftsman and an artist, but rather a work of craftsmanship, produced with artistic intent (assessed objectively with reference to expert evidence[112]), and judged by the court not to manifest a complete absence of artistic quality when considered in isolation and having regard to expert opinion.

The courts have tended to treat WACs as a special category of LDMA work, and have been cautious when considering the other categories of looking beyond aspects of a subject matter's form lest they offend the long-standing principle—statutorily entrenched for artistic works in section 4(1)(a)—that copyright is neutral as to considerations of artistic merit or worth. However, when faced with the prospect of supporting copyright protection for the types of subject matter above, they have

[110] For a fuller discussion see J Pila, 'Works of Artistic Craftsmanship in the High Court of Australia: The Exception as Paradigm Copyright Work' (2009) 36 Federal Law Review 365.

[111] ibid. See especially the speech by Lord Simon (87–95), whose reasoning was adopted by the High Court of Australia in *Burge v Swarbrick* [2007] HCA 17, (2007) 232 CLR 336.

[112] ibid. See also the speeches by Lords Morris and Simon, the latter referring to the need for a work to manifest the vocational aim and impact of an artist (at 95); *contra* Lord Kilbrandon, supporting a requirement for artistic intent but subjectively conceived (at 97).

sometimes done this, ie they have sometimes looked beyond a subject matter's form to consider its non-formal aspects, as the following examples demonstrate.

3.3.1.1 Not Every Collection of Letters is a Literary Work

According to the Court in *Exxon v Exxon Insurance Corp*,[113] the question to be asked when identifying a literary work under the CDPA is not, as the Act suggests, 'is there a work and of LDMA nature?' (two questions), but rather, 'is there an LDMA work?' (one question); the term 'literary' in the statutory phrase 'literary work' colouring and extending the meaning of 'work'. The result, according to the Court, is that a work might have a literary form but not be a literary work for the purpose of copyright. Considering what aside from a literary form would be required, the Court identified intentional, representational, and expressive properties; accepting as a literary work any subject matter 'intended to afford instruction, or information, or pleasure in the form of literary enjoyment'.[114] Applying this definition it held that the word 'exxon' was not a literary work, despite satisfying the statutory definition of literary works above.

The decision in *Exxon* is inconsistent with the more recent decision of the Court of Appeal in *Meltwater*. That decision followed the Court of Justice's judgment in *Infopaq*, discussed in section 2.3.1 above, that 'a headline is plainly literary as it consists of words,' consistent with the EU understanding of literary works as selections and arrangements of words. While *Exxon* involved a single word, which is not an authorial work within the meaning of this EU understanding, its general conception of authorial works is plainly inconsistent with the conception supported in *Infopaq*, and with the Court of Appeal's decision in *Meltwater* adopting that (*Infopaq*) conception.

3.3.1.2 Not Every Scribble, Painted Surface, or Handmade Three-dimensional Object is an Artistic Work

According to Pincus J in *Roland Corporation v Lorenzo & Sons*,[115] a distinction must be drawn for copyright purposes between random scribbles and simple images 'drawn with care',[116] affirming the view of Megarry J in *British Northrop v Texteam Blackburn Ltd*[117] that simplicity is no bar to artistic copyright, and suggesting further that what distinguishes an image fixed in lead from a drawing is the expressive intent of its creator. Similarly in *Harpbond*, the Court of Appeal's decision that an image fixed in paint on a face is not a painting can be seen to have been influenced by the purpose of the subject matter's creator, which was not to create a painting as such, but rather to create a commercial object in the form of the Adam Ant stage character. And finally, in *Metix (UK) Ltd v GH Maughan (Plastics) Ltd*,[118] Laddie J rationalized the Court's refusal in *Davis (J & S) (Holdings) Ltd v Wright Health*

[113] *Exxon v Exxon Insurance Corp* [1982] Ch 119 (CA) (*Exxon*). [114] ibid 143.
[115] *Roland Corporation v Lorenzo & Sons Pty Ltd* (1991) 33 FCR 111, 22 IPR 245.
[116] ibid [17]. [117] *British Northrop v Texteam Blackburn Ltd* [1974] RPC 69 (ChD).
[118] *Metix (UK) Ltd v GH Maughan (Plastics) Ltd* [1997] FSR 718 (ChD) (*Metix*).

Group Ltd[119] to treat dental impression trays as sculptures for copyright purposes with reference to the nature of sculptures as objects created by an artist's hand with a view in part to non-functional aspects of shape or appearance;[120] affirming that three-dimensional objects created to serve as the step in a production process and having no significance independent of that process are not sculptures for the purpose of UK copyright.[121]

Metix was applied by Mann J in *Lucasfilm Ltd v Ainsworth*,[122] involving the Stormtrooper helmet and other armour from the *Star Wars* films. There the Judge affirmed Laddie J's view that 'not every three dimensional representation of a concept can be regarded as a sculpture', and that for a work to be a sculpture 'it should have, as part of its purpose, a visual appeal in the sense that it might be enjoyed for that purpose alone, whether or not it might have another purpose as well'.[123] According to Mann J, the decisions in *Breville Europe Plc v Thorn EMI Domestic Appliance Ltd*[124] and *Wham-O*—that plaster shapes made for the production of die-casting moulds for toasters, and a model of a mass-produced Frisbee, are 'sculptures', despite having a purely mechanical or functional nature—were wrongly decided. The purpose of a sculpture, he said,

> is that of the creator. This reflects the reference to 'artist's hand' in the judgment of Laddie J in Metix, with which I respectfully agree. An artist (in the realm of the visual arts) creates something because it has visual appeal which he wishes to be enjoyed as such. He may fail, but that does not matter (no judgments are to be made about artistic merit). It is the underlying purpose that is important.[125]

In support of this statement, Mann J also drew the following helpful distinction, in a reference to Carl André's work, *Equivalent VIII*:

> A pile of bricks, temporarily on display at the Tate Modern for 2 weeks, is plainly capable of being a sculpture. The identical pile of bricks dumped at the end of my driveway for 2 weeks preparatory to a building project is equally plainly not. One asks why there is that difference, and the answer lies, in my view, in having regard to its purpose. One is created by the hand of an artist, for artistic purposes, and the other is created by a builder, for building purposes.[126]

Mann J's reasoning has since been supported by both the Court of Appeal and the Supreme Court.[127] In particular, those Courts have each affirmed the multi-factor test that Mann J derived from *Davis* and *Metix*. According to that test, whether an object is a sculpture for copyright purposes must be determined having regard to the ordinary meaning of 'sculpture', unconstrained by one's view of artistic worth or of what one might expect to find in an art gallery. In supporting this test the

[119] *Davis (J & S) (Holdings) Ltd v Wright Health Group Ltd* [1998] RPC 403 (Ch).
[120] See *Metix* (n 118) 721–22. [121] ibid.
[122] *Lucasfilm Ltd v Ainsworth* [2008] EWHC 1878 (Ch), [2009] FSR 2 (*Lucasfilm* Ch).
[123] ibid [118] (vi).
[124] *Breville Europe Plc v Thorn EMI Domestic Appliance Ltd* [1995] FSR 77 (Ch).
[125] See *Lucasfilm* Ch (n 122) [118] (vi). [126] ibid [118] (viii).
[127] See *Lucasfilm Ltd v Ainsworth* [2009] EWCA Civ 1328, [2010] Ch 503; *Lucasfilm Ltd v Ainsworth* [2011] UKSC 39, [2012] 1 AC 208 (*Lucasfilm*).

Supreme Court emphasized its fact-specific nature and the deference it therefore requires to the judgment of the trial judge. Consistent with this, the Court agreed with the view of Mann J that: '[i]t would not accord with the normal use of language to apply the term sculpture to a 20th century military helmet used in the making of a film'.[128]

Lucasfilm is binding UK authority on what constitutes a 'sculpture' for the purposes of the CDPA. It is also an important authority on the need to look beyond the form of a subject matter in order to determine whether it is an LDMA work within the meaning of section 1(1)(a) more generally. Having said that, in reasoning its decision the Supreme Court relied on the special position within copyright of three-dimensional objects, and on a distinction between the 'graduated' protection conferred on such objects by copyright and design right, and the 'indiscriminate protection of literary copyright'.[129] Given this, its opinion may be interpreted by future courts as having nothing to say for works other than sculptures or artistic works, or perhaps—given its reference to the 'indiscriminate protection of literary copyright'[130]—as supporting the expansive (formalistic) conception of literary works from *Infopaq* to which the Court of Appeal in *Meltwater* subscribed; noting that the Supreme Court's judgment in *Lucasfilm*—the copyright aspects of which were decided without reference to EU law—was published on the same day as the Court of Appeal's decision in *Meltwater* (implementing *Infopaq*) was published.

In the United States, a different test of copyright subsistence in utilitarian objects exists. Under §101 of the 1976 Copyright Act (17 USC), the design of a 'useful article'—defined to be 'an article having an intrinsic utilitarian function that is not merely to portray the appearance of the article or to convey information'—is deemed to be a work entitled to artistic copyright 'only if, and only to the extent that, such design incorporates pictorial, graphic, or sculptural features that can be identified separately from, and are capable of existing independently of, the utilitarian aspects of the article'. The meaning of this provision was recently considered, in the context of cheerleading uniforms, by the US Supreme Court in *Star Athletica, LLC v Varsity Brands, Inc.*[131] According to the majority's decision, where the design of a useful article incorporates artistic features, the eligibility of those features for copyright must in all cases be determined by means of the so-called 'separability test' of § 101, regardless of whether the features might otherwise be regarded as works fixed on the medium of the article.[132] This means, the majority held, that in any case involving a pictorial, graphic, or sculptural feature incorporated into the design of a useful article, the protectability of the feature by copyright will depend on whether it

[128] ibid [44]. [129] ibid [48]. [130] ibid.

[131] *Star Athletica, LLC v Varsity Brands, Inc* 580 US (2017) (*Star Athletica*).

[132] *Contra* the opinion of Justice Ginsburg (concurring), whose treatment of the features as works fixed on the medium of the cheerleading uniforms reflects the statement of Lord Mustill in *Ford Motor Co Ltd's Design Applications* [1995] RPC 167 (HL) 178, in the context of UK design law, that useful articles 'form the media through which' designs are put into effect. (For a discussion see ch 7 s 2.1.)

(1) can be perceived as a two- or three-dimensional work of art separate from the useful article and (2) would qualify as a protectable pictorial, graphic, or sculptural work—either on its own or fixed in some other tangible medium of expression—if it were imagined separately from the useful article into which it is incorporated.[133]

On the facts of *Star Athletica*, this test of conceptual separability[134] was held to be satisfied. The reasons were first, that the surface decorations on the cheerleading uniforms incorporated artistic features of relevant type, and second, that those decorations could be separated from the uniforms and applied onto other media 'without replicating' the uniforms themselves.[135] Only Justice Breyer and Justice Kennedy rejected this finding. In Justice Breyer's analysis, supported by Justice Kennedy, even accepting the majority's conceptual separability test, the designs could not be perceived as works of art since, when perceived separately from the cheerleading uniforms, they depicted the uniforms of which they were part.[136] 'The upshot' of this analysis was the view

that one could copyright the floral design on a soupspoon but one could not copyright the shape of the spoon itself no matter how beautiful, artistic, or aesthetically pleasing that shape might be: A picture of the shape of the spoon is also a picture of a spoon; the picture of a floral design is not.[137]

The distinction between the majority and minority decisions in *Star Athletica* can be explained with reference to different conception of the useful articles in question. For the majority, the uniforms were tokens that ceased to exist when represented two-dimensionally. By contrast, the minority treated them as types the existence of which was evidenced by their (two-dimensional) representation. In the context of a discussion of intellectual property subject matter, the minority's conception must be right. Further, the majority's approach effectively replaced the statutory question of whether artistic features incorporated into the design of a useful article might exist independent of the utilitarian aspects of the article with the question of whether those utilitarian aspects might exist without the artistic features. Since the same cheerleading uniforms could plainly be manufactured without the artistic features, its conclusion that they existed independent of the uniforms was inevitable. This was notwithstanding its insistence that the § 101 inquiry focus 'on the extracted feature and not on any aspects of the useful article that remain after the imaginary extraction'.[138]

Of additional interest regarding *Star Athletica* from a European and UK perspective is the majority's rejection of the reasoning of the UK Supreme Court in *Lucasfilm*, discussed above. That rejection can be seen in the majority's decision that the functional nature of an object, such as a uniform or lamp, does not make it unsuitable for protection by artistic copyright regardless of the history of its production, and whether it was created with the intention to exist as such.[139] As the majority said,

[133] See *Star Athletica* (n 131) majority opinion, 1–2.
[134] ibid 14–15. [135] ibid 10. [136] ibid dissenting opinion 1.
[137] ibid majority opinion, 5. [138] ibid 13. [139] ibid 8–10.

affirming earlier US Supreme Court authority, a statuette might have been 'intended for use as a lamp base' and nonetheless protected by copyright as a work of (artistic) authorship, such protection depending on 'how the article and features are perceived, not how or why they were designed'.[140] Further, the proper perception of a given article and its artistic features was treated by the majority as uninformed by the history of its treatment within society.

3.3.1.3 Not Every Collection of Sounds or Movements is a Musical or Dramatic Work

According to Mummery LJ in *Sawkins*, music is to be distinguished from noise as 'intended to produce effects of some kind on the listener's emotions and intellect'.[141] The performative nature of dramatic works, emphasized in *Norowzian*, supports an equivalent distinction between drama and movement, establishing that not every collection of sounds and movements is a musical and dramatic work respectively.

3.3.1.4 Words and Short Phrases, and Other Trivial Subject Matter: The *De Minimis* Principle

The principle *de minimis non curat lex* (the law does not concern itself with trifling matters) has been applied by courts in the UK to deny copyright to trivial subject matter, including particularly words and short phrases. The classic authority is *Francis Day & Hunter v Twentieth Century Fox*,[142] where the Privy Council held that as a general rule 'a title does not involve literary composition, and is not sufficiently substantial to justify a claim to protection' as an independent work,[143] with the result that the title 'The Man Who Broke the Bank at Monte Carlo' was not protected by literary copyright. More recent authorities in support of the same principle include *Football Dataco Ltd v Brittens Pools Ltd*,[144] where Floyd J held that individual entries in football fixtures, such as 'Hull v Wigan at 7.45 pm on February 20', are not the subject of literary copyright,[145] and *Football Dataco Ltd v Sportradar GmbH*,[146] where the Court of Appeal, in a discussion of copyright infringement, held that data involve no intellectual creation and are therefore also not protected by literary copyright.[147] In the other direction is *Meltwater*, where the Court of Appeal noted the possibility of literary copyright in titles and headlines recognized by the *Francis Day & Hunter* line of cases, and affirmed the trial judge's finding 'that newspaper headlines are capable of being original literary works' as 'plainly correct' and 'unassailable'.[148] While this decision does not support any new principles of law, it indicates an increased willingness on the part of the courts to find that short phrases are

[140] ibid 13. [141] See *Sawkins* (n 73) [53].
[142] *Francis Day & Hunter v Twentieth Century Fox* [1940] AC 112 (PC). [143] ibid 123.
[144] *Football Dataco Ltd v Brittens Pools Ltd* [2010] EWHC 841 (Ch), [2010] RPC 17 (*Football Dataco* Ch).
[145] ibid [69].
[146] *Football Dataco Ltd v Sportradar GmbH* [2011] EWCA Civ 330, [2011] FSR 20.
[147] ibid [14]–[16]. [148] See *Meltwater* (n 73) [22].

protected by literary copyright, ie that the general rule of *Francis Day & Hunter* does not apply on the facts of a particular case, following the Court of Justice's decision in *Infopaq* that short strings of words may reflect sufficiently an author's own intellectual creation to require protection under the Information Society Directive. Once again, this is an area in which traditional UK and current EU legal principles exist in tension.

While well established in the cases, it is questionable whether the *de minimis* principle adds anything of substance to the requirement for an LDMA work. The reasoning in *Exxon* supports this suggestion. Specifically, it suggests that the reason that words and some short phrases are not protected by literary copyright is not that they are too trivial to attract protection, but that they are not 'original literary works' properly defined. This is consistent with the reasoning in both *Meltwater* and *Infopaq*. Further, it is consistent with the common law courts' approach to the *de minimis* principle in the context of artistic works, where what seems to be important is not whether a subject matter is simple, but whether it is an authorial (artistic) work.[149] As seen in section 2, the Court of Justice took a similar view in the *Painer* case when it found that a photographic portrait may be original and thus protected by copyright despite the simplicity of its subject matter due to the scope that photographic portraits in general provide for the exercise of free and creative choices in their production.

3.3.1.5 Conclusion

In conclusion, it seems clear from the cases that at least some types of LDMA works require something in addition to the features of LDMA form described above, namely, a history of production that is not inconsistent with them being LDMA works. In practice this means that the mere presence of letters (or some other form of notation), properties of visual significance supported by a three-dimensional object, or combination of sounds or human movement, may not be enough to make a subject matter a literary, artistic, musical, or dramatic work within the meaning of the CDPA: the intent of the person who created the subject matter and/or view of society with respect to its nature needing also to be considered to determine whether they are consistent with the subject matter's categorization as a work of LDMA authorship and thus suitable for protection by LDMA copyright. The result is similar to that produced by the European legal requirement for works to have a certain history of production, considered above,[150] and suggests that if faced with a subject matter that seems to satisfy the statutory definition of one of the categories of LDMA works, but that stretches non-legal understandings of what ought properly to fall within that category, it may not be an LDMA work as a matter of UK law after all. One example of such a subject matter is a literary transcript of a literary work of the type at issue in *Walter v Lane* or other recreation of an LDMA work, which will possess the formal properties of an LDMA work but lack a history

[149] See eg *Roland Corporation v Lorenzo & Sons* (1991) 22 IPR 245 (FCA).
[150] Cf Pila and Torremans (n 31) 282.

of production consistent with it being such a work: perfect copies of LDMA works being created with the intent to exist, and perceived by society to exist, as records or material fixations of LDMA works rather than as LDMA works themselves.

3.3.2 Authorial Works are Original, ie the Product of Independent Skill and Labour

3.3.2.1 The Applicability of the Common Law and EU Law Tests of Originality
For copyright to subsist in an LDMA work, the work must be original.[151] In the CDPA, originality is defined for databases only. That definition is contained in section 3A(2), which transposes Article 3(1) of the Database Directive (providing that 'databases which, by reason of the selection or arrangement of their contents, constitute the author's own intellectual creation shall be protected as such by copyright. No other criteria shall be applied to determine their eligibility for that protection') as follows:

> For the purposes of this Part a literary work consisting of a database is original if, and only if, by reason of the selection or arrangement of the contents of the database the database constitutes the author's own intellectual creation.

As seen in section 2, and consistent with the provenance of section 3A(2) in the Database Directive, the requirement that a work be 'the author's own intellectual creation' is the EU test of originality/authorship, derived from the Berne Convention. Aside from the Database Directive, it is contained in Article 6 of the Term Directive for photographs and Article 1(3) of the Software Directives for computer programs, and has been held by the Court of Justice in a series of cases beginning with *Infopaq* to apply to all authorial works within the meaning of the Information Society Directive.[152] However, it has only been implemented domestically in the UK for databases, notwithstanding the UK's transposition of other provisions of the Term, Software, and Information Society Directives.[153] Given this, it might be inferred that the legislature only intended the EU test to apply with respect to databases, and that for all other LDMA works—including photographs and computer programs—the traditional common law test of originality continues to apply instead. However, and for as long as the UK remains an EU Member State at least, *Marleasing SA v La Comercial Internacional de Alimentacion SA*[154] requires

[151] CDPA s1(1)(a).

[152] See *Infopaq* (n 33) [37] ('copyright within the meaning of [Article 2(a) of the Information Society Directive] is liable to apply only in relation to a subject-matter which is original in the sense that it is its author's own intellectual creation'), interpreted by the Advocate General in Case C–393/09 *Bezpečnostní softwarová asociace—Svaz softwarové ochrany v Ministerstvo kultury* ECLI: EU:C:2010:611 [71] as authority for the proposition that 'copyright applies to a work when it is original in the sense that it is the author's own intellectual creation'.

[153] See Duration of Copyright and Rights in Performances Regulations 1995 (SI 1995/3297); Copyright (Computer Programs) Regulations 1992 (SI 1992/3233); Copyright and Related Rights Regulations 2003 (SI 2003/2498).

[154] Case C–106/89 *Marleasing SA v La Comercial Internacional de Alimentacion SA* [1990] ECR I–4135 (*Marleasing*).

the UK courts to read the CDPA so far as possible to be consistent with the Term, Software, and other EU copyright directives. To the extent that the traditional UK and EU definitions of originality differ, and in the absence of any statutory entrenchment of the former, the UK courts can therefore be said to be required to adopt the EU test of originality for all LDMA works under the CDPA in order to meet their EU legal obligations of consistent interpretation in accordance with the *Marleasing* principle. This view is moreover supported by the statement of the UK Court of Appeal in *SAS Institute* that the Court of Justice in *Infopaq* made up for the EU Legislature's failure in the Information Society Directive to have defined the subject matter in which copyright subsists by deciding that copyright subsists in all literary and artistic works that express an author's own intellectual creation as defined above.[155]

Despite this, it is not the case, or not clearly the case, that the EU test of authorship/originality now applies for all LDMA works under the CDPA. In *Meltwater*, for example, the Court of Appeal read the CJEU's comments in *Infopaq* as merely underlining the connection between originality and authorship, which connection, as discussed below, has always been recognized in the UK.[156] Hence its conclusion that the 'decision of the [CJEU] in *Infopaq* [has not] qualified the long standing test established by the [UK] authorities';[157] a conclusion that suggests that, even while the UK remains an EU Member State, the EU test of originality applies under the CDPA in respect of databases, and perhaps also in respect of photographs and computer programs (by reason of the Term and Software Directives), but not in respect of other types of LDMA works, to which the traditional common law test of the UK consequently still applies. When the UK leaves the EU, the applicability of that common law test will likely extend further to photographs and computer programs, in the absence of any provision in the CDPA applying the EU test to either type of subject matter, unless the UK courts elect to maintain the latter to ensure consistent subsistence standards within UK law and across Europe more generally.

The question arises from this discussion of whether the EU and UK tests of originality/authorship differ in substance. The view among UK courts, expressed also by the Court of Justice in *Football Dataco*, has been that the EU test of originality is more difficult to satisfy than the common law test. According to Floyd J in *Football Dataco*, for example, in a remark repeated later by Lewison LJ in *SAS Institute*,[158] it 'raises the bar' for UK copyright subsistence by imposing a requirement for 'creativity' in the creation of a work.[159] This emphasis on creativity aligns

[155] See also *SAS Institute Inc v World Programming Ltd* [2013] EWCA Civ 1482, [2014] RPC 8 (*SAS Institute* CA) [29] (Lewison LJ, remarking that while 'the Information Society Directive does not expressly deal with the scope of copyright protection (i.e. what is capable of being protected by copyright) [n]evertheless the ECJ (and latterly the CJEU) has supplied the omission').

[156] See *Meltwater* (n 73). [157] ibid [20].

[158] See *SAS Institute* CA (n 155) [37] (Lewison LJ, remarking: 'If the Information Society Directive has changed the traditional domestic test, it seems to me that it has raised rather than lowered the hurdle to obtaining copyright protection').

[159] See *Football Dataco* Ch (n 144) [53].

the EU originality requirement with the US originality requirement, as defined in *Feist Publications Inc v Rural Telephone Service Co Inc*,[160] and is the basis for the courts' view that the EU conception of originality is more difficult to satisfy than the traditional UK conception.

As seen above, the Court of Justice has supported Floyd J's analysis in *Football Dataco* with its decision that the EU test of originality for databases requires that the author 'possess a creative element, or in some way express its creator's personality'.[161] This is consistent with its decision in *Painer* that a photograph is original within the meaning of European copyright law if its subject matter leaves scope for sufficient 'formative freedom' that the photographer has exploited so as to produce a work that reflects her personality,[162] and with its decision in *Infopaq* that the source of a work's originality lies in those of its expressive aspects that can be attributed to its creator.[163]

3.3.2.2 The Common Law Test of Originality: The Requirement for Independent Labour and Skill in the Creation of a Work

3.3.2.2.1 Originality as Independent Origination

As seen above, the UK Legislature introduced the requirement for originality with its enactment of the Copyright Act 1911. The classic authority on the meaning of 'original' at common law remains one of the earliest decisions to consider it: *ULP*. In that case the requirement was defined by Petterson J to mean independent origination, in the sense of expending independent skill and labour to create a work. Applying this test, the judge held the plaintiff's mathematics papers to be original on the ground that they had originated from the examiners, albeit drawing on common mathematical knowledge and spending little time in their production. That definition was affirmed by the House of Lords in *Ladbroke v William Hill (Football) Ltd*,[164] and continues to be frequently cited.

As defined in *ULP*, and as under European law, originality is the other side of the authorship coin, with the result that any work having an author will be original for copyright purposes.[165] This explains why *Walter v Lane* continues to be regarded as good law, despite having been decided in 1900 before the statutory requirement for originality was introduced: namely, because it concerned the question of who is an author for the purposes of copyright. It may also help to explain why the common law test of originality has persisted alongside the stricter EU test, namely, because it has the weight of House of Lords authority behind it.

[160] *Feist Publications Inc v Rural Telephone Service Co Inc* 499 US 340 (1991) (*Feist*). Cf the view of the Canadian courts that 'intellectual creation' is not the same as (and does not necessitate) creativity: see eg *Tele-Direct Publications Inc v American Business Information Inc* [1998] 2 FC 22, 1997 Can L II 6378 (*Tele-Direct*); *CCH Canadian v Law Society of Upper Canada* [2004] 1 SCR 339 (*CCH*), discussed below.

[161] See *Football Dataco* (n 43) [36].

[162] *Painer* (n 40) [42], [99].

[163] See *Infopaq* (n 33) [47], [50].

[164] *Ladbroke v William Hill (Football) Ltd* [1964] 1 WLR 273 (HL) (*Ladbroke*).

[165] See *Sands and McDougall v Robinson* (1917) 23 CLR 49; also *Sawkins* (n 73).

The premise of *ULP* and *Walter v Lane* is that for a work to be original at common law it must have originated from the author in the sense of being the product of her independent labour and skill. Hence the central questions in this area of what constitutes independent labour and skill, and what constitutes labour and skill in the creation of a work specifically.

The leading modern authority on the common law test of originality is *Sawkins*, the majority judgment in which was delivered by Mummery LJ, with a separate opinion by Lord Justice Jacob. In *Sawkins*, the Court of Appeal found new performing editions of existing (17th century) musical works to be original musical works by reason of their production by the plaintiff's investment of 'substantial and independent effort, skill and time'[166]—or in the trial judge's language, approved by the Court of Appeal, 'considerable skill and labour'—in their creation.[167] The fact that the plaintiff in *Sawkins* had 'to a very large degree, reproduced the musical contents of the Lalande source material',[168] and that for three of the four editions he had not composed any new notes or sounds,[169] was irrelevant: his act of making the Lalande music playable by 'transpos[ing] the source material into conventional modern notation, correct[ing] it where necessary and ma[king] certain other additions' was sufficient to confer originality.[170]

The implication of *Sawkins* is that originality requires the creation of a work by labour and skill; labour being insufficient and judgement or creativity perhaps being unnecessary. The fact that part of Dr Sawkins's labour and skill was directed to copying was irrelevant; the only restriction on the labour and skill that can be counted in determining originality being that it must be labour and skill invested in the creation of the work. The point was made by Mummery LJ in the case as follows:

> Although I agree that some aspects of the claimant's exertions, such as time and labour spent on the discovery or retrieval of the original scores and in their layout on the page, are irrelevant to the subsistence of copyright in a musical work, I do not accept the narrow approach advocated by the defendant as to the type and nature of the work required to attract musical copyright. The defendant's emphasis is on the necessity for composition or re-composition of new notes of musical, as in a musical adaptation or arrangement, in order to produce an original combination of sounds appreciated by the ear, rather than on the exacting scholarly exertions of the claimant on the notation of the scores and the inclusion of performing indications and directions.[171]

Lord Justice Jacob's supplementary opinion in *Sawkins* is also important, primarily for its suggestion that labour and skill directed *entirely* to copying—as in the case of a perfectly recreated painting—might support a claim of LDMA copyright in the copy; a result supported by his Lordship with reference to the effect of granting copyright in such copies in promoting public access to the copied work.[172] This suggestion is in keeping with the common law tradition of utilitarian thinking in the field of copyright, and with the expansive view of creation that underpins the European conception of the invention discussed in Chapter 4. However, it is out

[166] See *Sawkins* (n 73) [16]. [167] ibid [23]. [168] ibid [24]. [169] ibid.
[170] ibid [25]. [171] ibid [44]. [172] ibid [87].

of kilter with the continental tradition of deontological thinking that informs the EU view of copyright particularly, and with the focus even of UK law traditionally on supporting the creation and dissemination of *authorial* works. That focus is reflected in the suggestion of *ULP* that a copy of an existing LDMA work is not itself an original LDMA work entitled to copyright, since it is not the product of *independent* skill and labour. To similar effect is the Privy Council's decision in *Interlego* that: '[a] well executed tracing involves much skill and labour but remains what it is, a tracing'.[173] Having said that, *Interlego* involved specific facts—the plaintiff was seeking to extend its intellectual property monopoly in respect of Lego blocks by revising the production drawings and claiming a new copyright in respect of the revised drawings—which makes it a somewhat specific authority. In addition, to the extent of its inconsistency with *Walter v Lane*, it was held to be wrong by the Court of Appeal in *Sawkins* as a matter of precedent. However, and as discussed above, *Walter v Lane* is itself dubious legal authority on the question of literary copyright, casting doubt over the correctness of the Court's treatment of it in *Sawkins* as requiring the rejection of the principle of *Interlego* against LDMA copyright in LDMA recreations.[174]

3.3.2.2.2 Originality as Independent Origination of an LDMA Work

In emphasizing the requirement for labour and skill in the creation of a work, *Sawkins* underlines the importance of conceiving properly the work when determining its originality. This has been a central issue in the context of compilations and databases, as *Ladbroke, Football League*, and *Football Dataco* demonstrate. Of note also is how the courts have strained their conception of works in certain contexts to support a particular finding on originality. Aside from *Walter v Lane*, discussed above, examples include *Interlego* (regarding artistic copyright in production drawings) and *Antiquesportfolio.com Plc v Rodney Pitch & Co Ltd*[175] (regarding artistic copyright in photographs).

Ladbroke, Football League and Football Dataco—*Compilations and Databases*
A compilation, as a literary work, has historically been conceived as a selection and arrangement of information or other material, with the result that only labour and skill in selecting and arranging material counts when determining a compilation's originality.[176] The question that arises is whether this includes labour and skill in deriving or gathering the material itself.

The implication of *Ladbroke* is that it does, on the ground that it is inappropriate to divide the authorial process into its expressive and pre-expressive stages. Thus, in *Ladbroke*, copyright was held to subsist in a compilation of betting coupons on

[173] See *Interlego* (n 75) 263.

[174] See in this regard *Raft Ltd v Freestyle of Newhaven Limited* [2016] EWHC 1711 (IPEC) (*Raft v Freestyle*) [8] (citing *Interlego* (n 75) as supporting the conclusion that a design derived from copying an existing design and altering part of it is not original *in toto*).

[175] *Antiquesportfolio.com Plc v Rodney Pitch & Co Ltd* [2001] FSR 345 (Ch) (*Antiquesportfolio*).

[176] J Pila, 'Compilation Copyright: A Matter Calling for "a Certain … Sobriety"' (2008) 19 Australian Intellectual Property Journal 231.

the basis of the skill and labour expended in calculating the odds, which, in the majority's opinion, overcame the minimal skill and labour in reducing them to the expressive form of the compilation itself. Central to the majority's reasoning was its rejection of the distinction between the expressive and pre-expressive stages of authorship, with the result that in some cases at least, deriving material for compilation would be part of the process of selecting and arranging it.

The same principle explains the earlier decision in *Football League Ltd v Littlewoods Pools Ltd*,[177] where copyright was held to subsist in football fixture lists as compilations on the basis of the labour and skill in both scheduling the games (ie deriving the fixtures) and reducing the schedules to writing. In Upjohn J's analysis, the defendants' argument that these two stages of work needed to be distinguished, and only the latter considered when determining copyright subsistence, was wrong. 'In my judgment', he held,

> [o]n the facts of this case, it is not open to the defendants to try and dissect and break down the efforts of the author in the way suggested. Accordingly in my judgment the plaintiffs are entitled to copyright in the chronological list.[178]

Thus, again, the Court treated the principle against dissecting the authorship of a work into its expressive and pre-expressive stages as requiring that the labour and skill in deriving information contained in a compilation be treated as part of the labour and skill in the creation of the compilation, and thus part of the labour and skill which needed to be considered when determining its originality. Recently, this view of *Football League* was affirmed by Floyd J in another case involving football fixture lists: *Football Dataco*. Nonetheless, the principle that it (and *Ladbroke*) supports has now been rejected by the decision of the Court of Justice—contrary to the decision of the trial judge in *Football Dataco*—that when determining whether copyright subsists in a database, the intellectual effort and skill of creating the data must be excluded. The only relevant effort and skill, the Court of Justice held, is that which expresses 'originality in the selection or arrangement of the data which [the] database contains', where 'selection or arrangement' does not include adding important significance to a pre-existing item of data (by, for example, fixing the date of a football match).[179] Further, the EU test of 'author's own intellectual creation' has been held to require more than significant labour and skill from the author; in particular, and as seen above, it requires that the author 'through the selection or arrangement of the data which [the database] contains ... expresses his creative ability in an original manner by making free and creative choices' to produce a work that reflects his 'personal touch'[180]—a test that would not be 'satisfied when the setting up of the database is dictated by technical considerations, rules or constraints which leave no room for creative freedom'.[181] From a UK perspective, the effect of the decision in *Football Dataco* is to underline the effect of the introduction of database copyright with the Database Directive in rendering compilation copyright redundant.

[177] *Football League Ltd v Littlewoods Pools Ltd* [1959] 1 Ch 637 (ChD) (*Football League*).
[178] ibid 656. [179] See *Football Dataco* (n 43) [46]. [180] ibid [38], [42].
[181] ibid [39].

Originality and Compilations/Databases—A Comparative Look at Telephone Directories

Compilations have tested legal definitions of originality in all common law jurisdictions, producing divergent originality standards reflecting divergent ideas of what copyright exists to protect. At one end of the originality spectrum sits the former Australian 'sweat of the brow' test of copyright subsistence from *Telstra*,[182] and at the other end sits the US 'modicum of creativity' test from *Feist*,[183] with the Canadian 'intellectual creation' test from *Tele-Direct* (also rejecting such protection) purportedly in the middle[184] but in reality very close to the US end.[185]

Telstra, Feist, and *Tele-Direct* all involved the question of copyright subsistence in alphabetically arranged local area telephone directories. In *Telstra*, Finkelstein J held the directories to be original notwithstanding the absence of skill or judgement. In reaching this decision, his Honour emphasized the case as one in which a creative or even new method of selection and arrangement was precluded by 'functional considerations or commercial reasons';[186] his point being that where you have an exhaustive compilation of factual material—ie a compilation that contains all facts of a particular kind (such as a local area telephone directory)—there can be no selection as such, and no feasible method of arranging the material other than the obvious ones of alphabetical, chronological, or sequential grouping. Hence the Judge's quandary—analogous to the quandary that Jacob LJ addressed in *Sawkins* regarding recreations of an artistic work—that the very qualities that make the work more valuable (meaning costly to produce and successful in the market) are also the qualities that threaten its originality and thus its entitlement to copyright protection. In the case of compilations those qualities are accessibility, accuracy, and coverage of data, while for recreations of an artistic work they are fidelity to the original.

The question arises of whether the courts ought to be troubled by copyright's failure to protect what makes an object valuable to the public and/or expensive to produce. Clearly it ought only to do so if the (commercial) value of a work and/or economic expenditure in creating it are legitimate reasons for granting copyright. Finkelstein J in *Telstra* thought that they were, emphasizing precisely these factors as additional justifications for his finding of copyright subsistence in the directory at issue in that case. Canadian and US courts have taken a different view, however, which has now been adopted in Australia too, leading to a successful re-litigation of the *Telstra* dispute.[187] In

182 *Telstra Corporation Ltd v Desktop Marketing Systems Pty Ltd* [2001] FCA 612, (2001) 51 IPR 257 (*Telstra*) (upheld on appeal in [2002] FCAFC 112 but rejected in *IceTV Pty Ltd v Nine Network Pty Ltd* [2009] HCA 14 (*IceTV*)).

183 *Feist* (n 160) 362.

184 See *CCH* (n 160) [22] (McLachlin CJ, rejecting the sweat of the brow standard of originality while also stating 'I would not, however, go as far as [the US Supreme Court] in requiring that a work possess a minimal degree of creativity to be considered original').

185 This is apparent not only from the European interpretation of the 'author's own intellectual creation' test as requiring the exercise of free and creative choices in a work's production, but also from the statement of the Court in *Tele-Direct* (n 160) itself that 'the word "author" conveys a sense of creativity and ingenuity'.

186 See *Telstra* (n 182) [74].

187 See *Telstra Corporation Ltd v Phone Directories Company Pty Ltd* [2010] FCA 44.

Tele-Direct, for example, the Canadian Federal Court, including particularly Décary J, applied something close to the EU conception of originality in support of the finding that telephone directories do not qualify as original intellectual creations and are thus not entitled to Canadian copyright protection. (That conception was later developed and refined by the Supreme Court of Canada in the non-compilation case of *CCH*, where it was held that for a work to be original under Canadian law it must be more than a mere copy of another work and involve 'an exercise of skill and judgment', but need not be creative in the sense of being novel or unique.[188]) Similarly in *Feist*, the Supreme Court rejected a claim to copyright in alphabetically arranged telephone directories, along with the principle of originality by 'industrious collection', and affirmed that under US law labour alone can never make a work original, there being a further need for a 'modicum of creativity'.[189] In the Supreme Court's words, 'copyright rewards originality, not effort',[190] meaning for factual compilations that a work must involve choices as to the facts' selection and arrangement that 'are made independently by the compiler and entail a minimal degree of creativity'.[191]

The question arises as to where on this spectrum the UK test of originality lies. According to a pervasive misconception, it lies at the far left owing to its support of 'sweat of the brow' copyright. Indeed, this was the view of Finkelstein J, whose primary justification for his decision in *Telstra* was English law.[192] It was also the view of McLachlin CJ for the Supreme Court of Canada in *CCH*.[193] Nonetheless, it is incorrect: there is no clear judicial authority for the proposition that modern UK law supports 'sweat of the brow' copyright.[194] On the contrary, the authorities that exist are against this proposition; a factor that influenced the High Court of Australia in its rejection of the principle of *Telstra* in *IceTV*.[195]

As for where on the spectrum the UK common law test is located: on the authority of *Sawkins* that the test is one of 'labour and skill', it is certainly to the right of the former Australian test. If the courts are correct, however, that EU law has 'raised the bar' for copyright subsistence in the UK, in the sense of imposing a requirement more onerous than the common law originality requirement,[196] it will be to the left of the Canadian and US tests. While the concept of 'labour and skill' does seem different from that of judgement or creativity, as suggested above, it is difficult to think of a subject matter that would be an original LDMA work within the meaning of UK law but not an authorial work within the meaning of EU law, suggesting that the difference may be more apparent than real.[197]

188 See *CCH* (n 160) [16] and [24]. 189 See *Feist* (n 160) [51]. 190 ibid [55].
191 ibid [16]. 192 See *Telstra* (n 182) [64]. 193 See *CCH* (n 160) [15].
194 See Pila, 'Compilation Copyright: A Matter Calling for "a Certain … Sobriety"' (n 176).
195 *IceTV* (n 182) [33]. 196 See *Football Dataco* Ch (n 144) [53].
197 See eg *Raft v Freestyle* (n 174) [7] and [9] (describing the UK test of originality as satisfied by the expenditure of 'aesthetic judgment', and suggesting that '[t]he difference may be only semantic').

Returning to *Ladbroke*, it is clear that the case would be treated today as involving a database rather than a compilation, and assessed with reference to the section 3A(2) test of originality, as with the football fixtures in *Football Dataco*. This is consistent with the Court of Appeal's suggestion in *Football Dataco v Yahoo! UK Ltd*[198]—subsequently supported by the CJEU[199]—that the copyright provisions of the Database Directive replaced existing national laws as to the subsistence of copyright in compilations. Thus, the *Ladbroke* compilation would only be original if, by reason specifically of the selection and arrangement of its data, it were held to constitute the author's own intellectual creation. And as suggested above, on the approach of *Football Dataco*, it seems clear that it would not be so held: not because of the shift from the UK to the EU originality standard, but rather on the ground that the calculation of the betting odds would no longer be regarded as part of the selection and arrangement of the odds, and thus, the labour and skill in calculating the odds would no longer count when determining the work's originality.

Interlego—*Production Drawings*

In *Interlego*, the Privy Council held that design drawings for Lego blocks created by adapting pre-existing drawings to new technical specifications manifested insufficient labour and skill to be original; its reasoning being that while the labour and skill in conceiving the technical specifications were substantial, they did not count for originality purposes on the ground that the specifications themselves were not part of the drawings (artistic works) for copyright purposes. This conception of the artistic work is difficult to accept, however, in that it focuses entirely on the drawings' formal properties, and ignores the other (non-formal) properties of LDMA works above. It also ignores the UK authorities that suggest that production and other working drawings need not be exclusively pictorial for copyright purposes. An example is *Solar Thomson Engineering Co v Barton*,[200] where the Court of Appeal distinguished mere concentric circles (alleged to be too simple to attract artistic copyright) from the circles in issue, being 'concentric circles drawn to the precise measurements which illustrate in plan the rubber ring to which the drawing relates'.[201] Another is *Lerose Ltd v Hawick Jersey International Ltd*,[202] where Whitford J rejected an argument that point patterns for knitting machines could not be regarded as artistic works by reason of their inclusion of technical (machine) instructions.[203] A third is *Wham-O*, where the New Zealand Court of Appeal disagreed that 'for copyright words and figures did not form part of the drawing and could not be taken into account in interpreting it', describing the statutory categories of drawing as each conveying 'in ordinary experience ... the concept of drawn lines in combination with words and figures'.[204] And finally, there is *Abraham Moon*, confirming that textual instructions for weaving fabric might be a graphic work if they have 'visual

198 *Football Dataco v Yahoo! UK Ltd* [2010] EWCA Civ 1380 [13]–[15].
199 *Football Dataco* (n 43) [52].
200 *Solar Thomson Engineering Co v Barton* [1997] RPC 537 (CA).
201 ibid 558.
202 *Lerose Ltd v Hawick Jersey International Ltd* [1973] FSR 15 (Ch).
203 ibid 21–22.
204 See *Wham-O* (n 83) 146.

significance' to 'an experienced fabric designer' such that the designer 'could look at [the instructions] and visualize what the fabric looks like',[205] and provided also that they are recorded.[206]

Antiquesportfolio.com—*Photographs*

Antiquesportfolio.com involved the question of photographic originality. In this context, the nature of the work is a statutory given—it is 'a recording of light or other radiation on any medium on which an image is produced or from which an image may by any means be produced, and which is not part of a film',[207] consistent with the international and EU view of photographs above.

How then is the originality of a photograph to be determined; and, in particular, what makes a photographer an author? According to Lloyd J in *Creation Records*, the act of taking a photograph is itself an act of origination sufficient to confer originality, unless the photograph was taken under direction (making the photographer, in the language of *Walter v Lane*, 'a mere scribe'[208]). The implication of the judge's decision, as *Antiquesportfolio.com* makes clear, is that it is the choice and positioning of the subject matter and other factors affecting the final visual effect of the photo itself (eg the lighting, the camera angle etc) that make a photographer an author for copyright purposes and a photograph original. On this view, any intentionally taken photograph of a single, static, or non-spherical three-dimensional object (eg an antique)—and perhaps of a single, static, and two-dimensional object as well—will be original on the basis of the photographer's responsibility for the visual properties of the resulting photograph. This is broadly consistent with the approach of the CJEU in *Painer*, discussed in section 2. So too the Court's decision in *Painer* that, once found to subsist, copyright in a photograph is as extensive as copyright in other original LDMA works is consistent with the decision of Judge Birss QC in *Temple Island*.

3.4 Conclusion

An authorial work within the meaning of UK copyright law is any bounded expressive object comprising an original LDMA work. For a subject matter to satisfy this definition it must have a certain LDMA expressive form produced by a person's

205 See *Abraham Moon* (n 102) [203]; also [103] ('[T]he fact the ticket was not produced by drawing lines must be irrelevant. The ticket was produced by someone with sufficient artistic skill to record the visual appearance he wanted to create in the form of the numbers and letters on that document. If Mr Aveyard had sketched out a picture of Skye Sage, then derived the details for the ticket stamp, and thrown away the sketch as superfluous, the result would be the same but Mr Turner could not then deny the existence of an artistic work recording the appearance of Skye Sage. I do not see why it matters that there was no sketch because the artist did not need to draw one in order to record the visual impression he wanted to create and thereby fix it in a material form').

206 ibid [104] ('Fixation is an important aspect of literary and artistic copyright (cf art 2 Berne Convention). Although s 3(2) of the 1988 Act only refers to literary, dramatic and musical work, and s4 has no corresponding provision, I presume that is just because it is assumed that s4(1) inevitably requires a record of the work in a material form. If the image of Skye Sage had not been fixed, that would be a different matter, but the ticket acts as a record of the image').

207 CPDA s 4(2). 208 See *Walter v Lane* (n 73) 554.

exercise of independent skill and labour the recognition of which as an authorial work of LDMA type is not inconsistent with the intention of that person and/or the view of society with respect to its nature.

4. Entitlement: Copyright Is for Authors

Legal conceptions of the subject matter protected by copyright are necessarily influenced by legal conceptions of the nature, aims, and beneficiaries of that protection, including most directly the principles governing copyright entitlement, and *vice versa*. Given this—and in particular given the nature of copyright subject matter and of copyright, and the particular deontological and utilitarian values that underpin it[209]—it is hardly surprising that in Europe, the United Kingdom, and other jurisdictions such as the United States and Canada, copyright is presumptively a right of creators, and more specifically of authors.[210]

Under section 11 of the CDPA, LDMA copyright is first owned by the author of the work or, for LDMA works made in the course of employment, by the employer of the author, subject to certain exceptions for works of the Crown, parliament, or international organizations, and subject also to any contrary provision by contract. An 'author' for these purposes is defined in section 9 of the CDPA to mean, for LDMA works, the creator of the work or, for computer-generated works, the person who makes the arrangements necessary for the work's creation. As for inventors, authors within the meaning of UK and also European law are clearly natural persons. Section 10 further defines joint authors as two or more authors who collaborate to contribute indistinct contributions to a work.

According to the courts, the principle that authors first own copyright in their works is valid also for commissioned works, subject still to any contrary provision by contract. As for what is required to make a person an author or joint author of a work: in *Robin Ray v Classic FM Plc*[211] it was held that contributing ideas to a work without any 'penmanship' will rarely suffice.[212] This is consistent with the more general principle expressed by the trial judge in *Fisher v Brooker*,[213] and supported on appeal by the Court of Appeal and House of Lords in that case, that an author of an LDMA work and joint owner of its copyright includes any person who makes a significant contribution to that which earns the work its protection, regardless of any industry custom—except perhaps an 'invariable and certain' one—of denying such persons a legal interest in the work.[214] In *Fisher v Brooker* itself, the result was

[209] See ch 2.

[210] See *Tele-Direct* (n 160) ('The use of the word "copyright" in the English version of the Act has obscured the fact that what the Act fundamentally seeks to protect is "*le droit d'auteur*" ').

[211] *Robin Ray v Classic FM Plc* [1998] FSR 622 (Ch).

[212] ibid 636.

[213] *Fisher v Brooker* [2006] EWHC 3239 (Ch), [2007] FSR 12 (*Fisher v Brooker* Ch); [2009] UKHL 41, [2009] 1 WLR 1764 (*Fisher v Brooker*).

[214] See *Fisher v Brooker* Ch (n 213) [11] and [60]. One of the two reasons given by the trial judge for granting permission to the defendants in *Fisher* to appeal his decision was their 'insistence ... that the

a finding that the author of the organ solo included within Procol Harum's tune *A Whiter Shade of Pale* was among the authors of that tune; the solo being, in the Court's decision, a distinctive and significant contribution to the musical composition as a whole, and the product of originality.[215]

5. Conclusions: Authorial Works as Artifact Types Having Certain Properties and Arranged in Categories that Express and Reflect those Properties

Returning once again to the analytic framework discussed in Chapter 3, it remains to answer the questions derived from it for the copyright (author's rights) regime.

(a) What are the categories of subject matter protected by the regime, and what are those subject matters' essential properties?

The main category of subject matter protected by copyright is the category of authorial works. In Europe and the UK, this category is understood to contain every original expressive production in the literary, artistic, or scientific domain and every original literary, dramatic, musical, and artistic work respectively. Thus defined, the essential properties of authorial works are: (a) their possession of a certain (in the UK, LDMA) expressive form; and (b) the history of their production. With respect to (b), the relevant property may be more specifically described as the property of having derived from a process involving the exercise of free and creative choices by one or more persons to produce a bounded expressive object that reflects their personality or personal touch (Europe), or of having been produced by the exercise of independent skill and labour and not having been intended and/or accepted by society to exist as something *other than* an authorial work of LDMA type (UK).

It is clear from this conception that the copyright work, as an expressive object the existence of which depends on the productive actions and intentions of one or more human beings, being the authors of the object in question, conforms closely to the paradigmatic conception of IP subject matter as artifacts considered in Chapter 3. While it may be objected that the physicality of works of visual art deprives them of the intangibility of such subject matter, making them (in some

decision would have a widespread and dire effect on the way that the music industry has operated in the past.' In the Court of Appeal, Mummery LJ, with whom the other Judges agreed, decided that the trial judge had been 'entitled to find that Matthew Fisher made a creative contribution to the Work', and 'right to grant a declaration as to his co-authorship' of the Work, but wrong to declare him co-owner of its copyright (*Brooker v Fisher* [2008] EWCA Civ 287, [2008] FSR 26 [114], [89]). In his Lordship's decision, the equitable considerations raised by Fisher's 38-year delay in asserting his ownership claim prevented it from succeeding. This decision was overturned by the House of Lords on appeal, which reinstated the trial judge's decision that Fisher co-owned copyright in the Work on the basis of his co-authorship of it (see *Fisher v Brooker* [41] (Lord Neuberger, others agreeing)).

[215] See *Fisher v Brooker* Ch (n 213) [11].

cases at least) tokens for which there exists no type, this is not consistent with the legal position in Europe or the UK. According to the UK position, while most artistic works *do* require a certain materiality to come into existence, accounting for the absence of any fixation requirement for them under the CDPA—contrary to the position of literary, dramatic, and musical works, and unless they are first realized in literary or other non-artistic form[216]—once found to exist they are protected by copyright in the same manner as other authorial works, namely, as intangible expressive objects, and thus independent of the fact and form of their fixation per se. Given this, we can say that artistic works are intangible in nature, and that it is in their conception as artifact types specifically that they are protected by copyright. In addition, however, and as remarked in Chapter 3, UK and European law is sensitive to the different nature of artistic and non-artistic works, taking account of that difference in its tests of copyright subsistence and infringement, as well as in its recognition of the additional rights of certain artists to profit from re-sales of the original fixation of their works of visual art.[217]

In addition to being intangible, authorial works are intellectual creations in the sense considered in section 2.2 of Chapter 3. Further, and as conceived under both European and UK law, authorial works may be said to satisfy the more restrictive view of the human acts triggering the recognition of property rights supported by the High Court of Australia in *Doodeward v Spence*,[218] in contrast to the performances, broadcasts, phonograms, films, and typographical arrangements of published editions protected by related rights, which satisfy the less restrictive view supported in *Yearworth v North Bristol NHS Trust*.[219] The reason is the requirement in both jurisdictions for a transformative act on the part of one or more natural persons giving rise to a new authorial work, in the sense not of an LDMA work that differs from that which existed previously, but rather of a work that can be said to have originated with the relevant persons rather than having been copied from someone else. In Europe, this requirement is reflected in the restriction of copyright to works that express the intellectual creation of an author (ie works that result from a putative author's exercise of free and creative choices and reflect her personal touch), and in the UK it is reflected in the restriction of copyright to works produced by independent skill and labour. Only if the decision in *Walter v Lane*, or the opinion of Lord Justice Jacob in *Sawkins*, were accepted as good law, and LDMA copyright accepted as capable of subsisting in verbatim transcripts and other recreations of existing LDMA works, would a different conclusion be required in the case of UK law specifically. In that situation, the different conclusion would be that under UK law, even the act of recreating an existing LDMA work is sufficient to

[216] This is why, in *Abraham Moon* (n 102) [104], Birss J underlined the need for a literary depiction of an artistic work to be fixed in order for the work to be protected by artistic copyright on its basis, notwithstanding the absence of any reference to artistic works in CDPA s 3(2). See n 206.

[217] See Directive 2001/84/EC of the European Parliament and of the Council of 27 September 2001 on the resale right for the benefit of the author of an original work of art [2001] OJ L 272/32.

[218] *Doodeward v Spence* [1908] HCA 45, (1908) 6 CLR 406 (*Doodeward*).

[219] *Yearworth v North Bristol NHS Trust* [2009] EWCA Civ 37, [2010] QB 1 (*Yearworth*).

justify the recognition of copyright, consistent with the principle of *Yearworth* and the view of public policy expressed by Lord Justice Jacob in *Sawkins*, namely,

> [t]hat the sort of work done by [a recreationist] should be encouraged. It saves others the time and trouble of recreation of near-lost works, but in no sense creates monopoly in them. If someone wants to use the claimant's short cut, they need his permission.[220]

It is on this basis, it might be said, that the acts of acting, singing, delivering, declaiming, playing in, or otherwise performing an authorial (LDM) work, [221] and fixing such acts, transmitting electronically images, sounds, or other information for reception by the public,[222] fixing sounds, [223] fixing moving images with or without accompanying sounds,[224] and arranging printed literary, musical, or dramatic material for publication,[225] are recognized as acts triggering the protection of intellectual property in the form of related rights,[226] notwithstanding the absence of any transformative act of human creation in the *Doodeward* sense.

Finally, legal conceptions of the work as an intangible expressive object that needs to be recorded in order to be protected but that exists independent of the fact and form of its recording—and the IP rights in which are infringed by its unauthorized instantiation in whole or substantial part—reflect a view of works as norm kinds, namely, objects (types) of which there exist properly and improperly formed examples (tokens), and moreover as Platonic entities, namely, ideals represented in their tokens. Similarly with respect to legal conceptions of related rights subject matter as expressive objects the IP rights in which are infringed by their unauthorized instantiation in whole or substantial part, which reflect a view of those subject matter also as norm kinds at least.

The view of authorial works and related rights subject matter as norm kinds makes the possibility of their imperfect exemplification important in the context of infringement particularly. To consider this further, it is useful to return to Nicholas Wolterstorff's phenomenology of art and its examples.[227] With certain exceptions, including its treatment of paintings as intangible (authorial) objects, and thus as artifact types, copyright law may be said to reflect that phenomenology. Central to it are three distinctions. The first is between the fields of performing and non-performing arts. The second, within the field of performing arts, is between performance works (ie works capable of performance), performances of them (being occurrences or events that occur at a certain time and place), and copies of each. And the third, within the field of non-performing arts, is between object works (ie works of which there can be an impression, casting, or example etc), objects of them (being physical entities in the form of impressions, castings, examples etc),

220 See *Sawkins* (n 73) [87].
221 See Rome Convention art 3(a); WPPT art 2(a); CDPA s 180(2).
222 See Rome Convention art 3(f); WPPT art 2(f); CDPA s 6(1).
223 See Rome Convention art 3(b); WPPT art 2(b); CDPA s 5A(1).
224 See CDPA s 5B (1) and (2).
225 ibid s 8(1).
226 See Information Society Directive arts 2–4 and recitals; CDPA ss 1(1)(b)–(c) and 180(1)–(1A).
227 See N Wolterstorff, 'Toward an Ontology of Art Works' (1975) 9 *Noûs* 115.

and copies of each.[228] In Wolterstorff's treatment, performance works and performances, as well as object works and objects of object works, can all properly be regarded as authorial works (in his language, 'works of art'), in contrast to copies of them. That copyright and related rights law depends broadly on the same phenomenology can be seen in its distinction between the performing and non-performing arts, reflected in the UK legal view of musical and dramatic works as combinations of sounds and movements intended and suitable for realization in performance, of LDM works as capable of performance, and of LDMA works (excluding dramatic and musical works from the category of literary works[229]) as works of which there can be an impression, casting, or example (including for LDM works a published edition). It can also be seen in the law's distinction between the authorial works protected by copyright, which it defines to include performance works, object works, and certain objects of object works (such as impressions of a print), and the subject matter protected by related rights, which it defines to include performances and most objects of object works (including sound recordings, films, and broadcasts). Third, it can be seen in the law's distinction between (performance and object) works on the one hand, and objects of object works, performances, and copies of each and of (performance and object) works on the other, which corresponds broadly to the distinction between the authorial works protected by copyright, and the instantiations or tokens of those works: (a) the creation of which is necessary in the UK to trigger the subsistence of literary, dramatic, or musical (and potentially artistic) copyright;[230] and (b) the production or public communication of which is also necessary in the UK or Europe to infringe their copyright. And finally, and closely related to this, it can be seen in the law's distinction between objects of object works and performances on the one hand, and copies of them on the other, which corresponds broadly to the distinction between the non-authorial expressive productions protected by related rights and the tokens of those productions the creation of which will be necessary to infringe their related rights.

(b) How is each subject matter individuated within the regime?

Every subject matter protected by copyright and related rights must be capable of individuation *qua* authorial work or related rights subject matter. This is supported by the UK cases emphasizing the need for a single and clearly identifiable work in order for copyright to be said to subsist and to have been infringed. It is also supported by the UK legislative requirement that LDM works be recorded in writing or otherwise in order to be protected—whether or not by their authors, and whether or not the recording survives—in order to help to establish the existence and nature of each work protected by copyright. Recalling the different metaphysical and epistemic notions of individuation considered in previous chapters, it is

228 ibid 117.

229 See eg CDPA s 3(1).

230 With an exception for performances of works, which will be insufficient to trigger copyright in them. On the potential need for such instantiations or tokens to trigger artistic copyright see *Abraham Moon* (n 102).

clear that the same reliance is not placed on the perspective of experts when deciding whether a subject matter is an individual work of relevant type as when deciding whether a subject matter is an invention in the patent field.[231] This might be said to reflect the comparative accessibility of the subject matter protected by copyright and related rights, and the wider and more general nature of the audience to whom authorial works and related rights subject matter on the whole are directed. It might also suggest a prioritizing of the view of authorial works and related rights subject matter as needing to be capable of individuation in the metaphysical sense of being whatever it is that makes them the single works and subject matter that they are over the view of them as needing to be capable of being singled out (*qua* authorial works and related rights subject matter) as distinct objects of perception by a certain intelligent individual; a suggestion that is perhaps supported in copyright by the tendency of the courts to focus on the formal properties of authorial works and related rights subject matter when individuating them. However, and as remarked in the context of plant varieties in Chapter 4, an essential feature of the law is its claim to authority, and the process of individuating the subject matter protected by copyright in particular depends essentially on predicting what the courts, comprised of intelligent individuals, would single out as distinct objects of perception. Further, it is clear that where a given subject matter *is* directed to a specialist audience, the courts will consider how it is perceived in fact by members of that audience.[232] Given this, individuation in the epistemic sense is also of central importance in copyright. Further, the same can be said regarding related rights for the simple and obvious reason that an object not perceived by the courts to be a single performance, broadcast, phonogram, film, or typographical arrangement will not be protected as such.

Some insight into the law's understanding of how works and related rights subject matter are individuated and identified is provided by its requirements for fixation and infringement. In EU and UK law—in contrast to the position in US law—performances are not authorial works protected by copyright. While plainly an instantiation of an authorial work, a performance of a work will not itself suffice to trigger or infringe copyright in the work. Only if the performance is recorded will copyright be triggered in the work performed, and then by virtue of the recording (rather than the occurrence of the performance itself); and only if the performance is recorded or in public will copyright in the work

[231] See eg Case T–68/11 *Kastenholz v Office for Harmonisation in the Internal Market (Trade Marks and Designs) (OHIM)* ECLI:EU:T:2013:298 [16]–[21] (denying a request to permit a professor of art to give expert evidence in a case involving artistic copyright on the basis that 'whether or not copyright protection exists for the original idea underlying a work of art is an assessment of a legal nature which, in the context of the present proceedings, does not fall within the competence of an expert on art').

[232] See eg *Designers Guild* (n 96) 2423 (approving reliance on 'expert evidence in identifying those features of an artistic work which enable it to produce a particular visual effect', which effect as above is part of what constitutes an artistic work as such); *Designers Guild* (n 96) 2423 (Lord Hoffmann); *Newspaper Licensing Agency Limited v Marks & Spencer plc* [2001] UKHL 38, [2002] RPC 4 (*NLA v Marks & Spencer*) [21] (regretting the absence of expert evidence on the nature of the skill and labour involved in a typographical arrangement of a published edition); *Abraham Moon* (n 102) [103]. See n 205.

performed be infringed, and then by virtue of the recording or public communication of the work. Further, recordings and public performances are not the only instantiations of even performative works (such as musical and dramatic works) that the law recognizes as sufficient to trigger or infringe copyright. Rather, it also recognizes instructions for performing a performance work in the form, for example, of musical and dramatic scripts. Such instructions are not strictly speaking copies of the work at all, but rather descriptions of the idea for it, akin to the description of the idea for an invention that must be provided in any patent application, and to the description of the idea for a textile design accepted as being sufficient to establish the existence of that design as a graphic work in *Abraham Moon*. Nonetheless, and unlike the invention in patent law, works in copyright law are not conceived as ideas, but rather, and as noted above, as Platonic entities that have some independent existence and that are capable of being represented in a variety of different forms. This is consistent with the treatment of musical and dramatic scripts as imperfect 'recordings' or examples of the works that they describe, reinforcing the nature of works in general as norm-kinds, and raising the difficult question of how to tell whether a given script or other thing is a sufficiently correct example of a work to trigger its copyright.

In practice this question rarely arises. By contrast, the question of how to tell whether a thing is a sufficiently correct example of a certain work that its production or communication to the public infringes copyright in the work arises frequently.

For copyright or related rights to be infringed as a matter of European and UK law, a third party must, without the permission of the copyright owner, do one of the acts reserved to the owner with respect to the whole or a substantial part (UK),[233] or the whole or a part (Europe),[234] of the protected work or subject matter. In practice, determining this involves two questions. The first is whether the allegedly infringing act has been done with respect to the whole of a subject matter or a (substantial) part of it. And the second is whether, if it has been, the allegedly infringing act is among the acts reserved exclusively to the copyright or related rights owner. From the first of these questions one can formulate an identity criterion for individual works and subject matter that enables the determination of whether certain elements X represent a (substantial) part of subject matter Y, such that deriving X from Y will potentially infringe the copyright or related rights in Y. Differently formulated, the question being asked might be said to be whether X is a sufficiently correct or incorrect example of Y so as to be regarded as a token of it. When deciding this in the context of authorial works, the European courts ask whether X expresses the intellectual creation that is Y,[235] and the UK courts ask whether X expresses enough of the LDMA originality of Y.[236] In both jurisdictions, the focus is therefore on the extent to which X reflects that which earned

[233] See CDPA s 16(3)(a). [234] See Information Society Directive arts 2–4.
[235] See eg *Infopaq* (n 33) [48].
[236] See eg *Designers Guild* (n 96) 2423 (Lord Hoffmann); *NLA v Marks & Spencer* (n 232) [19].

Y its protection by copyright, with the same approach being taken in respect of related rights.[237] From this we can see that the test of (substantial) part infringement is essentially a test of identity and of intellectual creation (as conceived for the purposes of copyright and related rights respectively): if X reflects sufficiently that which makes Y the authorial work or related rights subject matter that it is conceived in law to be, in the sense of reflecting sufficiently that which earned the creator of Y its protection, then it will be a sufficiently important part of Y to make the act of copying or communicating it without permission an infringement of copyright or related rights. Where Y is an authorial work, the result of this test is effectively to require that X be a sufficiently important part of Y *qua* authorial work to make the person who contributes it an author of Y in the *Fisher v Brooker* sense. Hence, once again, the method of answering the identity question for works above reflects the earlier understanding of what individuates a subject matter *qua* authorial work. Similarly where Y is a related rights subject matter, its result will be to require the courts' assessment of the nature of the skill and labour required to produce a subject matter of relevant type. Given the role of technology in producing such subject matter particularly, this can be expected to change over time. Hence the decision of the House of Lords in *NLA v Marks & Spencer* that, while related rights for typographical arrangements of a published edition were introduced to protect the 'skill in designing the pages and labour and capital in setting up the type and keeping it standing',[238] in the context of modern typographical arrangements involving a newspaper, its purpose is rather to protect the skill and labour invested in selecting and arranging the fonts, columns, margins, and other aspects by means of which the arrangement of a newspaper's content is expressed.[239]

(c) What is the relationship between each subject matter and its tokens?

The tokens of an authorial work instantiate the work by reproducing or, in the case of LDM works at least, representing it. By contrast, the tokens of a performance, phonogram, broadcast, film, or typographical arrangement instantiate the subject matter by reproducing (rather than representing) it. Each work or subject matter is instantiated in its tokens. The work or subject matter is thus the object or occurrence that the tokens instantiate.

The tokens of a given subject matter have in common their expressive form, consistent with their reproduction of the subject matter. By contrast, the tokens of a given work will not necessarily have the same expressive form by virtue of their ability to represent rather than reproduce the work. Thus, a textual description of a graphic work will have a different expressive form from a copy of the work. However, tokens of works and related rights subject matter all share a causal

[237] See eg *NLA v Marks & Spencer* (n 232) [19]–[20] (regarding the method for determining the infringement of related rights in typographical arrangements of a published edition).
[238] ibid [21]. [239] ibid [23].

connection to the protected work or subject matter, owing to the requirement that any infringing act involve that work or subject matter.

(d) How is the existence of each subject matter and its tokens known?

In law the existence of an authorial work and related rights subject matter must be established by evidence, including in the UK the evidence provided by the material record of the work that triggered its protection, if that record still exists. The existence of one or more of a work's or subject matter's tokens is also known in the manner above, namely, from the existence of a thing or event (in the form of a communication) that the court would understand: (a) to incorporate or involve the whole or a (substantial) part of the protected work or subject matter that it has accepted to exist; and (b) to have been derived from it.

6

The Trade Mark, Other Product Designations, and Goodwill

1. Registered Protection for Trade Marks and Other Product Designations, and Unregistered Protection for Goodwill

1.1 Registered and Unregistered Protection for Trade Marks

Whereas inventions and plant varieties are protected by grant of a public authority following application and examination, and authorial works and related rights subject matter are protected automatically upon their creation, trade marks receive protection both by grant of a public authority following application and examination, and automatically, upon the development of goodwill in relation to them. They are thus the objects of registered and unregistered intellectual property (IP) rights.

As with plant variety rights, registered trade marks in Europe are governed by both domestic and European (EU) legislation, establishing two titles of IP right: the first domestic, and the second EU-wide. In addition, while domestic trade marks are governed by domestic legislation, that legislation has been extensively harmonized by an EU directive the provisions of which mirror those of the EU legislation governing the grant of unitary (EU) trade mark rights. As a result, registered UK trade mark protection is essentially governed by EU law. By contrast, unregistered domestic trade mark protection in Europe has not been harmonized, and is governed in the United Kingdom by common law.

Focusing first on registered trade marks, section 1(1) of the Trade Marks Act 1994 (UK) (Trade Marks Act) identifies the basic subject matter of protection as the 'trade mark', and defines that term to mean any 'sign', including a collective or certification mark, that is 'capable of being represented graphically [and] of distinguishing goods or services of one undertaking from those of other undertakings'. However, the existence of a trade mark is not sufficient for registered UK trade mark protection, and the relationship between the statutory definition of protectable subject matter and the other requirements for registration is a matter of some conceptual and practical difficulty.

Even a cursory look at European and UK trade mark legislation underscores this difficulty. The relevant instruments are the EU Trade Mark Regulation,[1] which governs the grant of unitary (EU) trade marks, the EU Trade Marks Directive,[2] which harmonizes the substantive trade mark law of EU Member States applicable in respect of domestic trade mark registrations, and the Trade Marks Act, which governs the grant of domestic (UK) trade marks. The important provisions of these instruments are Articles 4, 7, and 8 of the EU Trade Mark Regulation, and the corresponding Articles 3, 4, and 5 of the Directive and sections 1(1), 3, and 5 of the Trade Marks Act. These provisions distinguish between three types of subject matter. The first are 'signs' within the meaning of Article 4 of the Regulation, Article 3 of the Directive, and section 1(1) of the Trade Marks Act, which include 'in particular, words, including personal names, designs, letters, numerals, colours, the shape of goods or of the packaging of goods, or sounds'.[3] The second are 'trade marks' within the meaning of Articles 4 and 7(1)(e) of the Regulation, Articles 3 and 4(1)(e) of the Directive, and sections 1(1) and 3(2) of the Trade Marks Act, which are those signs capable of supporting protection as a trade mark, namely, signs as defined immediately above that are

> capable of: (a) distinguishing the goods or services of one undertaking from those of other undertakings; and (b) being represented on the Register of European Union trade marks ... in a manner which enables the competent authorities and the public to determine the clear and precise subject matter of the protection afforded to its proprietor

—and that do not consist exclusively of functional, technical, or aesthetic characteristics of goods.[4] And the third are registrable trade marks within the meaning of Articles 7 and 8 of the Regulation, Articles 4 and 5 of the Directive, and sections 3 and 5 of the Trade Marks Act, which are 'trade marks' as defined immediately above that do not fall within any of the absolute or relative exclusions from registration, and that may thus be registered for protection as a unitary (EU) or domestic (UK) trade mark.

[1] Council Regulation (EC) No 207/2009 of 26 February 2009 on the Community trade mark [2009] OJ L 78/1, as amended (Regulation).

[2] Directive (EU) 2015/2436 of the European Parliament and of the Council of 16 December 2015 to approximate the laws of the Member States relating to trade marks [2015] OJ L 336/1 (Directive).

[3] Regulation art 4; Directive art 3. This definition was introduced in 2015, and will take effect in Regulation art 4 on 1 October 2017 (see Regulation (EU) 2015/2424 [2015] OJ L 341/21 arts 1(8) and 4). Member States will have until 14 January 2019 to implement the amendments under Directive art 3. Until then a 'sign' within the meaning of the Regulation at least will include 'particularly words, including personal names, designs, letters, numerals, the shape of goods or of their packaging', consistent with the definition in Trade Marks Act s 1(1) (providing that a trade mark 'may, in particular, consist of words (including personal names), designs, letters, numerals or the shape of goods or their packaging'). Signs within the meaning of UK and European legislation include 'indications' of source: see eg Regulation art 7(1)(c) and (d); Directive art 4(1)(c) and (d); Trade Marks Act s 3(1)(c) and (d).

[4] Cf Trade Marks Act s 3(2), which reflects the pre-2015 wording of the Regulation and Directive in its exclusion only of shapes (and not other characteristics) of goods. According to the Advocate General in Case C–163/ 16 *Christian Louboutin SAS v Van Haren Schoenen BV* ECLI:EU:C:2017:495 (*Christian Louboutin v Van Haren*) [64], the absence of any transitional provisions in the 2015 Directive 'may indicate' a view that the law under each is the same.

Of immediate note regarding the statutory definition of the term 'trade mark' above is its difference from the definition contained in section 1(1) of the Trade Marks Act in its requirement that a sign not be comprised exclusively of functional, technical, or aesthetic characteristics of goods. That this requirement *is* part of the definition of 'trade mark' is clear from the description of the subject matter excluded by reason of their possession of the relevant characteristics as 'signs', in contrast to the description of the subject matter that fall within any of the absolute or relative exclusions from registration as 'trade marks'. It is also consistent with the Court of Justice's description of subject matter comprised exclusively of functional, technical, or aesthetic characteristics of goods as 'signs that do not constitute trade marks', and of the provisions excluding such subject matter as thus representing 'a preliminary obstacle' to establishing the protectability of a sign.[5] The only way in which this more restrictive definition of the term 'trade mark' might be reconciled with the more expansive definition contained in section 1(1) of the Trade Marks Act is if the signs excluded from protection by reason of their functional, technical, or aesthetic characteristics are regarded as lacking, by reason of those characteristics specifically, the essential properties of trade marks within the meaning of section 1(1)—either by virtue of their inability to distinguish the goods or services of one undertaking from those of others or, and less convincingly, by virtue of their inability to be represented graphically. The view of signs that consist exclusively of functional, technical, or aesthetic characteristics of goods as incapable of distinguishing goods or services might on its face seem compelling, since such signs are unlikely to have an existence of their own, independent of the goods to which they are applied, and are thus unlikely to be capable of indicating clearly those goods' relation to a commercial origin.[6] Nonetheless, it is inconsistent with the structure of European and UK trade mark legislation, and with the applicability of the relevant exclusion even to those signs that have acquired distinctiveness through use in relation to the goods in question under Article 7(3) of the Regulation, Article 4(4) of the Directive, and section 3(1) of the Trade Marks Act.[7]

In conclusion, the basic subject matter of registered trade mark protection under EU and UK legislation is the trade mark, where by 'trade mark' is meant any sign that is capable of distinguishing goods or services and of representation in the trade mark register, and that is not comprised exclusively of functional, technical, or aesthetic characteristics of goods. This definition of the trade mark is slightly different and more restrictive than the definition supported by section 1(1) of the Trade Marks Act, which reflects something more akin to the traditional common law conception of the trade mark as 'a seller's peculiar mark, whatever be the form of it, adopted and used by him upon his merchandise and distinguishing his merchandise from other merchandise of a similar kind sold by others'.[8]

[5] See Case C–299/99 *Koninklijke Philips Electronics NV v Remington Consumer Products Ltd* [2002] ECR I–05475 (*Philips*) [76].

[6] See W L P A Molengraaff, 'The Nature of the Trade-Mark' (1920) 29 Yale Law Journal 303, 303.

[7] See *Philips* (n 5) [75].

[8] T Bodley, 'What is a Trademark?' (1882) 2 Kentucky LJ 151, 152.

Moving finally to the unregistered protection of trade marks in the United Kingdom: its source is the passing off action, which protects not trade marks as such, but rather the goodwill developed in respect of a trader's goods or services by use of trade marks and other objects.[9] In the absence of either harmonizing or domestic legislation, such protection is governed by common law.

1.2 Registered Protection for Other Product Designations

While most trade marks distinguish the goods or services of an individual undertaking, they may also distinguish the goods or services of groups of undertakings with reference (in the case of collective marks) to those undertakings' membership of a certain association or (in the case of certification marks) to the goods' or services' compliance with the requirements imposed by a particular certification authority. In these cases, the protection they confer is similar to that conferred by other titles of IP right available with respect to signs in the form of product names specifically. Those titles—recognized domestically in Europe since at least the 15th century,[10] and internationally since the 1891 Madrid Agreement for the Repression of False or Misleading Indications of Source on Goods[11]—include at EU-level protected designations of origin (PDOs) and protected geographical indications (PGIs), each of which distinguishes the goods originating from a certain geographical area and possessing certain characteristics, and traditional specialities guaranteed (TSGs), which distinguish the goods having a certain traditional name and characteristics.

The European legislative schemes governing PDOs, PGIs, and TSGs were introduced to create EU-wide (unitary) rights in substitution for previously existing domestic rights in respect of agricultural products and foodstuffs, and continue to be confined in their coverage to such objects;[12] although, and as the discussion in this chapter underlines, there is nothing in the nature of the subject matter protectable by these schemes that requires their coverage to be thus confined. In contrast to that conferred by other EU IP rights, the protection they confer is both uniform

[9] *Starbucks (HK) Ltd v British Sky Broadcasting Group PLC* [2015] UKSC 31, [2015] WLR 2628 (*Starbucks*).

[10] See P S Kindstedt, *Cheese and Culture: A History of Cheese and its Place in Western Civilization* (Chelsea Green Publishing 2012) 214 (referring to 15th century French legislation restricting use of the name Roquefort to cheese made in Roquefort).

[11] Madrid Agreement for the Repression of False or Misleading Indications of Source on Goods (opened for signature 14 April 1891, entered into force 1 June 1963) 828 UNTS 168, as amended (Madrid Agreement). See also Lisbon Agreement for the Protection of Appellations of Origin and their International Registration (opened for signature 31 October 1958, entered into force 1 January 1977) 923 UNTS 205, as amended (Lisbon Agreement); Agreement on Trade-related Aspects of Intellectual Property Rights (opened for signature 15 December 1993, entered into force 1 January 1995) 1869 UNTS 299 (TRIPs Agreement) arts 22–24.

[12] For a discussion of some of the issues raised by extending the availability of PDOs and PGIs beyond agricultural products and foodstuffs to handicrafts see D Marie-Vivien, 'A Comparative Analysis of GIs for Handicrafts: The Link to Origin in Culture as Well as Nature?' in D S Gangjee (ed), *Research Handbook on Intellectual Property and Geographical Indications* (Edward Elgar Publishing 2016) 292.

and exhaustive throughout EU territory, with the result that Member States may no longer grant domestic rights in respect of the same subject matter.[13]

The primary European legislation in this area is the Quality Schemes Regulation, which governs the grant of each of the three titles of IP right above. As defined in Articles 5 and 17, the specific subject matter protectable as designations of origin, geographical indications, and traditional specialities guaranteed are names that identify respectively:

- A product (a) that originates in a specific place, region, or (exceptionally) country (b) whose quality or characteristics are essentially or exclusively due to a particular geographical environment with its inherent natural and human factors, and (c) the production, processing, and preparation steps of which all take place in the relevant area—subject to certain special provisions where the product's raw materials come from an area larger than or different from the one defined;[14]
- A product (a) that originates in a specific place, region, or country, (b) whose quality, reputation, or other characteristic is essentially attributable to its geographical origin, and (c) at least one of the production, processing, and preparation steps of which takes place in the relevant area;[15] and
- A product (a) that is produced, processed, or composed according to traditional methods or using traditional raw materials, and (b) that is, or the characteristics of which are, traditionally denoted by the name for which protection is sought.[16]

As with trade marks, the availability of registered protection for names as PDOs, PGIs, and TSGs is subject to certain absolute and relative exclusions, the main effect of which is to underline the similarity in their nature as signs of use to distinguish goods or services in the marketplace.

[13] See Regulation (EU) No 1151/2012 of the European Parliament and of the Council of 21 November 2012 on quality schemes for agricultural products and foodstuffs [2012] OJ L 343/1 (Quality Schemes Regulation) art 4(b) (describing the aim of the PDO and PGI schemes to include 'ensuring uniform protection of the names as an intellectual property right in the territory of the Union'); Case C–478/07 *Budějovický Budvar, národní podnik v Rudolf Ammersin GmbH* [2009] ECR I–07721 (*Budějovický Budvar*) [114] (deciding that the aim of Council Regulation (EC) No 510/2006 of 20 March 2006 on the protection of geographical indications and designations of origin for agricultural products and foodstuffs [2006] OJ L 93/12 was 'not to establish, alongside national rules which may continue to exist, an additional system of protection for qualified geographical indications ... but to provide a uniform and exhaustive system of protection for such indications'). Member States may provide national protection for subject matter falling outside the scope of the PDO and PGI schemes established by the Quality Schemes Regulation (ie for 'geographical designations relating to products for which there is no specific link between their characteristics and their geographical origin'), provided it complies with EU law, including by not undermining the objectives of the Regulation or free movement principles: Case C–35/13 *Assica - Associazione Industriali delle Carni e dei Salumi and Kraft Foods Italia SpA v Associazioni fra produttori per la tutela del Salame Felino* ECLI:EU:C:2014:306 [33].

[14] See Quality Schemes Regulation art 5(1); also art 5(3).

[15] ibid art 5(2).

[16] ibid art 18(1) and (2).

2. Trade Marks and Other Product Designations in Europe (Including the United Kingdom): Purpose-limited Signs the Protection of which Does Not Undermine Other Intellectual Property Regimes

2.1 Trade Marks

2.1.1 Introduction

According to EU legislation, and as seen in section 1, the protection of a subject matter by registered trade mark is available for and only for (a) signs (b) that are capable of distinguishing the goods or services of one undertaking from those of other undertakings, (c) that are capable of being represented in the trade mark register, and (d) that do not consist exclusively of functional, technical, or aesthetic characteristics of goods within the meaning of Article 7(1)(e) of the Regulation and Article 4(1)(e) of the Directive. In order for a subject matter of protectable type thus defined to be registered, it must also fall outside the statutory grounds for refusal contained in Article 7(1)(b) to (d) and (f) to (m) and Article 8 of the Regulation and corresponding provisions of the Directive.

Unlike in patent and copyright law, in trade mark law the courts adopt an explicitly teleological approach to protectability. Further, when interpreting the statutory definition of a trade mark, they emphasize not only the purpose of trade mark protection itself, but also the purpose of the trade mark register, in addition to those objectives of the EU Treaties by which the trade mark system is understood to be motivated. As a result of this approach, each of the statutory properties of a trade mark are defined with a view to promoting consumer protection and undistorted competition[17] by: (a) enabling the use of signs by traders to indicate the commercial origin of goods and services, and thereby enable the individual purchasing experiences of consumers to be repeated or avoided (the so-called 'essential function' of a trade mark);[18] and (b) enabling third parties—including particularly public

[17] See eg Consolidated Version of the Treaty on the Functioning of the European Union [2012] OJ C 326/ 47 (TFEU) Preamble ('the removal of existing obstacles calls for concerted action in order to guarantee steady expansion, balanced trade and fair competition') and arts 3(1)(b) conferring exclusive competence on the Union to establish 'the competition rules necessary for the functioning of the internal market') and 32 (requiring the Commission to carry out the tasks entrusted to it under Title II Chapter 1 of the TFEU with a view to promoting competition); TFEU arts 4(2)(f) (conferring shared competence between the Union and Member States in the area of consumer protection), 12 (requiring consumer protection requirements to be taken into account in defining and implementing other Union policies and activities) and 169 (requiring the Union to ensure a high level of consumer protection by means of harmonizing and other measures).

[18] See eg Case C–10/89 *SA CNL-Sucal v Hag GF AG* [1990] ECR I–3711 [13] and [14] ('Trade mark rights are . . . an essential element in the system of undistorted competition which the Treaty seeks to establish and maintain. Under such a system, an undertaking must be in a position to keep its customers by virtue of the quality of its products and services, something which is possible only if there are distinctive marks which enable customers to identify those products and services. For the trade mark to be able to fulfil this role, it must offer a guarantee that all goods bearing it have been produced under the control of a single undertaking which is accountable for their quality. . . . [T]he essential function

authorities and economic operators—to identify those subject matter that have been registered as trade marks and the scope of protection that their registration confers.[19]

In its focus on supporting methods of marketing that protect consumer interests, the purpose of trade mark protection is very different from the purposes of copyright and patent protection. By contrast, the public notice aims of trade mark registration are essentially the same as the public notice aims of the patent document.[20] Unlike in patent law, however, in trade mark law those aims inform the statutory definition of protectable subject matter itself, both directly through the requirement that a sign be capable of representation in the trade mark register in order to be a trade mark, and indirectly through the teleological approach to statutory interpretation described above.

2.1.2 Trade Marks are Signs

According to Article 4 of the Regulation, corresponding to Article 3 of the Directive, an EU trade mark may consist of

> any signs capable of: (a) distinguishing the goods or services of one undertaking from those of other undertakings; and (b) being represented on the Register of European Union trade marks ... in a manner which enables the competent authorities and the public to determine the clear and precise subject matter of the protection afforded to its proprietor.

It follows from this provision that registered trade mark protection may be obtained for and only for signs.

A sign within the meaning of EU trade mark law may be understood as any expressive object, including—as the indicative list of signs in Article 4 of the Regulation makes clear—any letters, numbers, lines, colours, sounds, or shapes in isolation or combination, as well as moving images, actions, tastes, and textures.[21]

of the trade mark ... is to guarantee the identity of the origin of the marked product to the consumer or ultimate user by enabling him without any possibility of confusion to distinguish that product from products which have another origin'.)

[19] See eg Case C–273/00 *Sieckmann v Deutsches Patent- und Markenamt* [2002] ECR I–11737 (*Sieckmann*) [49]–[51] ('the entry of the mark in a public register has the aim of making it accessible to the competent authorities and the public, particular to economic operators. On the one hand, the competent authorities must know with clarity and precision the nature of the signs of which a mark consists in order to be able to fulfil their obligations in relation to the prior examination of registration applications and to the publication and maintenance of an appropriate and precise register of trade marks. On the other hand, economic operators must, with clarity and precision, be able to find out about registrations or applications for registration made by their current or potential competitors and thus to receive relevant information about the rights of third parties').

[20] See ch 4 ss 3 and 5(b).

[21] See eg *Sieckmann* (n 19) (accepting an odour to be a sign, albeit not protectable for lack of representability); R443/2010-2 *Sony Ericsson Mobile Communications AB* (23 September 2010) (accepting an animated sequence of still images to be a sign capable of protection as a registered trade mark); German registered trade mark number 30259811 (the feel of the term Underberg in braille, registered as a three dimensional mark on 12 March 2003); R120/2001–2 *Eli Lilly* (4 August 2003) (accepting the taste of artificial strawberries to be a sign, albeit not protectable for lack of representability); Case C–445/02 P *Glaverbel SA v Office for Harmonisation in the Internal Market (Trade Marks and Designs) (OHIM)* [2004] ECR I–06267 (accepting a design applied to the surface of glass products to be a sign,

Thus, a subject matter need not be visually perceptible to be a sign.[22] Nor need it be novel or an authorial work, with existing (including natural) objects also capable of being signs. However, and as with the other categories of IP subject matter considered previously, a subject matter must have a discrete and independent existence to be a sign within the meaning of EU trade mark law.[23] It follows that mere properties of something else, and subject matter that otherwise lack a discrete and objectively discernible form—including by reason of their ability to take on a variety of different forms—will not be capable of registration as a trade mark.[24] The result is to confine the protection of each registered trade mark to a single and discretely defined expressive object, just as the protection of each patent and copyright is confined to a single and discretely defined invention and authorial work. According to the courts, if trade mark monopolies were not thus confined, the purposes of trade mark protection and registration above would be undermined.[25]

In conclusion, a sign within the meaning of European trade mark law is any expressive object. Properties of an object, such as its colour or texture, will not be a sign unless the context of their use is sufficient to transform them into an object having a discrete and objectively discernible existence, including an existence separate from the goods or services in respect of which they are used. In this important respect, the requirement for a sign overlaps with the other requirements of protectability—including those of distinguishability under Article 4(a) of the Regulation and Article 3(a) of the Directive, and of not being comprised exclusively of functional, technical, or aesthetic characteristics of goods under Article 7(1)(e) of the Regulation and Article 4(1)(e) of the Directive—as well as with certain of the

albeit not protectable for lack of distinctiveness); R708/2006 *Edgar Rice Burroughs, Inc* (27 September 2007) (accepting the sound of the yell of the fictional character Tarzan to be a sign, albeit not protectable for lack of representability). The definition of signs as expressive objects is consistent with that proposed by the Commission to the Court of Justice in Case C–321/03 *Dyson Ltd v Registrar of Trade Marks* [2007] ECR I–00687 (*Dyson*) [29], namely, a subject matter capable of perception by one of the five senses, and as thus not including a 'concept' that, by definition, 'appeals only to the imagination'.

[22] See *Sieckmann* (n 19) [45].

[23] This is now reflected in the reference in Regulation art 4(b) and Directive art 3(b) to the need for the subject matter represented in the trade mark register (ie the sign) to be 'clear and precise'. On the separate existence of signs cf J Aldred, 'The Economic Rationale of Trade Marks: An Economic Critique' in L Bently, J Davis, and J C Ginsburg (eds), *Trade Marks and Brands: An Interdisciplinary Critique* (CUP 2008) 267, 278 (noting that, unlike copyright books and patented inventions, intangible outputs such as brand identities are hardly ever capable of independent existence, and thus have no separate price in markets).

[24] See eg Case C–104/01 *Libertel Groep BV v Benelux-Merkenbureau* [2003] ECR I–03793 (*Libertel*) [27] (deciding that while a colour per se is normally a simply property of things, and thus not a sign, the context of its use may make it a sign); *Dyson* (n 21) [37] (deciding that a transparent bin or collection chamber forming part of the external surface of a vacuum cleaner was not sufficiently specific to be a sign by reason of its ability to take 'on a multitude of different appearances'); Case C–49/02 *Heidelberger Bauchemie GmbH* [2004] ECR I–06129 (*Heidelberger*) [34] (deciding that: '[t]he mere juxtaposition of two or more colours, without shape or contours, or a reference to two or more colours "in every conceivable form"', will allow numerous different combinations, and thus be incapable of functioning as a trade mark).

[25] See eg *Heidelberger* (ibid) [24] (describing the purpose of the requirement for a sign as being to prevent the abuse of trade mark law in order to obtain an unfair competitive advantage).

additional requirements for a trade mark's registrability, such as distinctiveness.[26] Given the explicitly teleological approach adopted by the Court of Justice when interpreting trade mark legislation, and its concern to ensure that such interpretation promotes the purposes of the trade mark system above and the EU values that motivate them, this overlap is unsurprising.

2.1.3 ...That are Capable of Distinguishing and Intended for Use to Distinguish Certain Goods or Services

In addition to being a sign, Article 4 of the Regulation and Article 3 of the Directive require that a subject matter be capable of distinguishing the goods or services of one undertaking from those of other undertakings in order to be protectable as a trade mark.

Two things are of immediate note about the requirement for distinguishability. The first is its direct reflection of the purpose of trade mark protection to guarantee the essential function of a trade mark as an indicator of the commercial origin of goods or services. And the second is its anticipation of the absolute ground for refusing registration under Article 7(1)(b) and (3) of the Regulation and Article 4(1)(b) and 4(4) of the Directive for any trade mark that is devoid of distinctive character[27] and that has not become distinctive

[26] See eg Case T–433/12 *Margarete Steiff GmbH v Office for Harmonisation in the Internal Market (Trade Marks and Designs) (OHIM)* ECLI:EU:T:2014:8 (deciding that a sign comprising the position of the attachment of a button or label in the middle of the ear of soft toys was devoid of distinctiveness on the related bases that the attachment did not by itself enable the average European consumer to recognize the commercial origin of the soft toy, and would not be regarded by the average consumer as existing separate from the toy); Case T–85/13 *K-Swiss, Inc v Office for Harmonisation in the Internal Market (Trade Marks and Designs) (OHIM)* ECLI:EU:T:2014:509 (deciding that a sign comprising five parallel stripes was devoid of distinctive character on the basis that it could not be apprehended without the intrinsic characteristics of the products (shoes) to which it was applied being simultaneously perceived). Cf *Star Athletica, LLC v Varsity Brands, Inc* 580 US (2017), discussed in ch 5 s 3.3.1.2 (deciding that surface decorations on cheerleading uniforms could be protected separate from the uniforms).

[27] A trade mark will be devoid of distinctive character within the meaning of Regulation art 7(1)(b) and Directive art 4(1)(b) if, among other things: it might in normal usage in trade serve to designate a property of the relevant goods or services, which property is easily recognizable by the consumers for whom those goods or services are intended (Regulation art 7(1)(c); Directive art 4(1)(c)); or it has become customary in the current language or bona fide and established practices of the trade (Regulation art 7(1)(d); Directive art 4(1)(d)). See Case C–51/10 P *Agencja Wydawnicza Technopol sp z oo v Office for Harmonisation in the Internal Market (Trade Marks and Designs) (OHIM)* [2011] ECR I–01541 (*Agencja Wydawnicza Technopol*). On the scope of the more commonly invoked art 7(1)(c) and art 4(1)(c) see eg Joined Cases C–53/01 to C–55/01 *Re Linde AG, Winward Industries Inc* and *Rado Uhren AG* [2003] ECR I–03161; Case C–383/99 P *Procter & Gamble Company v Office for Harmonisation in the Internal Market (Trade Marks and Designs)* [2001] ECR I–06251 (*Procter & Gamble*); *Agencja Wydawnicza Technopol*; Case T–318/09 *Audi AG and Volkswagen AG v Office for Harmonisation in the Internal Market (Trade Marks and Designs) (OHIM)* [2011] ECR II–03841 (*Audi*). In US law, trade marks within the scope of paragraph 1(d) of Regulation art 7 and Directive art 4 above are referred to as 'generic marks', namely, marks that 'refe[r] to the genus of which the particular product is a species', and denied trade mark registrability. By contrast, trade marks within the scope of paragraph 1(c) are referred to as 'descriptive marks', namely, marks that 'convey[] an immediate idea of the ingredients, qualities or characteristics of the goods', and recognized as capable of acquiring distinctiveness through use (or in the US, 'secondary meaning'). See *Abercrombie & Fitch Co v Hunting World, Inc* 537 F2d 4 (2nd Cir 1976) (*Abercrombie*) 9–11; *Two Pesos, Inc v Taco Cabana, Inc* 505 US 763 (1992) (*Two Pesos*) 768–69.

by reason of its use.[28] As a preliminary expression of the requirement for distinctiveness, the distinguishability criterion does not exclude from protection any subject matter that would not later be excluded by the absolute ground for refusal above.[29] However, the converse is not also true: a subject matter that satisfies the distinguishability requirement and possesses the other essential properties of a trade mark might nonetheless lack distinctiveness and thus not be registrable. In effect, therefore, the Article 4 and Article 3 requirement for distinguishability is a more general version of the requirement for distinctiveness. According to the Court in *Philips*, its purpose is 'essentially to exclude from registration signs which are not generally capable of being a trade mark'.[30] Only if a sign is so capable (and is otherwise a trade mark) will its distinctiveness in respect of the specific goods or services for which its registration is sought need to be considered and decided.

As noted above, Article 7(3) of the Regulation and Article 4(4) of the Directive recognize the ability of any trade mark to be distinctive by saving from exclusion those marks that, while inherently devoid of distinctiveness, have nonetheless acquired distinctiveness through their use in relation to the goods or services for which their registration is sought. Given this, it is difficult to avoid the conclusion that any subject matter will, by virtue of its nature as a sign, have the distinguishability required by Article 4 of the Regulation and Article 3 of the Directive. This is consistent with the Court of Justice's definition of distinguishability in *Libertel* as requiring only that a sign be 'capable of conveying specific information, in particular as to the origin of a product or service',[31] as distinct from 'conveying certain associations of ideas [or] arousing feelings';[32] a definition that any expressive object ought to satisfy.[33] Further, it reaffirms that the significance of the distinguishability requirement is not to filter out non-protectable from protectable subject matter in the manner of the requirement for a sign, but rather to give trade mark authorities an initial opportunity to engage with the nature of the subject matter at issue in a case, and to consider the particular hurdles if any that that subject matter will face when being assessed for distinctiveness. Conceptually, it also underlines that the subject matter protected by registered trade mark is not the expressive object

[28] See also Regulation art 51(1)(b); Directive art 12(2)(a) (providing for the revocation of any registered trade mark that has become the common name in the trade for a product or service in respect of which it is registered and thereby lost its distinctiveness in respect of that product or service 'in consequence of acts or inactivity of the proprietor'). On the meaning of these provisions see Case C–409/12 *Backaldrin Österreich The Kornspitz Company GmbH v Pfahnl Backmittel GmbH* ECLI:EU:C:2014:130 (*Backaldrin*).

[29] See *Philips* (n 5) [39].

[30] ibid [37].

[31] See *Libertel* (n 24) [39].

[32] ibid [40].

[33] See in this regard the distinction between expression and impulsion in the works of John Dewey, which might be said to capture the *Libertel* distinction between conveying information and arousing feelings. In Dewey's work, 'impulsion' involves a visceral or unmediated response to a basic human need, while 'expression' involves 'an ordering of impulsion by way of incorporating values of prior experiences': T Leddy, 'Dewey's Aesthetics' in E N Zalta (ed), *The Stanford Encyclopedia of Philosophy* (Winter 2016 edn) para 2.4.

comprising the sign, but rather that object *qua* signifier of (among other things) the goods' or services' commercial origin.[34]

The consideration of a sign's distinguishability under Article 4 of the Regulation and Article 3 of the Directive takes place in the abstract, without regard to the nature of the goods or services in respect of which its registration is sought. However, as a preliminary expression of the requirement for distinctiveness, it is approached with the same general principles as govern the determination of distinctiveness in mind. Above all, this means that it is considered as the type of sign indicated in the application for registration,[35] and—subject to that restriction—from the perspective of the public, as well as having regard to those public interest considerations of consumer protection and undistorted competition that are regarded as 'manifestly, indissociable from the essential function of a trade mark'.[36] It is also considered with reference to the sign as a whole, and may thus not be rejected on the basis that a subject matter comprises elements that are themselves lacking in distinguishability.[37] Because of the linguistic, cultural, social, and economic factors of relevance to distinctiveness, it will not follow from a sign's lack of distinguishability in a given Member State that the sign lacks distinguishability in another Member State, which must accordingly be assessed independently.[38] Further, while prior decisions in other jurisdictions concerning the same or a similar sign may be considered,

[34] See in this regard *Qualitex Co v Jacobson Products Co* 514 US 159 (1995) (*Qualitex*) 164 ('It is the source-distinguishing ability of a mark—not its ontological status as color, shape, fragrance, word, or sign—that permits it to serve these basic purposes [of a trade mark]'); also B Beebe, 'The Semiotic Analysis of Trademark Law' (2004) 51 UCLA Law Review 621 (offering a semiotic account of trade mark law).

[35] See eg Case C–170/15 P *Enercon GmbH v Office de l'harmonisation dans le marché intérieur (marques, dessins et modèles) (OHIM)* ECLI:EU:C:2016:53 (*Enercon*) [26]–[30] (rejecting the argument that a trade mark should have been assessed for distinctiveness as a figurative mark, rather than as a colour mark, despite it having been described in the application as a colour mark, and on the ground that the relevant public would have perceived it as a figurative mark). See also Case T–293/10 *Seven Towns Ltd v Office for Harmonisation in the Internal Market (Trade Marks and Designs) (OHIM)* ECLI:EU:T:2012:302 (*Seven Towns*) (deciding that an application for registration of the Rubik's cube as a colour mark represented by seven coloured squares with black borders was invalid due to the 'inherent contradiction' that the description contained regarding 'the true nature of the sign at issue' ([66])).

[36] Case C–329/02 P *SAT.1 SatellitenFernsehen GmbH v European Union Intellectual Property Office* [2004] ECR I–08317 (*SAT.1*) [23]–[27].

[37] ibid [28] (concerning distinctiveness). For a subject matter the component parts of which are devoid of distinctiveness to be distinctive, there must be a perceptible difference between it and the sum of its parts—whether because of the unusual nature of their combination in relation to the goods or services, or because the sign creates an impression that is sufficiently far removed from that produced by the combined meanings of its parts (Case C–363/99 *Koninklijke KPN Nederland NV v Benelux-Merkenbureau* [2004] ECR I–01619 [100]). The same principle informed the Court of Justice's decision in *Procter & Gamble* (n 27) ([43]–[44]) that the trade mark BABY-DRY was not descriptive of nappies within the meaning of art 7(1)(c). In the Court's assessment, while the trade mark 'unquestionably allude[d] to the function' of drying nappies that the products were intended to fulfil, its 'syntactically unusual juxtaposition' of the words 'baby' and dry' to create an expression that was not familiar in English, either for designating nappies or for describing their essential characteristics, made it a 'lexical invention bestowing distinctive power on the mark so formed', putting it outside the scope of art 7(1)(c).

[38] Case C–421/04 *Matratzen Concord AG v Hukla Germany SA* [2006] ECR I–02303 (*Matratzen*) [25]; Case T–393/02 *Henkel KGaA v European Union Intellectual Property Office* [2004] ECR II–04115 (*Henkel*).

consistent with the principles of equal treatment and sound administration, the resolution of individual cases must prioritize respect for legality.[39] Thus, the fact of a sign having been the subject of national and international registrations cannot be determinative of its distinguishability within the meaning of Article 4 of the Regulation and Article 3 of the Directive.[40]

The view of the requirement for distinguishability as giving trade mark authorities an initial opportunity to engage with the nature of the sign at issue in a case, and to consider the particular hurdles if any that that sign will face when being assessed for distinctiveness, implies that different categories of signs may be treated differently for the purpose of such assessment. Initially this might appear inconsistent with the principle of equal treatment of different subject matter, which principle is as central to trade mark law as it is to patent and copyright law.[41] However, and as in those other IP regimes, the principle of equal treatment means only that the same criteria must be applied when establishing the protectability of different subject matter, and not that those criteria will produce the same impact regardless of the relevant subject matter's type.[42] On the contrary, it is clear from both the policy and factual considerations that inform the interpretation and application of the requirements for trade mark protectability that those requirements will impact differently on different categories of signs. Specifically, this is clear from the different impact that trade mark monopolies for different types of signs can be expected to have on the values of consumer protection and undistorted competition that the EU's teleological approach to the interpretation and application of trade mark legislation prioritizes.[43] In addition, it is clear from the different identity and characteristics of consumers of different types of signs,[44] and from the different

[39] See *Agencja Wydawnicza Technopol* (n 27) [73]–[75]; also *Audi* (n 27) [20]–[24].

[40] ibid.

[41] See eg *Philips* (n 5) [48] ('Article 2 of the Directive makes no distinction between different categories of trade marks. The criteria for assess the distinctive character of three-dimensional trade marks ... are thus no different from those to be applied to other categories of trade mark'); Joined Cases C–344/10 P and C–345/10 P *Freixenet, SA v Office for Harmonisation in the Internal Market (Trade Marks and Designs) (OHIM)* [2011] ECR I–10205 (*Freixenet*) [50]–[51] (deciding that the General Court had erred in finding that signs representing frosted white and black matt bottles were unable to distinguish the goods of the applicant from those of others, on the basis of evidence that no such bottles had ever been sold without a label or equivalent, with reference in part to the per se exclusion from protection of marks comprising the appearance of product packaging that does not contain any inscription or word elements that such finding supported).

[42] See eg *Audi* (n 27) [25] ('The principle of equal treatment is ... infringed only where comparable situations are treated differently or different situations are treated in the same way').

[43] See eg *Libertel* (n 24) [54]–[56] (deciding that the impact of permitting the registration of colours as trade mark on competition is relevant to the issues of protectability and registrability under the Directive).

[44] Compare, for example, the profile of the average consumer, 'who is reasonably well informed and reasonably observant and circumspect', and who must be enabled by a trade mark 'to distinguish the product concerned from those of other undertakings without conducting an analytical or comparative examination and without paying particular attention' (see *Henkel* (n 38) [53]) with the profile of the specialist consumer, who will pay a higher degree of attention to trade marks than his or her non-specialist counterpart (Case C–311/11 P *Smart Technologies ULC v Office for Harmonisation in the Internal Market (Trade Marks and Designs) (OHIM)* ECLI:EU:C:2012:460 (*Smart Technologies*) [47]–[48]).

likelihood of those consumers reading in different types of signs the message of commercial origin required for distinctiveness.[45] As a result of this combination of factors, the category neutrality of trade mark protection gives way in practice to a test of distinctiveness in which the category of sign at issue plays a central part.

This can be illustrated with reference to four categories of sign that have faced particular difficulties in the realm of distinctiveness. Those categories are pure or abstract colours, tastes, shapes, and slogans. While subject matter falling within these categories will, by virtue of their nature as signs, be distinguishable, they will rarely if ever be distinctive for two reasons. The first is the empirical assumptions of EU tribunals that the public will have a limited capacity to distinguish them, and will not be in the habit of drawing conclusions from them about the origin of goods or services.[46] And the second is the normative assumption of EU tribunals that restricting the freedom of commercial operators to use these subject matter in respect of the same goods or services as the trade mark owner would undermine the system of undistorted competition created by the EU Treaties.[47] As a result of these assumptions, colours, tastes, and basic geometrical shapes will very rarely if ever be regarded as inherently distinctive, with the result that they will only be registrable as trade marks if they can be shown to have acquired distinctiveness through use in the market.[48] In addition, for the shape of a three-dimensional product or packaging or its two-dimensional representation to be inherently distinctive, it will need to depart significantly from the norm or customs of the relevant market;[49] and for a

[45] See eg *Henkel* (n 38) [52] ('the perception of the average consumer is not necessarily the same in the case of a three-dimensional trade mark, consisting of the packaging of a product, as it is in the case of a word or figurative mark which consists of a sign that is independent from the appearance of the goods it denotes'); *Libertel* (n 24) [65] ('The perception of the relevant public is not necessarily the same in the case of a sign consisting of a colour *per se* as it is in the case of a word or figurative mark consisting of a sign that bears no relation to the appearance of the goods it denotes'). On the relevance of the category of the goods and services themselves see also Case C–342/97 *Lloyd Schuhfabrik Meyer* [1999] ECR I–3819 [26] (noting that the relevant public's perception of a trade mark will be influenced by its level of attention, 'which is likely to vary according to the category of goods or services in question').

[46] A similar position is adopted in the United States. See eg *Qualitex* (n 34) (regarding colours); *Wal-Mart Stores, Inc v Samara Brothers, Inc* 529 US 205 (2000) (regarding product designs).

[47] See eg *Eli Lilly* (n 21) [14] (referring to the need to protect the freedom of manufacturers to add the flavour of artificial strawberries to their products as a reason for denying the distinctiveness of the taste of artificial strawberries); *Libertel* (n 24) [54] (referring to the need to prevent exhaustion of the entire range of colours available to competitors as a relevant consideration when assessing the potential distinctiveness of a colour as a trade mark).

[48] See eg *Libertel* (n 24) [66] ('In the case of a colour *per se*, distinctiveness without any prior use is inconceivable save in exceptional circumstances, and particularly where the number of goods or services for which the mark is claimed is very restricted and the relevant market very specific'). The nature of a sign as a colour, taste, or shape depends on its description in the trade mark application (see eg *Enercon* (n 35)). The question whether a shape is a basic geometrical shape so as to be presumptively lacking in inherent distinctiveness is a question of fact not open to review on appeal: Case C–653/15 P *Bopp v Office de l'harmonisation dans le marché intérieur (marques, dessins et modèles) (OHMI)* ECLI:EU:C:2016:277 [3] and [6].

[49] See eg Case C–97/12 P *Louis Vuitton Malletier v Office for Harmonisation in the Internal Market (Trade Marks and Designs) (OHIM)* ECLI:EU:C:2014:324 [18]. It was on the basis of this principle that the Board in R 513/2011-2 *Société des Produits Nestlé SA v Cadbury Holdings Ltd* [2013] ETMR 25 (*Nestlé v Cadbury*) held the sign comprising the three-dimensional shape of the four-finger Kit Kat chocolate bar to lack inherent distinctiveness within the meaning of art 7(1)(b). In its decision, 'there is no aspect of the trade mark ... which may be easily and instantly memorised by a public displaying a normal level

slogan to be inherently distinctive, it will need to 'possess . . . a certain originality or resonance, requiring at least some interpretation by the relevant public, or setting off a cognitive process in the minds of that public'.[50] If they cannot, they also will only be registrable as trade marks if they can be shown to have acquired distinctiveness through use in respect of the goods or services for which their registration is sought.

In sum, any sign will by virtue of its nature as a sign be capable of distinguishing the goods or services of one undertaking from those of other undertakings within the meaning of Article 4(a) of the Regulation and Article 3(a) of the Directive. Nonetheless, the requirement for distinguishability is not vacuous, but rather performs a procedural and conceptual function. Its procedural function is to provide a preliminary opportunity for authorities to consider the particular hurdles that different categories of signs will face in avoiding the absolute exclusion from registrability of subject matter devoid of distinctiveness; and its conceptual function is to underline that the basic subject matter of registered trade mark protection is not the sign as such, but rather the sign *qua* trade mark, ie the sign of use for the purpose of signifying the commercial origin of the goods or services in respect of which it is registered. In this regard, trade marks may be conceived as purpose-limited signs similar to the purpose-limited subject matter protectable by patent grant.[51] On this view, every trade mark includes among its constitutive properties the putative trade mark owner's intention or purpose with respect to the sign represented in the trade mark register. This explains the requirement that each trade mark applicant also designate the specific goods or services in respect of which the sign is to be used. Continuing the analogy with the position of purpose-limited subject matter in patent law: that requirement is equivalent to the requirement that the applicant for a genetic product patent disclose the function of the product in the patent document in the sense of limiting the protectable subject matter with reference to the goods or services

of attentiveness, not previously exposed to the sign and educated, and which would make it possible for it to be perceived immediately as an indication of the commercial origin of the goods in question' ([38]). The fact that the sign was original was, the Board held, insufficient, since it nonetheless failed to differ substantially from the basic shapes of the goods in question commonly used in the trade ([41]).

[50] Case C–398/08 P *Audi AG v Office for Harmonisation in the Internal Market (Trade Marks and Designs) (OHIM)* [2010] ECR I–00535 [57]. In the Court's decision in *Audi AG v OHIM*, the words 'Vorsprung durch Technik', which mean to advance or lead through technology, were regarded to be precisely an example of such a distinctive subject matter, since they suggested 'at first glance, only a causal link and accordingly require[d] a measure of interpretation on the part of the public' ([59]), in addition to 'exhibit[ing] a certain originality and resonance which ma[de] it easy to remember' ([59]).

[51] See ch 4 s 2.2.1.In US law, all inherently distinctive marks are classified according to their degree of distinctiveness, as 'suggestive' ('Tide' laundry detergent), 'arbitrary' ('Camel' cigarettes), or 'fanciful' ('Kodak' film): *Abercrombie* (n 29) 9; *Two Pesos* (n 29) 768; *Wal-Mart Stores, Inc v Samara Brothers, Inc* 529 US 205 (2000) 201–11. A 'suggestive' mark has been defined as one that 'requires imagination, thought and perception to reach a conclusion as to the nature of goods', and that is (therefore) 'neither exactly descriptive on the one hand nor truly fanciful on the other' (*Abercrombie*, 10–11). A 'fanciful' mark has been defined as one 'invented solely' for its use as a trade mark (*Abercrombie*, n 12). And an 'arbitrary' mark has been defined as 'a common word . . . applied in an unfamiliar way' (*Abercrombie*, n 12).

that the applicant designates.[52] This explains why the same two signs registered in respect of dissimilar goods or services are conceived at law as different trade marks,[53] why UK law requires registered trade mark applications to be supported by a statement regarding the current or intended use of the trade mark in relation to the relevant goods or services,[54] and why failure to use a registered trade mark for a continuous period of five years is grounds for revocation of its registration.[55]

2.1.4 ... That are Capable of Representation

In addition to being a sign that is capable of distinguishing the goods or services of one undertaking from those of others, Article 4(b) of the Regulation and Article 3(b) of the Directive restrict the subject matter capable of protection by registered trade mark to subject matter that can be

> represented on the Register of European Union trade marks ... in a manner which enables the competent authorities and the public to determine the clear and precise subject matter of the protection afforded to its proprietor.

This definition was introduced in 2015 to have effect in the Regulation from 1 October 2017 and to be implemented by EU Member States by 14 January 2019, and replaces the earlier requirement—still reflected in section 1(1) of the Trade Marks Act—that a sign be capable of 'being represented graphically'.[56] While the requirement for graphic representability might have implied a view of signs as two- and three-dimensional subject matter having some literary and artistic (ie visually perceptible) form—especially given the then inclusive definition of representable signs as comprising 'particularly words ... , designs, letters, numerals, [and] the shape of goods or of their packaging'—no such implication was drawn. Thus, provided a subject matter was capable of graphic representation, it was able to fulfil the representability requirement for protectability as a trade mark.[57] Nor has the amendment to the representability criterion changed the form of representation required. In the case of unitary (EU) trade marks, that form is governed by the Implementing Regulations, which continue to require representation in graphic form, while also allowing electronic (.mp3) recordings of sound signs to support their representation in graphic form. Given this, the question might be asked why

[52] See Regulation art 26(1)(c) and EUTM Implementing Regulations art 1, rule 1(c); Trade Marks Act s 32(2)(c).

[53] Albeit one may still be infringed by or invalidate the other if it has a reputation in the relevant jurisdiction and use of the other would take unfair advantage of, or be detrimental to, its distinctive character or reputation: see Regulation arts 8(5) and 9(2)(c); Directive arts 5(3)(a) and 10(2)(c); Trade Marks Act ss 5(3) and 10(3).

[54] Trade Marks Act s 32(3).

[55] Regulation art 51(1)(a); Directive art 19(1); Trade marks Act s 46(1)(a) and (b).

[56] See n 3.

[57] See n 21 (regarding odours); Case C–283/01 *Shield Mark BV v Joodst Kist hodn Memex* [2003] ECR I–14313 (*Shield Mark*) [35] (regarding sounds).

the amendment was made. The answer is provided by the report that recommended it. According to that report, the requirement for graphic representability encouraged a misconception of representability as being a 'crucial defining element of the notion of a (Community) trade mark' rather than merely an aspect 'of the registration system', and was therefore best deleted.[58]

That the requirement for representability is a 'crucial defining element' of a trade mark remains clear from the terms and structure of the Regulation and Directive. As seen in sections 1 and 2.1, those instruments support a conception of the basic subject matter of registered trade mark protection as the 'trade mark', defined with reference to the aims of the trade mark system and the values motivating them. As also seen, those aims are: (a) to ensure a mechanism by which consumers can identify without confusion the commercial origin of goods and services, and thereby repeat or avoid with certainty their prior purchasing experiences; and (b) to ensure a mechanism by which third parties—including particularly trade mark authorities and competitors—can know what trade mark monopolies have been granted, and the scope of the protection afforded to them. While these aims are commonly cast as substantive and bureaucratic or administrative aims respectively, they both inform the statutory requirements of trade mark protectability and are relied on by the courts when interpreting those requirements. In the context of representability specifically, this is apparent from the Court's decision in *Heidelberger* that the depiction of two or more colours without shape or contours, and the written reference to those colours 'in every conceivable form', failed to establish the sign's capacity to be represented graphically on the grounds that such depiction and reference

> would not permit the consumer to perceive and recall a particular combination [of colours], thereby enabling him to repeat with certainty the experience of a purchase, any more than they would allow the competent authorities and economic operators to know the scope of the protection afforded to the proprietor of the trade mark.[59]

Implicit in this reasoning is that the representability requirement exists as much to protect consumers in their engagement with the sign as used in respect of goods or services as to protect third parties in their engagement with the sign as represented in the trade mark register.[60] In this regard, trade mark law follows patent law in treating the representation of a sign in the public document as the formal description of the protected subjected matter, which description must be sufficient to support the indefinite repetition of the subject matter by those for whose benefit it is intended.[61] While this requirement has a bureaucratic appearance in its focus on the sufficiency of the formal description of the protectable subject matter, it is

[58] Max Planck Institute for Intellectual Property and Competition Law, *Study on the Overall Functioning of the European Trade Mark System* (15 February 2011) para 2.12.

[59] See *Heidelberger* (n 24) [35].

[60] See also Joined Cases C–337/12 P to C–340/12 P *Pi-Design AG v Yoshida Metal Industry Co Ltd* ECLI:EU:C:2014:129 (*Pi-Design*) [57] (describing graphic representability as ensuring 'that a sign may always be perceived unambiguously and in the same way so that the mark is guaranteed as an indication of origin').

[61] See ch 4 ss 2 and 5(a).

supported by the definition of the invention itself as an indefinitely repeatable subject matter. As seen in Chapter 4, the rationale for this definition is that the grant of a patent for a product or process that cannot be repeated indefinitely would create a type of monopoly anathema to IP.[62] So too, one might reason, to grant a trade mark monopoly for a sign the signification or message of which cannot be repeatedly perceived and recalled would create the same type of non-IP monopoly.

At the heart of a sign's ability to support repeated perception and recall by the consumers for whom it is intended is its ability to be represented in a precise, clear, and stable or uniform manner. This is consistent with the decision of the Court of Justice in the *Sieckmann* case—which decision has now been reproduced in the recitals of the Regulation and Directive[63]—that a sign will only satisfy the representability requirement if it is capable of representation in a manner that is 'clear, precise, self-contained, easily accessible, intelligible, durable and objective'.[64] Once again, when formulating these criteria of representability in *Sieckmann*, the Court of Justice reasoned from *both* the need for a sign to perform the essential function of a trade mark as a mark of commercial origin[65] *and* the need for the trade mark register to inform third parties of the identity and protective scope of each trade mark registered.[66]

For the most part EU courts have supported this position. Specifically, they have excluded certain types of signs from protection by reason of their inability to be represented in the manner required, and have not allowed the nature of a sign to influence the interpretation of that requirement.[67] In so doing they have underlined that the subject matter protected by registered trade mark is not in law the sign but rather the trade mark.

[62] See ch 4 n 21, and accompanying text.

[63] See Regulation recital 9 ('A sign should be permitted to be represented in any appropriate form using generally available technology, and thus not necessarily by graphic means, as long as the representation is clear, precise, self-contained, easily accessible, intelligible, durable and objective'); Directive recital 13 ('In order to fulfil the objectives of the registration system for trade marks, namely to ensure legal certainty and sound administration, it is also essential to require that the sign is capable of being represented in a manner which is clear, precise, self-contained, easily accessible, intelligible, durable and objective. A sign should therefore be permitted to be represented in any appropriate form using generally available technology, and thus not necessarily by graphic means, as long as the representation offers satisfactory guarantees to that effect').

[64] See *Sieckmann* (n 19) [55].

[65] ibid [53] ('in order to fulfil its role as a registered trade mark a sign must always be perceived unambiguously and in the same way so that the mark is guaranteed as an indication of origin'). See also *Seven Towns* (n 35) [60] ('In order to fulfil its role as a registered trade mark, a sign must always be perceived unambiguously and uniformly, so that the function of mark [sic] as an indication of origin is guaranteed' (citing *Heidelberger* (n 24))).

[66] See *Sieckmann* (n 19) [52] ('If the users of the register are to be able to determine the precise nature of a mark on the basis of its registration, its graphical representation in the register must be self-contained, easily accessible and intelligible'); also *Seven Towns* (n 35).

[67] See eg Case T–305/04 *Eden SARL v Office for Harmonisation in the Internal Market (Trade Marks and Designs) (OHIM)* [2005] ECR II-04705 (*Eden*) [25] ('the requirements relating to the validity of a graphical representation may not be modified or relaxed in order to facilitate the registration of signs whose nature makes their graphical representation more difficult').

This unconcern with the impact of the representability requirement on the nature of the signs protectable by registered trade mark may be illustrated with reference to odours, tastes, and sounds. While accepted to be signs, odours have effectively been held by the Court of Justice to be incapable of representation in the manner required. This occurred with the Court's decision in the *Sieckmann* case that none of a chemical formula for the substance creating an odour, a written description of an odour, nor the deposit of a sample of an odour, was a sufficiently intelligible, clear, precise, objective, and durable representation of the odour to satisfy the (then version of the) Article 4 and Article 3 requirement.[68] Further, since none of these three forms of representation was itself capable of satisfying the requirement, a combination of them was also unable to satisfy it.[69] The result in *Sieckmann* was to deny the validity of an application for registration of an olfactory sign comprising the pure chemical substance methyl cinnamate, which had been supported by the deposit of a sample of the odour in a container, a written description of the odour as 'balsamically fruity with a slight hint of cinnamon', and the structural formula for the odour ('C_6H_5-CH=CHCOOCH_3').[70] Soon after this decision the Second Board of Appeal of the EUIPO remarked, in relation to an application for registration of 'the taste of artificial strawberry flavour', that the Court of Justice's decision in *Sieckmann* that the written description of an odour would not satisfy the representability requirement would appear also to apply 'to gustatory signs'.[71]

So too the representability requirement was originally held to limit the protectability of signs comprising sounds. An early indication of this was given by the decision of the Court of Justice in *Shield Mark* that the *Sieckmann* criteria were not satisfied by several of the methods deployed by the applicant to represent the sound signs at issue in that case: the first nine notes of Beethoven's *Für Elise*, and the sound of a cock crowing. The methods rejected involved the description of the sequence of notes comprising the first of these signs ('E, D#, E, D#, E, B, D, C, A'),[72] an onomatopoeia suggesting in Dutch the second ('Kukelekuuuuu'),[73] and a written description of both ('the first nine notes of *Für Elise*' and 'a cockcrow').[74] By contrast, the Court affirmed that the depiction of the opening notes of *Für Elise* by means of

> a stave divided into bars and showing, in particular, a clef . . . , musical notes and rests whose form . . . indicates the relative value and, where appropriate, accidentals . . . determining the pitch and duration of the sounds

[68] See *Sieckmann* (n 19) [69]–[71]. [69] ibid [72]–[73].

[70] ibid [12], [13], [58]. See further *Eden* (n 67) [33]–[34] (finding that the written description of 'the smell of ripe strawberries' was not sufficiently objective, clear, and precise to satisfy the representability requirement in respect of a sign comprising the smell of ripe strawberries on the bases of evidence that the smell of strawberries differed for different varieties, and of the absence of a generally accepted international classification of smells).

[71] See *Eli Lilly* (n 21) [12]. [72] See *Shield Mark* (n 57) [61]. [73] ibid [60].

[74] ibid [59]. See also *Edgar Rice Burroughs, Inc* (n 21) (deciding that the description of a sound sign as a 'yell of the fictional character Tarzan' was insufficiently clear and self-contained to satisfy the *Sieckmann* (n 19) criteria).

might be sufficient to satisfy the representability requirement by reason of its 'faithful representation of the sequence of sounds forming the melody in respect of which registration is sought'.[75] The fact that the representation might not be immediately intelligible was, the Court held, irrelevant: what mattered was that the representation might be *easily* intelligible, 'thus allowing the competent authorities and the public, in particular traders, to know precisely the sign whose registration as a trade mark is sought'.[76]

The effect of the decision in *Shield Mark* was to allow registered trade mark protection for notes or combinations of notes, but not for other sounds or collections of sounds that could not be represented on a stave using traditional musical notation, such as the crow of a cock. In a subsequent case concerning the protectability of 'the yell of the fictional character Tarzan', the Fourth Board of Appeal of the EUIPO underlined this effect of *Shield Mark* in its decision that the graphic depiction of such a sound in the form of a spectrogram could not of itself fulfil the *Sieckmann* criteria of being self-contained, clear, intelligible, or easily accessible, since it could not enable third parties viewing it either to discern any specific sound or melody, or to transform it into a sound, whether mentally or by use of technical means.[77] By the time of this decision, however, the rules governing the representation of unitary (EU) trade marks for sounds had been amended to *require* graphic representation of, 'in particular a musical notation', while also permitting any person filing his application electronically to support it with 'an electronic file containing the sound'.[78] While such a file may not substitute for the graphic representation itself, it has been accepted in combination with such a representation—including a spectrogram of the type submitted in *Edgar Rice Burroughs, Inc* concerning the yell of Tarzan—to meet the *Sieckmann* criteria.[79]

As seen above, another type of sign for which the representability requirement has created difficulties is colours, by reason of the *Sieckmann* criteria of precision, uniformity, durability, and clarity. When the protectability of colours was first considered, these criteria were held not to be satisfied either by the simple written description of a colour as, for example, 'orange',[80] or by samples of a colour that might deteriorate with time and/or fail to represent the colour's appearance on media other than paper.[81] The reasons given were the inability of such descriptions and samples to support *either* the essential function of a trade mark by enabling

[75] See *Shield Mark* (n 57) [62]. [76] ibid [63].

[77] *Edgar Rice Burroughs, Inc* (n 21) [20], [23], cf [35].

[78] Commission Regulation (EC) No 2868/95 of 13 December 1995 implementing Council Regulation (EC) No 40/94 on the Community trade mark [1995] OJ L 303/1, as amended (EUTM Implementing Regulations) art 1, rule 3(6). See also Regulation art 26(1)(d) (requiring the filing of a representation of the mark that satisfies the requirements of Regulation art 4(b)); Decision No EX-05-3 of the President of the Office of 10 October 2005 concerning electronic filing of sound marks (amending Decision No EX-02-2 of the President of the Office of 7 November 2002 governing the electronic filing of EU trade mark applications following the introduction of rule 3(6) above to regulate the submission of electronic files of sound signs).

[79] See registered trade mark EU005090055 https://www.ipo.gov.uk/tmcase/Results/4/EU005090055?legacySearch=False (last accessed 5 June 2017).

[80] This was the written description of the sign in *Libertel* (n 24). [81] ibid [32].

the consumer 'to perceive and recall' the relevant colour or combination of colours sufficiently to be able 'to repeat with certainty the experience of a purchase'[82] *or* the public notice aims of the trade mark register by enabling competent authorities and commercial operators 'to know the scope of the protection afforded' by the registration of the colour or colours as a trade mark,[83] supported by consideration of the detrimental impact that granting trade mark monopolies for colours would have on competition.[84]

At the same time, however, it was accepted by the Court of Justice that colours are capable of representation in a manner that satisfies the *Sieckmann* criteria. To this end, all that is required is that the colours in question be represented by a sample in combination with a textual description that refers to an internationally recognized colour identification code,[85] such as the Pantone Colour Chart.[86] An amendment to the rules governing the representation of signs in the trade mark register has supported this by expressly requiring this form of representation of colour marks.[87]

According to some commentators, this resolution of the representability problem for colours has not secured their protectability by registered trade mark, but rather created other obstacles to that end.[88] The reason is the view that any colour represented in the manner thus required is likely to be defined too specifically to be capable of stable perception and repeated recall by consumers.[89] If this were true, colours thus represented would be incapable of fulfilling the essential function of a trade mark, and would thus be unregistrable for lack of distinctiveness under Article 7(1)(b) of the Regulation and Article 4(1)(b) of the Directive. This, combined with the inability of a colour's representation to fulfil the public notice function of the trade mark register, might explain the practice of some domestic tribunals of construing signs involving colours as hybrid signs comprising colours and shapes rather than colours per se.[90]

[82] See *Heidelberger* (n 24) [35]; also *Libertel* (n 24) [39]–[41].

[83] See *Heidelberger* (n 24) [35].

[84] See *Libertel* (n 24) [54]–[56], [60].

[85] ibid [38]; see also *Heidelberger* (n 24) [42].

[86] See http://www.pantone-colours.com (last accessed 5 June 2017).

[87] EUTM Implementing Regulations art 1, rule 3(5).

[88] See eg G Humphries, 'A Selective Review of Colour Mark Issues and Case Law in the EU', paper delivered at the Fordham Intellectual Property Conference (2013) http://fordhamipconference.com/wp-content/uploads/2013/03/2013.humphries.design.paper_.pdf 4 (last accessed 5 June 2017).

[89] ibid.

[90] See eg Case KG ZA 13-123 *Christian Louboutin v Van Haren Schoenen BV* ECLI:NL:RBDHA:2013: BZ7844 (Rechtbank's-Gravenhage), currently on appeal; Case 2014/AR/843 *Christian Louboutin v Dr Adams Footwear* (Cour d'appel de Bruxelles) (deciding that the subject matter for which protection was sought was the colour Pantone 18-1663 TPX Chinese Red https://www.pantone.com/color-finder/18-1663-TPX (last accessed 5 June 2017) applied to the sole of high-heeled shoes and not the colour as such, which was a property of the shoes rather than an object in and of itself). See also *Enercon* (n 35); *Lambretta Clothing Co Ltd v Teddy Smith (UK) Ltd* [2004] EWCA Civ 886, [2005] RPC 6 [39] (distinguishing in the context of design protection between 'colours in the abstract' and 'colours applied to shapes', and describing the latter as not able 'physically nor conceptually [to] exist apart from the shapes of the parts of the article').

Ultimately, the difficulty of establishing the representability of colours reflects the same policy concerns as the difficulty of establishing colours to be signs that are capable of distinguishing goods or services. Those concerns relate to the impact of trade mark monopolies on the two objectives of the trade mark system above by reason: (a) of their restriction of the freedom of commercial operators to use basic elements of human expression in the marketing of their goods and services, and the distortion of competition that such restriction (it is said) would create; and (b) of the legal uncertainty that colour marks create—owing to the uncertain expressive boundaries of objects of colour and the uncertain scope of the monopolies conferred on them by registered trade mark—and the harm to consumer welfare, legal certainty, and competition to which such uncertainty gives rise.[91]

Having noted the connection between the trade mark requirement of representability and the patent law requirement of sufficient description above, it bears emphasis that the precision required of the representability of the sign in the trade mark register has been far less than that required of the description of the invention in the patent document, and more akin perhaps to that required of the description of a plant variety, or even more so to that required of the material fixation of an authorial work in copyright. Given the nature of signs and works respectively as expressive objects, and of inventions and plant varieties as ideas for a certain product or process, this is unsurprising. In effect, all that has been required to satisfy the precision aspect of the representability requirement of trade mark law is that the nature of and relationship between the expressive properties of the object comprising the sign be capable of clear identification, without any additional requirement for precision in the representation of their dimensions. Hence the Court of Justice's decision in *Apple Inc v Deutsches Patent- und Markenamt*[92] that the representation in the trade mark register of a sign comprising 'the distinctive design and layout of a retail store' did not need to indicate the size and proportions of the store in order to fulfil the requirement for representability.[93]

As noted at the outset of this section, the requirement for graphic representation has recently been replaced in the Regulation and Directive with a requirement for representation on the register 'in a manner which enables the competent authorities and the public to determine the clear and precise subject matter of the protection afforded to its proprietor'.[94] In recommending this amendment, the Max Planck Institute sought to make representability an evidentiary rather than a substantive requirement, and to support a conception of the basic subject matter of trade mark protection as the 'sign' rather than the 'trade mark'.[95]

[91] These concerns have been considered in detail by the courts and commentators. See eg *Christian Louboutin SA v Yves Saint Laurent America, Inc* 778 F Supp 2d 445 (SDNY 2011), overruled by *Christian Louboutin SA v Yves Saint Laurent America Holding, Inc* 696 F3d 206 (2nd Cir 2012); A Bartow, 'The True Colours of Trade Mark Law: Greenlighting a Red Tide of Anti Competition Blues' (2008) 97 Kentucky Law Journal 263; see also Humphries (n 88).

[92] Case C–421/13 *Apple Inc v Deutsches Patent- und Markenamt* ECLI:EU:C:2014:2070.

[93] ibid [19].

[94] See text associated with n 3.

[95] See text associated with n 58.

Implicit in this move was a rejection of the *Heidelberger* and *Sieckmann* view of graphic representability as serving the interests not only of those authorities and competitors who rely on the register to know the identity and protective scope of registered trade marks, but also of those consumers who rely on the sign as presented in the market to repeat or avoid past purchasing experiences. As long as the rules governing the representation of unitary (EU) and domestic (UK) trade marks continue to require their representation in documentary form, the amendment to the representability criterion can be expected to have no practical effect. Nonetheless, now that the term 'graphic' has been removed from the definition of 'trade mark', there is nothing to prevent the amendment of those rules to permit non-documentary—and thus, non-graphic—forms of representation, including representation by deposit of electronic recordings of sounds and moving images, and of tastes, textures, and other so-called 'exotic' signs, as is permitted for certain types of inventions in patent law, and as the amended recitals to the Regulation and Directive confirm.[96] It remains to be seen, however, whether the exclusive focus of the amended statutory criterion on meeting the requirements of the trade mark register will result in a reconception of that requirement as unconcerned with the capacity of a sign to operate as a signifier of commercial origin, and if it does, whether that reconception will affect the range of signs capable of protection as a registered trade mark.

In conclusion, for a sign to be a trade mark, it must be capable of representation on the trade mark register, which in turn requires that it be capable of depiction or portrayal in a manner that is clear, precise, self-contained, easily accessible, intelligible, durable, and objective. While this requirement is in many ways analogous to the patent and copyright law requirements for sufficient description of an invention and material fixation of an authorial work, it has historically differed in the important and related respects: (a) of ensuring the capacity of a sign to fulfil the essential function of a trade mark by supporting the repeated perception and recall by consumers of a message of commercial origin; and (b) of being a substantive rather than an evidentiary requirement, and of representing an essential rather than an accidental property of the subject matter protectable by registered trade mark. Among other things, this explains why the requirement for representability has not been interpreted and applied with a view to ensuring the protectability of all signs, and why certain types of sign, such as odours and tastes, are (for the moment at least) effectively excluded from protection on the basis of their inability to be represented in the manner required. Having said that, it is clear from the concept of representation itself that any sign comprising a trade mark will exist separate from its representation in the trade mark register, just as authorial works exist separate from their forms of material fixation and inventions exist separate from their definition in the patent claims and representation in the patent document.

[96] See n 63.

2.1.5 *. . . That are Not Comprised Exclusively of Functional, Technical, or Aesthetic Characteristics of Goods*

By provision of Article 7(1)(e)(i) to (iii) of the Regulation and Article 4(1)(e)(i) to (iii) of the Directive, a sign may not be registered as a trade mark if it consists exclusively of the shape or another characteristic of goods: (a) resulting from the nature of the goods themselves; (b) that is necessary to obtain a technical result; or (c) that gives substantial value to the goods. These paragraphs operate independently of one another as three separate exclusions from the category of protectable trade marks.[97] If any subject matter falls within any one of them, it will be denied protection regardless of its distinctiveness or other properties.[98]

In its focus on a certain category of signs, namely shapes and other characteristics of goods, Articles 7(1)(e) and 4(1)(e) represent an exception to the subject matter neutrality of European trade mark law.[99] According to the Court of Justice, a 'shape' within the meaning of these provisions includes the packaging of any goods (such as liquids and powders) that do not themselves possess any intrinsic shape, and that must therefore be packaged in order to be marketed.[100] It also includes shapes (in the form of a product or its packaging) depicted by means of a three-dimensional sign or by means of a two-dimensional sign representing the product figuratively. Whether it includes non-three-dimensional properties of goods, such as their colour, is a question before the Court of Justice currently. According to Advocate General Szpunar, however, it does, provided the colour is integrated into (and thus indissociable from) the shape of the goods.[101]

As with the other criteria of Article 4 of the Regulation and Article 3 of the Directive considered previously, when interpreting and applying Article 7(1)(e) and Article 4(1)(e) the courts have regard to the aims and policy objectives of the EU trade mark regime, including of especial importance the protection of consumer welfare and promotion of undistorted competition within the internal market. If it were possible to register as a trade mark some characteristic of a product that is necessary to obtain a functional or technical result or that gives the product substantial aesthetic value, they have said, the seller of the product would in effect obtain a perpetual monopoly in respect of that result or characteristic, undermining the aims of each of the trade mark, patent, and copyright/design right regimes. According

[97] Case C–205/13 *Hauck GmbH & Co KG v Stokke A/S* ECLI:EU:C:2014:2233 (*Hauck*) [39].

[98] See *Philips* (n 5) [75]; Case C–371/06 *Benetton Group SpA v G-Star International BV* [2007] ECR I–07709 [26].

[99] Case C–421/13 *Apple Inc v Deutsches Patent- und Markenamt* ECLI:EU:C:2014:2070.

[100] See *Henkel* (n 38) [33]–[34], [44]. Such packaging may also serve to designate characteristics of the packaged goods, including their quality, within the meaning of Regulation art 7(1)(c) and Directive art 4(1)(c).

[101] *Christian Louboutin v Van Haren* (n 4). This case concerns a preliminary reference from the Rechtbank Den Haag in the case referred to in n 90 above. The question referred is as follows: 'Is the notion of 'shape' within the meaning of Article 3(1)(e)(iii) of [the pre-2015 Trade Marks Directive, corresponding to Directive art 4(1)(e)(iii) but limited in its scope to shapes: see n 4] limited to the three-dimensional properties of the goods, such as their contours, measurements and volume (expressed three-dimensionally), or does it include other (non-three-dimensional) properties of the goods, such as their colour?' On the distinction between two-dimensional and three-dimensional products see *Lambretta Clothing Co Ltd v Teddy Smith (UK) Ltd* [2004] EWCA Civ 886, [2005] RPC 6 [24] ('All Articles (even thin flat ones) are 3 dimensional (using the practical Euclidean view of the world—not that of modern day physics)').

to their reasoning, a monopoly of this type would undermine the aims of the trade mark system by enabling trade mark protection to extend beyond signs that serve the essential function of a trade mark, and of the patent and copyright/design right systems by subverting their conferral of limited term exclusive rights in respect of functional, technical, and aesthetic subject matter on the persons responsible for devising or creating/designing them. It is in order to protect these purposes, and the integrity of each of the IP regimes that exist to fulfil them, that Article 7(1)(e) and Article 4(1)(e) are said to exist.[102]

In deciding whether a sign falls within the scope of one of the Article 7(1)(e) and Article 4(1)(e) exclusions, the Court of Justice begins by identifying the essential characteristics or most important elements of the relevant sign,[103] and then asks whether those characteristics or elements:

(a) Relate inherently to the generic function or functions of the goods, such that protecting the sign as a trade mark would make it difficult for competing undertakings to give their goods a shape or other characteristic suited to the use for which they are intended (paragraph (i));[104]
(b) Incorporate a technical solution—whether or not other existing shapes or characteristics can achieve the same technical result[105]—such that protecting the sign as a trade mark would 'impede the use of that solution by other undertakings' (paragraph (ii));[106] or
(c) Give substantial aesthetic or ornamental value to the product, such that protecting the sign would prevent competing undertakings from using the same aesthetic or ornamental element with respect to their own products (paragraph (iii)).[107]

The time for examining a sign under Article 7(1)(e) and Article 4(1)(e) is the date of filing, though evidence post-dating the filing—including evidence regarding the use of the trade mark after its registration—can still be considered if it helps to

[102] See eg *Philips* (n 5) [78] and [82] (describing Directive art 4(1)(e)(i) and (ii) as existing 'to prevent the protection conferred by the trade mark right from being extended, beyond signs which serve to distinguish a product or service from those offered by competitors, so as to form an obstacle preventing competitors from freely offering for sale products incorporated such technical solutions or functional characteristics in competition with the proprietor of the trade mark', and Directive art 4(1)(e)(ii) in particular as reflecting 'the legitimate aim of not allowing individuals to use registration of a mark in order to acquire or perpetuate exclusive rights relating to technical solutions'); Case T–508/08 *Bang & Olufsen A/S v Office for Harmonisation in the Internal Market (Trade Marks and Designs) (OHIM)* [2011] ECR II–06975 (*Bang & Olufsen*) [65] (describing the purpose of Directive art 4(1)(e)(iii) as being the same as that of Directive art 4(1)(e)(i) and (ii), namely, 'to prevent the exclusive and permanent right which a trade mark confers from serving to extend the life of other rights which the legislature has sought to make subject to "limited periods"').

[103] Case C–48/09 P *Lego Juris A/S v Office for Harmonisation in the Internal Market (Trade Marks and Designs) (OHIM)* [2010] ECR I–08403 (*Lego*) [69].

[104] See *Hauck* (n 97) [23]–[27].

[105] See *Philips* (n 5) [81]. That paragraph (ii) refers only to the manner in which the goods function and not also the manner in which they are manufactured was confirmed by the Court of Justice in Case C–215/14 *Société de Produits Nestlé SA v Cadbury UK Ltd* ECLI:EU:C:2015:604 [57].

[106] See *Lego* (n 103) [48].

[107] See *Hauck* (n 97) [31]–[36].

establish the position at the filing date.[108] Since the exclusions of each Article operate independently,[109] a sign the essential characteristics of which fall within a mix of their three exclusions will not for that reason be denied protectability: what is required is that its essential characteristics fall entirely within one or other of the relevant paragraphs.[110]

An important issue in the context of Article 7(1)(e) is the nature of the sign the essential characteristics of which must be identified. As noted above, implicit in the requirement that a sign be capable of representation in order to be a trade mark is that, while the representation of a sign serves the functions of identifying (and thereby enabling access to) the sign, in addition to defining the scope of its protection as a trade mark, the sign itself exists *qua* sign independent of its representation. This conception of the sign as existing separate from its representation is reflected in the method adopted by the Court of Justice for identifying the essential characteristics of a sign under Article 7(1)(e). That method might involve either a visual analysis of the representation of the sign in the trade mark register or, depending on the difficulty of the sign, a systematic examination of each of the sign's components in the light of any relevant evidence.[111] However, in any case in which it is not possible to analyse the relevant shape or characteristic of the goods solely on the basis of the sign's representation, the competent authority must look beyond that representation to consider evidence regarding the goods themselves.[112] Such evidence might include surveys or expert opinions, and data relating to prior IP grants in respect of the goods.[113] In the context of Article 7(1)(e)(iii) specifically, it might also include evidence regarding the nature of the goods, the artistic value of the shape and its dissimilarity from other shapes in common use on the relevant market, the existence of any price difference between the relevant goods and similar products, and the focus in the goods' marketing strategy on their aesthetic characteristics.[114]

A well-known example of a subject matter excluded from protection under Article 7(1)(e)(ii) is the red three-dimensional sign representing the shape of Lego blocks that was considered by the Court of Justice in the *Lego* case. In the decision under appeal in that case, the General Court had relied on certain findings of fact by the Grand Chamber, including: that the most important element of the sign consisted in the two rows of studs on the upper surface of the brick; that that element was necessary to obtain the intended technical result of the product; and that all other elements of the sign, with the exception of its colour, were also functional. In the absence of any evidence of distortion in these facts, the Chamber affirmed the General Court's decision as beyond the reach of its appellate jurisdiction. Nor, in the Chamber's judgment, had the General Court in *Lego* erred in its refusal to consider survey evidence regarding the public's perception of the sign in reaching

[108] See *Pi-Design* (n 60) [59]–[60]. [109] See *Hauck* (n 97) [39].

[110] ibid [41]–[43]. [111] See *Lego* (n 103) [71].

[112] Case C–30/15 P *Simba Toys GmbH & Co KG v European Union Intellectual Property Office (EUIPO)* ECLI: EU:C:2016:849 [48]–[51].

[113] See *Pi-Design* (n 60) [48]. [114] See *Hauck* (n 97) [35].

its decision: such evidence being in the Grand Chamber's decision a relevant factor at most and not in any case decisive under Article 7(1)(e)(ii).

The opposite decision was reached in respect of the shape of the Kit Kat chocolate bar in *Néstlé v Cadbury*. There the Second Board of Appeal of the EUIPO held that the sign, consisting of four identical trapezoidal bars aligned together on a rectangular base, was not excluded from protectability under Article 7(1)(e)(ii). In the Board's analysis, while the sign included certain functional features, such as the alignment of the bars and their joining through a thinner base that enabled the trapezoidal bars of the product to be portioned, those features were nonetheless not dictated by technical aims or considerations. In addition, it held, granting a trade mark monopoly for the sign would not prevent Cadbury's competitors from incorporating those features into any product that did not have the same non-functional elements (ie the trapezoidal shape of the bars) as the Cadbury sign.

Few would support the grant of trade mark monopolies for functional or technical characteristics of products given their impact on competition, making the exclusions of Article 7(1)(e)(i) and (ii) uncontroversial. Less accepted is the appropriateness of Article 7(1)(e)(iii), and the allegedly detrimental impact on competition of allowing aspects of product design that perform the essential function of a trade mark to be protected as trade marks.[115] Why, it has been asked, ought the law to protect the freedom of a trader's competitors to use those aspects of a product that, in addition to indicating its commercial origin, give it substantial aesthetic or ornamental value?[116] One answer might be that the rationale for the exclusion is not only to promote undistorted competition, but also to prevent overlapping IP (here, trade mark and copyright/design right) protection.[117] However, this seems not to be the position of EU law currently.

2.1.6 Conclusion

In conclusion, the subject matter for which registered trade mark protection may validly be granted are defined under European and UK law as any expressive objects (referred to as 'signs') that are 'generally capable of being a trade mark'[118] in the sense of supporting the two aims of trade mark protection and registration outlined above, and thereby promoting consumer interests and undistorted competition within the relevant (EU or UK) protective territory. In concrete terms, a trade mark thus defined is any expressive object that is capable of distinguishing the goods or services of one undertaking from those of other undertakings and

[115] See eg A Kur, 'Too Pretty to Protect? Trade Mark Law and the Enigma of Aesthetic Functionality' in J Drexl and others (eds), *Technology and Competition: Essays in Honour of Hans Ullrich* (Larcier 2009) 139; C Gielen, 'Substantial Value Rule: How it Came Into Being and Why it Should be Abolished' (2014) 36 European Intellectual Property Review 164.

[116] See Gielen (n 115) 167.

[117] Note in this context Regulation art 53(2) and Directive art 5(4)(b) (providing for the invalidation of any trade mark the use of which may be prohibited pursuant to an earlier EU or domestic intellectual property right).

[118] See n 30.

thereby enabling consumers to repeat or avoid indefinitely their prior purchasing experiences. To satisfy this definition, an object must not only be capable of conveying specific information as to the origin of a product or service—which it will be by virtue of its nature as a sign—but also capable of representation in a manner that is clear, precise, self-contained, easily accessible, intelligible, durable, and objective. Further, and consistent with the teleological terms in which trade marks are defined, a subject matter will only be protectable by registered trade mark if it is not a type of subject matter for which other limited-term IP rights exist, and more specifically, if its most important elements do not consist exclusively of functional, technical, or aesthetic characteristics of goods the protection by trade mark monopoly of which would prevent competing undertakings from giving their own goods the same functional, technical, aesthetic characteristics. A subject matter that satisfies this definition of a trade mark will be conceived as a purpose-limited sign, namely, a sign to be used for the purpose of indicating the commercial origin of the goods or services in respect of which it is registered, and liable to revocation if it is not so used.

2.2 Other Marks of Origin

2.2.1 Introduction

As seen above, European (and UK) law offers potentially indefinite protection for signs, including names, for use to distinguish certain goods or services, and referred to as trade marks. While the focus of the discussion in section 2.1 was on individual marks, being marks that distinguish the goods or services of an individual undertaking from those of other undertakings, EU and domestic (including UK) trade mark legislation also provides for the grant of non-individual marks, in the form of so-called 'collective' and 'certification' marks, which are still owned by an individual, but which are applied to distinguish the goods or services of collectives or groups of undertakings with reference (for collective marks) to those undertakings' membership of a certain association or (for certification marks) to the goods' or services' compliance with the requirements imposed by a particular certification authority. More specifically, and as defined by European legislation, a collective mark is the same as an individual trade mark except that, instead of distinguishing the goods or services of an individual undertaking, being the owner of the trade mark, it distinguishes the goods or services of the members of an association of manufacturers, producers, suppliers, or traders, which association itself is the trade mark owner.[119] A certification mark is the same as a collective mark except that it distinguishes those goods or services that have been certified by a given authority, being the owner of the trade mark, as possessing certain predefined characteristics.[120] A well-known example of a collective mark is the UK's NHS (National Health Service) trade

[119] See Regulation art 66. A collective mark can also be obtained by a legal person governed by public law: art 66(1).

[120] See Regulation art 74a.

mark, which is made available for access and use by any persons working within the NHS in an explicit effort to discourage the use of alternative logos that might compete with and compromise the integrity of the NHS brand.[121] Well-known examples of certification marks are the different Woolmark trade marks, owned by Australian Wool Innovation and licensed for use by any third party in respect of products that satisfy the specifications associated with each.[122]

The aims and perceived benefits of collective and certification marks are the same as those of regular trade marks in their focus on promoting consumer protection and undistorted competition within the internal market, albeit in the case of certification marks by indicating more than the commercial origin of the relevant goods or services. Particularly when combined, the protection they confer is very similar to the protection conferred by PDOs, PGIs, and TSGs. As with certification marks particularly, the aim of these titles of IP right is to promote fair competition and consumer protection by enabling undertakings to convey reliable information to consumers about the origin and quality of their products.[123] Also like certification marks, they encourage the producers of products to make 'a genuine effort to improve [their] quality in order to be able to use' the protected sign[124] and, as with some certification marks at least—such as the various Halal and Kosher marks used to signify a product's compliance with particular halal-related and kashrut-related specifications—recognize and promote the importance of different products for different European social and cultural communities and traditions,[125] and of the particular environment with which those products are associated.[126] In the context of PDOs and PGIs particularly, a primary aim of protection is to encourage and protect (against the multifarious forces of globalization especially) the idea and nature of products as gastronomical expressions of the environmental and cultural characteristics of the place from which they originate: their *goût de terroir* (*terroir*).[127] It is in this way that the law seeks to enhance the quality of the relevant products, and to protect their consumers and producers against the unauthorized use of the names, such as PROSCIUTTO DI PARMA,[128] that distinguish their origin and

[121] See https://www.england.nhs.uk/nhsidentity/why-its-important/ (last accessed 5 June 2017).

[122] See http://www.woolmark.com/brands/ (last accessed 5 June 2017).

[123] Quality Schemes Regulation recitals 3, 20 and 39, and art 1.

[124] See *Budějovický Budvar* (n 13) [112].

[125] See Case C–317/95 *Canadane Cheese Trading AMBA v Hellenic Republic* [1997] ECR I–04681 (AG) (*Canadane*) [10] ff (discussing the place of cheese in Western food and culture). For a justification of GIs that combines cultural and economic theory to argue for their role as instruments by which to pursue goals of biodiversity, food security, and cultural identity, including by enabling indigenous and local communities to protect their own agricultural knowledge production, see T W Dagne, 'Beyond Economic Considerations: (Re)conceptualizing Geographical Indications for Protecting Traditional Agricultural Products' [2015] International Review of Intellectual Property and Competition Law 682.

[126] On the complex relationship between GIs on the one hand and identity, creativity, and place on the other see M Ferrari, 'The Narratives of Geographical Indications' (2014) 10 International Journal of Law in Context 222.

[127] See generally S Bowen, *Divided Spirits: Tequila, Mezcal, and the Politics of Production* (OUP 2015) ch 1.

[128] Use of the EU-registered PDO PROSCIUTTO DI PARMA in respect of a product signifies that it originates from the Parma area and has been developed according to certain traditional methods and

related characteristics.[129] Consistent with this, and in contrast to certification and collective marks (which distinguish goods or services with reference to a particular association and certification of quality respectively), PDOs and PGIs distinguish goods with reference to the geographical area from which they originate and the characteristics that they possess in consequence of doing so. Thus, while collective marks may serve to designate the geographical origin of goods, and certification marks may serve to designate the quality or characteristics of goods, including the geographical area from which they derive, neither has the essential function of a PDO or PGI to designate both (and their relationship),[130] and nor is either a communally-owned title of IP right.[131]

Within Europe currently, PDOs, PGIs, and TSGs are available only with respect to certain specified agricultural products and foodstuffs. For PDOs and PGIs these are beer; chocolate and derived products; bread, pastry, cakes, confectionery, biscuits and other baker's wares; beverages made from plant extracts; pasta; salt; natural gums and resins; mustard paste; hay; essential oils; cork; cochineal; flowers and ornamental plants; cotton; wool; wicker; scutched flax; leather; fur; and feather;[132] in addition to spirit drinks[133] and wine;[134] and are offered different levels of protection.[135] For TSGs they are prepared meals; beer; chocolate and derived products; bread, pastry, cakes, confectionery, biscuits, and other baker's wares; beverages made from plant extracts; pasta; and salt.[136] In contrast to the protection conferred by other EU IP rights, and as noted in section 1, the protection conferred by PDOs, PGIs, and TSGs is both uniform and exhaustive throughout EU territory, with the result that Member States may not grant domestic rights in respect of the same

standards of ham production developed since Etruscan times: *Consorzio del Prosciutto di Parma v Asda Stores Limited* [2001] UKHL 7, [2002] FSR 3 [2].

[129] See in this regard Madrid Agreement art 1(1) (requiring member countries to protect against 'false or deceptive indication[s]' of product origin); Lisbon Agreement art 3 (requiring member countries to protect against 'any usurpation or imitation' of appellations of origin, regardless of whether the usurpation or imitation involves a false or deceptive indication of product origin). The higher standard of protection required by the Lisbon Agreement reflects that required by TRIPs Agreement art 23 in respect of geographical indications for wines and spirits.

[130] See Case T–627/13 *The Tea Board v Office for Harmonisation in the Internal Market (Trade Marks and Designs)* ECLI:EU:T:2015:740 [41].

[131] See s 4.1 and A F Ribeiro de Almeida 'The Legal Nature of Geographical Indications and Designations of Origin' [2014] European Intellectual Property Review 640, 646–47 (arguing that designations of origin and geographical indications are not forms of coownership or Roman common property, but rather communal property (in the German conception of *Gemeinschaft zur gesammten Hand*)).

[132] Quality Schemes Regulation art 2(1) and Annex I.I.

[133] See Regulation (EC) No 110/2008 on the definition, description, presentation, labelling and the protection of geographical indications of spirit drinks and repealing Council Regulation (EEC) No 1576/89 [2008] OJ L 39/16.

[134] See Regulation (EU) No 251/2014 of the European Parliament and of the Council on the definition, description, presentation, labelling and the protection of geographical indications of aromatised wine products and repealing Council Regulation (EEC) No 1601/91 [2014] OJ L 84/14.

[135] GIs for wines and spirits confer strong protection against even honest and non-misleading uses of the protected subject matter, in contrast to GIs for agricultural products, which offer protection more along the lines of that conferred by registered trade mark.

[136] Quality Schemes Regulation art 2(1) and Annex I.II.

subject matter.[137] As at 6 December 2016 there were only sixty-one registered UK products, including twenty-four PDOs, thirty-four PGIs, and three TSGs.[138]

2.2.2 Designations of Origin and Geographical Indications

As seen in section 1.2, the primary legislation in this area is the Quality Schemes Regulation, which governs the grant of PDOs, PGIs, and TSGs in respect of the agricultural products and foodstuffs listed above, whether or not they originate from EU territory. Focusing on PDOs and PGIs specifically, the following subject matter are defined to be eligible for protection:

- For PDOs—names that identify a product (a) that originates in a specific place, region, or (exceptionally) country (b) whose quality or characteristics are essentially or exclusively due to a particular geographical environment with its inherent natural and human factors, and (c) the production, processing, and preparation steps of which all take place in the relevant area—subject to certain special provisions where the product's raw materials come from an area larger than or different from the one defined; and
- For PGIs—names that identify a product (a) that originates in a specific place, region, or country, (b) whose quality, reputation, or other characteristic is essentially attributable to its geographical origin, and (c) at least one of the production, processing, and preparation steps of which takes place in the relevant area.

As these definitions underline, designations of origin and geographical indications are types of trade mark. More specifically, they are purpose-limited signs (comprising names) that are capable of distinguishing and intended for use to distinguish certain goods (comprising the agricultural products and foodstuffs described above) and the protection of which does not undermine other IP regimes (including particularly the plant variety and trade mark regimes). Their main difference is the aspect of the product that they distinguish: rather than its commercial origin, as for trade marks, designations of origin and to a lesser extent geographical indications distinguish the product's *terroir*. In order for a subject matter to be a designation of origin, it must be a name that designates, directly or indirectly, a geographical area from which a product originates—being a place, region, or in exceptional cases a country[139] in which the production, processing, and preparation of the product have all taken place—the inherent (homogeneous) natural and human features of which distinguish it from adjacent geographical areas[140] and account essentially or

[137] See n 13.

[138] http://www.ahdb.org.uk/documents/Horizon_Brexit_Analysis_Report_GI_Highres_06December2016.pdf (last accessed 5 June 2017).

[139] On the inability of an area defined by linguistic or territorial criteria to constitute a geographical area see Case C–12/74 *Commission of the European Communities v The Federal Republic of Germany* [1975] ECR I–00181 (the *Sekt* case) [8].

[140] Joined Cases C–465/02 and C–466/02 *Federal Republic of Germany v Commission of the European Communities* ECLI:EU:C:2005:804 (*Germany v Commission*) [50].

exclusively for the product's quality or characteristics. According to the Court of Justice in the *Sekt* case, appellations can only fulfil their specific purpose of safeguarding producers against unfair competition and consumers from being misled if the product they describe does in fact possess qualities and characteristics that distinguish it from all other products and are due to its origination in a specific geographical area.[141] Since a method of production strictly defined will always, in the absence of exclusive rights, be capable of being practiced in other geographical areas, it will never alone be capable of determining the product's geographical origin.[142] Hence the requirement of Article 5(1)(c) of the Quality Schemes Regulation that a designation of origin refer to products the production, processing, and preparation steps of which all take place in the defined geographical area.[143]

Geographical indications are similar in nature to designations of origin. They include all such designations, in addition to other product names that identify a geographical area—including a country—in which at least one of the product's production, processing, and preparation steps have taken place, and the features of which account essentially for the product's quality, reputation, or other characteristics. In addition to supporting a wider notion of 'geographical area' to include (as a matter of course) areas defined by territorial and linguistic criteria,[144] this definition permits a looser connection between the area indicated by the name and the product, including by treating a product's reputation as among the 'characteristics' accounted for by the area. As remarked by the Advocate General in *Canadane*, this brings geographical indications closer to generic names than designations of origin are due to their ability to indicate a product's origination from a place that does not imbue it with any special quality or characteristics, and their protection notwithstanding the absence of any requirement that the product conform to specified standards. For this reason, the subject matter protectable as a PGI is closer to the subject matter protectable as a registered trade mark than to the subject matter protectable as a PDO: in essence, it comprises a sign (in the form of a name) of use for the purpose of indicating the commercial origin of certain goods or services (in the form of agricultural products or foodstuffs) rather than a sign of use for the purpose of indicating a product's embodiment or expression of certain *terroir* properties.

In sum then, designations of origin and geographical indications are particular types of sign, in the form of names, that are capable of distinguishing and intended for use to distinguish certain goods on the basis of their geographical origin and, to a greater or lesser extent, the specific qualities and characteristics that they possess by reason of that origin.[145] While the name in question will often indicate the origin of the goods directly, as in the case of JERSEY ROYAL POTATOES, registered as a protected designation of origin for kidney potatoes produced, processed, and

[141] See the *Sekt* case (n 139) [7]. [142] ibid [9].

[143] See Quality Schemes Regulation art 3 (defining 'production step' to mean 'production, processing or preparation').

[144] But not to include 'mountain': see Joined Cases C–321/94 to C–324/94 *Criminal proceedings against Jacques Pistre* [1997] ECR I–02343.

[145] See *Canadane* (n 125) [35]; also the *Sekt* case (n 139) [7].

prepared in the Island of Jersey in accordance with certain statutory production standards,[146] it may also do so indirectly. An example is WEST COUNTRY BEEF, which is registered as a protected geographical indication for beef raised, finished, and slaughtered in Cornwall, Devon, Somerset, Gloucestershire, Dorset, or Wiltshire, and at least 70 per cent forage fed.[147] Another is FETA, which was held by the Court of Justice in *Germany v Commission* to be a protectable designation of origin for white cheese soaked in brine and traditionally produced in mainland Greece and the Department of Lesbos from ewes' milk or a mixture of ewes' and goats' milk. According to the Court in that case, the relevant areas, from which were excluded non-negligible parts of the country Greece, represented a geographical area the homogeneous natural features of which distinguished it from adjacent areas and determined essentially or exclusively the quality and characteristics of the relevant cheese. In addition, while products had been lawfully marketed in relatively large amounts under the name FETA in other Member States since the 1930s, the widespread marketing of those products with reference to Greek cultural traditions and civilizations supported the Court's conclusion that the name had not become the common name of a product within the EU, so as to be 'generic' within the meaning of the Quality Schemes Regulation, and thus incapable of performing the essential function of a designation of origin.[148]

As with trade marks, PDOs and PGIs may not be granted where their protection would undermine other IP regimes, including particularly those that exist to regulate the protection of plant varieties and trade marks. Situations in which they will be regarded to do so include those in which the relevant designation of origin includes a name—(a) already approved for use as the denomination of a plant variety; (b) wholly or partially homonymous with a name already registered as a PDO or PGI; or (c) similar to a trade mark with a reputation and established use—the use of which as a designation of origin would be likely to cause confusion among consumers regarding the true origin or identity of the relevant product.[149]

3. Goodwill in England and Wales: 'The Attractive Force Which Brings in Custom'[150]

As seen in section 1, the trade mark system of some jurisdictions at least comprises both a registered (trade mark) right and an unregistered (allied) right. In

[146] https://www.gov.uk/government/uploads/system/uploads/attachment_data/file/271267/pfn-jersey-royal-potatoes.pdf (last accessed 5 June 2017).

[147] http://www.westcountrybeefandlamb.org.uk (last accessed 5 June 2017).

[148] See Quality Schemes Regulation arts 3(6) (defining 'generic terms') and 6(1) (prohibiting the registration of generic terms as PDOs and PGIs).

[149] ibid art 6.

[150] *Inland Revenue Commissioners v Muller & Co's Margarine Ltd* [1901] AC 217 (HL) (*IRC v Muller*) 224 (Lord Macnaughten), cited with approval in *Reckitt & Colman Products Ltd v Borden Inc* [1990] UKHL 12, [1990] RPC 341 (*Reckitt*) (Lord Jauncey).

England and Wales, the unregistered right is conferred by the common law action of passing off.

According to Lord Oliver in the classic passing off authority of *Reckitt*: 'The law of passing off can be summarized in one short general proposition—no man may pass off his goods as those of another'.[151] In the same opinion his Lordship expounded the three elements required to establish the action—goodwill, a misrepresentation, and damage—and noted with respect to the first as follows:

> [For a claimant to succeed] he must establish a goodwill or reputation attached to the goods or services which [the claimant] supplies in the mind of the purchasing public by association with the identifying 'get-up' (whether it consists simply of a brand name or a trade description, or the individual features of labelling or packaging) under which his particular goods or services are offered to the public, such that the get-up is recognized by the public as distinctive specifically of the plaintiff's goods or services.[152]

As this passage makes clear, the subject matter protectable by the action of passing off is not the trade mark or 'get-up' in which a trader's goodwill is embodied, but rather the goodwill itself. This is consistent with the description by Millet LJ in *Harrods Ltd v Harrodian School Ltd*[153] of the action as 'a wrongful invasion of a right of property vested in the [claimant]', and of the object of the property right protected by the action as 'the goodwill and reputation of his business which is likely to be harmed by the defendant's misrepresentation', and not 'the name or get up which the defendant has misappropriated'.[154] To the same effect was the statement of Lord Oliver in *Reckitt* that 'the proprietary right which is protected by the action is in the goodwill rather than in the get-up'; it being this, he noted, that 'distinguishes the protection afforded by the common law to a trader from that afforded by statute to the registered holder of a trade mark'.[155]

As an object of property particularly, goodwill is an elusive and amorphous concept. The authoritative definition remains that of Lord Macnaughten from 1901, who described it as 'the benefit and advantage of the good name, reputation and connection of a business', and 'the attractive force which brings in custom'.[156] This aspect of 'bringing in custom' is central, and is what distinguishes goodwill from reputation. Specifically, and as affirmed by the Supreme Court in *Starbucks* in 2015, 'a plaintiff who seeks passing off relief in an English court must show that he has goodwill, in the form of customers, in the jurisdiction of the court'.[157] Contrary to the position in other common law countries,[158] mere reputation in the jurisdiction is not enough.[159]

In sum, the basic subject matter protected by the passing off action is denoted by the term 'goodwill'. According to the courts, 'goodwill' is the attractive force that requires time and investment to develop and that, once developed, influences the

151 See *Reckitt* (n 150) 406. 152 ibid.
153 *Harrods Ltd v Harrodian School Ltd* [1996] RPC 697 (CA). 154 ibid 711.
155 See *Reckitt* (n 150) 418. 156 See *IRC v Muller* (n 150) 223–24.
157 See *Starbucks* (n 9) [32]. 158 On which see the discussion ibid [38] ff.
159 ibid [52].

public towards the centre or source from which it emanates.[160] While the development and appropriation of goodwill will be impossible without the vehicle of a sign in the trade mark sense, the subject matter protected by the action is the goodwill itself and not the sign. Nonetheless, in practice establishing passing off involves showing: (a) that the defendant has used some thing, be it an invented or descriptive word,[161] an artistic or personal image,[162] a product shape or packaging,[163] a slogan,[164] or some other object, that—as a result of the claimant's own activities—is distinctive of (in the sense of being associated by a significant section of the relevant public with) the claimant's goods or services in respect of which the claimant (therefore) has goodwill; (b) that such use involves a misrepresentation likely to deceive the public; and (c) that the misrepresentation has damaged the claimant's goodwill in some way.

4. Entitlement

4.1 Registered Trade Mark Protection is for Registrants

As seen in Chapters 4 and 5, patents and copyright are presumptively rights of natural persons, being inventors and authors respectively.[165] Thus, and subject to the mainly employment-related exceptions discussed, only the deviser of an invention or creator of an authorial work will be entitled to the protections of IP law in respect of it.[166] So too in the case of related rights subject matter and plant varieties: the persons presumptively entitled to protection are those natural or legal persons responsible for the existence of the protected subject matter.

At first glance the situation in trade mark law appears very different owing to the absence of any person approximating a creator or deviser of the protected subject matter. Given this, it might be said, it is not surprising that any natural or legal person is able to apply for and be granted a registered trade mark, regardless of their connection to or responsibility for the sign comprising the mark, and subject only to the absolute and relative grounds for refusal and invalidation of registration. While those grounds recognize the possibility for conflicting claims in respect of the same trade mark, they resolve such conflicts temporally, with reference to the

[160] See *IRC v Muller* (n 150) 224 (Lord Macnaughten).

[161] In relation to descriptive words see eg *Reddaway v Banham* [1896] AC 199 (HL) (deciding that the term Camel Hair had become distinctive of the claimant's belting).

[162] In relation to celebrity images see eg *Irvine v Talksport Ltd* [2003] EWCA Civ 423, [2003] 1 WLR 1576 (deciding that racing-car driver Mr Eddie Irvine had substantial goodwill and reputation in his name and image that he was able to protect from unauthorized appropriation by means of the passing off action).

[163] See eg *Reckitt* (n 150) (deciding that the use of plastic containers that resembled a lemon had become distinctive of the claimant's lemon juice).

[164] See eg *Cadbury Schweppes Pty Ltd v Pub Squash Co Pty Ltd* [1981] RPC 429 (HL) (*Cadbury Schweppes*) 490 (Lord Scarman, describing passing off as 'wide enough to encompass other descriptive material, such as slogans').

[165] See ch 4 s 4; also ch 5 s 4.

[166] ibid.

date of application for registration or protection by other means of the mark,[167] and having regard to the *bona fides* of the applicant[168] and any knowing acquiescence by the first owner of the registered trade mark in the subsequent use of the mark by another.[169]

However, the apparent anomaly regarding entitlement to registered trade mark protection is removed when it is remembered that the protected subject matter is not the sign as such but rather the sign *qua* trade mark, and in particular, when it is remembered that the protected subject matter is a purpose-limited object similar to the purpose-limited objects protectable by patent grant. In patent law, the inventor of such a product is conceived as the person who has the idea to use the product for the relevant purpose. So too in trade mark law, it is possible to conceive the person who has the idea to use the sign for the relevant purpose, being the purpose of indicating the origin of certain goods or services, as devising the sign *qua* trade mark. Provided that intention is *bona fides*—which is ensured by the absolute and relative grounds for refusal and invalidation of trade mark registration, including for having been filed in bad faith, and by the requirement that the sign by used for the purpose indicated—and the subject matter as protected really is the sign when used for the purpose of indicating the commercial origin of the relevant goods or services, then the person whose intention it is can rightly be regarded as the deviser of the subject matter protected by the registered trade mark, and thus the person presumptively entitled to that protection. The same applies mutatis mutandis with respect to collective and certification marks, and other product designations such as designations of origin and geographical indications. In the case of the latter, however, only 'groups' of people that 'produce or obtain' products having certain *terroir* properties can apply to register a name as a PDO or PGI in respect of the relevant products, and the result (if a group's application succeeds) is the right of any person whose products have the same *terroir* properties to use the PDO or PGI to distinguish them with reference to those properties.

Overall, the UK and European law governing entitlement to registered trade marks and other designations of origin makes it clear that such subject matter are expressive objects of any origin that are intended to be and actually put to genuine use in trade to distinguish the goods or services of one or more undertakings from those of other undertakings on the basis of: their commercial origin

[167] See Regulation art 8; Directive art 5; Trade Marks Act s 5.

[168] See Regulation art 52(1)(b); Directive art 4(2); Trade Marks Act s 3(6) (requiring the invalidation of any trade mark the application for registration of which was filed 'in bad faith'). When applying this provision, the courts are required to consider all of the relevant factors in the particular case, including but not limited to: (a) the fact that the applicant knew or should have known that a third party was using, in at least one EU Member State, an identical or similar sign for an identical or similar product liable to be confused with the sign for which registration was sought; (b) the applicant's intention of preventing that third party from continuing to use such a sign; and (c) the degree of legal protection enjoyed by the third party's sign and by the sign for which registration was sought (Case C–529/07 *Chocoladefabriken Lindt & Sprüngli AG v Franz Hauswirth GmbH* ECLI:EU:C:2009:361 [53]; Case T–635/14 *Urb Rulmenti Suceava SA v Office for Harmonisation in the Internal Market (Trade Marks and Designs) (OHIM)* ECLI:EU:T:2015:297 [31]ff).

[169] See Regulation art 54; Directive art 9; Trade Marks Act s 48.

(for trade marks); their originator's association with a particular collective (for collective trade marks); their certification by a particular authority (for certification trade marks); or their expression of certain *terroir* properties (for PDOs and PGIs). Provided a person (for trade marks, including collective and certification marks) or group (for PDOs and PGIs) seeks the registration of a sign for the purpose of such use—whether by or with the authorization of the applicant (for trade marks, including collective and certification marks) or by members of the group (for PDOs and PGIs)—and provided that such use is maintained sufficiently throughout the period of registration as required by the relevant regime, the person and his licensees or other successors in title, and the (changing range of) group members, will be entitled indefinitely to the protections conferred by IP law in respect of it. Further, the basis of their entitlement is the same as the basis of a person's entitlement to patent protection for a purpose-limited product, namely, that the person or group who conceived the idea to use the sign to indicate the relevant properties of the goods or services in question is responsible for having devised that object *qua* mark or designation. In the case of PDOs and PGIs, a further analogy can be drawn with plant varieties: the group applying for the relevant protection deriving products from the natural resources of a particular area that express its *terroir* properties, much as plant breeders derive their plant varieties.

4.2 Passing Off Protection is for those who Develop Goodwill

Passing off protects the goodwill that a claimant has in fact established in respect of certain goods or services. It follows that the only persons entitled to prevent others from the unauthorized misappropriation of goodwill are those natural and legal persons who have developed it in the course of their activities.

While the paradigmatic beneficiary of the passing off action will be a commercial entity involved in the sale of goods or the provision of services in the local market, non-commercial entities such as political, charitable, and professional organizations, might also establish the necessary goodwill on the basis of their activities, provided those activities are in some sense commercial. The Court of Appeal confirmed as much in *Burge v Haycock*,[170] when it decided that a non-profit lobbying group, the Countryside Alliance, had developed goodwill in England and Wales as a result of its campaigning for countryside interests. The reason was that such campaigning involved marches and other high-profile public events, and was supported by significant trading activities and the provision of a variety of products and other benefits to its members.[171] In that context, Lady Justice Hale remarked, its right to protection could not 'depend upon [its] precise legal status'.[172]

Since passing off is, like other IP rights, a territorial right, the goodwill that it protects must exist in the protecting territory. A foreign claimant with an established reputation but no goodwill in England and Wales will not be entitled to

[170] *Burge v Haycock* [2001] EWCA Civ 900, [2002] RPC 28. [171] ibid [9]–[11].
[172] ibid [68].

rely on the action to prevent third parties from passing their goods or services off as those of the claimant or damaging the claimant's reputation. Having said that, establishing goodwill in the local jurisdiction is relatively easy to do. All that is required is evidence of the existence of people in that jurisdiction 'who, by booking with, or purchasing from, an entity in this country, [have] obtained the right to receive the claimant's service [or product]', whether directly from the claimant, and whether they actually obtain it in the jurisdiction or abroad.[173] In explaining this position recently, Lord Neuberger invoked the balance that he described as 'aris[ing] in relation to any intellectual property right' between

> the public interest in not unduly hindering competition and encouraging development, on the one hand, and on the other, the public interest in encouraging, by rewarding through a monopoly, originality, effort and expenditure.[174]

The same balance, Lord Neuberger said, explains why a claimant who has merely advertised his products without actually marketing them has no rights under the passing off action, namely, since in that case he 'has given no consideration to the public in return for his claimed monopoly'.[175]

The entitlement of any person who has developed goodwill in respect of goods or services to legal protection against third party passing off explains the courts' recognition of the principle of so-called 'extended passing off'. According to that principle, the goodwill embodied in a term or other object will be shared by anyone who has, through her use of the object in connection with her goods or services, developed goodwill in respect of those goods or services. This principle has supported passing off actions by claimants whose use of such terms as GREEK YOGHURT and SWISS CHOCOLATE (which are distinctive by reason of their association by a significant section of the public with yoghurt made in Greece and chocolate made in Switzerland) has been sufficient to generate goodwill in respect of their goods and thereby entitle them to prevent third parties from using the same or a similar term in respect of different goods (ie products other than yoghurt made in Greece and chocolate made in Switzerland).[176]

In conclusion, the common law principles governing entitlement to relief under the action of passing off make it clear that the goodwill that that action aims to protect is the positive association and reputation that a trader or other undertaking develops among the public to elicit its loyalty and custom. For goodwill to exist, it must have been developed by the undertaking through the use of such reputational

[173] See *Starbucks* (n 9) [52].

[174] ibid [61]. See also *Cadbury Schweppes* (n 164) 490–91 (Lord Scarman, stating, in a passing off case brought by the manufacturers of the lemon squash drink SOLO, 'competition must remain free; and competition is safeguarded by the necessity for the [claimant] to prove that he has built up an "intangible property right" in the advertised descriptions of his product, or, in other words, that he has succeeded by such methods in giving his product a distinctive character accepted by the market').

[175] See *Starbucks* (n 9) [61].

[176] See *Fage UK Ltd v Chobani UK Ltd* [2014] EWCA Civ 5, [2014] ETMR 26; *Chocosuisse Union des Fabricants Suisse de Chocolat v Cadbury Ltd* [1999] EWCA Civ 856, [1999] RPC 826 (CA).

externalities as words and images, which externalities are then liable to protection by the undertaking as embodiments of its property.

5. Conclusions

5.1 Trade Marks as Artifact Types Having Certain Properties and Arranged in Categories that Express and Reflect those Properties

(a) What are the categories of subject matter protected by the regimes, and what are those subject matters' essential properties?

The main category of subject matter registrable as a trade mark is the trade mark. In Europe and the UK, this category is understood to contain every (a) expressive object (b) that is intended for use and capable of being used to indicate the commercial origin of goods or services, and thereby to support consumers' repetition or avoidance of their prior purchasing experiences, (c) that is capable of being represented in a manner that is clear, precise, self-contained, easily accessible, intelligible, durable, and objective in the trade mark register, and (d) the essential characteristics of which do not consist exclusively of functional, technical, or aesthetic characteristics of goods. Thus defined, the essential properties of trade marks are: (a) their possession of certain expressive qualities; (b) the purpose or intention of their putative deviser to use them to indicate the commercial origin of certain goods and services, and their capacity to support such intended use; and (c) their inherent unsuitability for the limited-term protection afforded by the patent, copyright, and design right regimes.

Thus described, and perhaps surprisingly, the trade mark can be said to conform to the paradigmatic idea of an artifact considered in Chapter 3. One reason for this is its intangibility as a (purpose-limited) expressive object, and another is its nature as an intellectual creation in the second and more expansive of the senses considered in section 2.2 of Chapter 3. With respect to their nature as intellectual creations: while trade marks need not be the product of any transformative human act giving rise to a new object in the *Doodeward v Spence*[177] sense, they do involve making an object (in the nature of a sign) available in a new and useful way (as a mark of commercial origin), and may therefore be described as intellectual creations in the more expansive sense of *Yearworth v North Bristol NHS Trust*.[178] Hence the importance of an applicant's intention to use a given sign—and later of his actual use of the sign—as a means of indicating the commercial origin of certain goods or services to the public. In this sense the essential properties of trade marks are similar to the essential properties of purpose-limited products within the meaning of patent law: they include an intention to use an object—which may be

[177] *Doodeward v Spence* [1908] HCA 45, (1908) 6 CLR 406.
[178] *Yearworth v North Bristol NHS Trust* [2009] EWCA Civ 37, [2010] QB 1.

a pre-existing and previously available object—to achieve a certain purpose.[179] As purpose-limited signs they might be regarded in effect as a hybrid of the work (as an expressive object) and the purpose-limited invention (as an idea for an object to be used for a certain purpose).

Just as the functional or technical aspects of a product are inappropriate for protection by copyright, so too they are inappropriate for protection by registered trade mark. The reason is not that purpose-limited signs in the sense just defined will never incorporate such aspects, which they might, but rather that the effect of protecting them *qua* trade mark would be to confer a monopoly right of potentially indefinite duration in respect of them, and thereby subvert the purpose of the trade mark and patent systems respectively to promote undistorted competition and confer time-limited protection for inventions. It is for this reason that protectable trade marks are defined not to include any purpose-limited sign that is comprised exclusively of characteristics of a product the functional or technical qualities of which make it prima facie appropriate for protection by patent. More difficult to explain is the corresponding exclusion from the subject matter protectable by registered trade mark of the aesthetic or ornamental aspects of a product, being those aspects prima facie appropriate for protection by copyright or design right. On the one hand, this exclusion also prevents the cumulation of different species of IP in respect of the same—or at least, of overlapping—subject matter. On the other hand, competition-based arguments are less compelling in respect of non-functional and non-technical aspects of a product. Thus, provided potential conflicts among different classes of right holder are appropriately resolved, and each species of right is defined only to confer such protection as it exists to confer (determined in the light of the subject matter it exists to protect), the appropriateness of the exclusion might be doubted.

In section 2 of Chapter 3 it was remarked that, while historically trade mark rights have rewarded the creation of an association in the minds of consumers between a sign and a commercial origin, more recently they have protected the sign itself, treating it in the way that copyright treats the authorial work. While this shift is most apparent in the law of trade mark rights and infringement, it is also reflected in conceptions of the subject matter protectable by registered trade mark as the 'sign' rather than the 'trade mark'. As seen above, what distinguishes a trade mark from a sign is the intention of the prospective trade mark proprietor that it be used for a certain purpose and its capacity to support such use. Hence the significance of the recently accepted proposal that European trade mark legislation be amended to clarify that the requirement for representability of a sign is an evidentiary rather than a substantive requirement focused exclusively on ensuring the capacity of each registered trade mark register to fulfil its public notice functions. By detaching the representability requirement from the function of a sign *qua* trade mark, this proposal supports a reconception of the protectable subject matter as

[179] See ch 4 ss 2.2.1 and 5.

the expressive object comprising the sign rather than that object in its capacity as a mark of commercial origin.

Similarly, the requirement that a trade mark be capable of supporting the repeated perception and recall of a sign in the minds of consumers confirms the nature of trade marks as types, and of their individual representations as tokens. So too the conception of trade marks as expressive objects that convey through their use a particular message of commercial origin explains the reliance on semiotic theory to explain the nature and function of trade marks, and the fact of the type/token distinction having been formulated by a semiotic theorist.

As a hybrid of the work and purpose-limited invention, trade marks may be classified as both norm kinds, namely, objects of which there exist properly and improperly formed examples (neither of which may lawfully be reproduced without the permission of the trade mark proprietor) and universals in the conceptualist philosophical sense, namely, ideas (or rather in this context, information) that can be repeatedly expressed by the use of concrete particulars in the form of representations or reproductions of the sign in connection with the goods or services for which the trade mark is registered.

The same analysis as offered above for trade marks applies with respect to collective and certification marks, as well as for PDOs and PGIs; the only difference, as explained in section 4.1, being the message that each is intended to convey regarding the products or processes in respect of which it is registered.

(b) How is each subject matter individuated within the regimes?

Every subject matter for which a registered trade mark is sought and granted must be capable of being distinguished *qua* trade mark—namely, as an indication of the commercial origin of certain goods or services—from the trade mark register. The reasons for this are similar to those discussed in Chapter 4 for subject matter for which a patent is sought.[180] Specifically, and as there stated for inventions, rule of law considerations require that restrictions on individual freedoms such as those imposed by trade mark monopoly be defined sufficiently clearly for the public to be able to organize their lives without infringing others' rights. In addition, however, where patent law emphasizes the contractual nature of the patent grant as a further reason for requiring a patent applicant to provide a clear and concise definition and description of the invention sufficient to enable it 'to be performed by a person skilled in the art',[181] trade mark law emphasizes two different considerations. The first is the function of trade marks themselves as a reason for requiring a trade mark applicant to provide a clear and precise representation of the sign sufficient to enable 'the consumer to perceive and recall a particular [expressive object], thereby enabling him to repeat with certainty the experience of a purchase';[182] and the second is the importance of trade mark authorities being in a position 'to fulfill their obligations in relation to the prior examination of registration applications and to

[180] See ch 4 s 5.
[181] EPC art 83; Patents Act 1977 (UK) s 14(3).
[182] See text associated with n 59.

the publication and maintenance of an appropriate and precise register of trade marks'.[183]

Recalling the two notions and requirements of metaphysical and epistemic individuation introduced in Chapter 3,[184] it is clear that both are reflected in the trade mark law provisions governing the representation of a trade mark in the register. Specifically, the requirement for evidence of a mark's metaphysical individuation can be seen in the requirement for its representation in the application for protection,[185] and the requirement for evidence of a mark's epistemic individuation can be seen in the requirement that such representation be sufficiently clear, precise, self-contained, easily accessible, intelligible, durable, and objective to enable: competent authorities to examine the mark for registrability and maintain a public register of protected marks; competitors of the trade mark proprietor to understand the implications of the mark's registration for their own freedoms; and consumers to perceive and recall the sign sufficiently to reach purchasing decisions in an efficient manner.[186] Clearly, of the two types of individuation, it is epistemic individuation that has especial importance in trade mark law. This is apparent in those areas concerned with establishing the identity of a subject matter *qua* trade mark—including the relative grounds of refusal of registration for trade marks that are identical or confusingly similar to an earlier trade mark, and infringement—which make it clear that such identity depends primarily on the perception of the public, and of the consumer specifically. This was confirmed by the Court of Justice in *LTJ Diffusion SA v Sadas Vertbaudet SA*[187] in its discussion of the test for deciding whether the registration of a trade mark is to be denied on the basis that there exists an earlier trade mark that is identical or confusingly similar to it (and that has been registered in respect of identical or confusingly similar goods or services). According to the Court, the identity of a trade mark[188] depends on the 'overall impression' that it produces in the mind of 'an average consumer who is . . . reasonably well informed, reasonably observant and circumspect'.[189] Since the average consumer will not have access to marks at all times, he is also deemed to 'place his trust in the imperfect picture of [it] that he has kept in his mind,'[190] which picture will reflect the variable degree of attention that consumers pay to trade marks applied to different categories of goods or services.[191] The same conception of a trade mark's identity is reflected in the approach adopted by the courts when considering whether the similarity of a trade mark to an earlier mark renders the former

[183] See n 19. [184] See ch 4 s 5.

[185] See Regulation art 26(1)(d) and EUTM Implementing Regulations art 1, rules 1(1)(d) and 3; Trade Marks Act s 32(2)(d).

[186] See n 59.

[187] Case C–291/00 *LTJ Diffusion SA v Sadas Vertbaudet SA* [2003] ECR I–02799 (*LTJ Diffusion*).

[188] In relation to the refusal of registration for trade marks identical to an earlier trade mark see Regulation art 8(1)(a), (1)(b), and (5); Directive art 5(1)(a), (1)(b), and (3)(a); Trade Marks Act s 5(1), (2)(a), and (3)(a). In relation to the rights conferred by registered trade mark to prevent third parties from using signs that are identical to the trade mark see Regulation art 9(2) and (4); Directive art 10(2) and (4); Trade Marks Act s 10(1) to (3).

[189] See *LTJ Diffusion* (n 187) [52]. [190] ibid. [191] ibid.

ineligible for registration, and whether the similarity of a registered trade mark to a mark used by the defendant supports a finding of infringement of the registered trade mark owner's rights.[192] According to that approach, what matters is how the average consumer, with the characteristics outlined above, would perceive the marks when considered overall. In determining this, the courts begin with the representations of the relevant marks in the register, where such representations exist, and interpret them in the light of any use that has been made of the marks thus represented. Where a claim of infringement is brought against a defendant for use of a sign that has not been registered, the courts will by necessity focus exclusively on the sign as used in the market. Either way, their task is an interpretive one, with their aim in particular being to identify the formal and conceptual similarity between the marks, having regard to their dominant components and the nature and extent of their distinctiveness, and with a view to deciding whether their co-existence on the market is likely to cause confusion on the part of the public such that registration ought to be denied or infringement found.[193] The result is to affirm the importance of the concept of epistemic (rather than metaphysical) individuation in trade mark law, and of the 'average consumer' as the hypothetical 'intelligent individual'[194] whose ability to single each trade mark out as a distinct object of perception is central to its legal status.[195] The result is also to affirm the centrality to each trade mark's identity of its expressive properties, and its capacity for use in the market to distinguish certain goods or services of one undertaking from those of others. Thus, the name PICASSO registered as a trade mark in respect of paints will not be the same subject matter as the name PICASSO registered in respect of cars; the specific goods or services in respect of which the trade mark is registered therefore being an additional means by which marks are individuated within the trade mark regime.

Reference to the importance of the goods or services in respect of which individual trade marks are registered to the identity and method of individuating trade marks raises an important distinction between trade marks on the one hand and PDOs and PGIs particularly on the other. That distinction concerns the different manner of specifying the goods and services in respect of which each type of IP right is registered. For trade marks, the goods and services must be specified clearly and precisely[196] by the applicant in her trade mark application[197] with reference

[192] In relation to the refusal of registration for trade marks similar to an earlier trade mark see Regulation art 8(1)(b) and (5); Directive art 5(1)(b) and (3)(a); Trade Marks Act s 5(2)(b) and (3)(a). In relation to the rights conferred by registered trade mark to prevent third parties from using signs that are identical to the trade mark see Regulation art 9(2)(b) and (c); Directive art 10(2)(b) and (c); Trade Marks Act s 10(2)(b) and (3)(a).

[193] See Case C–251/95 *SABEL BV v Puma AG, Rudolf Dassler Sport* [1997] ECR I–6191 [22]–[25].

[194] See E J Lowe, 'Individuation' in M L Loux and D W Zimmerman (eds), *The Oxford Handbook of Metaphysics* (OUP 2005) 75.

[195] But see *Enercon* (n 35).

[196] Case C–307/10 *Chartered Institute of Patent Attorneys v Registrar of Trade Marks* ECLI:EU:C:2012:361 [43] and [59].

[197] See eg Regulation art 26(1)(c); EUTM Implementing Regulations art 1, rule 1(c).

to the forty-five classes of goods and services contained in the Nice Agreement Concerning the International Classification of Goods and Services for the Purposes of the Registration of Marks.[198] As above, trade marks are then individuated on the basis in part of the goods or services thus specified. However, while PDOs and PGIs are also individuated on the basis in part of the goods in respect of which they are registered, consistent with their nature as purpose-limited signs, the manner in which those goods are specified is different in reflection of the different nature of the subject matter protectable as PDOs and PGIs. As seen above, the subject matter protectable as PDOs and to a lesser extent PGIs is a sign of use to indicate a product's embodiment of a certain *goût de terroir*. Thus, for PDOs especially, the individuation of the protected subject matter depends on the identification of both the sign (ie the product name) and the products that originate from the geographical area and embody the associated characteristics designated by it. Both are published in the EU's Database of Origin and Registration (DOOR).[199] In addition to listing the name comprising the PDO, the DOOR lists the type of product in respect of which the name is registered, and the conditions with which individual products of that type must comply in order to be marked with the PDO.[200] Those conditions, contained in the product specification that Article 8(b) of the Quality Schemes Regulation requires each group seeking registration of a PDO or PGI to provide,[201] are then the basis for determining whether the PDO or PGI may be used in respect of a particular product,[202] and what scope of protection is conferred by the PDO or PGI on its beneficiaries.[203] Thus conceived, the role of the product specification is very similar to that of the patent claims and plant variety description, even if its form and content is very different from the form and content of both of those documents. The scope of protection conferred by PDOs and PGIs is also more

[198] See eg EUTM Implementing Regulations art 1, rule 12(d). For the current edition of the Nice Agreement see http://web2.wipo.int/classifications/nice/nicepub/en/fr/edition-20170101/taxonomy/ (last accessed 5 June 2017).

[199] http://ec.europa.eu/idabc/en/document/5360/5637.html (last accessed 5 June 2017).

[200] The requirements imposed by product specifications may extend beyond methods of production to such matters as preparing the product for presentation on the market provided they are necessary and proportionate means of safeguarding the quality of the product and thus the reputation of the PDO or PGI itself: see eg Case C–388/95 *Kingdom of Belgium v Kingdom of Spain* ECLI:EU:C:2000:244 [58] (affirming the validity of the condition imposed by the PDO RIOJA specification that the product be bottled in the geographical area of origin); Case C–469/00 *Ravil SARL v Bellon import SARL* [2003] ECR I–05053 [67]–[67] (affirming the validity of the conditions imposed by the PDO GRANA PADANA specification with respect to grated forms of the product); Case C–108/01 *Consorzio del Prosciutto di Parma and Salumificio S Rita SpA v Asda Stores Ltd* [2003] ECR I–05121 (*Prosciutto di Parma*) [48]–[49] (affirming the validity of the conditions imposed by the PDO PROSCIUTTO DI PARMA specification that the product be sliced and packaged in the geographical area of origin).

[201] See also Quality Schemes Regulation art 7 (describing the information that each product specification must contain). For the rules governing amendment of the product specification see further Quality Schemes Regulation art 53.

[202] See also Quality Schemes Regulation art 37 (requiring verification by a competent authority of a product's compliance with the specification before it is placed on the market with a PDO or PGI).

[203] See *Prosciutto di Parma* (n 200) [47].

similar to that conferred by patents and plant variety rights than that conferred by registered trade mark, particularly in its extension to unauthorized 'misuse, imitation or evocation'.[204] There, however, the differences of current relevance end. For example, PDOs and PGIs are individuated with reference to the image that they produce in the mind of 'the average consumer who is reasonably well informed and reasonably observant and circumspect',[205] as for registered trade marks. If the phonetic and visual relationship between two names is such as to produce in the mind of the average European consumer the image of the same type of product, the one name will be regarded as 'evoking' the other, and thereby falling with the scope of the PDO or PGI monopoly.[206] In applying this test, the Court of Justice has further held that it is appropriate to consider advertising material or other evidence 'which suggests that the … similarity between the two names is not fortuitous', consistent with the inclusion among the constitutive properties of PDOs and PGIs of an intentional or purposive element, and consistent with the approach of domestic UK courts when determining the infringement of patents for purpose-limited inventions.[207] The same conception of a PDO's and PGI's identity is reflected in the approach adopted by the courts when considering whether the similarity of a name to an earlier name, trade mark, plant variety, or animal breed, renders the former ineligible for registration, and whether a name has become generic so as to preclude its protection by PDO or PGI.[208] According to that approach, what matters is the impact on the average consumer of the name when considered overall.[209]

(c) What is the relationship between each subject matter and its tokens?

Each trade mark and other product designation is realized or instantiated in the manner in part of an authorial work. Thus, the tokens of a given trade mark or designation have in common their expressive properties, consistent with the nature of a trade mark as an expressive object. However, merely representing a trade mark such as the slogan JUST DO IT or a PDO such as the name PARMIGIANO REGGIANO in verbal or written form will not suffice to instantiate it as such. Thus, a person who says 'just do it' to his colleague will not thereby instantiate the trade mark. Rather, for the slogan to be instantiated *qua* trade mark it will need to be

204 See Quality Schemes Regulation art 13(1) (defining the protection afforded to PDOs and PGIs to include, among other things, protection against 'any misuse, imitation or evocation', 'even if the true origin of the products or services is indicated or if the protected name is translated or accompanied by an expression such as "style", "type", "method", "as produced in", "imitation" or similar'). On the scope of the protection against unauthorized 'evocation' of a PDO or PGI specifically see Case C–87/97 *Consorzio per la Tutela del Formaggio Gorgonzola v Käserei Champignon Hofmeister GmbH & Co KG* [1999] ECR I–01301 (the *Gorgonzola* case) [25]–[29]; Case C–75/15 *Viiniverla Oy v Sosiaali- ja terveysalan lupa- ja valvontavirasto* ECLI:EU:C:2016:35 (the *Calvados* case).

205 See the *Calvados* case (ibid) [25].

206 See the *Gorgonzola* case (n 204) [25]; ibid [48].

207 See the *Gorgonzola* case (n 204) [28]; the *Calvados* case (n 204) [39] and [48]. In the patent context see eg *Generics (UK) Ltd v Warner-Lambert Company LLC* [2015] EWCA Civ 556, [2017] RPC 1.

208 See Quality Schemes Regulation art 6.

209 See eg ibid; Case C–132/05 *Commission of the European Communities v Federal Republic of Germany* [2008] ECR I–00957 [53]–[55] (treating the test of genericity as whether consumers have ceased to regard a name as an indication of the geographical origin of a product 'and come to regard it only as an indication of a certain type of product', as in the case of Camembert and Brie).

represented *qua* trade mark, namely, as a mark of commercial origin for goods or services of the same type as those for which the slogan is registered. The same applies with respect to the instantiation of the name PARMIGIANO REGGIANO as a PDO.

(d) How is the existence of each subject matter and its tokens known?

In trade mark law, the existence of a trade mark or PDO is known by reason of and reference to its representation in the register, as for the existence of an invention in patent law. The existence of one or more of its properly or improperly formed tokens is also known in the manner above, namely, from the registration or use of a subject matter that the average consumer would understand to be identical or confusingly similar to the protected trade mark in respect of identical or confusingly similar goods or services or (in the case of a PDO) to evoke the same type of product in respect of which the PDO is registered.

5.2 Goodwill as an Extrinsic Property of a Person

(a) What are the categories of subject matter protected by the regime, and what are those subject matters' essential properties?

The subject matter protected by the UK passing off action is goodwill, understood by the courts to mean the attractive force or favourable regard that the public has for the provider of goods or services, as demonstrated by the trader's custom.

It is difficult to think of goodwill as an artifact in the sense considered in Chapter 3. The main reason is that goodwill is less an object than a property of a person in the form of a trader. Further, since the property depends on the view of the public, goodwill is an extrinsic rather than an intrinsic property, or perhaps a relation between the trader and the public. Whether conceived as a property or relation, it is not easily conceived as an object since its existence at any particular time depends on the mind of the public at that time.[210]

Nor relatedly is goodwill readily conceived as an intellectual creation in either of the *Doodeward v Spence* or *Yearworth* senses above. For a start, the creation of goodwill does not involve any transformative human action producing an object, and nor does it involve making an existing object available in a new and useful state or form. The most that could be said in this regard is that goodwill is the product of labour and skill on the part of the trader, but the mere exertion of labour and skill to produce a feeling or relationship does not justify the grant of property rights on the authority of either of those cases, and nor more generally is it readily described as involving an act of human or intellectual creation.

This is consistent also with the difficulty of conceiving goodwill as a type, notwithstanding its capacity for instantiation in a variety of tokens, including product packaging and individual purchases.

[210] See the discussion of mind-dependent entities in G Rosen, 'Abstract Objects' in E N Zalta (ed), *The Stanford Encyclopedia of Philosophy* (Fall 2014 edn) s 3.

(b) How is each subject matter individuated within the regimes?

The goodwill of one trader is distinguished from the goodwill of another trader with reference to the trader's identity.

(c) What is the relationship between each subject matter and its tokens?

The tokens of a trader's goodwill exist as reputational externalities, ie concrete objects and events to which her reputation attaches.

(d) How is the existence of each subject matter and of its tokens known?

The existence of goodwill is known by evidence of a trader's relationship with her customers.

7

The Design

1. Registered and Unregistered Protection for Designs

Notwithstanding certain commonalities, the subject matter considered in Chapters 4 to 6—comprising ideas for solving a technical problem using particular technical means, works that express an author's own (literary, dramatic, musical, or artistic) intellectual creation, and signs that are capable of distinguishing and intended for use to distinguish the goods or services of one undertaking from those of other undertakings—are readily distinguishable inter se. Given this, their protection by separate legal regimes, each with its own requirements for and definitions of protection, is unsurprising.

Less easily distinguishable is the subject matter considered in this chapter and protected by so-called 'design right'. Denoted statutorily by the term 'design', this subject matter can be broadly defined as the appearance of the whole or part of a product, and is notable for its overlap with the other categories of intellectual property (IP) subject matter considered previously by reason of its functional and aesthetic qualities and its branding capacities.[1] For example, product inventions, graphic trade marks, and original artistic works are all capable of attracting design right protection—albeit not as inventions, trade marks, and authorial works as such, but rather as the appearance of the patented product, mark, and work respectively. For this reason, and as confirmed expressly by the European (EU) Designs Regulation[2] and Designs

[1] While decision-makers tend to emphasis the functional and aesthetic aspects of designs, consistent with their formal properties, the Commission has always understood designs as 'instrument[s] for marketing'. See eg Case R 690/2007-3 *Lindner Recyclingtech GmbH v Franssons Verkstäder AB* [2010] ECDR 1 (EUIPO Board of Appeal) (*Lindner*) [33] ('Good design involves two fundamental elements: the product must perform its function and it should be pleasant to look at'); European Commission, Green Paper on the Legal Protection of Industrial Designs, Doc 111/F/5131/91 (June 1991) (Green Paper on the Legal Protection of Industrial Designs) [5.4.1] (supporting a proposal for the creation of a Community design right with reference to the value of design right as a means of supporting 'design as an instrument of marketing').

[2] See Council Regulation (EC) No 6/2002 of 12 December 2001 on Community designs [2002] OJ L 3/1 (Designs Regulation) art 96 (describing the provisions of the Regulation to be 'without prejudice to any provisions of [EU or Member State domestic law] relating to unregistered designs,

Directive,[3] design right provides an additional or alternative form of IP protection for each of these three types of subject matter, which protection will, by reason of its different nature and scope, potentially enable the right owner (if she is the same as the owner of the patent, trade mark, or copyright[4]) to extend the range of unauthorized uses of the subject matter that she is able to prevent in reliance on her intellectual property.

Consistent with this overlapping nature of the subject matter protected by design right and other IP rights, the design right regime combines features of each of the patent, copyright, and trade mark regimes. For example, both EU and UK legislation offer registered and unregistered protection for designs, similar to the registered and unregistered protection offered for trade marks by the UK trade mark and (indirectly) passing off regimes.[5] Community design right also confers unitary and uniform protection throughout EU territory, similar to the protection conferred by registered EU trade mark and sought to be introduced by the unitary (EU) patent title, and, as with EU trade mark and future unitary (EU) patents, exists alongside domestic (including UK) design right, which are governed by domestic legislation harmonized (for the registered right only) by the Designs Directive. In relation to the rights conferred by design right specifically: by prohibiting, for a limited term of three to twenty-five years,[6] the unauthorized production and use of products in or to which the design is incorporated or applied[7]—and for unregistered UK design right, the unauthorized production of a design document recording the design for

trade marks or other distinctive signs, patents and utility models, typefaces, civil liability and unfair competition' (art 96(1)), and requiring that a design protected under the Regulation by registered or unregistered Community design right 'also be eligible for protection under the law of copyright of Member States as from the date on which the design was created or fixed in any form' on such conditions as each Member State decides (art 96(2))).

[3] Directive 98/71/EC of the European Parliament and of the Council of 13 October 1998 on the legal protection of designs [1998] OJ L 289/28 (Designs Directive) arts 16 and 17 (corresponding to Designs Regulation art 96(1) and (2) respectively). On the meaning of art 17 see Case C–168/09 *Flos SpA v Semeraro Casa e Famiglia SpA* [2011] ECR I–00181 (interpreting art 17 as requiring the protection by copyright in each EU Member State of all designs protected by a design right registered in or in respect of the relevant Member State, with the result that Italian legislation precluding copyright protection for designs after they had entered the public domain was invalid).

[4] Given the different skills required for invention, authorship, and design, it is unlikely that, for example, the inventor of a product and designer of its appearance will be the same person, unless both acts are undertaken in the course of employment with the same organization, in which case any rights in respect of the resulting invention and design will be presumptively owned by the employer.

[5] See ch 6.

[6] In relation to registered design right see Designs Regulation art 12 (defining the term of protection as initially five years from the date of filing, renewable in five-yearly terms to a total maximum period of twenty-five years), reproduced in Designs Directive art 10 and Registered Designs Act s 8(2). In relation to unregistered Community design right see Designs Regulation art 11 (defining the term of protection as three years from the date on which the design was first made available to the public within the EU). In relation to unregistered UK design right see Copyright, Designs and Patents Act 1988 (UK) (CDPA) s 216(1) (defining the term of protection as fifteen years from the end of the calendar year in which the design was first recorded or, if articles made to the design were made available for sale or hire within five years from that time, ten years from the end of the calendar year in which that occurred).

[7] See Designs Regulation art 19; Designs Directive art 12; Registered Designs Act s 7; CDPA s 226(1)(a).

the purpose of enabling such articles to be made[8]—regardless for registered design right of whether such use was the result of copying,[9] they resemble in different ways the rights conferred by each of copyright, patent, and registered trade mark. For example, copyright prohibits the unauthorized reproduction in three-dimensional form of two-dimensional artistic works[10] for the life of the author plus seventy years,[11] patents prohibit the unauthorized manufacture of products that embody a technical idea[12] for up to twenty years from the date of filing,[13] and registered trade mark prohibits the use of signs for the specific purpose for which they were intended and registered[14] for a potentially unlimited period. *Unregistered* design right also resembles the UK passing off action, in being conditional upon the design having been made available to the public (for the Community right),[15] and the copyright regime, in being conditional upon material fixation of the protected subject matter (for the UK right)[16] and requiring originality,[17] subsisting automatically without the need for registration, and protecting only against unauthorized copying[18] (for the Community and UK rights). And *registered* design right also resembles registered trade mark, in applying with respect to the appearance of the whole or part of a product[19] and conferring monopoly-like protection,[20] patents, in requiring

[8] CDPA s 226(1)(b).

[9] Compare in this respect Designs Regulation art 19(1), Designs Directive art 12, and Registered Designs Act s 7 with Designs Regulation art 19(2) and CDPA s 226(2).

[10] Directive 2001/29/EC of the European Parliament and of the Council of 22 May 2001 on the harmonisation of certain aspects of copyright and related rights in the information society [2002] OJ L 167/10 (Information Society Directive) art 2(1); CDPA s 17(3).

[11] Directive 2006/116/EC of the European Parliament and of the Council of 12 December 2006 on the term of protection of copyright and certain related rights [2006] OJ L 372/12 art 1(a).

[12] Agreement on a Unified Patent Court [2013] OJ C 175/1 (UPC Agreement) art 25(a) and (c); Patents Act 1977 (UK) s 60(1)(a) and (c).

[13] Convention on the Grant of European Patents (opened for signature 5 October 1973, entered into force 1 January 1977) 1065 UNTS 199, as amended (EPC) art 63(1).

[14] Council Regulation (EC) No 207/2009 of 26 February 2009 on the Community trade mark [2009] OJ L 78/1, as amended (Trade Mark Regulation) art 9(2)(a) and (b); Trade Marks Act 1994 (UK) s 10(1) and (2).

[15] In the law of passing off this requirement is implicit in the need for goodwill or reputation: see ch 6 s 3. In the law of unregistered Community design right it is an explicit requirement of Designs Regulation art 11(1).

[16] See CDPA ss 3(2) (copyright) and 213(6) (unregistered design right).

[17] In relation to copyright see Information Society Directive arts 2 to 4 (discussed in ch 5 s 2); CDPA s 1(1)(a). In relation to unregistered design right see Designs Regulation arts 4(1) and 8 (and ss 2.2 and 2.3 below); CDPA s 213(1).

[18] In relation to copyright see Information Society Directive arts 2 to 4; CDPA s 16. In relation to unregistered design right see Designs Regulation art 19(2); CDPA, 226(2). See also *Farmers Build Ltd v Carrier Bulk Materials Handling Ltd* [1999] RPC 461 (CA) (*Farmers Build Ltd*) 480 (describing the unregistered UK design right as 'plainly a right in the nature of copyright: the only exclusive right conferred is restricted to the copying of the design').

[19] In relation to registered trade mark see Trade Mark Regulation art 4; Trade Marks Act 1994 s 1(1). In relation to registered design right see Designs Regulation art 3(a); Registered Designs Act s 1(2).

[20] In relation to registered trade mark see Trade Mark Regulation art 9; Trade Marks Act 1994 s 9. In relation to registered design right see Designs Regulation art 19(1); Registered Designs Act s 7.

novelty[21] and conferring monopoly-like protection,[22] and copyright, in protecting the appearance of the whole or part of a product[23] and requiring originality.[24]

Thus, when viewed as part of the wider intellectual property family, the design right regime presents a complex picture by reason of its intersections with and borrowings from each of its patent, copyright, and trade mark siblings.

The starting point for considering the subject matter protectable by design right under European and UK law today is Article 3 of the Designs Regulation, which defines that subject matter for the purpose of unregistered and registered Community design right as comprising

> the appearance of the whole or a part of a product resulting from the features of, in particular, the lines, contours, colours, shape, texture and/or materials of the product itself and/or its ornamentation;

where a 'product' is defined separately to mean

> any industrial or handicraft item, including inter alia parts intended to be assembled into a complex product, packaging, get-up, graphic symbols and typographical typefaces, but excluding computer programs.[25]

According to the Designs Regulation, any design thus defined—excluding any features that are dictated solely by the product or part's technical function or by requirements of interoperability[26]—is entitled to protection by both registered and unregistered design right, 'to the extent that it is new and has individual character',[27] and provided it is not contrary to public policy or morality.[28] For protection by unregistered right, the design must also have been made available to the public within EU territory.[29]

The definitional and subsistence provisions of the Designs Regulation mirror the corresponding provisions of the Designs Directive,[30] regulating the grant of domestic registered design right in all EU Member States.[31] By contrast, and as noted previously, the subsistence of domestic unregistered design right has not been the subject of EU harmonization, accounting for the differences between Member States' unregistered design right regimes, and between the UK statutory provisions governing the subject matter protectable by registered and unregistered (UK) design right respectively.

[21] In relation to patents see EPC art 52(1); Patents Act 1977 s 1(1). In relation to registered design right see Designs Regulation art 5; Registered Designs Act s 1B(1).

[22] In relation to patents see UPC Agreement art 25; Patents Act 1977 s 60. In relation to registered design right see Designs Regulation art 19; Registered Designs Act s 7.

[23] In relation to copyright see Information Society Directive arts 2 to 4 (discussed in ch 5 s 2); CDPA s 1(1)(a) and (4). In relation to registered design right see Designs Regulation art 3(a); Registered Designs Act s 1(2).

[24] In relation to copyright see Information Society Directive arts 2 to 4 (discussed in ch 5 s 2); CDPA s 1(1)(a). In relation to registered design right see Designs Regulation arts 4(1) and 8 (and ss 2.2 and 2.3 below); Registered Designs Act ss 1B and 1C.

[25] Designs Regulation art 3. [26] ibid art 8. [27] ibid art 4(1).

[28] ibid art 9. [29] ibid art 11. [30] Designs Directive arts 1, 7, and 8.

[31] ibid art 2 (including as Benelux designs).

The provisions governing the registered UK design right are contained in the Registered Designs Act 1949, and reflect the provisions of the EU Designs Regulation and Designs Directive. Thus, under sections 1, 1B(1), 1C, and 1D of the Act, registered UK design right may be obtained for any subject matter comprising the appearance of the whole or part of a product resulting from its features and/or ornamentation—excluding any features dictated solely by the product's technical function or by requirements of interoperability—to the extent that it is new and has individual character, and provided it is not contrary to public policy or morality. By contrast, the provisions governing unregistered UK design right are contained in section 213 of the CDPA, and differ from the corresponding provisions of EU legislation. According to section 213, unregistered UK design right subsists in any 'shape or configuration (whether internal or external) of the whole or part of an article'—excluding any features that (a) are a method or principle of construction, (b) enable the article to be connected to, or placed in, around, or against, another article so that either may perform its function, (c) depend upon the appearance of another article of which it is intended to form an integral part, or (d) comprise surface decoration[32]—provided it is 'original', including by not having been commonplace in the design field at the time of creation,[33] and that it has been recorded in a design document or incorporated in/applied to a manufactured article.[34] It follows that when considering the subject matter protectable by European and UK design law, two categories of design must be kept in mind: those registered designs eligible for registered Community and UK design right protection under the Designs Regulation and Registered Designs Act respectively; and those unregistered designs eligible for unregistered Community and UK design right protection under the Designs Regulation and CDPA respectively. In this chapter both categories of subject matter are considered. To that end regard will also be had to the further following provisions of European and UK legislation of importance for conceptions of each type of design right subject matter:

- Article 36(1)(c) and (2) of the Designs Regulation (corresponding to rules 4(1)(b) and 5(2) of the UK Registered Designs Rules 2006), requiring applications for registered design right to contain a pictorial representation of the design suitable for reproduction (or, in some cases, a specimen of the design), and an indication of the products in which it is intended to be incorporated or to which it is intended to be applied.
- Article 14 of the Designs Regulation (corresponding to section 2 of the Registered Designs Act[35] and section 215 of the CDPA), vesting Community design right in the designer (referred to in section 2(1) of the UK Act as the 'author' of the design) or his successor in title, with an exception for designs

[32] CDPA s 213(3)–(6). [33] ibid s 213(2).

[34] ibid s 213(6) ('Design right does not subsist unless and until the design has been recorded in a design document or an article has been made to the design').

[35] See also Designs Directive art 11(c) (requiring the refusal of registration for a design if the applicant is not entitled to the design right under the law of the relevant Member State).

developed by an employee in the execution of his duties or following instructions given by his employer.

- Article 10 of the Designs Regulation (corresponding to Article 9 of the Designs Directive, section 7 of the Registered Designs Act, and section 226(2) of the CDPA), defining the scope of protection conferred by design right.
- Article 19 of the Designs Regulation (corresponding to Article 12 of the Designs Directive, section 7(2) of the Registered Designs Act, and section 226 of the CDPA), defining the primary rights conferred by registered and unregistered design right, respectively.

2. The Registered and Unregistered Design in Europe, and the Registered Design in the United Kingdom: An Original Appearance of the Whole or Part of a Product

2.1 A Design Is the Appearance of the Whole or Part of a Product

As we have seen, a design within the meaning of European legislation is defined as the appearance of the whole or part of any industrial or handicraft item ('product')—including such intangible products as symbols and typefaces—resulting from the item's features and/or ornamentation. From this definition it is apparent, as noted above, that the category of subject matter protectable by registered and unregistered Community design right includes the appearance, among other things, of certain (product) inventions,[36] authorial (artistic) works, and (graphic) trade marks, and that design right thus provides an additional or alternative form of IP protection for each of these subject matter. Thus, a machine, fruit, or other physical object suitable for industrial exploitation—being an industrial product[37]—might be protected by both patent and design right;[38] a dress or other handmade object—being a work of craftsmanship[39]—might be protected by both copyright

[36] See in this regard Joined Cases T–22/13 and T–23/13 *Senz Technologies BV v Office for Harmonisation in the Internal Market (Trade Marks and Designs)* ECLI:EU:T:2015:310 (*Senz Technologies*) (in which the validity of a Community Designs Registration in respect of the appearance of umbrellas was challenged with reference to a patented umbrella).

[37] This conception of industrial products is from patent law: See eg T898/05 (*Hematopoietic receptor/Zymogenetics*) ECLI:EP:BA:2006:T089805.20060707; *Human Genome Sciences Inc v Eli Lilly* [2011] UKSC 51, [2012] RPC 6.

[38] Contrast the view of the EUIPO Board of Appeal, which has held that the appearance of a living product such as—in Case R595/2012-3 *Groente en fruit* (EUIPO Board of Appeal, 18 February 2013)—a tomato cannot be a design on the grounds that a living product is not an 'industrial item', and that the appearance of such a product is not the result of any industrial or manual process. As above (ibid), the view that a living product is not an industrial item is inconsistent with the understanding of patent law. In addition, there is no requirement that the appearance comprising a design be the result of an 'industrial or manual process'. Rather, and as discussed in s 2 below, European law requires that it be the result of free and creative choices by its putative creator-designer.

[39] This conception of works of craftsmanship is from copyright: see eg *George Hensher Ltd v Restawile Upholstery (Lancs) Ltd* [1976] AC 64 (HL) 77 (Lord Reid, describing a work of craftsmanship

and design right;[40] and a figure, word, or other expressive object that is capable of conveying information—being a symbol[41]—might be protected by both trade mark and design right. Having said that, the protection conferred by each species of IP differs, in some cases substantially, by reason of their different aims and conceptions of protectable subject matter. This is illustrated by the case of *Kastenholz*,[42] where the claimant sought to rely on his design right protection in respect of the appearance of certain watch dials and parts to prevent the unauthorized reproduction of their underlying idea. In its decision, the General Court made it clear that since such protection does not extend to a product's functionality, the claimant's ability to prevent others from constructing watch dials that made it possible to tell the time on the basis of their colours, as his watch dials did, depended on his ability to establish a different type of IP infringement.[43] While the claimant sought to do this in reliance on copyright, it was clearly a patent on which his claim depended.[44]

Kastenholz underlines that design and patent protection, while capable of co-existing, ought rarely if ever to conflict in the sense of conferring overlapping protection. The only exception to this is where the appearance of a product is dictated by its technical function, such that preventing third parties from reproducing that appearance would in effect prevent them from reproducing the technical solution that the product embodies. This is one of the reasons given for excluding from Community design right protection the appearance of any and all aspects of a product or product part that are dictated solely by its technical function or by interoperability requirements.[45] As discussed in section 2.2 below, in addition to ensuring that any design rights and patents subsisting in respect of the same subject matter will not overlap and thereby conflict, this exclusion confines design right protection to the appearance of products, and thus to designs as statutorily defined.

The same might be said with respect to design and trade mark protection. Specifically, since design right protects the appearance of products, including graphic symbols, for the purpose of application to or incorporation in a product, while registered trade mark protects such appearance for the different purpose of indicating the commercial origin of goods or services,[46] there is or ought to be no inconsistency in allowing both to subsist in respect of the same symbol.

By contrast is the position regarding design right and copyright, the protections of which overlap more directly by reason of their shared concern with preventing the unauthorized reproduction of expressive forms. It is with a view to limiting

as a 'durable useful handmade object') and 84 (Viscount Dilhorne, describing a work of craftsmanship as 'something made by hand and not something mass produced').

[40] For a recent example from the United States see *Star Athletica, LLC v Varsity Brands, Inc* 580 US_ (2017) (*Star Athletica*), discussed in ch 5 s 3.3.1.2.

[41] This conception of symbols is from trade mark law: see eg Case C–104/01 *Libertel Groep BV v Benelux-Merkenbureau* [2003] ECR I–03793 [39].

[42] Case T–68/11 *Kastenholz v Office for Harmonisation in the Internal Market (Trade Marks and Designs) (OHIM)* ECLI:EU:T:2013:298 (*Kastenholz*).

[43] ibid [72]. [44] ibid.

[45] See eg Designs Regulation recital 10; Designs Directive recital 14; also *Lindner* (n 1) [30] (discussed in s 2.2 in this chapter).

[46] Hence the conception of trade mark protection in ch 6 as purpose-limited protection.

the impact on third parties of such overlap that UK legislation precludes reliance on copyright to prevent the unauthorized use of design documents and models[47] or acts done in reliance on a (UK or Community) registered design right,[48] and that it limits the potential liability of third parties for acts that simultaneously infringe unregistered (UK) design right and copyright to liability for infringement of copyright.[49]

It is clear from the statutory definition of the subject matter protectable by Community design right as 'the appearance' of the whole or part of a product that the design has the formal properties of an artistic work protectable by copyright, in the sense of comprising a product the external and visible[50] aspects of which support new (created) properties of visual significance.[51] This accounts for the special provision in EU legislation for designs that are applied to or incorporated in a product that constitutes a component part of a complex product.[52] According to Article 4(2) of the Designs Regulation and Article 3(2) of the Designs Directive, such designs will only be protected if the part, once incorporated into the complex product, remains visible during its normal use, and to the extent that those visible features of the part are themselves new and have individual character. Since the 'normal use' provision is specific to Article 4(2) and Article 3(2), it does not apply with respect to other types of subject matter, which must accordingly relate to those external aspects of a product that are themselves visible, independent of their use. This was confirmed in *Biscuits Poult*, where the General Court decided that since the layer of chocolate filling inside a cookie became visible if and only if the cookie were broken, the appearance of that layer was not part of the appearance of the cookie, and could thus not be considered when assessing its novelty and individual character.[53] The fact that the cookie was always broken to reveal the layer of chocolate filling during its normal use of being consumed was, the court held, irrelevant, since the 'normal use' test is confined to designs applied to

[47] See CDPA s 51. According to Jonathan Parker J in *Mark Wilkinson Furniture Ltd v Woodcraft Designs (Radcliffe) Ltd* [1998] FSR 63 (Ch) (*Mark Wilkinson Furniture*) 65, the effect of this section is to render '[t]he twin concepts of copyright and design right ... mutually excusive', although—and as held by the Court of Appeal in *Lambretta Clothing Co Ltd v Teddy Smith (UK) Ltd* [2004] EWCA Civ 886, [2005] RPC 6 (*Lambretta Clothing*) [36]–[37]—without any guarantee of seamless IP (copyright and design right) protection.

[48] CDPA s 53. [49] ibid s 236.

[50] See Case T–494/12 *Biscuits Poult SAS v Office for Harmonisation in the Internal Market (Trade Marks and Designs) (OHIM)* ECLI:EU:T:2014:757 (*Biscuits Poult*) [20]. In its 2016 review of the EU design right regime, the Commission recommended that the visible nature of designs be made explicit, and perhaps linked to the informed user's perspective. See European Commission, Legal review on industrial design protection in Europe, MARKT2014/083/D (15 April 2016) (2016 Commission Review) 13 (Recommendation 6).

[51] See ch 5 s 3.2. This is notwithstanding the definition's recognition of the capacity of a product's tactile features to contribute to its appearance and thus to inform the conception of design right subject matter. See also *PMS International Group Plc v Magmatic Ltd* [2016] UKSC 12, [2016] WLR(D) 126 (*PMS v Magmatic*) (deciding that lack of ornamentation can be a feature of a design).

[52] A complex product is 'a product which is composed of multiple components which can be replaced permitting disassembly and re-assembly of the product': Designs Regulation art 3(c); Designs Directive art 1(c).

[53] See *Biscuits Poult* (n 50) [24]–[25].

or incorporated in a component part of a complex product, and a cookie is not a complex product.[54]

While designs comprise the appearance of the whole or part of a product, they exist separate from both individual (tangible) products and (intangible) types of product. Their separateness from individual products is a function of their own intangibility, and reflects their similarity to the authorial works protected by copyright.[55] As explained by Lord Mustill in a pre-Directive case involving the then registered UK design right, design law

> is concerned not with finished articles but with the design sought to be registered, *ex hypothesi* before the articles are made; and the articles themselves are relevant only because they form the media through which the designs intended to be registered under the statute will be put into effect.[56]

In deciding protectability, Lord Mustill said, in a decision underlining the purpose-limited nature of designs as expressive objects intended for application to or incorporation in a product, '[o]ne must therefore look, not to the history of the articles which already exist, but to the characteristics which they will have when the design fulfils its intended purpose' of being applied to or incorporated in them.[57]

This plainly holds under current European law, and is further underlined by the additional distinction that EU legislation draws in its definition of protective scope between a design and the types of product in or to which it is intended to be incorporated or applied. Specifically, while an application for registered Community design right must be supported by an indication of the products in which the design is intended to be incorporated or to which it is intended to be applied[58]—just as the subsistence of unregistered Community design right will often be triggered by the design's application to or incorporation in a product that is then made available to the public[59]—the protection conferred by registered and unregistered Community design right extends in each case to the unauthorized use of the design in respect of *any* type of product, and is not limited to such unauthorized uses as involve the type of product indicated in the application or by means of which the design secured its protection by unregistered right.[60] Consistent with this, designs

[54] ibid [27]–[28]. On the meaning of 'normal use' see also Case T–39/13 *Cezar Przedsiębiorstwo Produkcyjne Dariusz Bogdan Niewiński v Office for Harmonisation in the Internal Market (Trade Marks and Designs) (OHIM)* ECLI:EU:T:2014:852 [28] (deciding that the 'normal use' of a product might include potential uses, but not purely hypothetical uses, of it).

[55] See in this regard Joined Cases T–83/11 and T–84/11 *Antrax It Srl v Office for Harmonisation in the Internal Market (Trade Marks and Designs) (OHIM)* ECLI:EU:T:2012:592 (*Antrax*) [67] ('the protection sought relates to designs, irrespective of the actual dimensions of the products to which those designs are intended to be applied').

[56] *Ford Motor Co Ltd's Design Applications* [1995] RPC 167 (HL) 178.

[57] ibid. This brings to mind the purpose-limited nature of other forms of IP protection, including patent and trade mark protection, discussed in ch 4 s 2.2.1 and ch 6, ch 2. However, even the authorial works protected by copyright may be regarded as purpose-limited subject matter in the sense of being intended for instantiation (by reproduction in material form or communication).

[58] Designs Regulation art 36(2). [59] ibid art 11.

[60] ibid art 19(1) (referring to '*a* product' (emphasis added): see Case T–15/13 *Group Nivelles v Office for Harmonisation in the Internal Market (Trade Marks and Designs)* ECLI:EU:T:2015:281 (*Group Nivelles*) [115] ('Taking into account, inter alia, Article 36(6) ... and the reference to "a product" in the sense sentence of Article 19(1) ... the conclusion must be drawn that a registered Community

do not presumptively include among their essential properties the specific types of product to or in which they are in fact or intended to be applied or incorporated, and may therefore be said to exist at a higher level of abstraction than the authorial works protected by copyright.

In sum, the subject matter protectable by registered and unregistered Community design right is the appearance of the external (ie visible) features of the whole or part of a tangible or intangible product, including those features of a part intended for assembly in a complex product that remain visible during the product's normal use, ie it is a product supporting new (created) properties of visual significance. Thus defined, the identity of a design depends on the products in which it is able to be incorporated or to which it is able to be applied—which products might clearly change over time—regardless of the specific types of product in or to which it is in fact or was at the time of creation intended to be incorporated or applied. Further, this is reflected in the protection it receives.

2.2 ... Excluding Any Features Dictated Solely by Technical Function or Interoperability Requirements

According to Article 8 of the Designs Regulation, consistent with Article 7 of the Designs Directive:

1. A Community design shall not subsist in features of appearance of a product which are solely dictated by its technical function.
2. A Community design shall not subsist in features of appearance of a product which must necessarily be reproduced in their exact form and dimensions in order to permit the product in which the design is incorporated or to which it is applied to be mechanically connected to or placed in, around or against another product so that either product may perform its function.
3. Notwithstanding paragraph 2, a Community design shall under the conditions set out in Articles 5 and 6 subsist in a design serving the purpose of allowing the multiple assembly or connection of mutually interchangeable products within a modular system.

Of note regarding this provision is its exclusion from Community design right protection of certain *features* of appearance, rather than certain appearances *per se*. It must follow either that a design for the purpose of EU law excludes such features, or that such features, while part of a design, are incapable of supporting its protection by design right or a claim of design right infringement,[61] much as for the non-technical features of an invention in patent law.[62] On either reading, the Article

design confers on its holder the exclusive right to use on any sort of product ... the design in question and, under Article 10 ... any design which does not produce on the informed user a different overall impression')). See also Designs Regulation art 36(6) (stating that the specification of products in the application for registration of a design 'shall not affect the scope of protection of the design as such').

[61] See Designs Regulation recital 10 (stating that 'features of a design which are excluded from protection for these [technical function/interoperability] reasons should not be taken into consideration for the purpose of assessing whether other features of the design fulfil the requirements for protection'), reproduced in Designs Directive recital 14.

[62] See ch 4 s 2.

informs the legal conception of protectable subject matter. The question is what exactly it tells us about the nature and properties of that subject matter.

According to recital 10 of the Designs Regulation and recital 14 of the Designs Directive, the aim of the Article 8 and Article 7 exclusion is to prevent design right protection from impeding technological innovation and product interoperability. In pursuit of that aim, each Article restricts such protection to those features of a subject matter that can be attributed to the person claiming to have developed the design, as distinct from external constraints imposed by the nature of the product or product part. The effect is to support a conception of the design as a human creation, and more particularly, as a product of creative freedom, and as thus having historical as well as formal (artistic expressive) properties.[63]

This view of the technical function and interoperability exclusions of EU legislation as supporting a conception of the design as a product of creative freedom is consistent with the Commission's original (1991) understanding of those exclusions.[64] In that understanding, if an aspect of appearance were unable to be changed to any degree by reason of the impact of such change on the relevant product's functionality, no scope for creative freedom on the part of the designer could be said to exist, making design right protection inappropriate.[65] A later (1993) draft of the technical function exclusion made its link to the nature of designs explicit. By provision of that draft, Community design right was not to subsist in any 'design to the extent that the realization of a technical function *leaves no freedom* as regards arbitrary features of appearance'.[66] Once again, the Commission explained this exclusion as preventing the extension of design right protection to those 'extremely rare' cases where the form of a design follows the function of the relevant product or product part so as to have 'no individual character'.[67] In such cases, the Commission proposed, design right protection would be inappropriate, since the design could not be attributed to any 'personal creativity' on the part of its putative designer.[68]

The intended purpose of the technical function and interoperability exclusions to support a conception of the design as a work of personal creativity and (relatedly) of individual character continues to be reflected in its interpretation by the EUIPO Board of Appeal. This is notwithstanding that such interpretation expands the exclusion's sphere of application beyond the 'extremely rare' cases that seem to have been envisaged by the Commission in 1991. According to that interpretation,

63 See comparatively ch 5 ss 2.2 and 2.3.

64 Green Paper on the Legal Protection of Industrial Designs (n 1) [2.6.1].

65 ibid [2.6.2]. If protection were to be offered in such a case, the Commission said, it would need to be by means of patent law.

66 European Commission, Proposal for a European Parliament and Council Regulation on the Community Design, COM(93) 342 final 50, 57 (draft art 9(1), emphasis added).

67 ibid 14.

68 ibid. The memorandum continues (at 15): 'It is unlikely, however, that the whole design will be unprotectable. In most cases, only specific features will, without possibilities of variations, be dictated by function. Therefore, the provision provides for unprotectability to the extent only that there is no freedom as regards arbitrary elements of design'.

adopted in *Lindner*, and consistent with the interpretation of the corresponding exclusion of EU trade mark legislation,[69] the exclusion covers any and all features of a product or product part's appearance that are solely dictated by the function of the product or part, regardless of the existence of alternative appearances capable of achieving the same function. According to the Board, only this interpretation of the exclusion is capable of realising its dual aims of 'prevent[ing] design law from being used to achieve monopolies over technical solutions' without satisfying 'the more restrictive conditions imposed by patent law',[70] and ensuring that design right protection is confined to *designs*. With respect to the latter, the Board in *Lindner* held as follows:

> The significance of limiting protection to the visual appearance of products is that aesthetic considerations are in principle capable of being relevant only when the designer is developing a product's visual appearance. Most of the time the designer will be concerned with both elements of good design: functionality and eye appeal. In some cases functionality will be the dominant preoccupation of the designer. The need to make a product that works will be uppermost in the designer's mind and will largely determine the appearance of the product. As long as functionality is not the only relevant factor, the design is in principle eligible for protection. It is only when aesthetic considerations are completely irrelevant that the features of the design are solely dictated by the need to achieve a technical solution. This is not, it must be stressed, tantamount to introducing a requirement of aesthetic merit into the legislation. *It is simply recognition of the obvious fact that when aesthetics are totally irrelevant, in the sense that no one cares whether the product looks good, bad, ugly or pretty, and all that matters is that the product functions well, there is nothing to protect under the law of designs.*[71]

Implicit in this passage is a view of the technical function exclusion of Article 8 and Article 7 as helping to ensure the restriction of design right protection to those subject matter that can be attributed, to some extent at least, to a concern on the part of the person who develops them with their aesthetics or so-called 'eye appeal'. As made explicit by the Commission in its early proposals for design right legislation, this restriction implies a conception of the design as a product of free and creative choices by one or more natural persons, consistent with the European conception of copyright subject matter considered in Chapter 5.

The Board in *Lindner* has been criticized for interpreting the technical function exclusion as capable of extending even to features of a product's appearance for which there exist alternatives capable of supporting the same functionality.[72] According to the Board, provided a feature would be regarded by 'a reasonable

[69] See ch 6 s 2.1.5. Cf the US courts' treatment of functionality in the context of product packaging and product designs: *Two Pesos, Inc v Taco Cabana, Inc* 505 US 763 (1992) 775 ('a design [of product packaging] is legally functional, and thus unprotectible, if it is one of a limited number of equally efficient options available to competitors and free competition would be unduly hindered by according the design trademark protection'); *Inwood Laboratories, Inc v Ives Laboratories, Inc* 456 US 844 (1982) 850 fn 10, regarding product designs ('[i]n general terms, a product feature is functional if it is essential to the use or purpose of the article or if it affects the cost or quality of the article') (quoted with approval in *TrafFix Devices, Inc v Marketing Displays, Inc* 532 US 23 (2001) 32).

[70] See *Lindner* (n 1) [30]. [71] ibid [35] (emphasis added).

[72] See eg 2016 Commission Review (n 50).

observer' to have been determined by 'purely functional considerations', it will be caught by the exclusion.[73] In supporting this interpretation in *Lindner*, the Board expressly rejected the so-called 'multiplicity-of-forms' view of the exclusion as covering only those features of appearance that offer no scope for creative freedom in their development.[74] In effect, and recalling the discussion of originality in Chapter 5, the difference between these two interpretations relates to the two stages of the EU's test of originality in copyright.[75] While the more restrictive (multiplicity-of-forms) interpretation covers only those features of appearance that offer no scope for creative freedom in their development, thereby operating at the first stage of the originality test, the more expansive (*Lindner*) interpretation covers these features *as well as* a limited range of other features of appearance that, while offering scope for creative freedom, are not in fact the result of any creative choices by the putative designer, thereby operating at that test's first *and* second stages.

In its 2016 review of the EU design right regime, the Commission criticized the *Lindner* approach to the technical function exclusion, expressing its preference instead for the more restrictive multiplicity-of-forms interpretation that seems to have motivated the exclusion originally.[76] It recommended in the result that 'clear legislative guidelines be incorporated' into the Designs Directive and Designs Regulation to ensure that due consideration is given when applying the exclusion to whether the designer 'has some freedom in the development of features of appearance of the design'.[77] Instead of adopting the mantle of the so-called 'reasonable observer', the Commission also proposed that the question of creative freedom be decided with reference to the prior art, and that the presence of differences between the contested and previously available designs be accepted as establishing 'that the designer had some freedom'.[78] As above, the effect of this amendment would be to recast the technical function exclusion as reinforcing the first stage of the originality enquiry only, and as thus not applicable in any case in which more than one appearance for the given product was possible at the time of the appearance's creation without affecting the product's functionality.

The same analysis applies mutatis mutandis with respect to the interoperability exclusion. Specifically, any features of a product or product part's appearance determined exclusively by the needs of interoperability—ie required to permit the product to be mechanically connected to or placed in, around, or against another product

[73] See *Lindner* (n 1) [36]. See also Case R 1997/2012-3 *TrekStor GmbH v ZAGG, Inc* [2015] ECDR 6 (EUIPO Board of Appeal) [28] (deciding that the reasonable observer looking at the appearance of the protective cover of a tablet at issue 'would believe that the aesthetic function of the protective cover was a relevant factor and that the purpose of this specific body shape of the product is also to enhance its visual appearance').

[74] See *Lindner* (n 1) [28]–[29].

[75] The first stage excludes subject matter of a type that leave no scope for creative freedom in their production, and the second stage excludes subject matter that do not reflect their creators' exploitation of such scope to produce a subject matter that bears their creators' personal touch. See ch 5 ss 2.3.1 and 2.3.2.

[76] See 2016 Commission Review (n 50) 88 (describing *Lindner* (n 1) as having 'not helped matters') and 91 (recommending an approach focused on 'designer's freedom and multiplicity of forms').

[77] ibid 14 (Recommendation 9).

[78] ibid. For the Commission's full analysis see 85–92.

to enable either one to perform its (technical) function—will by definition not be a product of personal creativity, and will for that reason lack the originality required of a subject matter protectable by unregistered and registered Community design right.

2.3 … To the Extent that It Has Individual Character

The conception of the design as an author's (designer's) own intellectual creation is further supported by the provision in Article 4(1) of the Designs Regulation and Article 3(2) of the Designs Directive that a design shall only be protected 'to the extent' that it is new and has individual character.

Despite its different wording, the first of these requirements, that a design be protected to the extent of its novelty, is similar (albeit not identical) to the requirement that an invention be new in order to be patentable. Thus, a design will be new 'if no identical design has been made available to the public' previously.[79] By further statutory provision, and consistent with the test of identity recently adopted for inventions in UK patent law, '[d]esigns shall be deemed to be identical if their features differ only in immaterial details'.[80]

Consistent with the European conception of novelty in patent law,[81] the requirement for novelty in design law is treated as a secondary rather than a primary requirement of protection, relating to an accidental rather than an essential property of the protectable subject matter. Put differently, the question of whether a subject matter is new is treated as analytically separate from and independent of the question of whether it is inherently suited for protection as a design.[82] In effect, Article 4(1) and Article 3(2) prevent a right holder from relying on a feature of her design that is identical to a feature of a prior art design in order to establish infringement.

So too, and as again in patent (and also trade mark) law, the public policy/morality exclusion of Article 9 of the Designs Regulation and Article 8 of the Designs Directive has been treated as applying without prejudice to the nature of a given subject matter, and as thus capable of excluding from protection designs.[83] Given this, it would seem safe to conclude that the legal conception of the design has neither a moral and public policy nor a novelty aspect.

Different is the relationship between the requirements for a design and individual character. As seen above,[84] the Commission's 1993 design right proposal

[79] Designs Regulation art 5(1); Designs Directive art 4. The date for determining this is the date on which the contested design was first made available to the public (for unregistered design right) and the date of filing or priority (for registered design right). The same definition applies with respect to individual features of design.

[80] Designs Regulation art 5(2); Designs Directive art 4. On the corresponding test in patent law, presented as a test of identity and equivalence, see *Actavis UK Ltd v Eli Lilly and Co* [2017] UKSC 48 (discussed in ch 4 s 6.2).

[81] On which see ch 4 s 2.

[82] In patent law this has been made explicit. See eg T154/04 (*Estimating Sales Activity/Duns Licensing Associates*) [2007] EPOR 38 (*Duns Licensing*) [5].

[83] Green Paper on the Legal Protection of Industrial Designs (n 1) [8.9.2] (distinguishing invalidity for lack of protectable subject matter (eg in the case of applications for the protection of literary or musical works) and public policy or morality objections (eg in the case of applications for the protection of 'a swastika decorating a product with the clear intention of provoking the public') respectively. In relation to the corresponding exclusion from patent protection see ch 4 s 2.3.2.

[84] See the text accompanying n 67.

expressly connected these requirements by treating individual character as an essential property of a protectable design. The same connection is also suggested by the similarities between the concepts of individual character and originality, the latter of which: (a) underpins the technical function and interoperability exclusions of EU design law;[85] (b) is an express requirement of unregistered UK design right subsistence;[86] (c) was previously a requirement of registered design right protection in several EU Member States;[87] and (d) is—notwithstanding the initial appearance to the contrary—an essential property of the subject matter protectable by copyright.[88] It is also suggested by the courts' understanding of the requirement for individual character.[89]

Individual character is defined in Article 6 of the Designs Regulation and Article 5 of the Designs Directive. According to that definition, a design

> shall be considered to have individual character if the overall impression it produces on the informed user differs from the overall impression produced on such a user by any design which has been made available to the public

before the date of publication (for unregistered Community design right) or filing/priority (for registered Community design right), and taking account of 'the degree of freedom of the designer in developing the design'. This definition connects directly to the scope of design right protection, which extends to 'any design which does not produce on the informed user a different overall impression', assessed once again with reference to 'the degree of freedom of the designer in developing his design'.[90]

The restriction of Community design right protection to those aspects of a product or product part's appearance that—when compared to one or more specific, individualized, defined, and identified designs from among those previously made available to the public[91]—produce a different overall impression on the informed user,[92] and the extension of such protection to all designs that produce the same

[85] See s 2.2 in this chapter. [86] See CDPA s 213(1).

[87] See eg Registered Designs Act 1949 s 1(2) as originally enacted (restricting registered UK design right protection to designs that were 'new or original'); U Koschtial, 'Design Law: Individual Character, Visibility and Functionality' [2005] International Review of Intellectual Property and Competition Law 297 (discussing the pre-EU requirements for registered design right protection in continental European countries).

[88] See ch 5.

[89] On the courts' approach to determining individual character see Case T–526/13 *H&M Hennes & Mauritz BV & Co KG v Office for Harmonisation in the Internal Market (Trade Marks and Designs) (OHIM)* ECLI:EU:T:2015:614 [32] (supporting a four-stage approach to individual character: identifying the industrial sector to which the products in which the design is intended to be incorporated or to which it is intended to be applied belong; identifying the notional informed user of those products in accordance with their purpose, and her level of awareness of the prior art; deciding the degree of freedom afforded by the products to the designer in developing her design; and comparing the designs at issue, taking account of the industrial sector, the designer's degree of freedom, and the overall impressions produced on the informed user by the contested design and any earlier designs that form part of the prior art).

[90] Designs Regulation art 10; Designs Directive art 9.

[91] Case C–345/13 *Karen Millen Fashions Ltd v Dunnes Stores and Dunnes Stores (Limerick) Ltd* ECLI:EU:C:2014:2013 [25].

[92] See Designs Regulation art 6; Designs Directive art 5.

overall impression on that user, make it clear that the identity of designs depends on the overall (visual[93]) impression that they produce in the mind of others. When combined with the requirement that the individual character of a design (and scope of its protection) be assessed with reference to the degree of freedom accorded to the designer in developing it, such restriction also underlines that what merits a subject matter the protection of Community design right is very similar to what merits a subject matter the protection of copyright, namely, the fact of it being a type of subject matter that leaves scope for formative freedom in its creation, which scope its putative creator (the designer) has exploited in the particular case to produce an appearance of the whole or part of a product that—instead of bearing the creator's personal touch (as required for copyright[94])—produces an overall visual impression on the notional informed user of the product that differs from the overall visual impression produced on that user by previously available designs. The result is a test of individual character that combines the originality requirement of copyright with the inventive step requirement of patent law in its demand for a design that, when judged from the perspective of its intended audience, can be said to differ sufficiently in its expressive (visual) aspects from prior art designs[95] in ways attributable to its individual creator's or creators' exercise of creative freedom. Unlike copyright and patent legislation, although not dissimilar to the position adopted by the courts in the copyright and patent fields,[96] design legislation requires that the scope of protection conferred with respect to a design be modulated with reference to the

[93] See Case T–9/07 *Grupo Promer Mon Graphic, SA v Office for Harmonisation in the Internal Market (Trade Marks and Designs) (OHIM)* [2010] ECR II–00981 (*Grupo Promer Mon Graphic*) [50] (remarking that given the nature of designs, the different overall impression that must be produced is necessarily a visual one).

[94] See ch 5 s 2.3.2.

[95] On the nature of the prior art see Designs Regulation art 7; Designs Directive art 6. In contrast to the definition contained in European patent legislation (on which see ch 4 s 5(b)), EU design legislation defines the prior art to include only those designs the (non-prejudicial) disclosure of which could 'reasonably have become known in the normal course of business to the circles specialized in the sector concerned, operating within the Community' (on which see further Case C–479/12 *H Gautzsch Großhandel GmbH & Co KG v Münchener Boulevard Möbel Joseph Duna GmbH* ECLI:EU:C:2014:75) (*H Gautzsch Großhandel*)), excluding any designs made available to the public within twelve months preceding the relevant filing/priority date by or as a result of information provided or action taken by the designer or his successor in title. Hence the need, when identifying the prior art of a given design, to consider the likelihood of all previously disclosed designs having become known in the industrial sector to which the contested design relates. So too, and as the recitals of the Designs Regulation and Designs Directive each confirm, when deciding whether the overall impression produced by a contested design differs from that produced by a prior art design, the courts must consider 'the nature of the product to which the design is applied or in which it is incorporated, and in particular the industrial sector to which it belongs' (Designs Regulation recital 14; Designs Directive recital 13). In its 2016 review of the EU design right regime, the Commission recommended that these recitals be given the force of operative provisions: 2016 Commission Review (n 50) 13 (Recommendation 5).

[96] In both patent law and copyright, determinations of infringement are made having close regard to that which merits a subject matter its protection, be it a technical contribution to the prior art (for patents) or expressive (eg literary or artistic) originality (for copyright). See eg *Schütz (UK) Ltd v Werit UK Ltd* [2013] UKSC 16 (discussed in ch 4 s 4); *Designers Guild Ltd v Russell Williams (Textiles) Ltd* [2000] 1 WLR 2416 (HL) (discussed in ch 5 s 5(b)).

scope of creative freedom permitted to the designer when developing it.[97] Given this especially, and noting also the intuitive difficulty of accepting that a person who develops the appearance of a product of a type that offers no options—ie no freedom—in that regard is a 'designer', a case can be made for treating *either* the individual character of a design as a whole *or* the fact of a design being the product of a person's exercise of creative freedom, as among its essential properties for the purpose of Community design right.

As discussed in Chapter 6 for goodwill,[98] the dependence of a design's individual character as a whole on external factors—namely, the overall impression that it produces on a notional informed user in comparison with that produced on the same user by previously made available designs—would make it, in part at least, an extrinsic rather than an intrinsic property, or in other words, a relation between the appearance comprising the design and both a person (the user) and the prior art. By contrast, an appearance's dependence for its existence on the exercise of creative freedom by its putative designer can more readily be seen as an intrinsic property akin to that of originality in copyright. Given this, and the possibility of a person independently designing the appearance of a product that produces a strong overall impression on the informed user which impression is nonetheless not different from that produced by previous designs, the 'purist' view would seem to be that those aspects of individual character akin to originality in copyright are essential properties of the subject matter protectable by Community design right, in contrast to those aspects of individual character akin to inventive step in patent law, which, and as for inventive step in its European and UK conceptions,[99] are more appropriately conceived as among its accidental properties. As for novelty above, this is notwithstanding the express restriction of a design's protection by Article 4(1) of the Designs Regulation and Article 3(2) of the Designs Directive '*to the extent that* it ... has individual character [emphasis added]', which serves not to alter the nature of a design itself, but rather to limit the scope of protection conferred in respect of it.

When deciding whether the appearance of a product (or product part) is of a type that leaves scope for formative freedom for the purpose of EU design legislation,

[97] See Designs Regulation art 10(2); Designs Directive art 9(2). In relation to copyright cf Case C–145/10 *Painer v Standard Verlags GmbH* [2011] ECR I–12533 (*Painer*) (deciding that once found to subsist, copyright in a photographic portrait confers the same protection as conferred by copyright in other types of authorial works, notwithstanding the more limited scope for creative freedom that such portraits afford on account of their comparative realism and simplicity: see ch 5 s 2.3.2). In relation to patent law see T409/91 *Fuel Oils/Exxon* [1994] EPOR 149 [3.3] (expressing the general principle that 'the extent of the patent monopoly, as defined by the claims [under EPC Article 69 and Patents Act 1977, section 125], should correspond to the technical contribution to the art in order for it to be supported or justified'), discussed in ch 4 s 3.

[98] See ch 6 s 5.2.

[99] European jurisprudence treats the requirements for inventive step and patent protectable subject matter as independent of each other: see *Duns Licensing* (n 82) [5], discussed in ch 4 s 2. By contrast, UK jurisprudence treats them as related. Specifically, while inventive step is not regarded as an essential property of the invention, a subject matter must, in order to be an invention, make a technical contribution to the art, whether or not that contribution is sufficient to make the invention inventive: see ch 4 s 3.

the courts ask whether any constraints were imposed at the time of its creation by either the technical function of or statutory requirements applicable to the product or part,[100] reaffirming again the connection between individual character and the technical function exclusion above. Where such constraints *were* imposed, the affected features of the product or part are treated as having been standardized,[101] and the designer's scope for creative freedom as having been restricted accordingly so as to make it more difficult to produce a design applicable to (or capable of incorporation in) the relevant product or part that has individual character. In recognition of this increased difficulty, the law acknowledges the capacity of comparatively small differences in the overall impression produced by an appearance on the notional informed user as sufficient to give it individual character—exactly as the law in copyright acknowledges the capacity of comparatively minimal creativity in the production of a subject matter of a type that leaves only limited scope for creative freedom (such as photographic portraits) as sufficient to give it originality.[102] An example of an equivalent product in design law is the tazo considered by the General Court in *Grupo Promer Mon Graphic*. Since the tazo—a paradigmatically small, flat or slightly curved disc made of plastic or metal and used as game pieces for children or promotional items—offers little scope for formative freedom in design, the court accepted that even minor differences between the objective features of different tazo appearances could be sufficient to produce the different overall impression on the informed user required for individual character. By contrast was its view of the scope for formative freedom afforded by the internal combustion engine considered in *Kwang Yang Motors*. According to the court in that case, while certain components of the engine, such as its fuel tank and vent, were essential to its functionality, thus constraining the freedom of designers to conceive an appearance for it, the shape, configuration, and placement of the engine in the lawnmower in which it was intended to be incorporated were not themselves dictated by any functional (or statutory) constraints, leaving such matters for the designer to decide.[103] The result was to recognize the essentially unlimited creative freedom afforded by the engine, and the comparative difficulty therefore of showing that minor differences between objective features of different engine appearances would produce the different overall impression on the informed user required for individual character.

In *Grupo Promer Mon Graphic*, the existence of a certain paradigm for the product was held to constrain the freedom of designers so as to make it more difficult for them in fact to produce an appearance having individual character. The reason for this finding seems to have been the Court's acceptance of the paradigm as a

[100] See *Grupo Promer Mon Graphic* (n 93)[67]. [101] ibid. [102] See ch 5 s 2.3.1.

[103] This view was held to be supported by the variety of shapes and configurations that the corpus of internal combustion engines used in those lawnmowers contained in the prior art revealed. See similarly Case T–357/12 *Sachi Premium-Outdoor Furniture, Lda v Office for Harmonisation in the Internal Market (Trade Marks and Designs) (OHIM)* ECLI:EU:T:2014:55 [21] (agreeing with the EUIPO Board of Appeal's view 'that the freedom of the designer of armchairs is almost unlimited since armchairs can take any combination of colours, patterns, shapes and materials, and that the only limitation for the designer is the fact that armchairs have to be functional, that is, they must include at least a seat, a backrest and two armrests').

manifestation of the tazo's exclusive use and value as a game piece for children and as a promotional item.[104] Consistent with this, the court referred approvingly to the finding of the EUIPO Board of Appeal in the proceedings below that a tazo not conforming to this paradigm was 'unlikely to be accepted in the marketplace'.[105] Nonetheless, the courts have stressed that the degree of design freedom afforded by a given product or product part is to be determined without regard to aesthetic or commercial factors.[106] An example is *Shenzhen*, where it was held that mere trends in the design of a given product or product part cannot be regarded as limiting such freedom in respect of that product or part.[107] This principle was explained in *Antrax* with reference to the point of design freedom (and of design right generally) as being precisely to support innovation in product appearance, including new design trends.[108] In the same case the court emphasized that while a saturation of the state of the art by designs having certain features might be relevant when assessing an appearance's individual character, considerations of an appearance's aesthetic quality or commercial success will be irrelevant.[109]

In sum, the subject matter protectable by Community design right may be defined as an appearance of the whole or part of a product that is original in the sense of having been determined by its putative designer's exploitation of such scope for creative freedom as the relevant type of product affords. Thus conceived, designs are very similar to the artistic works protectable by European copyright, namely, products supporting new properties of visual significance that reflect the free and creative choices of one or more natural persons, being their creator-designer.[110] Their creation for addition to or incorporation in products might be said also to give them the performative aspect of a musical or dramatic work, consistent with the discussion of production drawings in Chapter 5 section 3.3.2.2.2.

2.4 Conclusion

While the category of subject matter protectable by unregistered and registered Community design right is denoted by the term 'design', the EU legislative definition of that term is incomplete, and the statutory framework governing the availability of Community design right in general confusing. As defined statutorily, a design is the appearance of those external (ie visible) aspects of the whole or part of a handicraft or industrial item—defined broadly to include not only those concrete objects made by hand or applicable in industry, but also intangible expressive objects such as figures, words, and other symbols—including those aspects of a product part intended for assembly in a complex product that remain visible

104 See *Grupo Promer Mon Graphic* (n 93) [67]–[70]. 105 ibid [68].

106 Cf *Star Athletica* (n 40) 16 (majority, declining to consider (a) whether the design of the cheerleading uniforms reflected 'the designer's artistic judgment exercised independently of functional influence' or (b) whether the artistic features incorporated into the uniforms' design were likely still to be marketable without the uniforms' utilitarian function).

107 Case T–153/08 *Shenzhen Taiden Industrial Co Ltd v Office for Harmonisation in the Internal Market (Trade Marks and Designs) (OHIM)* [2010] ECR II–02517 (*Shenzhen*) [58].

108 See *Antrax* (n 55) [95]. 109 ibid [96].

110 Designs Regulation art 14; Registered Designs Act s 2.

during the product's normal use. However, not all subject matter within the category of designs thus defined will possess the essential properties required to make it protectable by design right. The reason is the additional requirement—supported by the technical function and interoperability exclusions from Community design right protection, and the restriction of such protection to the extent of a subject matter's individual character—that a design be original in order to be protectable, in the sense of including aspects of appearance that result from the free and creative choices of one or more persons, which features alone comprise the subject matter protectable by Community design right. It follows that a design within the meaning of EU law is appropriately conceived as those new (created) properties of visual significance capable of addition to or incorporation in a product or product part that express the intellectual creation of a putative creator (designer).

3. The Unregistered Design in the United Kingdom: An Original Appearance of the Whole or Part of an Article

3.1 Introduction

As seen in section 1, UK legislation also provides for the subsistence of unregistered design right in designs.[111] Rather than the appearance of the whole or part of an industrial or handicraft item, however, a 'design' for the purpose of unregistered UK design right is defined exhaustively to mean 'the design of the shape or configuration (whether internal or external) of the whole or part of an article'.[112] Thus defined, the category of subject matter in which unregistered UK design right subsists is both more and less expansive than the category of subject matter in which unregistered Community design right subsists. It is more expansive in its inclusion of 'the design of the shape or configuration' of the whole or part of an 'article', rather than 'the appearance' of the whole or part of an 'industrial or handicraft item' (ie a 'product'), as well as the appearance of the internal aspects of a product or product part; and it is less expansive in its exclusion of the appearance of a part intended for incorporation in a complex product.[113] Looking beyond the definition of design to the other criteria for design right subsistence and exclusions from design right protection, it is also different in its requirement for originality[114] (in place of individual

[111] See CDPA s 213(1).

[112] ibid s 213(2). See also *Christopher Tasker's Design Right References* [2001] RPC 2 (Patent Office) (*Tasker's Design Right References*) [65]–[66] (construing a claim to the 'whole external shape and configuration' of a wardrobe door system as being to the component parts of the entire system, whether or not this included more than one could see when looking at the wardrobe); *Lambretta Clothing* (n 47) [14] (confirming that designs may relate to the shape or configuration 'whether internal or external' of the whole or part of an article).

[113] See *Farmers Build Ltd* (n 18) 480 (describing the aim of the 1988 rules governing unregistered UK design right as having been to reduce the previously available protection for the appearance of industrially produced articles, and to remove such protection altogether in the case of such articles' spare parts).

[114] Defined inclusively in CDPA s 213(4) to mean designs that are not 'commonplace in the design field in question at the time of its creation'.

character and novelty), and its exclusion of any features of shape or configuration dictated by interoperability or so-called 'must-match' requirements, or comprising surface decoration or a method or principle of construction[115] (in place of aspects of appearance dictated solely by technical function or interoperability requirements).

In addition to the requirements above, a subject matter must have been 'recorded in a design document or an article ... made to the design' in order to be protected by unregistered UK design right.[116] This provision is in place of the corresponding provision of European law that for unregistered Community design right to subsist, the design must have been made available to the public within EU territory,[117] where by 'made available to the public' is meant 'published, exhibited, used in trade or otherwise disclosed in such a way that, in the normal course of business, these events could reasonably have become known to the circles specialised in the sector concerned, operating within the [EU]'.[118] It is unclear what if any significance the difference in these subsistence requirements has, and whether the requirements of publication and fixation afford a designer the same freedom to define or exemplify her subject matter as the requirement for representation in a registered design right application affords her.

Either way, the fixation requirement of unregistered UK design right can be said to serve the same evidentiary function as the corresponding provision in copyright, while also underlining the intangible nature of the protected subject matter. This is consistent with the view of Peter Hayward for the Patent Office in *Tasker's Design Right References* that 'the implication of the word "until" is that the design could be created some time before being recorded in a design document or making an article to the design',[119] and with the statement by Lord Mustill quoted above.[120] By contrast is Mann J's description of a design within the meaning of section 213 of the CDPA in *Rolawn Ltd v Turfmech Machinery Ltd* as 'a physical manifestation of an idea, not some underlying abstraction' that does not exist until 'actually reduced ... to a particular form'.[121] To the extent that this description conflates the abstract and intangible qualities of designs, it ought to be rejected. To the extent that it recognizes that designs, like some authorial works of visual art, require a certain materiality in order to come into existence, without entailing the consequence that such existence is then dependent on the fact and form of their material fixation,[122] it is consistent with the conception of artistic works in copyright discussed in Chapter 5 sections 3.2.3 and 5(a). On this basis, too, Mann J's statement that a subject matter 'is not a design while it is a conception in the designer's head, and ... becomes a design when it takes physical shape on paper or in the flesh'[123] is

[115] ibid s 213(3)–(6).

[116] CDPA s 213(6). A 'design document' is 'any record of a design, whether in the form of a drawing, a written description, a photograph, data stored in a computer or otherwise': CDPA s 51(3).

[117] Regulation art 11(1).

[118] ibid art 11(2).

[119] See *Lambretta Clothing* (n 47) [52].

[120] See text accompanying n 57.

[121] *Rolawn Ltd v Turfmech Machinery Ltd* [2008] EWHC 989 (Pat), [2008] RPC 27 (*Rolawn*) [79].

[122] The view of a design's existence as depending on the fact and form of its material fixation can be seen in the treatment by the majority of the US Supreme Court in *Star Athletica* (n 40) of the articles capable of incorporating a design as (and only as) physical products: see the discussion in ch 5 s 3.3.1.2.

[123] *Rolawn* (n 121) [79].

consistent with the position in copyright that until an idea is given a certain expressive form, it has no existence as an authorial work as such.[124]

3.2 A Design Is the Shape or Configuration (whether Internal or External) of the Whole or Part of an Article

An initial question that arises when considering the subject matter protectable by unregistered UK design right is the difference between an 'article' within the meaning of section 213(2) of the CDPA and a 'product' within the meaning of Article 3 of the Designs Regulation and Article 1 of the Designs Directive. According to Laddie J in *Ocular Sciences Ltd v Aspect Vision Care Ltd*, the term 'article' is not appropriately defined so as only to include inanimate objects that are not and have never 'been alive',[125] but rather includes living and natural products such as animals and even—as in *OSL* itself—human body parts. While this view has been criticized,[126] it is consistent with the ordinary meaning of the term 'article', and with the expansive definition of 'product' in European design law to include industrial items such as living phenomena and expressive objects such as symbols and typefaces. Given this, the better view is that Laddie J's decision is correct, and that an article within the meaning of section 213(2) of the CDPA is the same as a product within the meaning of EU design legislation as interpreted above rather than by the EUIPO.

Of course, unregistered UK design right does not subsist in articles as such, but rather in 'the design' of their 'shape or configuration'. This raises the second difficulty of the section 213(2) definition of 'design', which concerns the nature of a 'design of the shape or configuration' of a product.

The CDPA definition of 'design' is regrettably circular in its inclusion of the very word it purports to define. In addition, the words at its heart—'shape or configuration'—were taken from pre-EU design legislation,[127] notwithstanding judicial uncertainty regarding their meaning. At the base of that uncertainty has been the issue of what if anything the word 'configuration' adds to 'shape', and more particularly, whether a design comprises more than the appearance of the physical components of a product. According to Pumfrey J in *Mackie Designs Inc v Behringer Specialised Studio Equipment (UK) Ltd*,[128] interpreting the definition of design contained in the CDPA, the 'configuration' of an article is different from

[124] See ch 5 s 3.2.1.

[125] *Ocular Sciences Ltd v Aspect Vision Care Ltd* [1997] RPC 395 (Pat) (*OSL*) 425 (considering the must-fit exclusion of CDPA s 213(3)(b)(i) in a case involving the design of contact lenses).

[126] See eg 2016 Commission Review (n 50) 112–13.

[127] See eg Registered Designs Act s 1(3), as originally enacted (defining 'design' exhaustively to mean 'features of shape, configuration, pattern or ornament applied to an article by any industrial process or means, being features which in the finished article appeal to and are judged solely by the eye, but does not include a method or principle of construction or features of shape or configuration which are dictated solely by the function which the article to be made in that shape or configuration has to perform').

[128] *Mackie Designs Inc v Behringer Specialised Studio Equipment (UK) Ltd* [1999] RPC 717 (Ch) (*Mackie Designs*).

its 'shape' or 'geometry',[129] comprising instead the nature and arrangement of its components.[130] It was on the basis of this understanding that the court held a circuit diagram, depicting in graphic form the nature of and relationship between the electronic components of an electric circuit, to be a design document within the meaning of section 51(1) of the CDPA, as a record of a design of a circuit board capable of protection by unregistered UK design right. Thus conceived, the circuit diagram was held to exist independent of the appearance of the circuit board, ie the 'particular layout on the board',[131] just as the London Underground Map, as a record of the design of the London underground train system, exists independent of the real-world positioning of the stations included within it.[132]

The conception of 'design' supported in *Mackie Designs*, which continues to represent settled law at first instance,[133] has been widely criticized by commentators for confusing 'mere schematic' depictions of products with the 'real-world' products that they depict.[134] In effect, the criticism is that such depictions lack the expressive specificity or stability of designs properly conceived: a circuit board representing instructions for manufacturing a product (a circuit) capable of having different physical appearances and thus different visual (expressive) properties. Given this, it might be said, to treat the board as a design is to support a conception of design right subject matter as closer in nature to the inventions protected by patents than the authorial works protected by copyright; a view consistent with the statement of Pumfrey J in *Mackie Designs* that selecting and arranging those aspects of a functional product that give the product 'its particular merit' as such are part of the work of a designer.[135]

The decision in *Mackie Designs* is consistent with non-legal views of the process of product design as involving the determination of a product's 'elements and their relationships'.[136] Further, it reflects the EU legal conception of designs as existing separate from the types of product to or in which they are intended to be applied or incorporated.[137] However, and as noted above, it also threatens the view of designs as expressive rather than technical objects. Hence the importance of conceiving the configuration of a product or product part as an object of expressive (visual) significance suitable for application to or incorporation in a product or product part. If it is instead conceived as a method of constructing a product or product part, its protection will not only be inappropriate in the light of the aims of the design right

[129] ibid 721. [130] ibid 723. [131] ibid.

[132] The analogy to the London Underground map is from *Lambretta Clothing* (n 47) [27] (citing Laddie and others, *The Modern Law of Copyright and Designs* (3rd edn, Butterworths 2000) paras 53.6–10).

[133] *Magmatic Ltd v PMS International Ltd* [2013] EWHC 1925 (Pat) (*Magmatic v PMS* Patents Court) [81].

[134] See *Lambretta Clothing* (n 47) [27] (referring to the criticisms expressed in Laddie, Prescott, and Vitoria (n 126)).

[135] *Mackie Designs* (n 128) 723.

[136] See eg J S Gero, 'Design Prototypes: A Knowledge Representation Schema for Design' (1990) 11 AI Magazine 26, 28 (defining the process of product design as involving the creation of a representation of a product's 'elements and their relationships').

[137] See s 2.1.

and patent regimes, it will also be prohibited by section 213(3)(a) of the CDPA, as discussed below.

Provided it can be (and is) properly conceived *qua* expressive object, the protection of a product's or product part's configuration under section 213 ought not to entail unregistered design right subsistence in mere 'abstraction[s] of ideas' or 'underlying design concept[s]', although without prejudice to the scope of protection conferred in respect of a design by such right.[138] Having said that, by treating designs as including selections and arrangements of product components, *Mackie Designs* clearly permits the protection *qua* design of subject matter capable of instantiation in products of non-identical appearance. This explains the case's cold reception among commentators and even judges. Recently, for example, Judge Hacon has proposed[139] that the principle of *Mackie Designs* be rejected as inconsistent with the definition of 'design' contained in section 213(2) of the CDPA, amended since *Mackie Designs* was decided. That amendment restricted the definition from '*any aspect of* the shape or configuration (whether internal or external) of the whole or part of an article' (emphasis added) to 'the shape or configuration (whether internal or external) of the whole or part of an article'.[140] According to Judge Hacon, while deleting the words 'any aspect of' was plainly not intended to bring section 213 into line with EU law, it might nonetheless 'for policy reasons of consistency' be treated as having had 'as close as possible' to that effect.[141] He continued:

> One route to such a result would be to interpret the effect of [the amended definition of 'design'] as being that it no longer permits a claim to unregistered design right to extend to designs other than those specifically embodied in all or part of the claimant's article, i.e. no more UK unregistered design rights in abstract designs.[142]

This view, repeated by the judge in *Action Storage Systems Ltd v G-Force Europe.Com Ltd*,[143] has merit in so far as *Mackie Designs* supports protection of an abstract idea for a product or product part constituted by its possession of certain interconnected components. However, if *Mackie Designs* is read more restrictively to support a claimant's ability to protect the expressive (visual) properties of such a product or product part (in its entirety), it need not be rejected.

Finally, it is important to note that even the expansive view of 'shape or configuration' supported in *Mackie Designs* is insufficient to include decoration or

[138] Cf in this regard *Rolawn* (n 121) [80] and [83] (Mann J, rejecting a claim that the protection conferred by unregistered design right extended to the 'generalised abstraction' underlying the protected designs, analogous to the extension of literary copyright in a play to its underlying plot, on the ground that a person 'is not entitled to claim design right in the abstraction of ideas' or in an 'underlying design concept', and that the generalized abstraction for which protection was sought 'would be appropriate for patents, if appropriate for protection at all').

[139] In *DKH Retail Ltd v H Young (Operations) Ltd* [2014] EWHC 4034 (IPEC) (*DKH Retail*).

[140] Intellectual Property Act 2014 (UK) s 1(1).

[141] *DKH Retail* (n 139) [16]. See also *Action Storage Systems Ltd v G-Force Europe.Com Ltd* [2016] EWHC 3151 (IPEC) [15].

[142] *DKH Retail* (n 139) [16].

[143] ibid.

ornamentation, such as colours and patterns. It follows, as the Court of Appeal affirmed in *Lambretta*, that such features of a product or product part are not included in the subject matter protectable by unregistered UK design right, independent of the express exclusion of such features by section 213(3)(c) of the CDPA.[144]

In sum, a design within the meaning of section 213(2) of the CDPA is the outline (shape) or structure (configuration) of any product or product part of two or three dimensions.[145] Thus defined, and notwithstanding *Mackie Designs*, it shares the formal (expressive) properties of an artistic work within the meaning of copyright, in comprising certain (physical) properties of visual significance that are capable of addition to or incorporation in a product or product part, albeit existing at a higher level of abstraction than the level of abstraction at which authorial works in copyright are conceived to exist.[146]

3.3 ... Excluding any Method or Principle of Construction, Must-fit or Must-match Features of Shape or Configuration, and Surface Decoration

As with EU law, UK law excludes from unregistered design right protection certain subject matter. Under the CPDA, those subject matter are defined to be: (a) any method or principle of construction;[147] (b) any aspects of shape or configuration that (i) enable the article to be manufactured so as to be connected to, or placed in, around, or against, another article—including the human body[148]—so that either article may perform its function,[149] or (ii) depend on the appearance of another article of which the article is intended by the designer to form an integral part, in the sense of needing to be as they are in order to maintain the appearance or identity of the former article;[150] and (c) surface decoration,[151] whether in two or three dimensions,[152] without also serving a significant

[144] See *Lambretta Clothing* (n 47) [22] and [25]–[29].

[145] On the distinction between two-dimensional and three-dimensional products see ibid [24].

[146] This view of designs is consistent with the UK courts' prior conception of *aspects* of design as only such features of a design as are visually significant, discernible, or recognizable: see eg *Dyson Ltd v Qualtex (UK) Ltd* [2006] EWCA Civ 166, [2006] RPC 31 (*Dyson*) [22]–[23], citing also *Volumatic v Myriad* (ChD, 10 April 1995). Since the restriction of the statutory definition of 'design' in the CDPA, not every visually significant feature of the design of a product or product part will be protectable *qua* design. However, the basic conception of designs as comprised of such features remains.

[147] CDPA s 213(3)(a).

[148] See *OSL* (n 125) 425 (interpreting CDPA s 213(3)(b)(i) as excluding 'all interface features', including living or formerly living things, such as eyes and other body parts).

[149] CDPA s 213(3)(b). The fact that a differently designed feature might have enabled the same function is irrelevant: *Ultraframe (UK) Ltd v Eurocell Building Plastics Ltd* [2004] EWHC 1785 (Pat), [2005] RPC 7 (*Ultraframe v Eurocell*) [114]; see also *Dyson* (n 146) [28].

[150] CDPA s 213(3)(b)(ii). Thus, the internal (invisible) features of an article are not excluded: *Ultraframe (UK) Ltd v Fielding* [2002] EWHC 1964 (Ch), [2003] RPC 23 (*Ultraframe v Fielding*) [70].

[151] See CDPA s 213(3)(c).

[152] See eg *Mark Wilkinson Furniture* (n 47) 72–73 (deciding that beading and engraving in the form of grooves on kitchen units were surface decoration); also *Lambretta Clothing* (n 47) [30] (confirming that the surface decoration exclusion covers colours, however deep beneath the surface of the article they run).

function.[153] When interpreting these exclusions, the courts have emphasized their basis in considerations of public policy. For the method or principle of construction exclusion, the relevant policy consideration has been the concern to prevent the extension of design right protection beyond 'one particular individual and specific appearance' to 'several different appearances, which all embody the general features' of the subject matter claimed,[154] so as to 'create an effective monopoly over articles made in a particular way'.[155] For the must-fit exclusion, it has been the concern to ensure a competitive market in consumable or spare parts.[156] For the must-match exclusion, it has been the concern to exclude from protection those aspects of shape and configuration that can be said to have been determined by something other than the designer, owing to the absence of any design freedom in respect of the article to which they relate.[157] And for the surface decoration exclusion, it has been the concern to prevent the protection by design right of three-dimensional embellishments of an article on the basis that such embellishments are more appropriately protected, if at all, by copyright.[158]

As seen in section 3.2, the last of the section 213(3) exclusions, covering surface decoration, is also a function of the statutory definition of 'design' itself, as the design of the shape or configuration of a product or product part, and is thus strictly speaking unnecessary. Also clear from the discussion in section 3.2 is that the first of the exclusions, covering methods or principles of construction, is similarly a restatement of the statutory requirement for the design of a shape or configuration of a product or product part. At the very least it can be seen as informing the legal conception of protectable subject matter. The reason is that, by denying protection to the design of any shape or configuration that supports 'several different appearances', the exclusion confines unregistered UK design right protection to those expressive properties of visual significance that represent an 'individual and

[153] See *Lambretta Clothing* (n 47) [31]; also *Dyson* (n 146) [83] ('Trivial additional function may not matter—for instance the function of covering cracks as in the case of the beading considered in *Mark Wilkinson* [*Furniture* (n 47)] (if indeed you regard that as function at all, which, like the judge, I doubt—covering visible cracks for appearance reasons is hardly functional').)

[154] *Landor & Hawa International Ltd v Azure Designs Ltd* [2006] EWCA Civ 1285, [2007] FSR 9 (*Landor & Hawa*) [13] (quoting with approval from M Howe, *Russell-Clarke and Howe on Industrial Designs* (7th edn, Sweet & Maxwell 2005) para 3–80)); see also *Tasker's Design Right References* (n 112) [30].

[155] See *Landor & Hawa* (ibid) [14]; also *Tasker's Design Right References* (n 112) [32] (rejecting a claim to the protection as a design of 'the configuration of MDF [medium-density fibreboard] moldings bonded onto the aluminium extrusion with the objective of concealing the aluminium' on the ground that it covered 'the general concept of using MDF moldings of unspecified shape or configuration to conceal an aluminium extrusion likewise of unspecified shape or configuration' and was thus a method or principle of construction within the meaning of s 213(3)(a)).

[156] See eg *Ultraframe v Fielding* (n 150) 458.

[157] See eg *Dyson* (n 146) [63]–[64] ('The more there is design freedom the less is there room for the exclusion': [64]).

[158] See *Lambretta Clothing* (n 47) [31]; *Dyson* (n 146) [81]. See in this regard Registered Designs Act 1949 s 1(4), as originally enacted (permitting the Board of Trade to make rules to provide for the exclusion from registration of designs for articles that 'are primarily literary or artistic in character').

specific appearance'. The challenge is then to reconcile this restriction with the statutory definition of protectable subject matter as including the configuration of a product or product part. Clearly *Mackie Designs* presents difficulties here, owing to its express support for the protection of subject matter capable of application or incorporation to or in products of different appearance. At the end of the day, the answer must lie in understandings of the concept of different appearance, and of the point at which the expressive properties comprising a given subject matter *qua* design are no longer the properties applied to or incorporated in a given product or product part.

This analysis, as above, is consistent with longstanding legal conceptions of design as concerned with what products look like, and relatedly, with the overall visual impressions that they create on the people who use the products in or to which they are incorporated or applied.[159] In addition, it ensures that the expansive definition of 'design' in section 213(2), combined with the nature of design documents and models as representations rather than examples of design right subject matter, do not result in the protection of generally defined properties of visual significance, as outlined above.[160]

That leaves the second and third of the exclusions, which, like the corresponding technical function and interoperability exclusions of EU design law, support a legal conception of the design as an original subject matter.

3.4 ... That Is Original, Including Not Commonplace

In 1988, when the unregistered UK design right regime was introduced, the protection conferred by registered UK design right was confined to subject matter that had eye appeal. The new regime differed in not requiring any corresponding aesthetic element: originality sufficed. In the first appellate case to consider this concept, involving a machine for separating manure into solid and liquid parts, the Court of Appeal held 'original' to mean the same as in the copyright chapters of the CDPA, subject only to the statutory exclusion, on originality grounds, of subject matter that was 'commonplace in the design field in question at the time of its creation'.[161] According to the courts, it follows that for a design to be protected by unregistered UK design right, it must pass two tests. First, it must be the product of independent skill and labour expended by its putative creator, rather than having been copied from a previous design,[162] consistent with the common law

[159] See eg *Procter & Gamble Co V Reckitt Benckiser (UK) Ltd* [2008] FSR 8 (CA) [3] and [27] (discussing registered design right), quoted with approval by the Supreme Court in *PMS v Magmatic* (n 51) [10].

[160] See in this regard *Magmatic v PMS* Patents Court (n 133) [94] (Arnold J, rejecting unregistered design right protection for certain designs comprising aspects of a product's configuration as methods or principles of construction, and remarking '[i]t is more like a patent claim than an identification of particular aspects of configuration of the [product]').

[161] CDPA s 213(4) ('A design is not "original" for the purposes of this Part if it is commonplace in the design field in question at the time of its creation').

[162] See *Farmers Build Ltd* (n 18) 475 and 481. In so doing he implicitly invoked the classic statement of the meaning of originality in copyright from *University of London Press v University Tutorial*

conception of copyright originality discussed in Chapter 5.[163] And second, it must, in some not necessarily significant respects, differ from those designs previously available in the relevant field so as not to be regarded as 'trite' or 'trivial'[164]—ie *de minimis*[165]—by a notional designer working in that field having regard to those designs with which he would be familiar.[166]

It is clear from design law's incorporation of the copyright conception of originality that designs are creations of one or more natural persons. This is consistent with the statement in *Fulton v Grant Barnett*, citing the CDPA's definition of design in section 213(2) and reference to a design's creator in section 214(1), that 'if a shape or configuration is to qualify for design right, it must have been consciously designed by somebody', and thus be said to have 'resulted from a design process'.[167] In the same case, the court also emphasized the designer's consciousness or state of mind in its discussion of whether a design is commonplace. In its judgment, even a design that 'differs from earlier designs in the same field only by small shifts in (for example) lines, angles and arcs' might not be commonplace if the designer can be said to have 'set out to create a new and different design'.[168] This view of unregistered design right subsistence as depending, in part at least, on the putative designer's intention was important in supporting the court's decision that the shape of the umbrella case at issue was not commonplace. According to the court, the reason for this decision was that each of the design's features was 'the result of a conscious design choice' by the designer, rather than of functional constraints imposed by the relevant product's need to case an umbrella.[169] This reasoning brings to mind the view of the courts in copyright that what distinguishes a *de minimis* scribble from an original artistic work protectable by copyright is the expressive intent of

Press [1916] 2 Ch 601, discussed in ch 5 s 3.3.2.2.1. See in this regard *Tasker's Design Right References* (n 112) [63] (regarding Mummery LJ's reference specifically in his discussion of 'commonplace' to designs made by persons other than the parties).

163 See s 3.3.2.2. This was recently expressed in *Raft Ltd v Freestyle of Newhaven* Ltd [2016] EWHC 1711 (IPEC) [7] with reference to *Sawkins v Hyperion Records* [2005] EWCA Civ 565, [2005] RPC 32 and *Walter v Lane* [1900] AC 539 (HL) as requiring 'that a designer has expended some sort of effort or skill, such as by way of aesthetic judgment, above merely copying an earlier design in a manner that can be described as slavish or servile'. According to Judge Hacon, the fact that the test for originality in copyright has moved on from the traditional UK test by reason of European law is irrelevant, since European-led developments in the UK law of copyright originality 'can have no direct bearing on design right law under the 1988 Act' ([9]).

164 See *OSL* (n 125) 429; also *Dyson* (n 146) [103]–[105].

165 On the exclusion of subject matter from copyright on *de minimis* grounds see ch 5 s 3.3.1.4.

166 See *Lambretta Clothing* (n 47) [45]. When deciding this, the courts are required to bear in mind the legislature's intention to protect the appearance of even non-aesthetic functional articles, regardless of novelty, except in those cases where doing so 'would create practical difficulties' by making substantial similarities in later designs inevitable: see *Farmers Build Ltd* (n 18) 481. See further *A Fulton Co Ltd v Grant Barnett & Co Ltd* [2001] RPC 16 (Ch) (*Fulton v Grant Barnett*) 273 (inferring from this that a design will not be denied unregistered protection 'merely because the defendant, in researching what is often referred to as the "prior art", discovers an obscure article which is fairly similar to the design in which design right is claimed').

167 See *Fulton v Grant Barnett* (ibid) 272 ('A shape or configuration which arose accidentally, without being designed, could not attract statutory protection').

168 ibid 276. 169 ibid.

its creator,[170] and suggests that the requirement that a design not be commonplace adds little if anything to the requirement that it be original within the meaning of UK copyright, notwithstanding its assessment against the prior art.

This discussion supports two related conclusions. The first is that originality is an essential (rather than an accidental) property of the subject matter protectable by unregistered UK design right, as for the subject matter protectable by registered design right and unregistered Community design right.[171] And the second is that, unlike the position in European law, where design right protection is expressly limited to the extent of a design's individual character (including its originality), thereby obviating the statutory exclusions from protection of aspects of design dictated by technical function or interoperability requirements, unregistered UK design right subsists in original designs as a whole. It follows that the must-fit and must-match exclusions of section 213(3)(b) perform an important role in expressly excluding from the scope of unregistered UK design right protection those aspects of shape or configuration that cannot be attributed to the designer's exercise of independent skill and labour in the creation of her design. In effect, this gives section 213(3)(b) a role analogous to the role of the idea/expression distinction in European copyright legislation.[172]

3.5 Conclusion

The courts have criticized section 213 of the CDPA over the years as leaving 'much to be desired' and being 'full of uncertainty', owing to its unclear language and policy basis.[173] Some of its perceived deficiencies were addressed in 2014, with the restriction of its definition of protectable subject matter to exclude such collections of aspects of a product's appearance as a claimant might find it expedient, in the light of the subject matter used by a defendant, to claim as her design.[174] Since that amendment, unregistered UK design right subsists in and only in those subject matter that comprise the original, including not commonplace, shape or configuration of a product or product part. Expressly excluded from such subject matter are those aspects of shape or configuration that: (a) originate not with the designer and her conscious acts of design, but rather with the constraints of product interoperability or matching; (b) reflect the surface decoration of the product

[170] See ch 5 s 3.3.1.2.

[171] Unlike registered design right protection, however, which only covers the original aspects of a design, unregistered design right subsists in the design as a whole. See eg *Farmers Build Ltd* (n 18) 482 (suggesting that a design might include commonplace features but not be commonplace overall); also *Ultraframe v Eurocell* (n 149) [117].

[172] See ch 5 s 3.2.1.

[173] See *Dyson* (n 146) [14]; *Mark Wilkinson Furniture* (n 47) 72.

[174] Intellectual Property Act 2014 (UK) s 1(1). Before this amendment, unregistered UK design right subsisted in *any aspect of* the shape or configuration of an article or part of an article. Nonetheless, the continued subsistence of unregistered (Community and UK) design right in respect of product parts still enables a claimant to 'trim his design right claim to most closely match what he believes the defendant to have taken' (*OSL* (n 125) 422), albeit less so than before 2014, and represents an important difference between the subject matter protectable by unregistered design right and the subject matter protectable by copyright.

or product part; or (c) lack the clear and discrete expressive boundaries of a specific and individual appearance, such that protecting it would create a monopoly in a method or principle of product construction. The result is a conception of the protectable design that is similar to that supported by European legislation. The main differences are its extension to the expression of a product or product part's internal shape or configuration, its exclusion of the appearance of surface decoration, and its requirement for clear and precise expressive properties (of visual significance). Thus defined, a design for the purpose of unregistered UK design right is appropriately conceived as an original artistic work protectable by UK copyright, with one important difference: unlike the latter, designs need not possess the historical property of having been intended by their creator and/or regarded by society to exist as a work of original artistic expression.

4. Entitlement: Registered and Unregistered Design Rights are for Designers (ie for Authors)

Under Article 14 of the Designs Regulation, unregistered and registered Community design right vests initially 'in the designer or his successor in title', with corresponding provision for jointly developed designs,[175] subject to an exception for designs developed in the course of employment. According to the Court of Justice, and as in the field of UK copyright,[176] this applies equally for commissioned designs, subject to any contractual arrangement to the contrary.[177]

That the 'development' of a design entails an act of creation, making the 'designer' an author within the meaning of copyright, is confirmed by the UK's transcription of the Designs Regulation's entitlement provision in section 2 of its Registered Designs Act. According to that provision, '[t]he author of a design shall be treated for the purposes of this Act as the original proprietor of the design', where 'the "author" of a design means the person who creates it'. So too under the CDPA, with an exception for employee-created designs, unregistered UK design right is first owned by the design's 'designer',[178] defined in section 214 to mean 'the person who creates it'.

In sum, and consistent with the conclusions above that originality is an essential property of a protectable design under European and UK law—and the design in consequence an authorial work—that law recognizes that designs are by definition

[175] See Designs Regulation art 14(2) ('If two or more persons have jointly developed a design, the right to the Community design shall vest in them jointly').

[176] See ch 5 s 4.

[177] Case C–32/08 *Fundación Española para la Innovación de la Artesanía (FEIA) v Cul de Sac Espacio Creativo SL* [2009] ECR I–05611 [51] (deciding that the rules governing the first ownership of design right in respect of commissioned designs are as for those governing the first ownership of design right in respect of designs developed outside the context of employment).

[178] CDPA s 215(1).

creations of one or more 'author(s)', being natural (rather than legal) persons referred to as 'designer(s)'.

5. Conclusions: Registered and Unregistered Designs as Artifact Types Having Certain Properties and Arranged in Categories that Express and Reflect those Properties

(a) What are the categories of subject matter protected by the regime, and what are those subject matters' essential properties?

In the UK and Europe, the statutory category of design right subject matter is denoted by the term 'design', which covers the subcategories of 'registered design' and 'unregistered design' respectively. In Europe each category is understood to contain any appearance of the external features of a product or product part, including those features of a part intended for assembly in a complex product that remain visible during the product's normal use, and excluding any features that are not the product of free and creative choices by the subject matter's putative designer. Thus defined, a registered design and an unregistered design is a type of original (artistic) work within the meaning of EU copyright, and is comprised of the same formal and historical properties. While UK law supports the same conception of registered design, it defines the term 'unregistered design' differently. According to that definition, an unregistered design is an original work comprising a specific and individual expression of the external or internal shape or configuration of a product or product part—being the expressive (visual) properties of the shape or configuration of a product or product part conceived in its entirety, not comprising a method or principle of construction or surface decoration—produced by a person exercising independent labour and skill, and excluding any aspects of appearance attributable to interoperability or interchange requirements. Thus defined, an unregistered design under the CDPA is a type of original artistic work within the meaning of traditional UK copyright authorities, excluding the requirement for an authorial work not to have been intended by its creator and/or regarded by society to exist as something other than an original artistic work, which requirement was formulated precisely to exclude from copyright those designs and other subject matter that possess the formal properties of original literary and artistic works but are nonetheless not appropriately conceived as works of literary and artistic authorship or originality.[179]

The complexity of these definitions, and in particular of the statutory provisions by which they are articulated, goes some way to explaining the dissatisfaction of UK courts with the legislation in this field of IP, and the description of design law in general as having the appearance of 'a particularly abstruse branch of metaphysics'.[180] Nonetheless, it is clear from the courts' interpretation of those provisions that both registered and unregistered designs—like original artistic works—are

[179] See ch 5 s 3.3.1.

[180] See *Dyson* (n 146) [79].

expressive objects of visual significance that depend for their existence on the productive actions and intentions of one or more human beings, being the designers of the object in question. As such, and as for original artistic works, they conform closely to the paradigmatic conception of IP subject matter considered in Chapter 3.[181]

Since designs comprise properties of visual significance intended for addition to or incorporation in a product or product part, their development must accommodate any functional constraints imposed by the latter, just as a woodcut must accommodate the constraints imposed by that particular printmaking medium. However, and as the analogy to woodcuts suggests, while such functional constraints materially affect the process of design creation, they do not alter the nature of designs themselves as original expressive objects. Further, since designs are expressive rather than functional or technical, they need not convey the information required to enable manufacture of the product or product part by means of which they are expressed.

As with other types of original works, designs within the meaning of EU and UK law are intellectual creations in the sense considered in section 2.2 of Chapter 3, and satisfy the more restrictive of the views of the human acts justifying the recognition of property rights considered in that section. The reason is the requirement for a transformative act on the part of one or more natural persons giving rise to new properties of visual significance, in the sense not of properties that differ from those which existed previously—though this is also required under the Designs Regulation and Designs Directive—but rather of properties that can be said to have originated with the relevant persons. In Europe this requirement is reflected in the restriction of design right protection to appearances (and those features of appearance) that express the intellectual creation of an author-designer, and in the UK it is reflected in the restriction of unregistered design right to non-trivial appearances produced by exercise of independent skill and labour.

Less clear is whether the law conceives the design as a Platonic entity in the manner of an original literary and artistic work or as an idea in the manner of an invention. The view of the subject matter protectable by unregistered UK design right as a specific and discrete intangible expressive object that needs to be recorded in order to be protected but that exists independent of the fact and form of its recording—and the IP rights in which are infringed by its unauthorized instantiation in whole or substantial part—suggests the former. Less clear is whether the same can be said for the design protectable by Community design right and registered UK design right. The main reason for this in the case of registered (Community and UK) design right is the freedom afforded to registered design right applicants to define their designs at a high level of generality in order to maximize the scope of their resulting property, which might suggest that such designs are as much ideas for the addition of certain expressive properties to a product or product part as they are original works within the meaning of copyright, consistent with their conception as purpose-limited expressive objects analogous to trade marks. Further, this is not inconsistent with the law's conception of even the designs protectable by registered design right as norm kinds or object works of which there can be perfect

[181] See ch 5 s 5(a).

or imperfect examples, being those properties that do not produce a different overall visual impression on the informed user. Nor is it inconsistent with the aim of the rights conferred in respect of the designs protectable by both registered and unregistered design right at enabling the designer to prevent third parties from using such examples without her authority. Adopting the design-specific phenomenology of John Gero,[182] we might describe the subject matter protectable by each title of design right in part at least as a representation of a product's elements and their relationships that—whether consciously or otherwise—reflects a routine, innovative or creative adaptation of a pre-existing design in the form of a prototype.[183] Since routine adaptations of a prototype are, by Gero's definition, comprised entirely of features that fall within a well-defined state space of design, in the sense of being directly instantiable from the prototype,[184] they will lack the individual character, if not the novelty, required for design right registration, and if copied from the prototype, the individual character, if not the novelty, and originality required for unregistered design right subsistence, and will also very likely infringe any design right protection in respect of the prototype. By contrast, since innovative adaptations of a prototype include, by Gero's definition, features that are not routine, albeit still within the state space of potential designs instantiable from the prototype,[185] they will be unlikely to infringe any Community or registered (UK) design right protection at least[186] in respect of the prototype, and will moreover possess the individual character or originality required for such protection in their own right. Even more so for creative adaptations of a prototype, being in Gero's phenomenology those appearances the features of which reflect an extension or moving of the state space of potential designs instantiable from the prototype,[187] which will not infringe any design right protection in respect of the prototype, including any unregistered UK design right protection, and will also be protectable in their own right under each of the Community and UK regimes. The fact that the designs protectable by registered design right are capable of definition at greater or lesser degrees of generality does not affect the applicability of this analysis, which offers a persuasive explanatory model for all design right regimes, regardless of whether designs are conceived as a type of authorial work or purpose-limited expressive object.

(b) How is each subject matter individuated within the regime?

EU and UK law require that the subject matter protectable by design right be capable of individuation in ways similar to the ways in which other IP subject matter are required to be. Each subject matter protected by registered design right must be capable of being distinguished *qua* design from the registration document, and in particular from the information that every application for registered design right is required and permitted to contain.[188] Especially important in this regard

[182] See Gero (n 136). [183] ibid 34–36. [184] ibid 34. [185] ibid.

[186] Less absolute is the correspondence between protectability and infringement under the unregistered UK design right regime owing to the different requirements for each.

[187] See Gero (n 136) 34–36.

[188] See Designs Regulation art 36 and Commission Regulation (EC) No 2245/2002 of 21 October 2002 implementing Council Regulation (EC) No 6/2002 on Community designs [2002] OJ L 341/28, as amended (Implementing Regulations) art 1.

is the representation or specimen of the design that Article 36(1)(c) of the Designs Regulation and rule 4(1)(b) of the UK Registered Designs Rules 2006 require. According to the UK Supreme Court in *PMS v Magmatic*, and as noted previously, the description of the design in the application is entirely a matter for the applicant, who may decide what properties of visual significance to include, and the level of generality at which to define them.[189] If the applicant defines his subject matter too generally, his right will be at risk of invalidation on the ground that his design lacks novelty and/or individual character.[190] If he defines it too specifically, he will limit the scope of protection to which he is entitled.[191] While design legislation does not impose the same requirements of sufficient description as patent legislation imposes,[192] consistent with the expressive nature of designs, and the absence of any need for the design document to enable the manufacture of products according to them, it is nonetheless clear that a representation that fails sufficiently to enable the claimed properties of visual significance to be identified will fail the statutory requirement for representation of the design, in addition to being a method or principle of construction within the meaning of section 213(3)(a) of the CDPA.

As well as performing the same definitional function as the patent document, the design right document supports the same requirements for evidence of its protectable subject matter. The first—reflected in the requirement for representation of the design—is metaphysical individuation, according to which an object is individuated by 'whatever it is that makes it the single object that it is'.[193] The second—reflected in the requirement for an appearance sufficient to produce in the mind of an informed user an overall (visual) impression that differs from the overall (visual) impression produced by prior art appearances—is epistemic individuation, according to which an object is individuated by the ability of a certain intelligent individual to single it out 'as a distinct object of perception'.[194]

Necessarily different are the means by which the subject matter protected by unregistered design right must be capable of individuation. While the subsistence criteria for unregistered Community and UK design right differ in their requirements that a design have been previously made available to the public[195] and 'recorded in a design document or an article'[196] respectively, the effect of each is largely the same, namely, to ensure that each protected subject matter has at some point in time been evidenced by reduction to material form. As with authorial works, this confirms again that the subject matter protectable by unregistered design right must be capable of individuation in the metaphysical sense of being whatever it is that makes them the designs that they are, as well as in the epistemic sense of being capable of being singled out *qua* designs as distinct objects of

[189] See *PMS v Magmatic* (n 51) [30]. [190] ibid. [191] ibid.

[192] See EPC arts 83 and 84 and Patents Act 1977 s 14(3) and (5)(a) to (c) (requiring a clear and concise textual definition and description of the subject matter for which protection is sought that is sufficient to enable the invention to be performed by a person skilled in the art).

[193] E J Lowe, 'Individuation' in M L Loux and D W Zimmerman (eds), *The Oxford Handbook of Metaphysics* (OUP 2005) 75.

[194] ibid. [195] Designs Regulation art 11. [196] CDPA s 213(6).

perception by the courts adopting the mantle (for unregistered Community design right) of the informed user.

With respect to the question 'how is each subject matter individuated?', therefore, the answer is metaphysically—by asking what properties of visual significance are represented in the design right registration document or prior art/recording (as applicable); and epistemologically—by asking what does the notional intelligent individual understand the properties thus represented as a distinct object of (visual) perception or impression to be? As in the areas of IP considered in previous chapters, in design law it is the second of these conceptions and methods of individuation that has especial importance. This can be seen clearly from those areas concerned with establishing the identity of a subject matter *qua* design—novelty and individual character for Community design right, and originality for unregistered UK design right.

Under European law and the UK Registered Designs Act, a design is 'new' if and only if 'no identical design has been made available to the public' previously,[197] where by 'identical design' is meant a design the features of which 'differ only in immaterial details',[198] and by 'made available to the public' is meant disclosed in such a way that 'could ... reasonably have become known in the normal course of business to the circles specialized in the sector concerned, operating within the Community',[199] regardless of whether the disclosure itself took place within the EU.[200] The fact that the individual features of a design existed previously in the public realm does not as such destroy its novelty. What matters is whether

> all the elements were made available to the public and it was clearly stated that those elements were intended to be combined to constitute a specific product, thus enabling the shape and features of that design to be identified. In other words, it cannot be accepted that a design is novel ... where it consists only of a combination of designs that have already been made available to the public and in respect of which it has already been stated that they were intended to be used together.[201]

Having established that a design is new, in the sense of incorporating one or more materially different features, the question arises of whether those features are sufficient to give it individual character, in the sense of producing an overall impression that differs from the overall impression produced by the relevant prior art on the informed user.[202] In this regard, design law follows trade mark and patent law, which also rely on the 'overall impression' and perception produced by a given subject matter in the mind of a hypothetical intelligent individual in its individuation of trade marks and inventions respectively. Further, according to the courts, the informed user whose impression of a design determines its individual character

197 Designs Regulation art 5(1); Designs Directive art 4.
198 Designs Regulation art 5(2); Designs Directive art 4.
199 Designs Regulation art 7(1); Designs Directive art 6(1).
200 See *H Gautzsch Großhandel* (n 95) [33]; also *Senz Technologies* (n 36) [29] (describing the question as whether, on the facts, it was not possible for the relevant circles to be aware of the disclosure, bearing in mind the degree of awareness of the prior art that could reasonably be attributed to them).
201 See *Group Nivelles* (n 60) [77]–[78].
202 Designs Regulation art 6; Designs Directive art 5.

is a cross between the comparably placed hypothetical persons of patent and trade mark law—the skilled technical addressee or 'sectoral expert', and the well-informed and reasonably observant and circumspect average consumer.[203] The thing of which she is presumed to be a user is the product in which the design is intended to be incorporated or to which it is intended to be applied, which the informed user is presumed to use in accordance with its intended use.[204] The sense in which she is presumed to be 'informed' is the sense of being particularly observant and having some awareness of the state of the prior art with reference to which the design's individual character is to be assessed.[205] She is also presumed to know the various designs that exist in the relevant sector, to possess a certain degree of knowledge regarding the features that those designs normally include, and, as a result of her interest in the products concerned, to pay a relatively high degree of attention when using them.[206] By contrast, she is not presumed to have any technical expertise beyond that which a person might be expected to acquire by use of the relevant product, and is thus not presumed to be able to distinguish (beyond the extent permitted by such use) those aspects of the product's appearance dictated by technical and arbitrary considerations respectively.[207] The result is to affirm the importance of the concept of epistemic individuation in design law, and of the 'informed user' as the hypothetical 'intelligent individual' whose ability to single each design out as a distinct object of perception is central to its legal status as a design; and also to affirm the centrality to each design's identity of both its formal properties (of visual significance capable of addition to or incorporation in a product or product part) and its historical properties (of having originated by exercise of it putative creator's free and creative choices). That the test of infringement is essentially the same test of 'individual character' further supports this analysis.

[203] See Case C–281/10 P *PepsiCo, Inc v Grupo Promer Mon Graphic SA* [2011] ECR I–10153 (*PepsiCo*) (describing the informed user as 'lying somewhere between that of the average consumer applicable in trade mark matters, who need not have any specific knowledge and who, as a rule, makes no direct comparison between the trade marks in conflict, and the sectoral expert, who is an expert with detailed technical expertise').

[204] See *Shenzhen* (n 107).

[205] See *Grupo Promer Mon Graphic* (n 93) [62].

[206] See *Shenzhen* (n 107) [47].

[207] ibid [48]. In Case T–11/08 *Kwang Yang Motor Co Ltd v Office for Harmonisation in the Internal Market (OHIM)* [2011] ECR II–00266, the General Court applied these principles in a case involving a design for a component part of a complex product in the form of an internal combustion engine capable of being incorporated into a lawnmower. In its decision, the informed user had been correctly identified by the Board of Appeal of EUIPO in the proceedings below as someone wishing to use a lawnmower who, for example, needed to purchase one and had thus become informed about them, regardless of the fact that the design was also sold to manufacturers of other products in which combustion engines were installed. These principles were extended by the decision in *PepsiCo* (n 203) that, because of his or her particularly observant nature, the informed user will be presumed to make a direct comparison between the designs at issue unless such comparison would be impractical or uncommon in the relevant sector, by reason either of specific circumstances or of the characteristics of the products to which the designs relate.

By contrast is the method by which the law of UK unregistered design right individuates each design, which follows more directly that adopted for authorial works in copyright, considered in Chapter 5.

(c) What is the relationship between each subject matter and its tokens?

Each protectable registered design is realized or instantiated by application to or incorporation in an individual product or product part. As with product inventions, the design as type or universal is thus instantiated in or exemplified by the products or product parts to which it relates.

The same applies for each protectable unregistered design. However, the tokens of unregistered designs also share a causal connection to the protected design, owing to the requirement that any infringing act involve a subject matter derived from that design, as in the field of copyright.

(d) How is the existence of each subject matter and its tokens known?

In design law, the existence of a registered design is known by reason of and reference to its representation in the design documentation itself, in accordance with and fulfilment of EU and UK legislative requirements. The existence of one or more of its tokens is also known in the manner above, namely, from the existence of a design that produces the same overall (visual) impression on the mind of the informed user of the relevant products as that produced by the design represented in the design documentation.

By contrast, the existence of an unregistered design must be established by evidence, as in copyright. The existence of one or more of its tokens is also known in the manner above, namely, from the existence of a subject matter that the court would understand: (a) to produce the same overall (visual) impression on the mind of the informed user as that produced by the protected design (for unregistered Community design right), or to incorporate the whole or a substantial part of the protected design that it has accepted to exist (for unregistered UK design right); and (b) to have been derived from it.

Index